Entangled Histories

JEWISH CULTURE AND CONTEXTS

Published in association with
the Herbert D. Katz Center for Advanced Judaic Studies
of the University of Pennsylvania

David B. Ruderman and Steven Weitzman, Series Editors

ENTANGLED HISTORIES

Knowledge, Authority, and Jewish Culture in the Thirteenth Century

EDITED BY

Elisheva Baumgarten,
Ruth Mazo Karras,
and Katelyn Mesler

PENN

UNIVERSITY OF PENNSYLVANIA PRESS

PHILADELPHIA

Publication of this volume was assisted by a grant from the Herbert D. Katz Publications Fund of the Center for Advanced Judaic Studies of the University of Pennsylvania.

Published by
University of Pennsylvania Press
Philadelphia, Pennsylvania 19104-4112
www.upenn.edu/pennpress

Printed in the United States of America on acid-free paper
1 3 5 7 9 10 8 6 4 2

A Cataloging-in-Publication record is available from the Library of Congress
ISBN 978-0-8122-4868-5

In memory of our friend and colleague

Olivia Remie Constable
1960–2014

Contents

PART III. TRANSLATIONS AND TRANSMISSIONS
OF TEXTS AND KNOWLEDGE

Introduction

Elisheva Baumgarten, Ruth Mazo Karras, and Katelyn Mesler

"Go now into the Jews' streets and see how many do business with them [the Christians] even on the holiday itself."[1]

This pronouncement was a central part of one of R. Yeḥiel of Paris's responses to Christian accusations against Jewish conduct during the trial of the Talmud (Paris, 1240). Yeḥiel, a prominent advocate for the Jewish community, was countering a common Christian accusation that "Jews are hostile toward and a danger to gentiles."[2] He argued that, although he and his contemporaries observed the Torah with "all their souls," they still performed many activities that were forbidden by the Talmud. He was alluding to different prohibitions in tractate 'Avodah Zarah that pertained to what was considered idolatry or to aiding idol worshippers but were commonplace activities among medieval European Jews.[3] In the context of the Talmud trial, a landmark event in the history of Jewish-Christian relations, his implication was that not every statement against gentiles in the Talmud need be read as evidence of contemporary anti-Christian activities.[4] Thus he emphasized the close relations between Jews and Christians that he witnessed in his everyday surroundings.

His text states: "For we are taught: For three days preceding the holiday of the gentiles it is forbidden to engage in trade with them. Go now into the Jews' streets and see how many do business with them [the Christians] even on the holiday itself. And further we are taught 'Do not board cattle in the barns of gentiles,' and yet every day we sell cattle to gentiles and make partnerships with them and are alone with them and entrust our infants to their households to be nursed; and we teach Torah to gentiles, for there are Christian clerics who know how to read Jewish books."[5] As Yeḥiel indicates, many of the topics he mentions are noted in the Talmud as actions that are to be avoided. Despite this, he clarifies that Jews regularly engaged in business with their Christian neighbors, involved them in their domestic arrangements,[6] and, most notably in light of the questions of the transmission of knowledge discussed in this volume, taught them the Jewish interpretation of Torah, or perhaps even how to read Hebrew.[7] In another passage, Yeḥiel noted that he was used to discussions with clergy and that this was the reason for his role in the trial.[8]

From Yeḥiel's "Jews' streets" to the secular courtroom, from the cult of saints to the Islamicate bureaucracy, and from shared reliance on Aristotle to shared polemics, this volume highlights a complex interdependence in thought and action among different groups of Jews, as well as between Jews and the Christian and Muslim majority cultures. The chapters, contributed by thirteen specialists in the history, society, and literature of the long thirteenth century, explore intricate interreligious and intercultural dynamics. The presence (though not always literal) of Jews was an integral part of life for medieval Christians and Muslims, who were affected by Jews just as Jews were affected by their situation as a minority culture, or set of cultures. The interaction born of these relationships, from love and friendship to hostility and violence, is best described as "entanglement."

Terms of Entanglement: Historiographies

The Paris Talmud trial represented a new sort of hostility in medieval Christian-Jewish relations: the Jews were accused of not only rejecting Christianity but of deliberately rejecting that which was valid in pre-Christian Jewish belief. It can be seen as a momentous event in a series of anti-Jewish intellectual developments running from the thirteenth century through the early modern period that built on earlier layers of Christian-Jewish hostility. Although the thirteenth century did mark a watershed in regard to interreligious polemics, the past decades of research have focused especially on the fact that Jews were not just on the receiving end of polemics, they also produced them, in some cases initiating polemical interchanges.[9]

At the same time, many scholars studying the accounts of the Talmud trial and other medieval texts have found it difficult to reconcile the deep religious animosity behind disputations, accusations, and persecutions with the routinely cooperative contacts between Jews and Christians mentioned within the very same texts.[10] The religious hostility and ongoing social ties are hard to discuss simultaneously, and in light of the further persecutions that led to the expulsion of Jews from the various regions of western Europe from the thirteenth to early sixteenth centuries, it is not surprising that scholarship has emphasized enmity rather than day-to-day coexistence and intellectual contact. Indeed, modern scholarship has tended to emphasize the distance between Jews and Christians, because the two communities have been studied by different groups of scholars, those familiar with Hebrew sources and those versed in Latin materials. Even shared events, like the Talmud trial, have been studied separately from the Christian and Jewish sides.

Yet over the past decades, scholars have gradually come to the understanding that separation and hostility were constantly in creative tension with economic, cultural, and intellectual exchange, and this seeming contradiction was at the foundation of Jewish existence in medieval Europe. While we encounter the designation "alienated minority" to describe the medieval European Jewish community, we also find other descriptions that affirm Jewish interactions with the Christian majority: "intimate and distant," "together and apart," "overlapping yet separate."[11] The complexity of coexistence began on the most basic level of the streets of the cities of medieval Europe, where Jews tended to live in specific neighborhoods but were not their exclusive residents. They lived alongside Christians and interacted with their neighbors in a variety of ways. Medieval sources tell of neighborly relations and cooperation as well as hostilities. Much of this cooperation took place among women; as Yeḥiel states, for example, Jewish families might hire Christian women to nurse their children, and Jewish women were involved in consumption loans to Christian women.[12] Women's daily interactions to a large extent flew under the radar and must be teased out from a variety of sources; recent scholarship on medieval encounters has increasingly focused on the role of women, although none of the chapters in this volume places it at the center.[13]

The interplay of cooperation and hostility, or separation and collaboration, between Jewish and Christian communities, as well as the complexity of the relations between Jewish communities living under Christian rule and those living under Muslim rule, and furthermore between the Jews of southern and northern Europe, is at the heart of this volume.[14] The terminology used by scholars to describe these complexities—and the debates and dilemmas that arise from that terminology—are key to their understandings of interfaith and intrafaith relations. While use of the term "influence" to describe the way ideas and practices were transferred and shared between religious groups and geographies has fallen out of favor, as scholars have rejected the implied passivity of the group being influenced, there is no generally accepted replacement. Some studies use the geometric metaphors common in the field of comparative history: parallels, intersections, convergences, vectors.[15] However, these geometric metaphors can be too binary, implying a rigid dichotomy: parallel lines never meet, converging lines intersect only in one place. They do not take account of ongoing contact, or of multiple vectors.

As a result, recent scholars have sought to indicate the complex relations between and among groups by employing terms like "embeddedness," "exchange," "acculturation," "appropriation," "overlap," "interpenetration," and "hybridity."[16] These all seek to express the near-paradox of simultaneous connection and separation: one can be embedded but not completely part of, acculturating but still distinct; when one appropriates, one makes something one's own, but not necessarily separate from the culture of origin. Such terms all imply transfer or absorption, in many cases a Jewish incorporation of a Christian or Muslim practice or idea during the medieval period, centuries after Christianity and Islam each incorporated elements of Judaism. The terms also allow for the possibility of ongoing dialogue and conscious decisions in reaction to the Other, as well as the possibility that what is absorbed may look and function very differently from the source. But such terms may lose sight of the other side of the coin: the environment of hostility, anti-Jewish legislation, efforts at conversion, and eventual expulsion. Scholars have used words like "exclusion," "difference," "distinctiveness," "isolation," "hostility," "persecution," "intolerance," and "alienated" to express these realities.[17]

The chapters in this volume seek to look at the Jews of medieval Europe during the thirteenth century as entangled in other cultures, creating connected histories between communities that may include hostile as well as tolerant encounters. Entanglement implies complexity; the things being tangled (threads, vines, branches) can cross many times, becoming difficult or impossible to pull apart, but still remain distinct, as with two colors of thread or two types of plant. They can run alongside each other separately, cross, diverge, and converge again.[18] Parallels, similarities and differences, exchange and appropriation, exclusion and persecution, can all be part of entanglement. "Entanglement" can sometimes be a negative term; we do not voluntarily let our hair, our computer cables, our relationships become tangled. Here we attempt to use it in a more neutral way, as in quantum entanglement where individual particles in a system cannot be described without describing the system as a whole.[19] The chapters in this volume seek to present rising antagonisms alongside shared cultures, privileging neither. Rather than resolve the contradictions between persecution and cooperation, many of the chapters seek to outline them and explain how they endured and coexisted. Complex and entangled coexistence operated not just between Jewish and Christian or Muslim communities, but also among communities within Judaism. Ashkenaz and Sepharad cannot be considered in isolation from each other any more than Jewish and Christian communities in the same region can. Further, as many of the chapters demonstrate, although these communities had their own unique customs and traditions, there was also overlap and appropriation between them.

Many of the chapters look at the way knowledge and ideas were transmitted across religious or geographical boundaries. Entangled transmission is not a static, unidirectional movement of an idea from point A to point B but rather a complex process that has the potential to affect everyone involved, to be rejected, to transform the context into something wholly unrecognizable. The recipients, whether from one Jewish cultural stream to another or from one religious community to another, do not passively absorb knowledge, texts, or practices, but rather make a choice of what to integrate and how to adapt it to be meaningful in its new context. The situation is very similar to what Itamar Even-Zohar has termed a "culture repertoire," which describes the collection of available options from which elements of culture are chosen and employed.[20] Using these terms, we turn now to three distinct foci of entanglement that run through this volume: interactions between intellectual communities; those between secular and religious authorities; and the act of translation as an example of transmission of knowledge between communities.

Intellectual Communities and Interactions in the Long Thirteenth Century

The comments attributed to Yeḥiel came at one of the most complex moments of Jewish existence in thirteenth-century France, and can be read as a moving attempt to deflect accusations being made against the Jews.[21] At the same time, they can also be seen as indicative of the routine contacts between Jews and Christians in thirteenth-century Paris. These levels of meaning allow for reflection both on contact between Jewish and Christian elites and on the daily interactions that took place between many members of both societies, as well as on the interplay of differing Jewish traditions.

Jewish Europe contained the regions of Tsarfat (broadly designating France and England, though often limited to northern France), Ashkenaz (in its broadest sense including northern France and England as well as German lands; in its narrowest sense referring only to German lands), Sepharad (Iberia), Provence (signifying all of southern France, and culturally close to Sepharad), and Italy, including some areas under Muslim rule.[22] In the thirteenth century, among the intellectual elite, one might find the Ḥasidei Ashkenaz (Pietists) in the Rhineland, the tosafists in northern France, Maimonideans and anti-Maimonideans in Provence, Nahmanides and his circle in Barcelona, and various kabbalistic groups across Iberia.[23] These different linguistic and cultural communities addressed many similar questions but through the lens of different intellectual traditions.[24]

Even within the one relatively confined discipline of *halakhah*, cultural difference is evident.[25] Ephraim Kanarfogel's chapter on rabbinic conceptions of matchmaking takes us via *halakhah* into areas of everyday life that differed across Jewish cultures. He examines the process of marriage formation in medieval Ashkenaz, where matchmakers loomed rather large, and Sepharad, where they did not. Sephardic halakhists, he notes, placed the responsibility for making a match on the parents or grandparents. Sephardic halakhists, as well, were more lenient toward the dissolution of a planned match, as long as the *kidushin* (betrothal) had not yet taken place. In France, by contrast, a communal ban and a financial penalty were imposed, because the breaking of the match was thought to be highly embarrassing to the couple and their families. Kanarfogel suggests that the reason for both these differences—the use of matchmakers and the greater penalties for breaking a match in Ashkenaz—stems from the greater responsibility put there on the bride and groom rather than on their families. In Sepharad, where parents made the decisions, they could pressure their children to stick with an unwanted match; matchmakers, however, could not bring such pressure on individuals who made their own decisions. Ashkenazic sources emphasize consent of the parties, even of very young girls, whereas Sephardic ones put more emphasis on the will of the Almighty.[26]

Yet, some Ashkenazic and Sephardic halakhists knew each other's work, and as a result it is often quite difficult to distinguish among aspects of halakhic traditions and schools. Jewish communities in different towns and indeed in different regions maintained close links, and several of the chapters demonstrate the processes and results of that intellectual contact in multiple areas of scholarly endeavor. Moses Nahmanides, the subject of Mordechai Cohen's chapter, is a good example, sitting astride several very different currents in Jewish culture. In his Torah commentary Nahmanides endeavored to incorporate midrashic sensibilities—often mediated through Rashi's glosses—in an otherwise Andalusian model of *peshat* (plain sense) represented by Abraham Ibn Ezra (1089–1164) and Moses Maimonides (1138–1204). At the same time, he integrated typological exegesis and kabbalistic modes of interpretation into his commentary, evidently to resolve hermeneutical tensions produced by a convergence of the Andalusian and northern French *peshat* models.[27] Cohen shows how Nahmanides selected elements from an available culture repertoire. His fourfold classification of ways of reading Scripture is reminiscent of the four senses known to Christian exegetes. A number of scholars have noticed parallels between Jewish quadripartite models and Christian ones, but the four ways of reading never corresponded exactly. Cohen shows that while Nahmanides may have gotten the idea of a fourfold schema from Christian sources, the schema he developed—*peshat*, midrash, typology, and mysticism—served to solve a very specific problem that he had, relating to questions that were fundamentally part of Jewish and not Christian biblical interpretation. Cohen points out that Nahmanides need not have read Latin to have learned of Christian typology and the fourfold division; he need only have spoken with Christian scholars, as he likely did.

Discussions between Christian and Jewish scholars also appear in Rami Reiner's chapter, which uses a report about correspondence between Rabbenu Tam (R. Jacob ben Meir, d. 1171) and Henry the Liberal, Count of Champagne from 1152 to 1181, to demonstrate another aspect of the entanglement of intra-Jewish and intercommunal processes of knowledge transmission. Biblical exegetes and halakhists were expected to be two different groups of specialists (much like theologians and canon lawyers in Christian society), although Rabbenu Tam's polymath grandfather Rashi and his brother Rashbam were exceptions. By Rabbenu Tam's generation the study of the law via the Talmud had become, in northern France, the most highly regarded field of study, while the major biblical exegetes of the period were located in the south of France and in Iberia. Yet, as Reiner shows, the line between the areas of specialization was hardly inviolable; a leading halakhist like Rabbenu Tam was expected to have encyclopedic knowledge of the Torah as well, and to demonstrate this in his work. As a powerful French lord (son-in-law of Louis VII), Henry the Liberal was patron of a major circle of intellectuals at his court, and it is likely that this activity is what prompted him to address to Rabbenu Tam queries about certain passages of the Bible, showing that the opinion of Jewish scholars was respected on the sacred texts that they shared with Christians. But it is even more remarkable that Rabbenu Tam was able to frame his answers not only in terms of Jewish traditions but also in terms of the Christian majority society; if not himself an intimate at the court, he was well aware of features of aristocratic life. The correspondence demonstrates the integration of a man totally immersed in a talmudic discourse community who was at home in the community surrounding Henry's court as well.

Rabbenu Tam lived in the small town of Ramerupt, but most Jews tended to be concentrated particularly in growing urban centers. Many towns, like the Jews themselves, had special relationships with the regional lord or monarch through grants of privileges. The contact described by R. Yeḥiel shows that activity like that of Rabbenu Tam continued, with Jews exchanging ideas with learned Christians. Some of them traveled a long way to do so, although most Jewish religious authority was local. As urbanization proceeded in Europe through the twelfth and thirteenth centuries, the Jews formed part of the economic lifeblood of towns.[28]

Towns were centers of knowledge as well as commerce, and the locus of Christian learning shifted to the universities that were established there. Studies at Christian universities fell into four areas: the arts, consisting of the study of language and linguistic logic, which were expanded after the reception of Aristotle by the addition of moral and natural philosophy; law, that is, canon and civil law, for which Bologna was the most famous; medicine, which became increasingly professionalized with the reception of Aristotelian theory and its separation from empirical practice, and for which Salerno and Montpellier were best known; and theology, the "Queen of the Sciences," whose home was in Paris.

The idea of the colleges that made up the medieval universities of the thirteenth century has a great deal in common with the madrasa of the Islamicate world, although the latter was largely dedicated to studying religious law.[29] Jewish yeshivot tended to be smaller than madrasas or the Christian universities—more like the colleges within the latter—and focused mainly on the study of Talmud.[30] However, in none of the religious traditions did education in the broadest sense remain restricted to these rarefied institutions of higher learning. The aids for preachers that proliferated after the Fourth Lateran Council (1215) demanded regular instruction of the laity, and later works of edification for the laity themselves drew upon theological teachings from the universities,[31] just as Jewish works attempted to summarize talmudic learning for a wider audience. Judah Galinsky's chapter on thirteenth-century halakhic compilations discusses the summaries and restatements of halakhic material that were written in the second half of the century, notably the *'Amudei golah* (Pillars of Exile), also known as the *Sefer mitsvot katan* or *Semak*, of R. Isaac of Corbeil, completed in 1276–77. Compared to works from earlier in the century, like the *Sefer ha-terumah* (Book of Offering) of R. Barukh ben Isaac, the *Semak* presupposes a much wider audience, and other works of the period fall somewhere in the middle of the spectrum. These compilations contrast with the scholarly work from the Rhineland in the eleventh century and from northern France in the twelfth. Somewhat similar compilations existed already in twelfth-century France in the form of *maḥzorim*, liturgical guides containing not only parts of the liturgy but also practical legal as well as ritual material. It is in the thirteenth century, however, as Galinsky demonstrates, that the genre of the practical legal treatise, at least the major points of which were eventually intended for study by all in the synagogue, came into its own.

Galinsky attributes this development partly to the influence of Maimonides and his *Mishneh Torah* and that of Ḥasidei Ashkenaz, both of which tended to push toward a more accessible presentation of *halakhah*. In part, however, he argues that these texts grew out of their context in the urban center of Paris, a center for the book trade. The rise of the University of Paris meant that a good deal of copying was done there in urban ateliers rather than in monasteries as previously. Besides textbooks, these ateliers produced works for the use of clergy in preaching and pastoral care, as well as works directed at laypeople, at least well-off ones. These three categories correspond roughly to the audiences Galinsky has identified: scholars for the *Sefer ha-terumah*, a secondary elite for works like Moses of Coucy's *Sefer ha-mitsvot*, and a wider group of laypeople for the *Semak*. All three were experimenting with audience and format, especially compared with static genres used in the Rhineland, and all three authors had ties to Paris. These works were written for no one but Jews; they were in no way explicitly in dialogue with Christian work. And yet, as Galinsky shows, the authors wrote within the setting of a wider Christian culture, and Christian texts may have spurred their thinking about form and audience, if not the content, of their work.

Secular and Religious Authorities

Jews and members of other communities were entangled not just by their ideas but also by the authorities that governed their lives. Sites of intellectual work (yeshiva, madrasa, university) were clearly demarcated by religious identifications, despite allowing for contact between select individuals; however, the circumstances within which most medieval Jews lived were immersed within those of the majority culture. Jews and Christians were in close daily contact by necessity and proximity as well as by choice. These mundane exchanges did not involve intellectual engagement of the kind that typified exchanges between learned men, but the practices and beliefs that were imparted and exhibited as part of these exchanges were no less consequential in determining the way Jews went about their daily activities and their religious rituals.[32] Sometimes Jewish activities depended upon the local secular power. In the thirteenth century cultural, religious, and intellectual developments collided with politics, marking a shift in the relations among Christianity, Judaism, and Islam. The entanglement of religious and secular authority deeply affected the position of Jews in medieval polities. This aspect of the period stands out in the work both of scholars working on the Jews within Islam and those working on Christian Europe.

Luke Yarbrough's chapter on the madrasa and non-Muslims focuses on how Jews, who formed part of the intelligentsia in Muslim as well as in Christian society, lost their previous connections with political authorities. Jews had often provided a significant part of the corps of administrative officials in Egypt, but in the thirteenth century they (along with Christians) began to be excluded from the administrative class. The madrasa played a role in this process, not, as previous scholarship has argued, because it strengthened group consciousness and a knowledge of Islamic jurisprudence that supported discrimination, and prepared Muslim religious scholars for debate with unbelievers. Rather, Yarbrough suggests that while elite audiences did not consider the madrasa related to state employment, through a long and gradual process madrasa patronage networks became intertwined with bureaucratic ones. Muslim scholars with certain personal connections competed successfully for administrative positions, thus marginalizing Jewish and Christian officials and their communities. Yarbrough's work fits into a tradition of scholarship on Jews in medieval Europe that suggests that the anti-Judaism that advocated political and legal marginalization was inevitably entangled with larger economic and political changes, here a closer relationship between political and religious elites occasioned by the rise of the madrasa (and, *mutatis mutandis*, the university).

Rebecca Winer's chapter, analyzing a corpus of Latin loan documents in notarial registers from thirteenth-century Perpignan, demonstrates how Jews were part of the notarial culture of their times. A Jewish notarial culture already existed in the thirteenth century, but the Crown attempted to increase its revenues by controlling this notarial system and regulating Jewish use of Latin notaries. The fact that Jews entered into transactions before Christian notaries is not at all surprising; the registers for Perpignan contain hundreds of such contracts, and Perpignan is not unusual in this regard within the Crown of Aragon. What is highly remarkable is that some of these Jews added Hebrew notations to the register, either their signatures or other phrases. These unexpected markings shed light on how the Jews and Christians viewed and behaved toward each other when they came together before the notary to acknowledge a transaction. Above all her chapter demonstrates the complexities involved in studying communities that interacted simultaneously on a variety of different levels, both religious and economic.

Winer's evidence points to a cooperation, if a grudging one, that was not always the case. In Europe, although relations between Christians and Jews had never been ideal, the thirteenth century saw the origins both of blood libels and of accusations of host desecration. Each instance of these accusations reflected its local circumstances, but a shared Christian culture made certain topoi available to local communities. Local communities were not the only ones who took advantage of accusations against the Jews to claim effective authority. The new mendicant orders, international in scope and eager to claim independence and a position of intellectual leadership in Christendom, deployed attacks on the Talmud as one of their tools.[33] And monarchies got in on the act as well. By the end of the century, the first of Europe's major expulsions of Jews—from England, in 1290—had taken place; even earlier, Jews in many places were considered "royal serfs" and monarchs' role in judging accusations like blood libel—even if they found in favor of the accused Jews—was an assertion of their power over them, as well as over their powerful Christian accusers.[34]

The exercise of royal, lordly, or papal power over the Jews, who were in many places granted special status that exempted them from legal authority other than their community's and the king's, cannot be seen in isolation.[35] It was part of a system in which monarchical power was evolving over the course of the thirteenth century, alongside the development of (Christian) representative institutions of various sorts.[36] The "crisis of Church and State" of the late eleventh and twelfth centuries had largely been resolved in favor of the hierarchical church, which constituted a monarchy of its own; Pope Innocent III (r. 1198–1216), who convened the Fourth Lateran Council, was the epitome of papal monarchy. This is not to say that all churchmen followed everything the pope said, any more than all secular people followed the secular laws of their jurisdiction; there were many competing entities within the church, including monastic orders, mendicants, and beguines, and different synodal regulations applied to different regions. There was considerable diversity of thought even within what was considered orthodox. Nevertheless the church was increasingly hierarchized and bureaucratized, much like the various kingdoms and principalities were coming to be.

This process worked at many levels, from the training of the parish clergy to the expansion of the papal chancery.[37] As R. I. Moore suggests, "The decrees of Lateran IV [1215] set forth a sweeping program which drew upon and synthesized the intellectual, administrative, and pastoral developments of the tumultuous century and a half since the Gregorian reforms. They provide yet another example, and one of the most successful, of the systematization which was the central characteristic of this age and culture, laying down with lucid precision the foundations and framework for the government of the church and much of European life for the rest of the middle ages and beyond."[38] Church and state worked hand in hand to suppress "heresy," when it suited monarchs to do so (as in the Languedoc), a development which has some parallels to the attacks on Jews; like Judaism, heresy was not a new concern, but ways of dealing with it were changing.[39] Ecclesiastical regulation, which had previously touched relatively lightly on Jews and relied on secular authorities for enforcement, began to exert wider jurisdiction over Jews in the thirteenth century, just as the church was also setting up new mechanisms—such as the role of inquisitors—for bringing its judicial apparatus to bear.[40]

Accusations against Jews—for which real Jews suffered—could serve hermeneutic functions within Christianity. For example, in the wake of the church's new emphasis on transubstantiation (made doctrine at the Fourth Lateran Council in 1215), host desecration accusations against Jews, along with their disseminated narratives, served to reinforce the truth of transubstantiation.[41] When host desecration narratives end, as they often do, with miracles that render Jesus' presence in the host manifest, the function of these narratives as a reinforcement of Christian faith is evident. Christian culture could also make a negative image of the Jew central to its own self-definition. The chapter by Kati Ihnat and Katelyn Mesler examines a particular aspect of material culture as a case study of how Christians used the figure of the Jew to think with. Over the course of the early and central Middle Ages, Christians developed a practice of making votive images of wax, to be venerated or offered to a saint in petition or in thanks for healing. Christian authorities found themselves in the position of supporting the use of such images, while developing concerns over correct theological understanding and proper devotional usage on the part of the votaries who offered them. These anxieties were, in effect, displaced onto the Jews. The concern with Jewish sacrilege against Christian holy objects was of long standing, and accusing Jews of desecrating wax images, or even of practicing sorcery with them, allowed Christians to delineate the boundaries of acceptable devotional practice. At the same time, such accusations, part of the Christian imaginary, had very real repercussions for the Jews involved.

The centerpiece of thirteenth-century confrontations between Jews and Christians, and a turning point in Jewish-Christian relations in the Middle Ages that represented a great expansion of authority over Jewish thought and religion, was the trial of the Talmud in Paris in 1240, which was followed by the disputation about the Talmud in Barcelona in 1263. In essence, the church was claiming the authority to judge Jews' relationship to their own Hebrew Bible by condemning additions and interpretive traditions that postdated the founding of Christianity.[42] In Paris, a certain amount of institutional apparatus was necessary in order to carry out the trial. The location of Paris provided the combination of a stronghold of royal power, a university that was in theory independent of local church authorities but that had its own governmental apparatus and papal allegiance, and the existence of an inquisitorial process.[43]

Nicholas Donin, one of the central figures in the 1240 Talmud trial, moves us beyond the imaginary into real political conflict. In his chapter Piero Capelli presents him as a key figure in the entanglement of differences (or what Donin saw as contradictions) between talmudic and other possible forms of Judaism, as well as deeply involved in political shifts within Christian polities. Donin was already considered an outsider by Jews before he turned to Christianity. Capelli argues, based especially on the textual history of the *Vikuaḥ rabenu Yeḥi'el* and other manuscripts, that Donin staked out a position against not only the Talmud but against all rabbinic interpretation of

Scripture, and that he was central to the changing attitude of various European states toward the Jews in this period. As Capelli demonstrates, he became a "chess piece" (although not necessarily a pawn) in games such as those between Louis IX and the counts of Toulouse, as Louis used an attack on the Jews as a means of gaining papal support in expanding into the south. Donin did not set out to be a mover and shaker in those larger political events; rather, he may have been set on his road by an opposition to the authority exercised by rabbis over Jewish communities on the basis of their knowledge of Talmud.

Translations and Transmissions of Texts and Knowledge

Donin represents a broader trend in which the number of converts in Christian Europe increased as a result of missionizing efforts, force, financial and social incentives, and the threat of expulsion. Jews in Muslim regions were subject to some, but not all, of these pressures, and their relation to the intellectual culture of the dominant group was different. As the Christian and Muslim worlds increasingly came into contact in the western Mediterranean in the twelfth and thirteenth centuries, so too did the Jewish communities there, but the Jews of the Islamicate world had access to a significantly unified culture stretching from Muslim Spain to Egypt and beyond, and they made use of it to develop an intellectual sophistication beyond, as they saw it, what was available in Christian lands. One effect of the perceived disparity was the movement, which began in Muslim Spain and flourished among emigrants from al-Andalus to Provence, to translate texts (science, philosophy, and medicine), disciplines (linguistics), and cultural elements (literary and poetic styles and themes) for the Jews in Christian lands, especially Christian Spain, southern France, and Italy. In transmitting new texts and ideas from one Jewish community to another, Jews also were at the interface of the translation movement at large: they facilitated the movement of texts, especially from Muslim to Christian culture.

The reception of Aristotle, new interpretations of whose writings came to the Jewish and Christian worlds via Maimonides and the Muslim scholars Avicenna (Ibn Sina) and Averroes (Ibn Rushd), and subsequent discussions about the appropriate role of rationalism in religion, particularly in the interpretation of sacred texts, was particularly prominent in the thirteenth century. In Christian history the pinnacle of this process was long considered to be Thomas Aquinas, a Dominican active at the University of Paris. Because much of this history in the modern era was written by Roman Catholic scholars who were themselves Thomists or came out of a Thomist background, the thirteenth century was seen as one of intellectual greatness.

Aristotelianism was important in the intellectual traditions of Judaism, Christianity, and Islam, but it was also a source of conflict within all three. It came under great suspicion in Christian culture, with many texts banned from study in the early part of the thirteenth century and certain Aristotelian and Averroist ideas condemned in Paris in 1277, although the authority of Aristotle eventually triumphed in the Thomist synthesis.[44] Christian Aristotelians, including Alexander of Hales, Albert the Great, and Aquinas, were indebted to Maimonides, and thus the intellectual life of the Christian thirteenth century had strong Jewish and Muslim roots.[45] On the Jewish side, the works of Maimonides had made their way to the south of France and Spain, where huge controversies over their use erupted, especially over the relationship between religious practice and reason, and the use of philosophy in the interpretation of Scripture. Among Jews it was a cultural as well as a doctrinal conflict, as Jewish leaders in Latin Christendom saw Maimonides as challenging the very beliefs, practices, and communal structures that had kept their communities together. His works also unsettled Jewish authorities in the Latin West because those works so obviously carried with them the marks of a cultural environment (that of the Jews of Islam) that was alien to them.[46]

The growth of Aristotelian knowledge, involving Christian universities and intra-Jewish controversies, is a good example of entanglement. On all social levels, knowledge—religious, philosophical, medical, linguistic—reached people through a complicated route. The chapters in this collection all deal in one way or another with the issue of transmission of ideas across linguistic, cultural, or geographical borders. To put this idea in terms employed elsewhere by Yossef Schwartz, "communities of knowledge" potentially share a variety of texts, in distinction to "communities of discourse," groups whose members discuss and interpret the texts in dialogue with each other.[47] Schwartz's chapter uses the example of two scholars living in Italy in 1289–90, Zeraḥyah ben Isaac ben She'alti'el Ḥen and Hillel ben Samuel ben Elazar of Verona, as an illustration of the ways different Jewish intellectual communities fit together. These two men, both of them physicians, philosophers, and translators (from Arabic to Hebrew and from Latin to Hebrew, respectively), were part of a shared community of knowledge but in some ways belonged to different communities of discourse, even though both were Maimonideans.

Their disagreement over the interpretation of Maimonides carried with it several subtexts, including the issue of who had the authority to interpret Maimonides, the virtues of practical versus theoretical medicine, and personal competition between these men. They disagreed over Maimonidean hermeneutics in exegesis—an issue, we recall, with which Nahmanides was also concerned—and its implications for specific readings.

One of the prominent characteristics of the long thirteenth century is the impact of translated texts like those undertaken by Hillel and Zeraḥyah. Latin, Hebrew, and Arabic were the primary literary languages of the cultures discussed here. Christians and Jews who lived in Muslim lands would have known Arabic, but in Western Europe (with the exception of Muslim Spain) Arabic was known only by a handful of specialists. Few Christians knew Hebrew and few Jews knew Latin. Communication between Christians and Jews took place in the vernacular they both spoke, whether Arabic or dialects of Italian, French, German, English, or Spanish. This meant that translations from Arabic and translations from Latin had different cultural roles: those from Arabic made texts that were widely available in the Islamicate world available to people outside it, but those from Latin were of texts available in the Christian world only to a handful of learned elite. The Hebrew philosophical-scientific canon came to consist of works originally written in Arabic by Jews, works originally written by Muslims in Arabic or texts translated into Arabic from Greek, and works translated from Latin that in many cases had been translated from Arabic, but these streams merged into one corpus. Yet, as Schwartz points out, the two different Jewish linguistic and cultural contexts developed along different paths, each with its own cultural resonances. When these two scholars translated and commented upon works that came to form part of this corpus, Hillel chose the systematic tract and disputation as formats, both typical of Latin university discourse, whereas Zeraḥyah chose the commentary form characteristic of Maimonideans. The choice of format reflected their different intellectual projects and the intra-Jewish split that characterized linguistic and philosophical communities.

The translation movement began earlier for Christians than for Jews. Toward the end of the eleventh century, Constantinus Africanus, working at Monte Cassino in Italy, made a corpus of Greco-Arabic medicine available in Latin. In the following century, translators working primarily in Spain translated numerous works of philosophy, science, astrology, and medicine from Arabic. The process of translating from Arabic into Latin was often aided by Arabophone Jews, who assisted the efforts in twelfth-century Spain as well as those in the thirteenth century at the courts of Alfonso X in Castile and Frederick II in Palermo.[48] Even with the help of Jews, however, translations from Hebrew into Latin were extremely rare before the Christian Hebraism of the late fifteenth century.

The translation movement for Jews began more slowly, with only a handful of translations from Arabic into Hebrew dating from before the second half of the twelfth century. These early translations include religious works from Judeo-Arabic, linguistic treatises, and astrology.[49] There was also a small but important movement of translation from Latin into Hebrew from the twelfth century, especially of medical texts, which included both works that had been translated from Arabic into Latin and original compositions in Latin.[50] Latin would become an increasingly important source of Hebrew translations over the following centuries, but it did not surpass Arabic in most domains until the fifteenth century, when translations from Arabic experienced a sharp decline.

In the twelfth and thirteenth centuries, however, Arabic remained the main source for translation into Hebrew. By the 1160s, Judah ibn Tibbon (ca. 1120–90) had emigrated from Andalusia to Provence and was engaged in the translation of Judeo-Arabic works, including fundamental works of Sa'adia Gaon, Baḥya ibn Paquda, Judah ha-Levi, and Solomon ibn Gabirol. His son, Samuel ibn Tibbon (ca. 1165–1232), continued by translating works of Averroes, Aristotle, and—most significantly—in 1204 Maimonides' *Guide of the Perplexed*. Although a second translation of the work was produced by Judah al-Ḥarizi (ca. 1205–13)—the version that was translated into Latin a few decades later—the dominance of the Tibbonid dynasty would continue to carry weight, with Samuel's son, Moses ibn Tibbon, and son-in-law, Jacob Anatoli, becoming two of the great translators of the middle of the thirteenth century. Samuel ibn Tibbon's translation of the *Guide*, more widely circulated, is word for word rather than sense for sense; it makes more difficult reading than al-Ḥarizi, but was valued as bringing the reader closer to the experience of reading the original.[51]

The influence of Maimonides sent shockwaves throughout the Jewish world, as Jews grappled with the implications of his Aristotelian philosophy. In her chapter S. J. Pearce traces one of those waves, demonstrating that transmission of knowledge took place not just across languages but across genres and across time as well as space. Like Galinsky and Capelli, she focuses on the material texts of the medieval Jewish tradition, the manuscripts. The particular manuscript she discusses—a Hebrew version of the "Alexander

Romance"—may not seem at first relevant to the Maimonidean controversies over the place of rationalism in Jewish thought. However, its colophon claims that the "Alexander Romance" too was translated by Samuel ibn Tibbon, an implausible suggestion based on sources used in the Hebrew text, and in so doing intervenes in the debate over the two translations of the *Guide of the Perplexed*. Pearce reviews possibilities for understanding the colophon's critique of al-Ḥarizi and what it has to say about translation theory as applied to a text about Alexander. She further reviews the manuscript's problematic history. Her investigation suggests that early modern Ashkenazic readers were building on literary traditions from al-Andalus through their choice of texts. They understood the complexity of the issues involved in the translation of the *Guide* and other texts from Arabic, and of debates over the place of Maimonides in Jewish culture.

Because of their role in selecting and interpreting the texts to be translated, translators served an important role as cultural mediators, providing the options that composed the intellectual repertoire for either Christians or Jewish communities. Yet transmission did not depend on text translation alone; one may speak of cultural translation, in which a text may remain in its original language but take on a different function or even be rephrased. The study of the Bible was mentioned by R. Yeḥiel as something that brought Jews and Christians together. In the twelfth century, Stephen Harding consulted with Jews to correct the text of the Old Testament; later in the century, monks at the Abbey of St. Victor in Paris were known to discuss Bible interpretation with Jews. Transmission and entanglement are also easily discernible in the medical profession. There was a great deal of personal contact between Jewish and Christian doctors, who learned from each other, cooperated, and—we see clearly from the case of Jacob ben Makhir ibn Tibbon at Montpellier at the end of the thirteenth century[52]—helped translate each other's texts. Jewish doctors did play an important role in the translation movement (with the exception of al-Ḥarizi, all the translators discussed above were physicians), but they also treated Christian patients, just as Christian doctors sometimes treated Jewish patients. Converts, ranging from the repentant Doeg ha-Edomi to the embittered Nicolas Donin, were also important mediators for oral and textual transmission. Other contexts include the relationships between Jews and Christian or Muslim officials and the implications of a shared legal system.[53]

There is even a degree of transmission discernible in the more hostile relations of Christians, Muslims, and Jews during the Crusades, as shown in

Uri Shachar's chapter on pollution and purity. He posits not a specific mechanism for transmission of a particular genre, but a similarity in rhetorical tropes across Jewish, Christian, and Muslim accounts of the crusades so notable as to imply the entanglement of a shared culture repertoire. In all three traditions, ideas of pollution and purity were used to distinguish between self and other; but, at the same time as each depicted the other as impure, they also used language that attributed to the other a significant role in the process of purification. Christian crusade rhetoric cast Muslims as contaminants of the sacred sites, earlier through deliberate desecration or, later, by their mere presence; scholarly attempts to explain this trope have treated it as isolated, whereas Shachar shows that it was intertwined with the use of a similar approach in Muslim and Jewish texts. Ayyubid jihad texts, which reacted to Christian holy war rhetoric, stressed the ritual sanctification of sacred sites, which unclean idolaters should not approach, and the contaminating influence of the enemy. The idea of "the Holy Land" did not have the same valence for Muslims as it did for Christians, but by the thirteenth century Muslims too were seeing land as something polluted that needed to be purified with a flow of infidel blood. As individuals were cleansed with water, territory could be cleansed with blood. In Christian thought the cleansing water was that of baptism rather than ritual ablution, but it could still be replaced by spilled blood. Shachar argues that Christians were well aware that Islamic texts required an act of metaphorical ritual cleansing to reclaim polluted land. Jews who immigrated to the Holy Land in the thirteenth century and attempted to prepare the land for the coming of the Messiah also wrote of a ritual bath, which could take the form of a rain of blood, to cleanse the impurity of immoral enemies from the land.

While Shachar identifies similar cultural work done by different texts in three religious traditions, Elisabeth Hollender demonstrates how one text within Jewish society could do different cultural work according to geography and context. The chapters by Kanarfogel, Cohen, and Galinsky show how distinct the intellectual cultures of the various regions in thirteenth-century Judaism could be. But alongside these distinct regional variations in Jewish practices and norms, the cultures of the communities in different geographies were deeply entangled with each other. The scholars Kanarfogel studies understood their shared talmudic texts differently, but they did not work in isolation from each other. Hollender reminds us just how soft the geographical and linguistic borders were. Her chapter questions the dichotomy between Sepharad and Ashkenaz by arguing for ongoing close contact between the two on the basis of the reception of Sephardic poetry in Ashkenaz. Cultural transmission requires more than just a text arriving in the company of a traveling scholar or merchant; shorn of its cultural context, it requires a new context. Transmitted texts do not always fulfill the same functions as they did in their original home, but rather undergo cultural translation. In the new cultural context, readers may put texts to a variety of experimental uses (in this case, liturgical contexts for poems that had previously been more personal) before fixing them into a manuscript tradition. Liturgy is one of the cultural spheres most susceptible to cultural transmission, and Hollender takes as her example the way in which Ashkenazic Jews used the poem *Tsiyon ha-lo' tish'ali* ("Zion, will you not inquire?") by Judah ha-Levi, making it part of the liturgy and adopting certain Sephardic aesthetic norms in the process, and using it as a model for additional Ashkenazic *kinnot* (laments) for the Ninth of Av. In contrast with the early modern period when the liturgy became more standardized, in the thirteenth century each congregation made decisions about which *kinnot* to include alongside *Tsiyon ha-lo' tish'ali*. The transmitted text gave rise to a new genre, not because the Sephardic poem was perceived to be superior to what was available in Ashkenaz but because it stimulated new Ashkenazic developments. The cultural translation that turned the poem into a *kinnah* had echoes in other Jewish cultures that accepted the Ashkenazic change of function.

* * *

The quotation with which we began calls us to the Jews' streets, streets that were not hermetically sealed but that were shared with their neighbors who constituted the majority culture. The different chapters in the book all present different environments in which Jews interacted with their surroundings, absorbed, rejected, and appropriated from them, and then produced the sources that historians study today. They touch on a number of central aspects of medieval life: learned and legal culture, polemics, exegesis, translation, and ritual. The spaces examined here, the court, scriptorium, madrasa, yeshiva, and university, were arenas of interaction and cultural production, as well as of distinction and appropriation, as were other spaces that are considered less intensively such as the church, the synagogue, the marketplace, and above all the home. The various types of entanglement presented here should make clear that the histories of medieval Christian, Jewish, and Muslim cultures can no longer be written in isolation.

PART I

Intellectual Communities and Interactions in the Long Thirteenth Century

Chapter 1

Rabbinic Conceptions of Marriage and Matchmaking in Christian Europe

Ephraim Kanarfogel

Recent studies have traced the parameters of matchmaking in medieval European Jewish society, seeking as well to identify attitudes toward marriage more broadly in both the northern and southern regions (Ashkenaz and Sepharad).[1] Based on the many texts that have been published or are still in manuscript, it is possible to propose an overarching theory that accounts for differences between the two regions, encompassing both those that have been noted heretofore and others that have not yet received attention. I first present the differences and amplify them, and then suggest some larger perspectives to clarify points of divergence.[2] Comparisons between these leading Jewish cultural entities have long been seen as illuminating, especially given the increasing contacts between Ashkenaz and Sepharad in the period under discussion.

The Presence of Matchmakers

Modern scholarship has detected a striking difference between Sepharad and Ashkenaz regarding the use and prevalence of matchmakers (*shadkhanim*). Spanish rabbinic literature during the twelfth and thirteenth centuries barely refers to matchmakers and does not discuss their function.[3] At the same time, a leading northern French tosafist, Samson ben Abraham of Sens (Rash mi-Shants, who emigrated to Israel c. 1210, where he died in 1214), points to effective *shadkhanim* who were operating freely in northern France by the late twelfth century.[4] Moreover, the German tosafist Simḥah of Speyer (d. c. 1230) writes that it was "common to pay *shadkhanim* quite handsomely,"[5] while a parallel ruling by R. Simḥah's contemporary, Barukh ben Samuel of Mainz (d. 1221), along with that of Barukh's son, Samuel Bamberg, confirm the regular presence of such figures.[6] *Sefer Ḥasidim*, the compendium of pietism and ethics that reflects Jewish life in Germany at this time, also acknowledges the role of *shadkhanim*.[7]

Indeed, precisely because matchmaking had become so entrenched in Ashkenaz by the thirteenth century, Meir ben Barukh (Maharam) of Rothenburg (d. 1293) sought to diminish the exorbitant payments that were being made even to less effective *shadkhanim*, especially in light of an incident that had occurred in Erfurt.[8] Nonetheless, while Maharam's recommendation, to pay the *shadkhan* only a base fee for his time, is recorded first in *Sefer Mordekhai* (composed by Mordekhai ben Hillel, Meir's student), the (earlier) view of Simḥah of Speyer, that the *shadkhan* must be paid whatever he was promised, is then cited as a counter-position. Moreover, *Sefer Mordekhai* indicates that additional support for R. Simḥah's position emerges from a ruling by Isaac ben Samuel (R"I) of Dampierre (d. 1189), that a diviner who adjured demons (*shedim*) in order to locate a lost object is entitled to receive the overly large sum that he had been promised, since this is what people expect to pay for such an important and unusual service. As reported by his student R. Judah Sirleon, R"I similarly applied his approach to allow for the overly generous payment of doctors or healers as well.[9]

A subsequent passage in *Sefer Mordekhai* shows that Maharam's insistence on the successes and standing of a *shadkhan* as the determinants of his compensation mirrored the thinking of Joseph ben Abraham, the son-in-law of one of R. Meir's northern French teachers, Yeḥiel of Paris.[10] Maharam's conclusion, however, was questioned by another of his own students, Ḥayyim ben Isaac Or Zarua'. Indeed, Ḥayyim broke with his teacher in this matter and supported the position of Samson of Sens, as his father Isaac ben Moses Or Zarua' had presented it: matchmakers are to be paid the agreed upon amount in any case. They are entitled to the large payments proposed by their clients since they possess special abilities.[11]

The discussions that took place between Meir of Rothenburg and his students about the payment of *shadkhanim* document the functioning of matchmakers within Ashkenazic society through the end of the thirteenth century and beyond. Indeed, by the end the fourteenth century, in both

Germany and northern France (in the aftermath of the Black Death), the role of *shadkhan* was often assumed by rabbinic leaders, who commanded large fees.[12]

Matchmakers were welcomed throughout medieval Ashkenaz because they increased the possibilities for finding appropriate mates, irrespective of what parents and other family members were doing. Indeed, in the initial passage presented above from Samson of Sens, the matchmaker was not hired by the parents but by the prospective bride. As with medical treatment and the locating of lost objects where a specialized agent could accomplish things that others could not, the successful matchmaker, by dint of his charisma, savvy, and persistence, was worth a great deal to his client. However, as noted above, rabbinic authorities in medieval Spain had no discussion of the *shadkhan* and his role, because their communities did not typically employ them.[13]

The Parental Role

Several responsa by Solomon ben Abraham ibn Adret (Rashba) of Barcelona (c. 1235–1310) stress that it was the parents (and grandparents) who were tasked by Hispano-Jewish society with finding a mate for their children. Rashba rules that the bond or surety that parents often pledged when a proposed marriage was agreed upon (to limit the possibility that either side would withdraw) did not have to be forfeited when a young lady rejected the groom selected by her parents, since this was a rare and unexpected occurrence (*ones*). In Rashba's words, "Jewish girls are modest, and do not go over the line by choosing their husbands without their fathers' consent."[14]

Similarly, a grandfather was released by Rashba from forfeiting the bond that he had pledged in Estella when his granddaughter refused to marry the groom that he had selected, since "he could not have foreseen the possibility of his granddaughter's refusal, because all girls, with rare exception, abide by the wishes of their parents and relatives." Rashba characterizes the (grand) daughter's refusal as an "unexpected occurrence of the highest order" (*ein lekha ones gadol mi-zeh*).[15] Although Yom Tov Assis is undoubtedly correct in his finding, based on archival evidence, that a greater number of daughters disagreed with their parents' choice than Rashba's various responsa suggest,[16] parents (and grandparents, or other immediate relatives) are the only ones involved in seeking a mate for their child, as confirmed by the near total absence of references to *shadkhanim* in medieval Spanish rabbinic literature.[17]

Parents and other family members were involved in trying to marry off their children in medieval Ashkenaz as well but, as we have seen, *shadkhanim* were quite active there already by the second half of the twelfth century.

Moreover, there is an additional dimension of rabbinic thought in each region that supports these distinctions regarding *shadkhanim* and the parental role. The leading Spanish authorities during the thirteenth century, Ramban (d. 1270), Rashba, and Ritva (Yom Tov ben Abraham ibn Ishvili, d. c. 1325), justified the large payments to which medical doctors were entitled (where the patient agreed to make such a payment) in accordance with a talmudic discussion (Yevamot 106) about making good on inflated payments promised in exchange for relief from acute physical circumstances. Nahmanides comments that a doctor is paid as much as he was promised since when healing the patient, "he sells his wisdom which is worth quite a lot," as opposed to one who provides a patient with medications but does not devise any therapeutic plan, who receives compensation only for the price of those medications.

Not surprisingly, these Spanish rabbinic authorities do not refer to *shadkhanim* in this context, or to diviners.[18] Ashkenazic talmudists and halakhists, on the other hand, link the high payment of doctors directly to the exorbitant payments that were given to *shadkhanim* and magical diviners as noted above.[19]

In sum, Spanish rabbinic authorities considered medical treatment to be a highly developed science or skill, while finding marriage partners or lost objects was not. Parents were fully capable of securing marriage partners for their children. Ashkenazic rabbinic authorities believed that effectively arranging for marriage partners (like seeking cures and finding lost objects) could be enhanced by turning to someone with unique skills that included a great deal of personal rapport and perhaps even a measure of magical arts.[20] Employing a gifted matchmaker provided for the greatest possibility of a suitable partner being found, beyond the efforts of parents and other family members. As we shall see below, these differences between Ashkenaz and Sepharad with regard to making *shidukhim* are also linked to the question of how much responsibility (and choice) a bride and groom had in arranging their own marriage.

Marriage of Minor Girls Under the Age of Twelve

Avraham Grossman has proposed other reasons that might explain the dichotomy between Sepharad and Ashkenaz regarding the use of *shadkhanim*. The emphasis on impeccable lineage (*yiḥus*) throughout Germany and northern France meant that the stature and economic viability of a family were greatly valued. Matchmakers were able to verify these criteria in the family of the proposed mate, and to locate suitable partners in places near and far whose families possessed these traits. Grossman also suggests that the young ages at which many marriages took place (in particular with brides who were below the age of twelve), and the fact that "for the most part, parents did not consult their children at all but rather suggested matches for them based on their own considerations of what was best," meant that one set of parents might turn to a matchmaker to assess the suitability of the match before moving forward.[21]

However, if matchmakers were particularly necessary (and effective) in overseeing marriages that involved younger couples, we would expect to find matchmakers operating in Spain as well, where evidence for the marriage of girls under the age of twelve is quite extensive (as Grossman had also noted), extending back to the geonic period.[22] Moreover, as Elisheva Baumgarten has argued, the incidence of girls below the age of twelve getting married within medieval Ashkenaz during the thirteenth century appears to have been much more limited than Grossman and others have imagined. Baumgarten supports her claim about such limitations in northern France with a passage in a Tosafot gloss to Tractate Kidushin, and a ruling of Rabbenu Perets that will be discussed presently (both of which, as she noted, were associated with the tosafist academy at Evreux), in addition to arguing for the absence of such marriages in Germany based on two responsa by Meir of Rothenburg, one of which (regarding the marriage of R. Meir's own daughter) will be discussed below.[23] In light of its important implications, the history of this rabbinic allowance and societal practice needs to be carefully examined.

The Tosafot gloss to BT Kidushin 41a is the best-known rabbinic text about child marriage in northern Europe. The amora Rav ruled that one should not marry off his daughter until she reaches the age of twelve (even though a father is permitted to do so earlier according to Torah law), since, as the tosafist commentator explains, she might not have agreed to this choice were she of age. The commentator then adds: "But nowadays we are accustomed to marrying off our daughters even under the age of twelve (*ketanot*), because each and every day, the weight of the exile overcomes us. If someone currently has the funds to provide a dowry for his daughter, he may not have enough money later, which will cause his daughter [not to be married and] to remain an *'agunah* forever."[24]

Grossman cites a similar justification recorded in the anonymous *Sefer Kol bo*, from Perets ben Elijah of Corbeil (d. 1297) in the name of R″M, whom Grossman identifies as Rabbenu Perets's senior colleague, Meir of Rothenburg: "This ruling [of Rav] was applicable in their day, when many Jews lived in one place. But nowadays when we are small in number, we regularly permit the marriage even of a *ketanah*, lest [when she becomes of age] another will marry her first."[25] Both of these justifications refer to the diminished position of Jews within medieval society. The Tosafot passage seeks mainly to protect brides, while the ruling of Rabbenu Perets is more concerned with the disappointment of the potential groom. Nonetheless, there is quite a bit of common ground between them.

The Tosafot to Kidushin were produced (in large measure) in the tosafist study hall at Evreux, which was headed by the brothers Moses, Samuel, and Isaac ben Shne'ur during the second quarter of the thirteenth century. All three are mentioned in these Tosafot, as is the student of Isaac who apparently edited them. Moses ben Shne'ur is referred to a number of times in these Tosafot by the initials R″M and, as suggested by Baumgarten, it is he, rather than Meir of Rothenburg, who is referenced to as R″M in the *Kol bo* formulation by Rabbenu Perets.[26] This formulation originated in Rabbenu Perets's glosses to *Sefer mitsvot katan* by Isaac ben Joseph of Corbeil (d. 1280); like Isaac, Rabbenu Perets had also been a student at Evreux.[27]

Moreover, the precise section of the Tosafot Kidushin passage under discussion is named, in a gloss to the published text of the *Sefer Mordekhai* to Kidushin (at sec. 505), as Tosafot Shitah, a textual title or appellation that applies, as far as I can tell, exclusively to Tosafot Evreux or to Tosafot Rabbenu Perets.[28] A more muted form of this allowance is found in Abraham ben Ephraim's *Kitsur semag* (composed c. 1265), in the name of his teacher, Tuvyah of Vienne, along with a less nuanced version of the reasoning enunciated by the tosafist commentator from Evreux. R. Tuvyah was a younger contemporary (and close colleague) of the brothers of Evreux.[29] As Baumgarten suggested, the thirteenth-century justification for the marriage of *ketanot* in northern France was expressed solely in the tosafist academy at Evreux and was adopted by its devoted student, Rabbenu Perets of Corbeil, in slightly different form. Indeed, this allowance does not appear (in either of its forms) within any of the other Tosafot collections to Kidushin that were compiled before Tosafot Evreux.[30]

An unremarked twelfth-century justification for the marriage of *ketanot* is found in *Sefer Mordekhai* in the name of Elijah ben Judah of Paris, an older contemporary of Rabbenu Tam (d. 1171).[31] R. Elijah's name, however, is not mentioned by Tosafot Evreux or in the passage by Rabbenu Perets just discussed, even as the reason that he provided accords precisely with the one given by Rabbenu Perets. Thirteenth-century northern French tosafists were apparently unaware of this earlier justification. Moreover, Rabbenu Tam's leading student and successor in the late twelfth century, R"I of Dampierre, explicitly disapproved of such marriages in most cases; only when the father of a *ketanah* had died could she be married before the age of twelve. In all other instances, R"I held that the ruling of Rav was to be followed, and her father was required to wait until she turned twelve so that she could fully acquiesce to the marriage.[32]

Three twelfth-century tosafist discussions involving Rabbenu Tam touch upon the marriage of minor girls. Rabbenu Tam questioned an interpretation of Rashi (to BT Ketubot 57b), that the passage at hand can be understood only according to the view of Rav. There is no indication here, however, that Rabbenu Tam thought that Rav's ruling should be not followed in practice.[33] In a case that came before him, Rabbenu Tam's student, Menaḥem ben Perets of Joigny, maintained that a mother and brother could not marry off a young daughter while her father was traveling far away from home, since it is possible that the father had already betrothed her in another locale. Rabbenu Tam argues that if R. Menaḥem's concern was well founded, the subsequent marriage of all daughters at any age would be problematic. Rabbenu Tam's formulation does not suggest that *ketanot* were typically married off by their fathers, only that there were many instances of men who traveled and subsequently died while away from home, leaving young daughters behind.[34] Rabbenu Tam and Menaḥem of Joigny also argued about an uncommon instance of marital confusion, in which someone had betrothed the daughter of a wealthy individual from a distant land without properly specifying which daughter he intended to marry, where it turned out that all three of this individual's daughters were minors.[35]

The sum of the evidence indicates that while justification for the marriage of *ketanot* was initially proposed in northern France during the twelfth century, the phenomenon did not become entrenched in any region until somewhat later. And given the narrow scope of the tosafists who offered justifications during the thirteenth century, it is difficult to argue that this practice was widespread in northern France even then.

Moreover, even if one were to assume more substantive activity in northern France already during the twelfth century, which was then expanded further during the thirteenth century, nothing of this marriage practice involving minor girls can be found in any German tosafist sources, and German rabbinic figures are hardly mentioned even in theoretical discussions about marrying a *ketanah*. A passage by Avigdor ben Elijah Katz of Vienna—who was likely born in northern France and lived for a good deal of the thirteenth century, studying mainly in Germany with Simḥah of Speyer and teaching there and in Italy before becoming the rabbinic leader of Vienna[36]—demonstrates that the silence in German lands was not coincidental.

In his commentary to the Torah, which includes many halakhic rulings, R. Avigdor writes (on Gen. 24:51, in which Rebecca's family tells Abraham's servant Eli'ezer to take Rebecca and return to Israel so that she could become the wife of Isaac): "[She was sent] even though she was still a *ketanah*. This is the basis for the practice in northern France to marry their daughters off when they are minors, for purposes of modesty."[37] R. Avigdor, who was aware of Jewish practices throughout northern Europe, asserts that marrying minor girls was done only in northern France. This was pointedly not the case in Germany, even though *shadkhanim* were visibly active there from the days of Simḥah of Speyer and throughout the thirteenth century, no less than in northern France. It would seem, then, that the need to oversee the marriage of young girls (*ketanot*) cannot explain the use of *shadkhanim* as Grossman had posited. The strong presence of *shadkhanim* in Germany (where *ketanot* were rarely married), and their near total absence in Spain (where *ketanot* were regularly married), belies this suggestion.

Indeed, the single documented, straightforward case of the betrothal of a minor girl from late thirteenth-century Germany reflects the hesitation of German rabbinic figures to allow the marriage of minor girls, while requiring the bride's full acquiescence at any age.[38] Meir of Rothenburg writes that when he married off his daughter who was a minor, he "instructed her to accept her *kidushin* (betrothal) only if she so desired." Maharam explains that although it is prohibited for a father to betroth his minor daughter in accordance with the view of Rav, it is permitted to have her accept the *kidushin* for herself. This is precisely what he did in the marriage of his daughter, making certain that she firmly agreed to the betrothal and that she controlled it.[39]

Such an approach fully honors the halakhic theory behind Rav's position—albeit not the practice that he had advocated—and is supported by the analysis of an earlier thirteenth-century German tosafist as well.[40]

Cancellation of a Marriage Commitment

Another significant difference in attitudes toward marriage between Ashkenaz and Sepharad is evident regarding the cancellation of a marriage commitment (known as *bitul shidukhin*). In Spain, the termination of a *shidukh* was not seen as cause for undue regret or embarrassment. This is enunciated most clearly in an early responsum which, as Avraham Grossman has suggested, was likely composed by Joseph ibn Avitur (c. 1000): "In this era, there is no embarrassment or blemish [for a terminated *shidukh*], for it is customary that several men speak to Jewish daughters about marriage, but they only marry the one who is meant for them (*she-'olot be-goralan*). For the matching of a woman to a man is surely a heavenly undertaking. The man who had been trying to marry this woman [but failed], what can he do—this was not the one intended for him (*lo' haytah be-goralo*). As the rabbis said, 'A person does not touch what has been set aside for another.'" The larger halakhic context of this passage is that a groom who does not betroth the woman with whom he had a marriage commitment does not have to pay any penalty.[41]

Indeed, the notion that the cancellation of a marriage commitment should not be met with deep concern had already been expressed in a more understated way by Sa'adia Gaon, in a situation where it was unclear as to which daughter the groom had intended to offer marriage: "The first offer by Simeon is to be ignored and no explanation need be provided; for if he had wished to back out of a marriage commitment [in any case], he may do so."[42] The implication is that guaranteeing the establishment of a match is ultimately beyond the control of either the bride or the groom. As such, the dissolution of a match (before the wedding) is considered an acceptable reality rather than a negative occurrence. To be sure, Sephardic rabbinic authorities may have been seeking to cultivate behavior that was not naturally inherent within the larger societal group, but the rabbinic values are clear—this is a matter of fate (*goral*), which is within the divine purview.

A passage in *Sefer ha-Shetarot* by Judah ben Barzilai of Barcelona (c. 1100) notes that a financial condition was commonly imposed on the families of the bride and groom to dissuade either side from backing out, and funds or bills of indebtedness were often placed in escrow for this purpose. This was, however, a monetary arrangement with no other ramifications, as was the *shtar pesikta*, a document that was signed by the parties to ensure that the wedding would not be postponed and that the various financial commitments would be executed. These sanctions were not treated as fines for improper interpersonal behavior, nor were they imposed in every locale.[43] The purely monetary nature of these arrangements in the Sephardic world emerges quite clearly from a formulation of Maimonides in *Mishneh Torah* about economic commitments.[44]

This approach to the payment of fines for breaking a *shidukh*, and the related question of whether there is any embarrassment (*boshet*), is roundly contradicted by a series of tosafists in both northern France and Germany. Simcha Emanuel has conclusively demonstrated that in northern France, the fine for breaking a *shidukh* was supplemented by a strong communal ban (*ḥerem*).[45] Ashkenazic sources further assert that the fine represents payment for inflicting personal damages and embarrassment (characterized as *pegam* and *boshet*, respectively), and is not merely compensation for wedding costs or other payments that might have been lost. By consistently referring to these payments as *demei boshet* (payment for embarrassment), Ashkenazic sources indicate that a canceled wedding commitment is a form of real damage that must be made good according to talmudic law. The Talmud rules that embarrassment by words alone is insufficient to obligate the payment of *boshet*; the embarrassment inflicted has to be physical or at least visceral.[46] In the view of Ashkenazic halakhists, a potential mate who has been rejected experiences palpable feelings of shame (as does the larger family) and must be compensated for this damage.

A passage by Samson of Sens describes the handing over of pledges at the time that a *shidukh* was agreed upon, in order to bind the two families to carry out the wedding and to support the young couple. R. Samson insists, however, that the fine that results from withdrawing from this arrangement (which the security pledges also helped to cover) is not simply an effective means of ensuring that these commitments be honored. Rather, it was meant to redress the embarrassment experienced by one father (or groom or family) if the other backed out. R. Samson compares this to the hiring of a tutor, which is accompanied by a formal commitment that the tutor will be fined if he quits and there is no appropriate replacement, since this disruption causes the student to suffer.[47] Elsewhere, Isaac Or Zarua‘ makes the same point about establishing binding marriage agreements: “Even if there is not a full monetary obligation (*kinyan*) that binds the two wedding parties, the potential fine is accepted by both sides since the one who reneges embarrasses his friend; [avoiding] this embarrassment is what causes both parties to accept these terms."[48] This conceptualization is also found in Tosafot ha-Rosh (which often reflect Tosafot Shants),[49] and in Moses of Coucy's *Sefer mitsvot gadol* (in the name of R"I of Dampierre), which also includes the comparison to a tutor.[50] In addition to these formulations by northern French tosafists, *Sefer Mordekhai* cites this approach in the name of the German tosafist Eli'ezer ben Joel ha-Levi (Rabiah, d. c. 1225),[51] as does *Hagahot Maimuniyot*.[52] Interestingly, this approach is found already within a responsum by Rashi, who indicates that it preceded him and goes so far as to suggest that an ad hoc penalty of corporal punishment might also be appropriate, given the broad embarrassment generated (*she-lo' levayesh bnot Yisra'el*).[53]

Ḥayyim ben Isaac Or Zarua' wonders whether the monies disbursed when a *shidukh* is terminated should be given to the parent or to the child, since both are embarrassed when the engagement is broken. It was suggested to him that the payment should go to the child who suffers the rejection of the future in-laws; parents always puts the suffering of their child ahead of their own.[54]

Joseph Ibn Avitur and other Sephardic rabbinic scholars sought to establish that there was no cause for *boshet* in the breakup of an agreed upon *shidukh*. The fines associated with canceling *shidukhin* in Spanish Jewish society were purely monetary, and were not ubiquitous in any event. The overwhelming opinion in Ashkenaz, however, was that the cancellation of a marriage commitment was a source of palpable embarrassment and suffering. These feelings were substantial enough to provide an iron-clad means of obligation (*kinyan*) for imposing the fines found throughout Germany, as well as the impetus for the additional *ḥerem* that was in vogue in northern France, which considered the cancellation an affront to the community as a whole. These penalties were imposed, at least in part, because it was not easy for a young man or woman to find another mate after this kind of traumatic breakup, which was therefore seen as causing them real damage. As Meir of Rothenburg put it, "If one backs out on the *shidukhim*, his fellow acquires all of the funds put aside for that purpose since he was embarrassed by the other, and will not be able to easily find as fitting a match moving forward, as would have been the case had this not occurred."[55]

Accounting for the Differences

A significant conceptual distinction concerning the nature of Jewish marriage appears to underlie the series of halakhic and procedural differences between Ashkenaz and Sepharad presented here. All agree that the *shidukh* enterprise is a partnership or an amalgam between the people who were most closely involved with it—the bride and groom, the parents and grandparents, perhaps even siblings—and the Almighty. Spanish rabbinic authorities, going back to the Muslim period and to at least several Geonim in the east as well, maintained that the divine role in bringing husband and wife together was the predominant factor in determining the existence of a marriage. The task of the parents and grandparents was to arrange the marriage within the earthly realm, of which they were quite capable. However, it was ultimately the divine agency that allowed the marriage to move forward.

Since the parents and family were charged with this responsibility, even the couple themselves had little input. Thus, it was expected that a daughter would always agree to the choice of her father (or grandfather). This also serves to explain why Solomon ibn Adret, as Avraham Grossman has pointed out, remained steadfast in his view that a father could force his minor daughter to marry the man of his choosing,[56] despite the fact that the trend in Christian Europe, from the twelfth century onward, was to give the couple themselves more choice and a greater say in the matter.[57] For the Sephardic rabbinic conception, the determination of whether a betrothal and wedding would come to fruition was made and directed within the divine realm, with the parents serving as emissaries. Thus, if a commitment to marry was broken, there was no cause for regret or embarrassment. This was a matter of the heavenly *goral* (fate) of the bride and groom that was not particularly given to human intervention.

Ashkenazic rabbinic authorities, on the other hand, in both northern France and Germany, believed that the driving force behind marriage consisted of the will and efforts of the bride and groom, along with those of others (parents and family members, as well as matchmakers) who acted on their behalf. The Almighty obviously played a crucial if inscrutable role in this process, but it was up to the human participants to expend whatever efforts and means available to bring about a marriage that was appropriate in their view. The cancellation of a marriage commitment was seen as a source of deep disappointment and embarrassment, and was to be avoided at almost any cost.

Since the bride and groom were the key actors on their own behalf, the bride had to agree explicitly to her *kidushin* (and even in the not altogether common case that she was still a *ketanah*) in accordance with the position of Rav, which was accepted as normative by an impressive array of tosafists. Although *Sefer ḥasidim* advised fathers to marry off their children at a relatively young age so that they would accept the choice of a mate presented to them,[58] it also strongly supported the concept of a marriage entered into on the basis of love or at least on the desire of the couple to marry one another. And, as has been noted, *Sefer ḥasidim* was among the many Ashkenazic works that approved of the use of *shadkhanim* as facilitators to help achieve that goal.[59]

An unnoticed halakhic statement by Rabbenu Tam may also reflect these values. An engaged woman (a *meshudekhet*), whose wedding party had already been invited to the impending marriage ceremony (*ḥupah*), suffered the loss of her brother. Rabbenu Tam allowed her to marry within the initial thirty-day mourning period since if the groom could not marry this woman, he would marry no other and his obligation to procreate would remain unfulfilled. Indeed, Rabbenu Tam asserts that even if this couple were not yet formally committed to each other, he would have allowed them to marry in this situation "since she wants only him, and he wants only her." Because the groom was committed to this woman and would not marry another, Rabbenu Tam was prepared to allow the couple to be married at this time under any condition.[60]

The two disparate conceptions in medieval Ashkenaz and Sepharad on the nature of Jewish marriage can be detected within the talmudic corpus,[61] and are manifest in other exegetical contexts as well. As noted above, Avigdor Katz of Vienna commented that northern French Jews derived support from the betrothal of Rebecca for allowing a *ketanah* to be married. At the same time, however, Samuel ben Kalonymus he-ḥasid of Speyer, father of Judah he-ḥasid, maintained, on the basis of a series of midrashic passages (as did several tosafist Torah commentaries), that Rebecca was actually fourteen when she married Isaac, an interpretation consonant with the practice throughout Germany of not typically allowing *ketanot* to be married.[62]

Rashi, while accepting the standard approach of the *Seder ʻolam* that Rebecca was three years old when she was betrothed to Isaac, nonetheless stresses that Rebecca's family made it a point to ask her if she wanted to marry Isaac. Indeed, Rashi asserts that this action demonstrates that a woman can be married only with her consent (*mi-daʻatah*), which suggested to others that his approach is fully aligned with the talmudic view of Rav, that a father should not marry off his daughter as long as she is a *ketanah*. Even in this unique situation, it was necessary for Rebecca to acquiesce and to represent herself (as in the case of Maharam and his daughter noted above).[63] Similarly, while Rashbam understands Genesis 24:50 ("from the Almighty the result has emerged") to mean that it is difficult to extrapolate from Rebecca because there was an explicit divine intervention that chose her for Isaac,[64] he explains that Rebecca was nonetheless asked if she wanted to return with Eli'ezer to marry Isaac (Gen. 24:58–59) because this was the common practice (*derekh erets*) for all marriage proposals.[65]

On the other hand, Baḥya ben Asher, a student of Ibn Adret in Spain in the early fourteenth century, interprets Genesis 24:50 to mean that this is the way that all matches are made; they emerge from the divine realm and are determined there. Baḥya adduces a series of talmudic and midrashic passages to show that the bride and groom, and even their parents, have little to do with initiating or determining who their mate will be. All is in the hands of Heaven, and they can only deal with what comes their way.[66]

In a similar vein, Ashkenazic sources interpreted the talmudic concept of *shema yekadmenu aḥer be-raḥamim* (BT Mo'ed Katan 18b), "lest another, through the power of his prayers, precede [the intended groom] in marrying this woman," to mean that through prayer, an individual can subvert the heavenly process that designates a woman to be the marriage partner of a particular man. According to the commentary to Mo'ed Katan attributed to a student of Yeḥiel of Paris, this tactic is effective even with regard to a first marriage, where it surely seems that the heavenly determination, rather than any human action, should be the controlling factor,[67] an approach found also in a Tosafot gloss to Sanhedrin.[68] For these Ashkenazic interpreters, intense efforts undertaken by the suitor can be highly effective.

Spanish commentators, on the other hand, understandably had a difficult time squaring this talmudic passage with their conception of marriage, since individuals should have no ability to interfere with the heavenly match of others, which is their "religious fate" (*goral*). How is it possible, then, for one man to take away another's chosen match through prayer? Ritva interprets this passage to mean that only on the basis of improved actions over the long term can a person aspire to a "better" match from Heaven; increasing one's merits over time can cause the original heavenly decree to be redirected. The *raḥamim* of which the Talmud speaks does not connote prayer (as it often does) for Ritva, since there is no immediate way for a person to redirect a *shidukh*, an understanding that accords with the larger Sephardic mindset.[69]

Nissim ben Reuven (RaN) of Gerona (d. 1376) and his student, Yosef Ḥaviva (author of *Nimukei Yosef*), point to an ensuing talmudic passage which suggests that although the prayers of the man who was not intended by the Almighty to marry this particular woman might be heard to an extent, they will ultimately fail. Reflecting the unequivocal approach found in the Jerusalem Talmud, that the newly constructed marriage will never last, RaN and *Nimukei Yosef* explain that divorce, or even the death of the interfering male, will surely follow, allowing the originally decreed marriage to take place.[70]

With regard to marriage, the Spanish rabbinic posture confidently rendered unto the Almighty what was his, and charted the human response accordingly. This is not the only instance in which Ashkenazic and Sephardic authorities (and societies) expressed such differences about individual choice in the face of divine will, suggesting that these differences regarding marital choice and matchmaking reflect more than diverse interpretations of the underlying talmudic and biblical texts.[71] There were significant intellectual linkages between Ashkenazic and Sephardic communities during the medieval period, and each cultural area also developed in the context of the majority culture in which it was embedded. However, some differences in social practice between the two regions cannot be attributed to transmission or adaptation or to differing majority contexts, but rather were due to features internal to the development of *halakhah* and religious values in these areas. This study has shown that the choice of marriage partner is one such example.

Chapter 2

Nahmanides' Four Senses of Scriptural Signification: Jewish and Christian Contexts

Mordechai Z. Cohen

Jewish, Christian, and Muslim scholars in the medieval period developed sophisticated methods of scriptural interpretation, which they applied to the Hebrew Bible, the Christian Bible, and the Qur'an, respectively. While these methods usually developed independently within each faith tradition, there were important points of contact among Jews, Christians, and Muslims that allowed for the exchange of hermeneutical concepts across the nominally impermeable boundaries of religion. Interfaith polemics, for example—whether oral or written, whether organized or ad hoc—represented a sort of intellectual entanglement that brought to light differences as well as commonalities in the ways that the three faith groups encountered their sacred scriptures.[1] Jewish scholars in Muslim lands, at least since the early tenth century, wrote biblical commentaries in Judeo-Arabic and inevitably absorbed hermeneutical concepts designed by Muslims for the interpretation of the Qur'an.[2] Jewish and Christian Bible interpreters in Western Europe lacked such a common scholarly language, as Jews there wrote in Hebrew, Christians in Latin. Yet there is evidence of the exchange of views between them, most likely through conversations in the vernacular languages they shared, especially from the thirteenth century onward.[3]

This chapter explores how such an exchange seems to have contributed to the interpretive thought and practice of Moses Nahmanides (1194–1270), a key Jewish Bible exegete who lived in Girona near Barcelona and spent his final years in Palestine. The chapter assesses Nahmanides' hermeneutical innovations in light of his Christian intellectual milieu and his Jewish interpretive heritage, especially the *peshat* traditions that had developed in the preceding centuries in al-Andalus and in northern France. Nahmanides innovatively delineates four interpretive modes: *peshat* (plain sense), midrash, typological interpretation (*remez*), and kabbalistic/mystical (*sod*) readings. This four-fold scheme is not found among earlier Jewish interpreters, which gives greater urgency to exploring the apparent parallel to the well-known "four senses" of Christian interpretation summed up in the medieval couplet: *Littera gesta docet, quid credas allegoria, moralis quid agas, quo tendas anagogia* (the Literal teaches deeds, Allegory what you believe, Moral how you act, Anagogical where you are going).[4]

Jewish four-layered exegetical commentaries become more defined in the late thirteenth century, as attested in the Pentateuch commentary of Baḥya ben Asher (composed around 1291), a student of Nahmanides' student Solomon ibn Adret, and in the Zohar, penned in the circle of Moses de Leon (1250–1305), where the four senses were associated with the acronym PaRDeS (*peshat, remez, derash, sod*). Gershom Scholem and Moshe Idel have discussed parallels to the Christian four-fold scheme in connection with the Zohar, and Albert van der Heide has done so in connection with Baḥya.[5] None of them asserted a precise correspondence between the four Christian and four Jewish senses; rather, they weighed the possibility that the notion that the Bible can be read in four distinct ways was influenced by Christian thought. Though a four-fold schema is visible already with Nahmanides—considerably older than Baḥya and de Leon, and a more pivotal figure in the Jewish exegetical tradition—the notion of influence, which implies passivity on the part of the writer being influenced, is not very useful to explain it. Rather than speak simply of Christian influence, this chapter argues that Nahmanides drew upon tools from his intellectual surroundings to answer pressing questions that arose within conflicting internal streams of Jewish learning.

The extent of Nahmanides' knowledge of Latin is unknown, but he conversed with Christians (at times in polemical contexts) about their doctrines and Bible interpretation.[6] The most compelling evidence that Nahmanides absorbed elements of Christian interpretation comes from his pronounced method of typological interpretation, which resembles the well-defined Christian allegorical mode of reading whereby Old Testament narratives are said to prefigure events in the Gospel.[7] Nahmanides read the Pentateuch narratives as prefiguring events in Jewish rather than Christian history, using his typological readings to suggest that divine providence directly charts its course. While this sort of interpretive move can be traced to the sages of the rabbinic period (as noted by Nahmanides), Nahmanides' special terminology betrays the influence of Latin interpretive conceptions.[8]

Yet it is not enough to note parallels and posit Christian influence on Nahmanides' hermeneutics. The parallels can help us more sharply define dynamics internal to the Jewish interpretive tradition. We must ask why Nahmanides felt the need to adopt a typological mode of reading that resembled its Christian manifestation, and why he found it useful to employ a four-fold scheme of interpretation that he would have known from Christian sources. The claim made here is that by appropriating the typological mode of reading and the four-fold scheme of signification, Nahmanides was able to respond to specific challenges posed by the convergence of Jewish exegetical traditions in the thirteenth century—some first encountered by the great Provençal commentator David Kimḥi (hereafter, Radak; c. 1160–1235).

In the introduction to his Pentateuch commentary, Nahmanides announces the primacy of the commentary of Rashi (Troyes, 1040–1105), which is largely made up of reworked midrashic sources, notwithstanding Rashi's professed valuation of *peshat*. Yet in reality, Nahmanides is bound by the "purer" grammatical-rationalistic Andalusian model of *peshat* represented by Abraham ibn Ezra (1089–1164) and Moses Maimonides (1138–1204).[9] Nahmanides also employs (for the first time in the Jewish exegetical tradition) kabbalistic modes of interpretation.[10] In fact, Nahmanides' four-fold scheme incorporates values from each of these interpretive streams, which at times seem incompatible. By drawing upon Christian hermeneutical modes, Nahmanides arrives at a new and complex (though not problem-free) Jewish interpretive model.

Preliminary Matters: Defining *Peshat* and *Sensus litteralis*

The relationship among the various senses of the Bible was a hot topic in late medieval Latin learning.[11] The early church fathers had hallowed the spiritual senses at the expense of the literal, following Paul's dictum, "The letter killeth, but the spirit giveth life" (2 Cor. 3:6). In the thirteenth century, new perspectives emerged regarding the relative valuation of the literal and various spiritual senses of Scripture. Drawing upon the twelfth-century exegetical work of the Victorines and the new Aristotelian learning that entered the cathedral schools in that same century, Thomas Aquinas equated the literal sense with authorial intention, making it epistemologically decisive. Aquinas insists that "from the literal sense alone can any argument be made," and not from the spiritual senses.[12] For Nahmanides to have been aware of these developments in Christian learning, he need not have read Latin himself. It would have been sufficient for him to have discussed Bible interpretation with Christian scholars—a likely scenario.

Within Jewish Bible interpretation, the twelfth century witnessed the dramatic development of the concept of *peshat*, or plain sense exegesis. Rabbinic-era interpretation was characterized by the associative, fanciful, and aphilological midrashic modes of reading. What came to be termed *peshat* exegesis, on the other hand, aimed to interpret sacred writ philologically and contextually. This occurred separately in two centers of Jewish learning. A nascent interest in *peshat* appears in Rashi's work, and the method was perfected by his students in northern France, primarily Joseph Qara (c. 1050–c. 1130) and Rashi's grandson, Rashbam (c. 1080–c. 1160). This coincided with the revolution in Ashkenazic talmudic learning, pioneered by Rashi's students and two of his grandchildren, Rashbam and his younger brother, Jacob Tam (c. 1100–1171), founders of the vibrant tosafist school. A parallel conception of *peshat* is represented by Ibn Ezra, who epitomized the tradition of Hebrew linguistics and Bible commentary written in Judeo-Arabic that had developed in al-Andalus in the eleventh century—with its roots in the work of the tenth-century Geonim of Babylonia, especially Sa'adia Gaon (882–942). As a Sephardi, Nahmanides was first trained in the Andalusian school. But as a student of the tosafists, he venerated Rashi—no *pashtan* (practitioner of *peshat*) by Andalusian standards.[13]

Modern studies of the *peshat* method and the *sensus litteralis* in Christian exegesis tend to equate these interpretive notions with the Bible's plain meaning in the modern sense, or what the Bible "really says." Beryl Smalley, for example, sees in the heightened interest in the *sensus litteralis* the beginnings of the "scientific study" of the Bible historically and philologically, whereas prior Christian interpretation focused on the Bible's "spiritual senses," prompting readers to "not look at the text, but through it."[14] Subsequent scholars, however, argue that Smalley's "valorization" of the *sensus litteralis* should be tempered with a clearer awareness of how this interpretive mode operated within the culture of medieval Latin conceptions of literary authorship.[15] Analogously, whereas many twentieth-century studies of *peshat* regarded it as a precursor of modern historical-critical Bible scholarship, recent scholarship has emphasized the importance of viewing the medieval *peshat* methods—as they emerged in different streams of Jewish learning—within their respective intellectual and cultural contexts.[16] At times this new relativistic scholarly perspective meets resistance, because the term *peshat* in modern Hebrew is indeed used to connote "correct" interpretation of the Bible (notwithstanding the complexities associated with such a concept per se). This definition is then retrojected onto the medieval usage, resulting in the homogenization of the concept of *peshat* throughout its different chronological and geographic manifestations. Yet in the formative medieval period, multiple *peshat* models were advanced, each developing in distinct trajectories in different centers of Jewish learning, an observation that illuminates the hermeneutical challenges Nahmanides sought to address. The various medieval manifestations of plain sense exegesis—whether termed *peshat* or *sensus litteralis*—were thus a set of theoretical constructions that different interpreters devised to frame their novel interpretive methods.[17]

Twelfth-Century *Peshat* Models

The maxim that "a biblical verse does not leave the realm [lit., hands] of its *peshat*" appears three times in the Talmud; but its meaning there is unclear, and in any case the principle it implies is ignored for the most part, as rabbinic exegesis is almost exclusively midrashic.[18] Only in the medieval period does the maxim become the touchstone for a new mode of analysis. The decisiveness of this innovation is reflected in the programmatic statement of Rashi: "There are many midrashic *aggadot* [ancient rabbinic sayings, traditions] and our Sages have already arranged them in their appropriate place in *Bereshit Rabbah* and other midrashim. But I have come only to relate *peshuto shel mikra* [the *peshat* of Scripture] and the [sort of] *aggadah* that conforms to [lit., settles] the words of Scripture."[19] In a culture that studied the Bible exclusively through a midrashic lens, Rashi sought to institute a philological, grammatical, and historically sensitive literary analysis, that is, *peshat*. Yet he most often drew upon midrashic sources—a conundrum that has plagued Rashi scholars for centuries.[20]

Particularly troubling are the cases in which Rashi arrives at a *peshat* interpretation, but then goes on to offer a midrashic one. If he clearly discerned "the *peshat*," what need did Rashi have to cite the midrash? Sarah Kamin persuasively argued that *peshuto shel mikra* was never Rashi's exclusive goal.

Rather, he used this new concept to establish a commentary that establishes the language of Scripture, providing a coherent and internally consistent running commentary that involves both *peshat* and midrash in a dual hermeneutic.[21] Recent scholarship offers support for this view by pointing to Rashi's Christian intellectual milieu, in which even those who privileged the literal sense still took it for granted that the essential meaning of Scripture is its spiritual sense. From this perspective, the *peshat* revolution in northern France might be regarded as a Jewish manifestation of the new spirit of contemporaneous Latin learning in which the language arts (grammar and rhetoric) were brought to bear on the sacred text in new ways that led to increasing attentiveness to its literal sense.[22] Rashi, likewise, manifests a new—but hardly exclusive—interest in the plain sense of Scripture, which was ignored in his talmudically centered intellectual milieu.

To understand the distinction Rashi had in mind between his *peshat* exegesis and the midrashim of the rabbis, it is helpful to cite James Kugel's characterization of the assumptions underlying ancient (Jewish and Christian) Bible interpretation—including midrash. Three of the assumptions identified by Kugel are relevant for our study:

1. The Bible is a cryptic document, in which the surface meaning hints at its truer, deeper meaning. The rabbis would formulate rules for deriving these deeper meanings, yielding lists of hermeneutical principles (*middot*), such as those of R. Elie'zer and R. Ishmael.[23]
2. Scripture is a "Book of Instruction" fundamentally relevant to readers in every generation, and is not merely a record of the past.[24]
3. Scripture is perfect, containing no mistake or superfluity. This led to the doctrine of "omnisignificance," whereby nothing in Scripture was said in vain or for rhetorical flourish. Every detail in the biblical text—including unusual words or grammatical forms, repetitions, etc.—was regarded as potentially meaningful.[25]

Though Rashi introduced the importance of *peshuto shel mikra*, he did not deny these axioms, which inform the midrashic interpretations he adopts. For Rashi, the study of *peshuto shel mikra* serves as a foundation for selecting the most fitting midrashic readings.

This outlook is most clearly articulated in Rashi's programmatic introduction to the Song of Songs, which he took to be a national allegory reflecting the relationship between God (the lover) and Israel (the beloved), as expounded in midrashic tradition:

> "One thing God has spoken; two things have I heard" (Ps. 62:12). "One verse can have [lit., goes out to] a number of meanings" (BT Sanhedrin 34a), but in the end "a biblical verse does not leave the realm of its *peshat* (*peshuto*)." . . . Although the prophets uttered their words in allegory (*dugma*), one must fit [lit., settle] the allegorical meaning (*dugma*) on its basis and sequence, according to the sequence of the Scriptures. Now I have seen many aggadic *midrashim* on this book . . . that do not fit [lit., are not settled upon] the language or the sequence of Scripture. I therefore decided to establish the literal sense (*mashma'*) of the verses, in order to settle their interpretation according to their sequence, and the rabbinic *midrashim* I shall set, one by one, each in its place.[26]

Though Rashi takes it for granted that the midrashic reading reflects the ultimate meaning of this biblical text, he introduces a contextual-philological analysis of the literal love tale it depicts. He thus interprets the Song of Songs on two methodological planes. The midrashic reading must parallel the text as expounded on the *peshat* level. But for Rashi, the midrashic interpretation of the Song of Songs is the more authoritative one. The true meaning of this text lies beneath its surface and provides theological instruction about the relationship between God and Israel. And here, Rashi seems to have a polemical motive: whereas Christian readings of the Song of Songs emphasized the rejection of Israel and her replacement with the Christian Church, Rashi argued that the book illustrates the eternal bond of love between Israel and God.[27]

While Rashi's methodological remarks regarding Scripture's dual signification are attached to a text he takes as allegorical, his comments elsewhere indicate that he applied this bifurcation to all of Scripture, as he often juxtaposes his *peshat* commentaries with parallel midrashic ones—each labeled accordingly.[28] Even Rashbam, who departed from his grandfather's model and made elucidation of "the *peshat*" the exclusive goal of his commentary, acknowledged the theoretical primacy of midrashic interpretation, which he terms "the essence" of Scripture. As he writes: "Our Rabbis taught us that 'a biblical verse does not leave the realm of its *peshat*,' even though the essence (*'ikar*) of Torah comes to teach and inform us—through the hints of the *peshat*—the *haggadot, halakhot,* and *dinim* (tenets, doctrines, and precepts of Judaism) by way of redundant language and through the thirty-two *middot* (hermeneutical rules) of R. Elie'zer . . . and the thirteen *middot* of R. Ishmael."[29] Rashbam, like Rashi, regarded *peshuto shel mikra* as the surface layer of the biblical text, but he did not question the assumption that what Scripture really comes to teach is beneath the surface—as conveyed by midrash.[30]

By stipulating the theoretical superiority of midrash, Rashbam freed himself from the need to adhere to the *halakhah* (Jewish law) when interpreting *peshuto shel mikra*. Manifesting ingenuity and originality in his analysis, which is often at odds with rabbinic halakhic interpretation, Rashbam effectively created an alternative, non-talmudic, shadow system of *halakhah* based on his reading of Scripture itself.[31] To justify this analytic mode, he writes: "I have not come to explain *halakhot*, even though they are the essence . . . and some of them are found in the commentaries of Rabbi Solomon my grandfather. . . . But I have come to interpret the *peshat* of the Scriptures. And I shall interpret the laws and *halakhot* according to 'the way of the world' (*derekh erets*). And yet, the *halakhot* [as interpreted by the Rabbis] are the essence (*'ikar*), as our Rabbis said: 'The *halakhah* uproots Scripture' (BT Sotah 16a)."[32] Since Rashi had interpreted the legal portions of the Pentateuch based on rabbinic halakhic exegesis, Rashbam could devote his energies to "the *peshat* of the Scriptures," which he characterizes as being "according to the way of the world," an expression he uses to connote his rationally inclined, linguistically sensitive exegetical approach.[33]

The tenor of Rashbam's comments is echoed in a remark by his contemporary Thierry of Chartres (d. slightly after 1156) in the preface to his *Hexameron*: "I am going to expound the first part of Genesis, and the seven days and the division between the six works in relation to physics and the literal sense (*secundum physicam et ad litteram*). . . . I shall proceed to the exposition of the historical literal sense, so I shall completely leave beside the allegorical and moral readings, which holy expositors have lucidly accomplished."[34] Both authors pay homage to earlier tradition, while focusing their attention on a newer scientific approach. Thierry's conceptual combination *secundum physicam et ad litteram* resembles Rashbam's association of *peshat* and "the way of the world" (*derekh erets*).[35]

A very different model of *peshat* was developed in Muslim Spain—and first brought to Jewish communities in Christian Europe by Abraham ibn

Ezra, who began his career writing Bible commentaries upon his arrival in Rome in 1040. Aiming to bring the philological Andalusian method to Jewish audiences in Christian Europe accustomed to midrashic commentary, Ibn Ezra offers a different construal of the talmudic *peshat* maxim: "Our early [Sages] . . . interpreted sections, verses, words, and even letters midrashically in the Mishnah and Talmud. . . . Of course they knew the straight path, and therefore said that 'a biblical verse does not leave the realm of its *peshat*,' whereas the midrash is an added idea. But the later generations made midrash the essence (*'ikar*) and foundation (*shoresh*; lit., root), like Rabbi Solomon of blessed memory, who interpreted Scripture midrashically. He thought that it is by way of *peshat*, but the *peshat* in his book[s] is less than one in a thousand. Yet the sages of our generation celebrate these books."[36] Rashi's claim to *peshuto shel mikra*, coupled with his popularity among Jews in Christian Europe, rankled Ibn Ezra, who located genuine *peshat* within his own Andalusian heritage. Furthermore, Ibn Ezra conceives of *peshat* differently than Rashi did, for in his usage the term implies a value judgment that his northern French predecessor did not share. The "way of *peshat*," for Ibn Ezra, connotes *methodologically correct interpretation*—"the straight path," which he refers to elsewhere in his writings simply as "the truth" (*emet*) or "the essence" (*'ikar*)[37]—whereas "the midrash is an added idea," superimposed on the biblical text. Elsewhere he clarifies the theoretical assumption underlying this conception: "The words of any author, whether a prophet or a sage, [have but] one meaning (*ṭa'am*), although those with great wisdom (the Rabbis) augment [this] and infer one thing from another thing . . . at times by way of *derash* or by way of *asmakhta* [aide memoire, artificial projection onto the text]. About this the early Sages, of blessed memory, said: 'A biblical verse does not leave the realm of its *peshat*.'"[38] Whereas Rashi posits the multivalence of Scripture ("One verse can have a number of meanings"),[39] which allows for *peshuto shel mikra* and midrash to coexist as layers of scriptural signification, Ibn Ezra regards *peshat* alone as the meaning of Scripture. This singular model can be traced to Sa'adia, whose hermeneutical system incorporates the Muslim conception that God's will (*murād allah*) is expressed in the clear, unambiguous verses of sacred scripture, undercutting the first midrashic assumption Kugel identified.[40]

Maimonides, the great philosopher and talmudist, takes the singular *peshat* model to its radical logical conclusion. He boldly asserts that only laws expressed by the *peshat* are of biblical force (*de-orayta*), whereas those derived through the thirteen midrashic *middot* are merely of rabbinic authority (*de-rabbanan*). The latter must therefore be excluded from enumeration among the 613 commandments—the enumeration cited in rabbinic literature to designate the essence of Judaism. The *de-orayta* versus *de-rabbanan* distinction appears in the Talmud, with an often fuzzy correlation of the former to the text of Scripture and the latter with rabbinic enactments. Maimonides recruits the *peshat* maxim to define this distinction sharply and systematically: "[The Sages] of blessed memory taught us . . .: 'a biblical verse does not leave the realm of its *peshat*' and the Talmud in many places inquires: 'of what does the verse itself speak?' when they found a verse from which many matters are learned by way of [midrashic] commentary and inference."[41] To make this connection between *peshuto shel mikra* and *de-orayta* status, he draws upon theoretical categories from Muslim jurisprudence. Using Arabic hermeneutical idioms, he characterizes the original core of the 613 biblical commandments as "roots" (*uṣūl*), which draw their authority directly from the *naṣṣ* ("the text" of Scripture itself), whereas the "branches" (*furūʿ*) are based upon the sort of inference known as *qiyās* (legal analogy or reasoning), the term he uses to characterize the midrashic *middot*.[42] In Maimonides' view, these hermeneutical rules were employed by the rabbis to scrutinize the text of the Bible and thereby augment the law given initially at Sinai. This outlook informs Maimonides' *Mishneh Torah*, his comprehensive code of Jewish law, in which he systematically cites plain sources from the Pentateuch—rather than midrashic derivations—to establish the basis of the *halakhah* that he regarded to be of *de-orayta* status.[43]

We can best appreciate Maimonides' construal of the *peshat* maxim by contrast with that of Rashbam, which is virtually its opposite. For the northern French talmudist, "The *derash* is the essence"; it is the ultimate source of *halakhah*. The prospect of denying the legal authority of *peshuto shel mikra* evidently was not problematic for Rashbam. This may seem surprising to a modern reader, especially one accustomed to thinking of *peshuto shel mikra* as the correct interpretation—as the term is used in modern Hebrew. Yet it would not have been strange in Rashbam's Christian intellectual milieu or against the backdrop of the midrashic tradition that did not grant ultimate authority to the surface layer of the biblical text. On the other hand, Maimonides, living in a Muslim intellectual milieu and inheriting the singular *peshat* model of Ibn Ezra, privileged *peshuto shel mikra* exclusively and relegated laws derived midrashically to the secondary *de-rabbanan* legal status.

Nahmanides' Rule of *Peshat*

Nahmanides raises a trenchant critique of Maimonides' rule of *peshat* primacy in his *hasagot* (critiques) on the latter's *Book of the Commandments*: "[This] principle . . . is shockingly beyond my comprehension, and I cannot bear it, for . . . if so . . . the truth is the *peshat* of Scripture alone, not the matters derived midrashically."[44] Nahmanides zeroes in on the sharp edge of Maimonides' reading of the *peshat* maxim, which implies that *peshat* alone is "the truth," the single authoritative sense of Scripture—precisely as Ibn Ezra stated. But Nahmanides argues that "the *midrashim* relating to the commandments . . . are all included in the language of Scripture . . . for the *peshat* [does not preclude the validity of midrash] as held by the Karaites [lit., Sadducees]. For 'the Torah of the Lord is perfect' (Ps. 19:8), with not a superfluous or missing letter, [but rather] all were written with wisdom."[45] As a student of the tosafists, Nahmanides adheres to a talmudic perspective that grants an essential status to midrashic derivations, and hints that the singular Andalusian *peshat* model comes dangerously close to the Karaite opinion. Nahmanides regards the Torah as a special sort of "perfect" text, in which something significant can be inferred from its every letter. Therefore, he explains, "all [matters] derived in the Talmud through one of the thirteen *middot* have biblical status [lit., are words of Torah], and they are an interpretation (*perush*) of the Torah given at Sinai."[46] As for the talmudic *peshat* maxim itself, Nahmanides offers his own construal as an alternative to that of Maimonides: "They did not say 'a biblical verse is not [to be understood] except according to its *peshat*,' but rather we have its *midrash* with its *peshat* and it does not leave the realm [lit., hands] of either one of them, since Scripture can bear all [meanings], both being correct [lit., true]."[47] Nahmanides' vociferous critique of Maimonides' singular *peshat* model (and, by implication, that of Ibn Ezra) and his insistence on the "essential" nature of midrashic derivations might make one think that he betrayed his Sephardic heritage and switched his intellectual allegiance to the camp of the talmudically oriented model of Rashi and Rashbam. Yet elsewhere, Nahmanides makes strongly dismissive statements about midrash that are thoroughly Andalusian. For example, in his disputation with Pablo Christiani (according to Nahmanides' account), he remarked: "We have . . . a book called *midrash*, that is to say sermons—rather like the case should a bishop get up and preach a sermon and one of the listeners like it and write it down. If one believes in it—well and good—and if one doesn't believe in it, there's no harm in that. . . . We also call this book *aggadah* . . . that is to say that they are merely things that one man tells another."[48] In this spirit, Nahmanides will often criticize Rashi's midrashic readings and instead offer his own interpretation "by way of *peshat*" that adheres more closely to Ibn Ezra's method. Furthermore, he regularly distinguishes between genuine applications of the midrashic *middot*, which (in his opinion) produce laws that are of *de-orayta* authority, and more tenuous midrashic "readings" that fall under the category of *asmakhta*, and therefore cannot be the genuine source of a *de-orayta* law.[49]

Indeed, Nahmanides privileged *peshuto shel mikra* in a way that Rashi and even Rashbam did not. Nahmanides consistently rejects the possibility that *peshuto shel mikra* may be interpreted in a way that does not conform to the *halakhah*—a possibility opened up by Rashbam's argument that the halakhic system is essentially based on midrash, and not the *peshat*, which therefore lacks legal authority. Furthermore, it would seem that Nahmanides regarded *peshuto shel mikra* as the first—and preferred—source of *halakhah*. Hence, wherever possible, he endeavors to demonstrate that a given precept is based on *peshuto shel mikra*, even if midrashic derivations are cited as its source in rabbinic literature—a move that Maimonides often makes.[50]

Nahmanides was well aware that the *middot* defy the rules of philological-contextual analysis. What he sought to accomplish in his critique of Maimonides' radical rule of *peshat* primacy was to endow the laws derived from the *middot* (but not from the less rigorous midrashic derivations by way of *asmakhta*) with a higher legal authority than they possessed in the Maimonidean system. From a hermeneutical perspective, however, he evidently accepted Maimonides' characterization of *peshuto shel mikra* as the primary meaning of the text, and the midrashic derivations through the *middot* as a secondary, derivative layer of meaning.[51]

Nahmanides' Typological Interpretation

The elevated status Nahmanides ascribes to midrashic interpretation in his critique of Maimonides' principle of *peshat* primacy would seem to be restricted to applications of the *middot*, which Maimonides and others in the Andalusian tradition characterized as a special mechanism that authorizes the rabbis to extrapolate laws from Scripture.[52] As a rule, Nahmanides does not grant the same status to non-halakhic (aggadic) midrash.[53] Yet there is a realm of aggadic midrash in which he constructs an analogous system of dual scriptural signification. At the beginning of his commentary on the patriarchal narratives in Genesis, Nahmanides remarks:

> I will tell you a principle by which you will understand all the coming portions of Scripture concerning Abraham, Isaac, and Jacob. It is indeed a great matter which our Rabbis mentioned briefly, saying [*Tanḥuma Lekh Lekha*, §9]: "Whatever happened to the patriarchs is a sign (*siman*) to the children." It is for this reason that the verses narrate at great length the account of the journeys of the patriarchs, the digging of the wells, and other events. Now someone may consider them unnecessary and of no useful purpose, but in truth they all serve as a lesson for the future: when an event happens to any one of the three patriarchs, it indicates what is decreed to happen to his children. . . . [E.g.,] The Holy One, blessed be He, had Abraham remain in Canaan to create similitudes (*dimyonot*) to what He intended to occur to his progeny.[54]

Nahmanides goes on to cite other examples: Abraham's travels in Canaan symbolize the map of the Israelites' entry, led by Joshua, into the land. Likewise, "Abraham's exile in Egypt . . . is an allusion (*remez*) to the exile of his children there," and "Isaac's exile . . . to the land of the Philistines . . . alludes to (*yirmoz*) the Babylonian exile."[55]

As observed by Funkenstein, this Nahmanidean strategy of reading bears a strong resemblance to the tendency of Christian interpreters to view Old Testament accounts as symbols or "types" of events and persons in the New Testament, especially Jesus Christ.[56] As Augustine writes: "Abraham our father was a faithful man who lived in those far-off days. . . . His wife Sarah bore him a son. . . . God . . . made them . . . to be heralds of his Son who was to come; so that not merely in what they said, but in what they did or in what happened to them, Christ should be sought and discovered."[57] The New Testament thus became a lens through which the deeper meaning of the Old Testament could be perceived. Events in the latter that seemed inconsequential were thereby endowed with significance. Not only was God's command to Abraham to sacrifice Isaac viewed as a "prefiguration" of God himself sacrificing his only son, but Isaac's carrying the wood was seen as a symbol of the cross Christ would bear.[58]

Beyond the obvious methodological similarity, Funkenstein notes that the terminology employed by Nahmanides—novel in the Jewish exegetical tradition—echoes that of Christian typological exegesis. Hence, in his review of the symbolic significance of the accounts of the Patriarchs in Genesis, Nahmanides remarks: "In the Book of Genesis . . . the Torah completed the account of how the world was . . . created, as well as an account of all the events which befell the patriarchs, who are a sort of creation to their progeny. All the events that happened to them were figures of [other] events [lit., things; *tsiyurei devarim*], indicating and foretelling all that was destined to come upon their progeny."[59] The distinctive Nahmanidean term "figures of events" echoes the Latin term *figura* employed in typological interpretation. Some might argue that one need not posit Christian influence to explain Nahmanides' typological readings, since he cites rabbinic sources for them. Indeed, the statement "whatever has happened to the patriarchs is a sign to the children" that Nahmanides cites as the basis for his typological strategy is rabbinic. Yet the meaning of this rabbinic statement is hardly unequivocal, and Nahmanides imparts it with special hermeneutical coloring, as a system of reading.[60]

A specific example of typological influence arises in Nahmanides' adaptation of Augustine's notion that the six days of creation in Genesis symbolically represent the "six ages of the world" (*sex aetates mundi*). According to this doctrine, which was highly influential in the medieval Christian world, each day of creation represents a thousand-year epoch of human history (based on 2 Peter 3:8, "One day with the Lord is as a thousand years, and a thousand years as one day"), from the formation of Adam to events of the Revelation, with the seventh epoch ("age") being eternal rest after the final judgment and "end of time," just as the seventh day of the week is reserved for rest. Nahmanides, likewise, remarks that "the six days of creation are [a foreshadowing of] all the days of the world, i.e., that its existence will be six thousand years. For this reason the Rabbis have said: 'A day of the Holy One, Blessed be He, is a thousand years' [*Bereshit Rabbah* 19:14]."[61] He goes on to offer specific parallels between the six days of creation and the six-thousand-year periods of world and Jewish history. Although Nahmanides cites the rabbis as the basis of this parallel, the actual method is unmistakably Augustinian.[62]

Nahmanides adopted this interpretive mode in the first place because there were specific problems in the Jewish exegetical traditions he inherited that he was uniquely able to resolve by adapting the Christian typological mode of reading. Rather than regarding this "borrowing" simply as

"Christian influence," we might say that Nahmanides drew upon tools made available by his Christian intellectual surroundings to perfect his Jewish reading of the Bible.

Largely ignoring the midrashic assumption that Scripture is written "for our instruction," the *peshat* methods that emerged in the twelfth century interpreted the biblical narrative within its historical context. However, for Rashi and Rashbam, *peshuto shel mikra* was effectively an ancillary aspect of scriptural signification; thus eternal "instruction" could always be secure in the midrashic readings, which Rashbam characterized as the "essence of Torah." For Ibn Ezra, though, the "way of *peshat*" precludes the midrashic assumptions and projections. Within the Andalusian school, the biblical narratives were valued for providing historical context for the Law, but were not mined for detailed "instruction" per se.[63]

While developing separately for most of the twelfth century, the northern French and Andalusian *peshat* schools functioned adequately, each with its own assumptions. But when they converged in the thirteenth century, a dilemma became apparent: how could an adherent of Ibn Ezra's rigorous *peshat* mode find moral or religious "instruction" in the biblical narratives? This dilemma faced the Provençal commentator Radak, whose father, Joseph Kimḥi (c. 1105–70), was an Andalusian émigré, who brought the learning of his heritage to Narbonne, which had been a bastion of midrashic interpretation. As a proud Sephardi, Radak fashioned his *peshat* method after that of Ibn Ezra and was an ardent Maimonidean. Yet this younger Kimḥi, evidently influenced by his Provençal milieu, was also a devotee of rabbinic literature, and valued Rashi's commentaries for their midrashic content.[64] Aware of the religious edification midrash provides, Radak aimed to replicate it in his *peshat* exegesis by devising a distinctive style of extrapolating religious and moral lessons from the narratives in Genesis, often prefaced with the formula "This story was written to inform us."[65] Nahmanides embraced this approach and even borrows his Provençal predecessor's distinctive phraseology, noting some such lessons where Radak had noted them—and, more importantly, applying the method independently.[66]

Yet Nahmanides would have perceived the limitations of this endeavor. As a *pashtan*, Radak refrained from midrashic speculations and aimed to deduce only modest conclusions well supported by the text. The result was a sparse coverage of the Genesis narratives: perhaps a dozen or so lessons in all. Nahmanides augmented this number a bit but could not go much further. Most significantly, while lessons might be derived from each biblical episode as a whole, the details they contain often elude deeper explanation. The midrashic impulse, of course, was to attribute significance even to the smallest details of the biblical narratives (the doctrine of omnisignificance). But this analytic style was criticized as irrational by both Ibn Ezra and Maimonides, as Nahmanides was well aware.[67]

So how could Nahmanides attribute deep meaning to the biblical narratives without offending the sensibilities of the Andalusian *peshat* school—which he had internalized? The typological mode of reading resolved this dilemma. Even while stipulating that on the level of *peshuto shel mikra* there is no specific lesson conveyed by the details of the Bible's historical episodes, Nahmanides could attribute to them a secondary symbolic significance. As he remarks on the episode of the wells Isaac dug in the land of the Philistines: "Scripture gives a lengthy account of the . . . wells, even though there would seem to be no purpose in the plain sense of the story (*bi-peshutei ha-sipur*). . . . But there is a hidden matter (*'inyan nistar*) here, as scripture conveys future events."[68] Nahmanides proceeds to explain how the name of every well dug by Isaac hints at another episode in Jewish history.

Nahmanides here clarifies the dilemma he faced: the *peshat* reading offers little of significance in terms of "doctrine." Why were these details included in the Pentateuch? To answer this question, he posits that Scripture conveys a secondary, typological level of signification. While Nahmanides may have drawn the notion of a distinct typological layer of scriptural signification from his Christian intellectual milieu, his motives for adapting it into his own reading of Scripture emerged from an internal Jewish hermeneutical tension.

Nahmanides' Kabbalistic Interpretation

In the early thirteenth century, the study of Kabbalah had reached maturity in the centers of Jewish learning in Provence and Catalonia. Nahmanides was deeply influenced by Kabbalah and incorporates it into his Bible commentaries, often prefaced with the marker "by way of truth," which might be compared with his corresponding marker "by way of *peshat*" inherited from Ibn Ezra and Radak. We will focus here on how the kabbalistic dimensions of Nahmanides' commentary interact with what he describes as *peshuto shel mikra* and other layers of scriptural signification.

In his introduction to the Pentateuch, Nahmanides refers to profound kabbalistic mysteries about creation and about the nature of God, and argues further that they are "all written in the Torah, either explicitly or by implication (*be-remez*)."[69] To be sure, the basic goal of his commentary is to "draw people's hearts with *peshat* interpretations and a few pleasant [midrashic] words." But he goes on to speak of a further goal of his, to convey "hints (*remazim*) . . . regarding hidden matters of the Torah (*sitrei Torah*) [discernable by none but] . . . an understanding recipient."[70] These remarks create the impression that the often cryptic notes prefaced by the expression "by way of truth" embedded in Nahmanides' commentary necessarily convey a layer of scriptural signification independent from his other modes of interpretation. However, David Berger and Bernard Septimus have argued that Nahmanides often invokes kabbalistic knowledge specifically in order to arrive at a most fitting *peshat* reading.[71] In such cases, he usually begins his commentary by pointing to the linguistic or conceptual deficiencies of earlier interpretations, which he resolves by drawing upon a kabbalistic doctrine. A prime example is his commentary on Deuteronomy 25:6, a verse about the law of the levirate marriage that Rashi had interpreted based on a talmudic halakhic midrash, which Ibn Ezra dismissed as a case of *asmakhta* and interpreted literally "by way of *peshat*."[72] The trouble is that the literal reading contradicts the *halakhah*, a situation that Nahmanides could not accept. Indeed, the Talmud (BT Yevamot 24a) notes this contradiction and therefore regards this verse as an exception to the rule that "a biblical verse does not leave the realm of its *peshat*." The traditions Nahmanides inherited thus presented him with two unacceptable possible readings: either a *peshat* interpretation that contradicts the *halakhah*, or a midrashic interpretation that violates the rules of *peshat* (which, for him, meant philological-contextual interpretation). Nahmanides rejects both of these possibilities and instead cryptically remarks, "But by way of truth, this verse is a promise, and thus it is according to its *peshat*."[73] In his view, then, there is only one correct interpretation of this verse, which he arrives at using a kabbalistic doctrine. The preponderance of such examples of "convergence" of *peshat* and "the way of truth" would suggest the centrality of *peshuto shel mikra* in his view.[74] In other words, unlike other kabbalists who tended to "devalue" *peshat*, Nahmanides used his kabbalistic knowledge in service of this Andalusian exegetical project.[75]

Yet at times Nahmanides indeed speaks of an esoteric layer of scriptural signification separate from *peshuto shel mikra*. Substantiating his claim that esoteric knowledge about the account of creation is "hinted at" in the Torah, he writes the following regarding the opening verse of Genesis: "By way of truth Scripture speaks about the lower realms and hints at (*yirmoz*) the higher realms. Thus the word *bereshit* ('in the beginning') refers covertly to the emanation called Wisdom, the first of all beginnings."[76] In discussing the Garden of Eden episode, Nahmanides writes: "All these things are twofold [in meaning] (*kefulim*), the overt (*galuy*) and the concealed (*ḥatum*) are both true (*emet*)."[77] He explains elsewhere: "The Garden of Eden exists somewhere in this world. . . . Everything appearing in Scripture in the Creation section is true in its plain sense (*peshat*), and in none of them does 'Scripture leave the realm of its *peshat*.' . . . But the secret of the issue is that the matters are twofold [in meaning], for the Garden of Eden, and the four rivers and the Tree of Life and the Tree of Knowledge . . . all are literal and according to their *peshat* . . . but also convey a wondrous mystery, for they are figures for [other] things (*tsiyurei davar*)."[78] By combining the *peshat* maxim that he defined in his critique of Maimonides with the notion of "figures" he employed in connection with his typological mode of reading, Nahmanides indicates that once again we are dealing with a dual hermeneutic. While he insists on preserving the integrity of *peshuto shel mikra*, he argues that Scripture also conveys another layer of meaning.

This mystical layer of meaning is distinct in Nahmanides' system from the other non-*peshat* modes of scriptural signification discussed above. It clearly has nothing to do with the realm of halakhic midrash. On the other hand, Nahmanides' use of the term "figures" suggests a similarity to his typological mode of reading. In his mystical readings, Nahmanides posits that the mundane realities described in the *peshat* layer correspond on a metaphysical level to the divine reality composed of dynamic potencies or emanations.[79] Whereas the transfer in Nahmanides' typological readings involves the progression of history—events that occurred at one time are said to prefigure events in a later time—his mystical readings entail a conceptual transfer whereby entities in the lower, mundane reality symbolize ones in a higher, supernal one—not unlike Augustine's discussion of the relation that holds between the "earthly" and "heavenly" Jerusalem.[80]

Nahmanides, in positing this additional layer of scriptural signification, opened up a way of incorporating several interpretive systems. While *peshuto shel mikra* offers no specific doctrine, on a deeper, mystical level Scripture is indeed "omnisignificant." In the very first remarks in the body of his Pentateuch commentary, he opens his gloss on Genesis 1:1 by citing the famous midrashic question posed by Rashi: given that the Pentateuch is a book of law, why does it even include an account of creation? Betraying Maimonidean influence, Nahmanides argues that the doctrine of creation could not have been omitted from the Pentateuch as it is one of the fundamental beliefs of Judaism. Yet, as a talmudist, Nahmanides was unwilling to reject the midrashic remark itself and thus reinterprets it in the following way: the doctrine of creation is conveyed briefly in Exodus 20:11 ("For in six days the Lord made the heaven and earth . . ."); the question is why the Pentateuch expends words on a detailed narrative of creation. This sort of question is typical of the midrashic outlook, which assumes that every detail of Scripture must contain instruction. Nahmanides therefore has no need to answer the question on the *peshat* level.[81] Yet it is conceivable that the same type of thinking that motivated him to posit a typological layer of scriptural signification, as described above, likewise motivated him to posit a mystical one in his commentary on this verse.

Jewish and Christian Conceptions of Scriptural Multivalence

Nahmanides was not the first Jewish interpreter to adhere to the doctrine of scriptural multivalence, which can be traced to the ancient rabbinic saying that "the Torah has seventy faces."[82] That vague notion was refined by Rashi and Rashbam, who articulated a dual hermeneutic by distinguishing between *peshuto shel mikra* and midrashic interpretation, and asserting that both inhere in Scripture.[83] The innovative move advanced by Nahmanides was to define three types of non-*peshat* scriptural signification more sharply: halakhic derivations using the midrashic *middot*, and typological and kabbalistic readings that expound the hints embedded in Scripture to future events and supernal realities, respectively. Whereas Rashi could cite halakhic and aggadic (including typological) midrashic interpretations in an undifferentiated way, Nahmanides felt compelled to define distinct mechanisms by which such interpretations can be ascribed to Scripture legitimately. In doing so, he responded to critiques of midrash implicit in the singular *peshat* models formulated by Abraham Ibn Ezra and Maimonides. Even while criticizing those Andalusian predecessors, the Catalan talmudist had to justify his conception of scriptural multivalence theoretically. As Septimus observes, for Nahmanides "there could be no return to the innocence of Rashi."[84]

In the case of halakhic midrash, Nahmanides could simply modify the Maimonidean scheme, within which the *middot* were defined as a secondary mechanism of extrapolation from the biblical text, and, as such, are distinct from *peshuto shel mikra*, which is the primary source of *halakhah*. Nahmanides did not need to debate this hermeneutical hierarchy. Without questioning the conceptual primacy of *peshuto shel mikra*, he could simply argue that the secondary extrapolations according to the *middot* also enjoy a *de-orayta* legal status. In this way, he rejected only their demotion to *de-rabbanan* status by Maimonides.

A different mechanism was required for non-halakhic midrash, and it would seem that here Nahmanides found it useful to appropriate the Christian notion of "figuration," which he terms *tsiyyurei davar/devarim* (figures of things). This hermeneutical model, as employed by Nahmanides, implies that the language of the biblical text itself has only one meaning, *peshuto shel mikra*. The things and events that the *peshat* signifies, in turn, hint at later events and supernal realities.[85]

There is little reason to ascribe significance to the fact that the precise number of senses of Scripture delineated by Nahmanides coincides with that of the Christian four-fold scheme. Nahmanides arrived at his "four senses" almost coincidentally, as a by-product of aiming to balance the Andalusian value of *peshuto shel mikra* with his talmudic-midrashic orientation influenced by the northern French school. Yet the fact that it was a commonplace within his broader (Christian) intellectual milieu that Scripture conveys four senses simultaneously may have made it easier for Nahmanides to break out of the straitjacket of the dual hermeneutic of his Jewish predecessors and construct his own four-layered scheme.

More important is the fact that Nahmanides' strategies for negotiating the complexities of the interrelation among the four modes of scriptural signification are comparable to some of those devised in contemporaneous Christian learning. As Rita Copeland explains, Thomas Aquinas built upon distinctions made by Augustine to devise a "definitive answer to the difficulties encountered by earlier generations of exegetes" by positing that "there are really only two senses of Scripture, the literal and the spiritual (the spiritual can be multiplied [into] . . . moral, allegorical, and anagogical). . . . Words point to things literally; and those things—events, objects, and facts—are ordained to yield up higher truth."[86] This perspective reflects "the new prestige and scope which the literal sense came to enjoy, within thirteenth-century schools of theology and beyond."[87] It would, for example, profoundly influence Alfonso de Madrigal (Ávila, c. 1400–1455), who enumerated the "ways in which the literal sense may be judged as superior to the spiritual sense."[88] Though the spiritual sense continued to dominate Christian interpretation, there was a new hermeneutical trend to tether it to—and even locate it in—the literal sense.[89]

Nahmanides' conception of "figuration"—a hermeneutical category he evidently drew from Christian sources—bears striking similarities to the one worked out by Aquinas. It would be a stretch to argue that Nahmanides was aware of the theories of St. Thomas himself, who was a generation younger than he—and whose major works were written late in his life. (Aquinas's theories would eventually reach Spain, as attested two centuries later by de Madrigal.) Yet Aquinas's hermeneutical thought was part of a larger context of scholastic Latin learning, represented, for example, by Robert Grosseteste (1175–1253), Guerric of St. Quentin (d. 1245), Alexander of Hales (1185–1245), and Albertus Magnus (1193 or 1206–80), who was Aquinas's own teacher. By the 1230s, those authors were beginning to draw upon newly introduced Aristotelian learning to understand the interrelation among the senses of scriptural signification in new ways.[90] It is not inconceivable that some of those intellectual currents came to Nahmanides' attention. In any case, Aquinas's emphasis on the literal sense as the only signification of the words of Scripture illuminates Nahmanides' endeavors to define the workings of the multiple layers of scriptural signification in relation to *peshuto shel mikra*. Both thirteenth-century thinkers endeavored to preserve the value of older, traditional forms of interpretation—whether midrashic or spiritual—in the face of the increasing prestige of the new exegetical conceptions that emerged and strengthened in the twelfth century (*peshuto shel mikra* and *sensus litteralis*).

Chapter 3

Bible and Politics: A Correspondence Between Rabbenu Tam and the Authorities of Champagne

Avraham (Rami) Reiner

The subject heading "The authorities in Champagne asked Rabbenu Tam about three matters" appears in two manuscripts containing biblical commentaries by the French tosafists,[1] close to the commentary to Genesis 5:24 ("Enoch walked with God, then he was no more, for God took him"). The writer concludes the correspondence by noting: "This is what Rabbenu Tam, may his abode in the Garden of Eden be honored, replied to the authorities as he saw fit."

The Rabbenu Tam referred to in this responsum is R. Jacob ben Meir, who was active his entire life in Ramerupt, in the Champagne district, almost until his death in the summer of 1171.[2] He is known as the foremost of the French tosafists, and, as such, legal questions were directed to him from throughout Europe. A query in the realm of Bible commentary, however, raises a question that has been asked in the past: was he also a Bible scholar, like his maternal grandfather Rashi and his brother R. Samuel, Rashbam, whose ties with non-Jewish French scholars are documented in his writings?[3] Additionally, the fact that the queries were posed by the authorities in Champagne is both surprising and intriguing. Did these authorities address Rabbenu Tam because of his fame as a Jewish scholar, because he was known as a Bible scholar? Or did this query have its roots in the political and social ties that led this ruler to turn to an outstanding Jewish scholar such as Rabbenu

Tam, even if the latter was not an important Bible scholar? The subject of the nature of this correspondence, which is at the center of this essay, must be preceded by a short discussion of the extent to which Rabbenu Tam engaged in Bible interpretation, and the degree to which he was accepted as an authority in this arena.

Did Rabbenu Tam Interpret the Bible?

A late tradition that appears in *Shem ha-gedolim* by R. Ḥayyim Joseph David Azulai (Hida, eighteenth century, Jerusalem/Livorno) attributes the following to Rabbenu Tam: "Just as my master, my grandfather, interpreted the Talmud, I do so as well, but a commentary to the Bible is beyond my powers, because I am not capable of this."[4] This testimony reflects the common assumption that Rabbenu Tam did not write a commentary to the Bible. An examination of contemporaneous sources, however, presents a more complex picture. The existence of a commentary to Job composed by Rabbenu Tam was first noted in the early twentieth century by Samuel Poznanski, who pointed to citations to it found in contemporary writings.[5] In 1993 Benjamin Richler published his identification of the commentary to Job in a manuscript in the holdings of the university library in Rostock.[6] Richler himself, however, found weaknesses in this identification. He wrote at the end of his article that the only certainty is that the commentary in MS. Rostock is French, and from the time of Rashbam, but we cannot be certain of Rabbenu Tam's authorship. The commentary was later published by Israel Ta-Shma[7] as the work of Rabbenu Tam, and again by Avraham Shoshana.[8] In contrast to these scholars, I find Richler's doubts still valid, and suggest three additional reasons to doubt his authorship:

1. A glossary that was written in Rouen, the manuscript of which is currently in Leipzig, contains more than twenty-two thousand biblical words with their French equivalents and their meanings in Hebrew.[9] Seven commentaries that are ascribed to Rabbenu Tam in this glossary relate to the book of Job. Four of these, however, originate in Rabbenu Tam's *Sefer ha-hakhra'ot*,[10] which is discussed below, and the other three neither appear in, nor are identical to, the commentary recently attributed to him.[11]
2. The commentary ascribed to Rabbenu Tam, when referring to

commentaries by Rashi, does not mention him by name; rather, it introduces the latter's commentary with "*yesh mefarshim*" (there are those who interpreted).[12] Such an allusion to Rashi is completely unknown elsewhere in Rabbenu Tam's writings. Moreover, the phrase "*yesh mefarshim*" is also used in the commentary to denote other commentators and compositions besides Rashi,[13] a matter that further undermines the attribution of the commentary to Rabbenu Tam, Rashi's grandson, who surely would have distinguished his famed grandfather from other commentators.

3. In *Sefer ha-hakhra'ot*, a linguistic study, Rabbenu Tam discusses the linguistic disagreement between Menaḥem ibn Saruq and Dunash ben Labrat. He examines twelve verses from the book of Job, in some of which the interpretation in *Sefer ha-hakhra'ot* corresponds to that in the Rostock commentary to Job.[14] In some instances, the correspondence could be explained in different ways, and does not constitute proof of their common authorship by Rabbenu Tam.[15] The commentary makes no mention of other verses discussed in *Sefer ha-hakhra'ot*,[16] while the interpretations in the two works contradict one another regarding still other verses.[17]

Further support for the argument that Rabbenu Tam did not write the Rostock commentary on Job, if not decisive proof, is the treatment of the clause from Job 41:12, "as from a steaming, boiling [*ve-'agmon*] cauldron." The commentary attributed to Rabbenu Tam states: "In *leshon Kna'an* [the language of Canaan], one implement is called *'agmon*.'" "The language of Canaan" refers to the language of Bohemia, the land of the Slavs. To the best of my knowledge, no additional instance appears in all of Rabbenu Tam's writings in which he refers to this language or translates from it, and there is no reason to assume he had any knowledge of this tongue. Furthermore, Rabbenu Tam's definitively attributed writings never once use the appellation "Canaan" to denote the Bohemian lands.[18] We therefore may conclude that Rabbenu Tam wrote a limited commentary to Job. The author of the commentary in MS. Rostock used the commentary by Rabbenu Tam, just as he drew upon additional sources. The language of the composition is not that of Rabbenu Tam, since it is practically inconceivable that he would include his grandfather Rashi in an amorphous group of "*yesh mefarshim*." The work's final redactor was probably a Torah scholar who was familiar with the French commentaries, including that of Rabbenu Tam. He might have been one of Rabbenu Tam's students who came from the land of "Canaan," and therefore was quite familiar with the commentary on Job of the French sages, and was also capable of adding an observation that was based on the language of "Canaan."[19]

Now we must turn from this commentary of doubtful authorship to a work that we know definitively was written by Rabbenu Tam. In *Sefer ha-hakhra'ot* Rabbenu Tam discussed one hundred and sixty objections by Dunash ben Labrat to the linguistic conception of Menaḥem ibn Saruq. These objections, all of which pertain to the language of the Bible, appear in the latter's *Maḥberet Menaḥem*.[20] Rabbenu Tam usually, but not always, defended Ibn Saruq's positions, thereby continuing the tradition of his grandfather Rashi. In the introduction to *Sefer ha-hakhra'ot*, Rabbenu Tam wrote a poem beginning with the Hebrew acrostic "*Ya'akov be-Rabbi Meir petah devarekha ya'ir*" (Jacob son of R. Meir, the words you inscribed give light [Ps. 119:130]). This acrostic, together with a single instance in which the author refers to Rashi as his grandfather, demonstrates that the author is R. Jacob ben Meir—Rabbenu Tam, Rashi's grandson.[21] A lengthy and detailed response by R. Joseph Kimhi (1105–70) of Spain, who was active in Narbonne, where he wrote *Sefer ha-galui*, attests to Rabbenu Tam's authorship of *Sefer ha-hakhra'ot*. Kimhi also asserted[22] that, despite Rabbenu Tam's halakhic and talmudic greatness, he "did not labor in grammar to find the depths of their [i.e., the written compositions] brightness, similar to our masters in the land of France and its surroundings, who are mainly occupied with the Talmud, and at times with the Bible . . . but not with linguistic use. Consequently, they have no mastery of it." In other words, the French sages are considered to be unparalleled in Talmud and *halakhah*, but their wisdom is much less with respect to the Bible and its interpretation, and their linguistic knowledge is so small that they seemingly should not put their hand to it at all. Thus, although the book was unquestionably composed by Rabbenu Tam and relates to the Bible, its major focus is linguistic. It would not likely lead to Rabbenu Tam's being seen as a Bible commentator in the eyes of the authorities in Champagne who had no knowledge of Hebrew and therefore would not be interested in Hebrew linguistics.

An additional genre that might likely preserve biblical interpretations by Rabbenu Tam is the tosafists' literature on the Torah. Once again, Poznanski was the first to describe these works. When he came to Rabbenu Tam's contribution, he wrote: "The collections of the tosafists on the Torah contain many of his interpretations of Pentateuchal passages, but they also include passages relating to Tosafot on the Talmud, halakhic matters, and the like. It is almost certain that he was confused with his student, R. Jacob of Orleans, who also was called Rabbenu Tam."[23]

Thus, according to Poznanski, Rabbenu Tam did not systematically interpret the Torah, and most of what is ascribed to him is the product of his talmudic and halakhic discussions. Admittedly, not all the Bible interpretations ascribed to Rabbenu Tam are of this sort, and "it is possible that he [Rabbenu Tam] interpreted some verses, and these interpretations were transmitted by his students."[24] These, however, do not suffice to change the general picture—that is, the decisive majority of the Bible interpretations attributed to Rabbenu Tam emerged from halakhic discussions or interpretation of the Talmud and rabbinic literature.

For example, *Sefer ha-gan*, a commentary to the Torah that was composed in France some seventy years after the death of Rabbenu Tam, mentions him twice, but each reference concerns a halakhic ruling by Rabbenu Tam that is only marginally related to Bible interpretation.[25] Likewise, a study of *Moshav zekenim* on the Torah (fourteenth century, author unknown)[26] teaches that of the nearly fifty references to Rabbenu Tam, only four are not directly related to rabbinic literature. Most of these passages have parallels in Tosafot on the Talmud and originate in the talmudic study hall. Patently, then, we do not have a commentary to the Torah per se by Rabbenu Tam.

The nature of Rabbenu Tam's subordination of Bible commentary to halakhic study is evident in his interpretation of the following talmudic dictum: "A person should always divide his years [of study] into three: a third [of this time] to Scripture, a third to Mishnah, a third to Talmud."[27]

According to Rabbenu Tam, this demand is fulfilled by studying the Babylonian Talmud, since Babylonia [*Bavel*] and its Talmud were defined by R. Johanan as follows: "Intermingled [*belulah*] with Scripture, intermingled with Mishnah, intermingled with Talmud."[28] Thus, by studying the Babylonian Talmud, one at the same time fulfills the demand to study Scripture and Mishnah, no longer being required to devote a third of his time to each.

Even if the primary goal of such an interpretation was to reconcile the talmudic dictum with the methods of study in twelfth-century France, it also indicates the limited and inferior place that Rabbenu Tam assigned to Bible study. In a similar vein, Rabbenu Tam wrote to R. Meshulam of Melun that Bible study should be reserved for children.[29]

Thus, Rabbenu Tam's commentary to Job, if he indeed composed one, was limited in scope and did not survive the ravages of time. *Sefer ha-hakhra'ot* is primarily concerned with grammar; its Bible commentary is decidedly of secondary importance. His other biblical interpretations originated in his talmudic discussions, and appear only if the Talmud itself related to Scripture.

Possible Reasons for the Count of Champagne's Query to Rabbenu Tam

If Rabbenu Tam rarely engaged in Bible commentary per se, we are left with the question of why the "authorities in Champagne" addressed him with questions related to comprehension of the Bible while Bible commentators such as Rashbam and R. Joseph Bekhor Shor, with whom non-Jewish scholars were undoubtedly familiar,[30] were active at the time in his surroundings and might just as easily have been queried. It may very well be that the ruler of Champagne had heard that Rabbenu Tam was a famous Jewish sage whose academy attracted students from all across Europe. Therefore, the count directed his questions to him, without drawing distinctions between biblical commentary and commentary on the Talmud and *halakhah*. This is certainly possible; but I wish to offer a more likely suggestion based on a consideration of the nature of the relationship between local Christian authorities and Rabbenu Tam.

Isaac Hirsch Weiss was the first to collect evidence of Rabbenu Tam's ties to the Christian authorities in northern France.[31] Weiss based his essay on an analysis of how various writings penned by Rabbenu Tam and his students were formulated. Thus, a query directed to Rabbenu Tam begins with the words: "Our great master, our holy master, our master Jacob, without whom no one would raise his hands and feet in all the land, kings will consult with you, and they will do naught, whether great or small, until the secret is disclosed to you."[32] Rabbenu Tam begins his responsum with the words: "Although your emissary came while I was troubled, due to the ministers who confronted their master, and your servant sees and the city is in an uproar, though ministers meet and consult with me, I did not refrain from responding to your questions."[33] Likewise, Rabbenu Tam wrote in an apologetic tone at the beginning of another responsum: "Labor is imposed on me by others, and the service of the king."[34]

These formulations imply that the "service of the king" was imposed on Rabbenu Tam, who functioned as a sort of political advisor to the lord and his ministers, a role that was not necessarily connected to Rabbenu Tam's standing within the Jewish community. Other sources indicate that Rabbenu Tam's internal leadership within the Jewish community was well known in the non-Jewish surroundings. Thus, in his depiction of the massacres of the Second Crusade, R. Ephraim of Bonn emphasizes Rabbenu Tam's being the "great one of Israel" as a factor leading the Crusaders to attack him.[35] We can also agree with the argument made by Robert Chazan that the effort to defend the Jewish community politically from the Blois blood libel in the summer of 1171 (the last summer of Rabbenu Tam's life) was initiated by Rabbenu Tam, who was well acquainted with the lords of Champagne.[36] This correspondence therefore adds another layer to our understanding of the nature of Rabbenu Tam's relationship with the count of Champagne. This tie was not limited to the political and economic spheres. The correspondence attests to a social and intellectual bond that was not based on Rabbenu Tam's "professional" reputation, for, as noted, the Bible and its interpretation were not areas in which Rabbenu Tam chose to engage and for which he was renowned both near and far.

The "authorities in Champagne" whose questions were addressed to Rabbenu Tam almost certainly refer to Henry I, Henry the Liberal, who was count of Champagne from the death of his father, Thibaut II, in 1152 to his own death in 1181.[37] Henry's brother was Thibaut V of Blois, in whose territory—and with whose support, in great deal—the Blois blood libel took place in the summer of 1171. After mentioning and castigating the behavior of Thibaut, the anonymous chronicle that describes these events presents Henry in a starkly different light: "The ruler Heinrich, the brother of the wicked one, was aggrieved by this, and said: We have not found in the Torah of the Jews that it is permitted to kill a non-Jew. Yesterday a report went forth on the eve of Passover in Epernay, but I did not believe it. "[38]

The author of the chronicle praised Henry, count of Champagne ("Heinrich"), for his skepticism about the accusations of ritual murder being leveled against the Jews. The chronicler thereby placed Henry together with his father-in-law, King Louis VII of France, who also refused to lend any credence to such a charge. Besides the fact of this refusal, obviously significant in its own right, the specific content of his objection is also illuminating. The author testifies that Henry said: "We have not found in the Torah of the Jews that it is permitted to kill a non-Jew." This sentence implies that the Hebrew author viewed Henry as one with some knowledge of the Torah and the laws of the Jews.

Henry did possess broad knowledge, as the chronicle implies. The court of Henry and his wife, Marie, was renowned throughout France as a cultural center. In 1157 he established in Troyes, near Rabbenu Tam's home, the Saint-Etienne monastery, a center in which many of the educated of the time were active,[39] with the support of Henry and the involvement of Marie. John F. Benton has revealed the central position occupied by of the Bible and its interpretation in Henry and Marie's intellectual and cultural world.[40] Thus, for example, after Henry's death, Marie commissioned a poem of more than twenty thousand rhymed lines that interpreted Genesis. The wealth of sources—including untraditional ones—is so impressive that it has been suggested that its author, Evrat, and even Marie, in whose court he was active, were connected to a nonconventional Christian movement.[41] Furthermore, when John of Salisbury was in Rheims after having been forced to leave England in 1163, Henry sent to him a delegation of intellectuals with questions pertaining to the books of the Bible and their authors.[42] John, dismissive of the count's intellect, initially avoided responding to Henry's questions, but eventually wrote back after being convinced by the abbot of the monastery, Pierre de Celle, that Henry was serious and sincere in his desire to learn. An analysis of the questions demonstrates that although Henry was appreciative of scholarship and sought the company of outstanding scholars, he was certainly no intellectual himself. It therefore is not surprising that such a person found his way to Rabbenu Tam—with whom he was already familiar in another context, and who was known as an outstanding Jewish leader—rather than to less prominent Jewish sages who were better known in Jewish communities for their Bible commentaries than was Rabbenu Tam. Bible commentators such as *Rashbam* and R. Joseph Bekhor Shor were active at this same time, and Christian scholars solicited their biblical knowledge. Henry's choice of Rabbenu Tam was conditioned by political and social reality as well as shared intellectual interests. This, however, does not fully explain the context of the count's request.

The first of Henry's questions dealt with Enoch, of whom the Bible states (Gen. 5:24): "Enoch walked with God, then he was no more, for God took him." Henry assumed that the taking of Enoch was death, and wondered why, if Enoch walked with God, he died relatively young, at the age of 365, while other biblical characters of his time lived so much longer. The second question, which I do not discuss here, related to Leviticus 14:34: "When you enter the land of Canaan that I give you as a possession, and I inflict the leprous plague upon a house in the land you possess." The way in which the verse is worded implies that the Israelites are promised that upon their arrival in the Land of Israel there will be a leprous plague upon the house in the land that it possesses. Henry asks on this: "What manner of tiding is this?" In the third and last question, Henry wonders about the kingship of David and Saul. In his opinion, David was a greater sinner than Saul, leading Henry to wonder why Saul was deposed while the Davidic line endured.

The circumstances of the passing of Enoch, whom the Bible says was "taken" by God, and not that he died, aroused the imagination and thought of writers in antiquity. Early Jewish traditions held that Enoch went to Heaven in his lifetime and served there as a celestial scribe and secretary,[43] while the books of Enoch and Jubilees teach that Enoch was the first astronomer and scientist.[44] Whatever Enoch's occupation, what is important for our discussion is the interpretive possibility that Enoch did not die, but rather went elsewhere in his lifetime. This position was already embraced by the New Testament, as in Hebrews 11:5: "By faith Enoch was taken up so that he should not see death; and he was not found, because God had taken him. Now before he was taken he was attested as having pleased God."

The preoccupation with Enoch as one who did not die and, more importantly, as one whose miraculous departure was a prototype for Jesus' passing (similar to that of Elijah) frequently appears in the Patristic literature. This view became prevalent, and accepted, in the Christian literature for centuries, and the rabbis, too, were aware that Enoch's departure was embraced by Christians as a model for passing that is not death. Thus, we find in the midrashic work *Bereshit rabah* (fifth century): "The *minim* [Christians] asked R. Abbahu, saying to him: 'We find that Enoch did not die.' He asked them: 'Why?' They replied: 'Taking is mentioned here [i.e., referring to Enoch], and taking is mentioned about Elijah.'"[45] R. Abbahu gave his answer, and his students praised his response. What is relevant for our discussion is that the Jewish sages were well aware of the Christian adoption of the early traditions regarding Enoch's departure.

With this in mind, Henry's question is quite surprising. He assumed that Enoch died like everyone else, and that his premature death was punishment for his sins. He therefore was forced to ask: "Why did the Holy One take Enoch rather than all the rest, for we see that his actions exceeded those of others?" Henry's question is accordingly not based on the common Christian notion that Enoch did not die, and it shows, once again, that Henry's court was open to views that did not correspond to the accepted Christian stance. In light of this, his turning to a Jewish sage such as Rabbenu Tam is a bit more understandable. Rabbenu Tam wrote in his response to this question: "Because he was the seventh, and the Holy One, blessed be He, seeks sevenths: the seventh day for the Sabbath, the seventh year for the Sabbatical year, the seventh heaven in which to dwell, and so in everything."

According to Rabbenu Tam, it was Enoch's good luck as a member of the seventh generation of the human race after Creation that caused him to be beloved by God and resulted in God's taking him, instead of causing his death. Unlike Henry's starting assumption that Enoch died like any mortal, Rabbenu Tam's interpretation indicates that, instead of dying, Enoch was taken by God because of His fondness for anything connected to the number seven. Rabbenu Tam found this interpretation in the midrashic works *Pesikta de-Rav Kahana* and *Vayikra rabah* (fifth to sixth century),[46] but his adoption of this explanation is noteworthy. The opinion that Rabbenu Tam chose to present, that Enoch did not die, is close to the traditional Christian stance, in contrast with the position of the rabbis, who maintained that Enoch died for his sins. This latter view appears in *Bereshit rabah*: "R. Hama son of R. Hoshea said: He is not inscribed in the scroll of the righteous, but rather in the scroll of the wicked. R. Aibo [said]: Enoch was insincere, at times he was righteous, at other times, wicked. The Holy One, blessed be He, said: While he is righteous, I will remove him [from the world]."[47]

This interpretation also appears, with minor changes, in the commentary of Rashi, Rabbenu Tam's grandfather. Rabbenu Tam, in contrast, disregarded this tradition, and instead suggested that Enoch did not die, but was chosen and accordingly was taken by God. Thus, this position is a response to Henry's assumption of Enoch's death, and teaches that the two correspondents, Henry and Rabbenu Tam, did not feel constrained by the dominant interpretive tradition prevalent in their respective faiths. The correspondence between Rabbenu Tam and Henry attests to the existence of an unfettered interreligious discourse between two individuals who viewed the Bible as the basis for their religious conception. The religious difference between them did not keep them from their desire to understand the hidden ways of the God they shared.

Henry and Rabbenu Tam shared a closeness of another sort that can be seen from a study of the third question and response in this correspondence. Henry asked about the rule and fate of Saul and David. In his opinion, David was a greater sinner than Saul, and Henry asked why Saul had been deposed while David was able to establish a royal line. Rabbenu Tam expressed his answer by means of the following parable:

> In regard to what you asked concerning Saul: I will relate to you a parable. What is this like? It is like a great king who was imprisoned in a foreign land. The great ones of the land came to him, and said: "You cannot be released from your imprisonment until you bring us much money."
>
> He said to them: "I have nothing now with which to pay."
>
> They said to him: "Swear to us that you will send it to us at the appointed time," and he so stipulated in his oath.
>
> He went to his land and collected the money, which he sent with his officials and servants, to go to them at the appointed time.
>
> When they had gone half the way, they came upon a lord who was selling his land cheaply. They said, "This land will be for our master from the money that we have with us. We will return, and take other monies to pay his debt." And so they did. When they came to the king, he asked them: "Why have you come so speedily?" They replied, "We did thusly."
>
> The king immediately became angry with them, and he said to them: "You have disgraced me before my ministers, for of what avail to me are riches, after I have lost my trust?"
>
> Thus said the Holy One to Saul: Go and proscribe Amalek, since I swore. But he spared the best of the sheep to sacrifice to Me. Then Samuel said: "Obedience is better than sacrifice" [I Sam. 15:22], attentiveness, than sacrifices offered to the dead. Accordingly, the kingdom was stripped [from Saul].

According to this parable, the sin that was the undoing of Saul—namely, undermining the promise by God, who swore to proscribe Amalek—was not committed by David. When Saul spared Amalek, God's oath was not fulfilled, and such an affront to Him could not be forgiven. Returning from the moral of the tale to its main character: if the king had stolen, murdered, or committed any other despicable act, his offense would not have been as grievous in his own eyes as his violation of the vow, which caused him to be despised by his inner circle.

Rabbenu Tam offered an innovative solution. In Tractate Yoma, the Talmud discusses the question of divine justice in the punishment of Saul and

David, which it left unresolved. All that the Talmud says is that the Lord was the support of David, but not of Saul, whose sin was lesser than that of David.[48] Unlike the Talmud, Rabbenu Tam describes in detail the nature of the sin as he grapples with this problem. Rabbenu Tam's solution, however, is more instructive regarding the sage himself than about the severity of the sin. The values of the society in which Rabbenu Tam lived are internalized in what he writes. This was a society based on the values of loyalty and the mutual commitment of vassal and lord. The honoring of such commitments was the social and ethical foundation of this society and ensured its security. This covenant was forged by means of homage, and its unilateral violation was a criminal act, to be punished severely: the violator was declared disloyal.[49] This value system finds clear expression in the parable related by Rabbenu Tam, which reaches its climax in the words of the king: "You have disgraced me before my ministers, for of what avail to me are riches, after I have lost my trust?" An oath of fealty was an integral component of this homage, and such an oath is highlighted in Rabbenu Tam's parable. Clearly, then, not only is the value system reflected in the parable about the importance of trust between vassal and lord, the manner in which the parable is fashioned emphasizes the place of the oath. When the copyist of the responsum completed presenting what Rabbenu Tam had written, he added a comment of his own: "This is what Rabbenu Tam, may his abode in the Garden of Eden be honored, replied to the authorities as he saw fit."

Rabbenu Tam's responsum, which drew upon the values and concepts of the society in which he lived, would have been warmly welcomed by Henry, who, in addition to being appreciative of scholarship, was also count of Champagne. Could we also suggest that Rabbenu Tam was part of the sociopolitical system of lordship, vassalage, service, and fief-holding?[50] Obviously, we would have difficulty in accepting such a proposal. Homage and its accompanying oath of fealty were Christian by nature, and we could hardly imagine a Jew such as Rabbenu Tam being a party to such a relationship. Furthermore, we have no substantive knowledge of any other Jew in northern Europe in that period who was part of this social structure. Notwithstanding this, at times Rabbenu Tam's language alludes to greater involvement in the system of lordship than is typically assumed. I illustrate this argument with two brief examples.

The ceremonies of homage and the oath of fealty included fixed and obligatory formulae, as indicated by contemporary French legal works: the would-be vassal proclaimed, "My lord, I wish to be your man," while the lord was required to state, "I accept and take you as my man."[51] Rabbenu Tam writes at the end of a lengthy responsum to the Paris rabbis: "If it were not for the heavy burden [of those troubles], until the indignation would pass [see Isa. 26:20], until *my ruler* will leave, I would have written at length, but my troubles are pressing upon me. Perhaps they will pass . . . and I would be master of my time."[52] The word "my," referring to the ruler who visits during the troubled time, is very reminiscent of the accepted "my lord"/"my man" formulation, and strongly indicates the consciousness, and perhaps also standing, of the speaker—Rabbenu Tam.

One additional example can be offered: one of the undisputed obligations of the vassal to his lord was that of giving counsel. This duty was already mentioned in the early eleventh century, and during the course of the twelfth century vassals were required to present themselves at their lord's estate for consultations.[53] Aaron ben Joseph, a student of Rabbenu Tam, wrote at the beginning of a query that he directed to his teacher: "Our great master, our holy master, our master Jacob, without whom no one would raise his hands and feet in all the land, kings will consult with you, and they will do naught, whether great or small, until the secret is disclosed to you. Accordingly, I have sent to draw water from the cistern of Bethlehem, to learn what is the law of the *yevamah* [levirate wife]."[54] The praises heaped on Rabbenu Tam by Aaron indicate that he saw his teacher as shaping the agenda of the royalty and noblemen who consulted with him. But this sentence could also be understood metaphorically. Rabbenu Tam's response, however, shows the concrete nature of the passage: "You are a man, and may there be many like you in Israel, my beloved, R. Aaron. Although your emissary came while I was troubled, due to the ministers who confronted their master, and your servant sees and the city is in an uproar, though princes meet and speak against me, I did not refrain from responding to your questions."[55]

We cannot know why the ministers were angry with their lord, or why the city was in an uproar. We do know, however, that when R. Aaron turned to Rabbenu Tam, he already knew that the latter was busy offering advice to those who in no way could be numbered among the sages of Israel, a fact confirmed in Rabbenu Tam's detailed response. Might we be able to surmise that Rabbenu Tam participated on occasion in the consultations in the court of the man whom he called "my ruler"?

Conclusion

We have here offered an interpretation of the singular correspondence between the count of Champagne, most probably Henry I, and Rabbenu Tam on the understanding of biblical passages.[56] Although Henry was appreciative of scholarship, he was certainly not a scholar himself. Rabbenu Tam was the premier French halakhic authority and talmudic commentator of the time, but hardly engaged in biblical commentary, and was by no means known in Jewish circles as a Bible commentator. I have proposed that the context for the correspondence was the relationship, with its social and cultural aspects, between the count of Champagne and Rabbenu Tam, whose standing, I suggest, was similar to that of a vassal. If this is the case, then we possess testimony to a relationship unparalleled in northern Europe. The events portrayed in various sources can now be understood in a new light.[57] Thus, we should reinterpret the fact that Rabbenu Tam, like his father, lived in the village of Ramerupt, close to Troyes, but not in the city itself. Most of the Jewish communities of the time were situated in the trade cities next to the rivers through which goods passed, as was the case with Troyes. The fact that both Rabbenu Tam's father and Rabbenu Tam himself took up residence in the rural area surrounding Troyes—quite atypical of the Jews of the period—supports the central argument of this essay.

Additionally, we have seen in a passage from a halakhic source: "*Rosh* [R. Asher ben Yeḥiel], of blessed memory, wrote in his additions that he had heard that when Rabbenu Tam wanted to eat from his falcon's prey, he would make for it silver nails like shoes"—to prevent the falcon from delivering its venom and thereby rendering the hunted animal unfit for consumption, according to the talmudic conception in Tractate Hullin.[58] Was Rabbenu Tam accustomed to going hunting, after the fashion of the French nobility? The description seems credible, especially since Rabbenu Tam demonstrated his knowledge of hunting practices an additional time.[59] This analysis has demonstrated that Rabbenu Tam was integrated into the French and Champagne court culture to an extent greater than has hitherto been imagined.

Chapter 4

Rabbis, Readers, and the Paris Book Trade: Understanding French Halakhic Literature in the Thirteenth Century

Judah Galinsky

In a recent study I suggested that thirteenth-century French Jewish legal scholars were more motivated to reach a broader reading audience, beyond the elite Talmud scholar, than their Rhineland contemporaries.[1] In their writing on Jewish religious law throughout the century, French scholars showed an interest in making their works more accessible, an impetus that would seem to have been absent from their western German counterparts until the last quarter of the century, when one finds the beginnings of a change in Germany within the school of Meir of Rothenburg.[2]

In France, the scholars who wrote works on religious law expended thought and effort devising tools that would make their work available even for readers less conversant than the scholar with the talmudic material. This can be seen as early as the turn-of-the-century work *Sefer ha-terumah* (The Book of Offering) by Barukh ben Isaac. Although the body of the work is complex and written in the "scholastic" style of the Tosafot,[3] the author appended to his work an abridgment that allowed a wider range of readers to consult his legal decisions without having to immerse themselves in the complexities of the talmudic discussion.

However, the most dramatic expression of this French characteristic can be found in the work *'Amudei golah* (The Pillars of Exile) or, as it became known, *Semak*, by Isaac of Corbeil, completed in 1276–77. As we shall see, this book was written with a broad audience in mind. The author even expected laypeople to dutifully study his work, albeit with the help of learned colleagues, on a daily basis. In between these two extremes, the scholastic *Sefer ha-terumah* and the popular *Semak*, we note the path-breaking code of Moses of Coucy, *Sefer ha-mitsvot* (The Book of Commandments) or, as it became known, *Semag*, completed circa 1250, and the abridgment of this work, *Sefer ha-simanim* (The Book of Reference) or *Kitsur Semag*, composed by Abraham ben Ephraim and completed circa 1260.[4] Both works had an agenda of reaching out to a reading audience beyond the learned scholar and his students, even if they did not expect their book to become a handbook for the layman, as Isaac of Corbeil believed of his own work. In western Germany, the Rhineland, there is no such long-term sustained development throughout this century.[5] It would seem that mainstream scholars active in this area, Eli'ezer ben Joel ha-Levi of Cologne, Simḥah of Speyer, Barukh of Mainz, and Isaac Or Zarua' of Vienna, had no real interest in simplifying the law in order to make it more accessible, nor did they care for an educational program that would familiarize the laity directly with the law via the written word.[6]

At first glance such a stark distinction may seem somewhat surprising, as many scholars who study northern European Jewish society and its learned culture usually group northern France and the Rhineland together under the rubric of "Ashkenaz" and "Ashkenazic culture" (*tarbut ashkenaz*).[7] In this study I explore a number of historical factors that I believe led to the thirteenth-century differentiation between these two proud cultures on the central issue of religious law and its dissemination. One of those central factors, in my opinion, is the emergence of the Paris Latin and vernacular book trade during that time.

The Eleventh Century: Between Germany and France

Avraham Grossman, in his *Early Sages of France* (*Ḥakhmei tsarfat ha-rishonim*), pointed to a number of differences between the rabbinic cultures of northern France and Germany during the eleventh and early twelfth centuries. He also argued that in many cases these differences were a result of closer ties between northern French culture and Andalusian Jewish culture.[8] One of these was the development of the maḥzor genre in France.[9] If we take as representative of its class the lone surviving work of this genre, the maḥzor of Simḥah of Vitry, a student of Solomon ben Isaac of Troyes (Rashi), written at the beginning of the twelfth century, then one could say that his literature took as its base the *Siddur*, or *Seder*, of Amram Gaon, written in the second half of the ninth century in Babylon. Following this Babylonian model, the work was a composite one, including both liturgical and legal components.[10] However, whereas in the earlier work the legal sections were limited to laws pertaining to prayer and synagogue service, in the French maḥzor tradition the legal section was expanded to include laws relating to the Sabbath, the various holidays, aspects of food preparation (*kashrut*), and more.[11] Besides the extant maḥzor of Simḥah (*Maḥzor Vitry*), Grossman observes that we have evidence for four other French maḥzorim. Three were authored by students of Rashi, sometime between the late eleventh to early twelfth century, such as those by Jacob ben Samson and Shemaiah.[12] However, the earliest mention of a French maḥzor comes from Joseph Tov-'Elem, who was also the earliest known talmudic scholar from the area, active during the first half of the eleventh century.[13] It is worth noting in this context the strong intellectual ties that Joseph had with the Babylonian Geonim, which were much more than his German contemporaries.[14]

It is not easy to explain why two closely connected cultures such as Germany and France differed on this point of literary history of religious works, already in the eleventh and early twelfth centuries. However, as mentioned above, Grossman has suggested that traditionally northern French religious scholars in contrast to their Rhineland counterparts were more open to influence from the trends and traditions that came from the Muslim-controlled areas of Babylon and Spain.[15] This may explain the French adoption of the work of Amram and its development into an instrument that could transmit basic religious law to communal leaders and teachers. The Geonim and the Spanish scholars had a tradition of writing works that combined liturgy and practical law that one does not find in Germany of this time.

A second avenue worth exploring and emerging as well from Grossman's important studies of eleventh-century Germany and France is the relative weakness of French talmudic culture. A survey of the surviving fragments of information from this time indicates that the Rhineland, especially Mainz and Worms, were cities of scholars. They were centers of Talmud study and their leadership was composed of merchant-scholars from the established families. In short, the religious tone of the area was determined by the scholarly families that had originally settled in these cities.[16] One cannot draw similar conclusions with regard to northern France of this period. Besides

Joseph Tov-'Elem mentioned above, it is difficult to even identify any talmudic scholar of note. Moreover, when a talmudic prodigy such as Rashi and others like him wanted to continue their talmudic education, they had no choice but to travel to Germany.[17] In short, it does not seem that Franco-Jewish society at this time was particularly learned or that the community was strong in its religiosity, as were the communities of Mainz and Worms in the Rhineland.[18] In this light one can understand the need to produce a work, such as the maḥzor, in order to educate the community, something that was less crucial for Rhineland Jewry, where oral instruction directly from learned individuals was readily available.[19]

Talmudic culture in France began to take the lead over Germany at the end of the eleventh century due to the impact of one man, Rashi, and as a result of the devastating Rhineland massacres in 1096 that left the famous study halls greatly weakened if not completely ruined.[20] It is in the next century, however, that we witness dramatic change, both in the style of study and in its development into the premier intellectual center of Talmud study.

The Twelfth Century: Intellectual Revolution in France

During the twelfth century northern France became the undisputed center of Talmud study. The French Tosafists, led by Jacob (Tam) and his nephew Isaac of Dampierre, developed a dialectical approach to the Talmud that had its roots already in Germany at the turn of the century. They sharpened the method considerably, however, and made it into a sophisticated instrument for the study of the Talmud and for deciding the law.[21] Due to their efforts Talmud study became synonymous with the Tosafot dialectical approach in the centers of learning in both France and Germany. If the eleventh century belonged to Germany, it is pretty clear that the French owned the twelfth. The beginning of the century was dominated by the straightforward Rashi commentary to the Talmud and the second half was dominated by the "scholastic" efforts of the tosafists. If in the eleventh century French students, such as Rashi, traveled to Germany to study Talmud, in the twelfth the tendency was in the reverse direction.

With all the effort being expended on developing a new approach toward interpreting the Talmud, namely, the introduction of contradictory sources and resolving them in a way that did away with the difficulty, it is understandable that one can hardly see any substantial advances in the sphere of practical legal writings.[22] The focus of the scholars of this era was on understanding the original talmudic text, and not in composing secondary works that summarized practical law. It would seem that throughout the twelfth century the *Maḥzor Vitry* retained its prominence in France as the primary reference for religious instruction pertinent to daily life.

The Thirteenth Century: Legal Developments in France

In addition to the continued development of the Tosafot glosses on the Talmud throughout the thirteenth century, one finds a newfound emphasis on works of practical religious law. The first work produced in the century, Barukh's *Sefer ha-terumah* (The Book of Offering), was completed circa 1202.[23] The author, a student of the famous Isaac of Dampierre, hailed from northern France, and can be found deciding cases of law in the city of Paris, as Simcha Emanuel has recently demonstrated.[24] Even if Barukh did not actually live in the city, he did reside in its vicinity. This work is an excellent example of the necessity to summarize the practical ramification of the previous century's insights and breakthroughs.

It is often that following periods of great creativity there will be a turn toward summary and codification,[25] and the title of Barukh's work, *ha-terumah*, indicates that this was his primary concern.[26] The biblical word *terumah* means an offering that is lifted or elevated from a larger quantity for some higher purpose. However, in the Talmud we find the term being used to signify the process of selecting or separating something of higher quality from a collection that has both lower- and higher-quality items. R. Simeon tells his disciples regarding his rules of legal reasoning, "Study my rules, for my rules are '*terumot* of *terumot*' of the rules of R. Akiba" (BT Gittin 67a). Rashi explains, "I have chosen and elevated [these rules] from the principal mishnayot [collection of legal rulings] of R. Akiba, that is, 'selection after selection (*berera aḥar berera*),'" or as the Soncino translation of the Talmud translates this phrase, "the cream of the cream."

In introducing his work, Barukh expected his reader to make the association with the talmudic passage cited above regarding the rules that have been selected carefully. He writes, "This work is called *Sefer ha-terumah* for its rules [laws] are taken from the *terumot* [selection] of the masters of cunning (*ba'alei mezimot*), the holy ones of the Rock, those who dwell on High."[27] It would seem that the author saw his contribution as one who collected from the choice sections of the previous generation of tosafist legal lore, just as R. Simeon actively selected from the teachings of R. Akiba. A quick glance at his book reveals that Barukh's primary act of summary and selection was his choosing to focus on those tosafist teachings that had clear practical ramifications, while ignoring their breakthroughs that did not. His decision to append an extended table of contents that could also serve as an abridgment to the work underscores his goal to aid in the circulation of the Tosafists' legal innovations. It should be noted that the content of the book was limited in scope, as it treated only certain major topics of the law.[28]

The story of halakhic literature in thirteenth-century France, however, cannot be attributed solely to the process of summation that typically follows creativity. The developments in the production of French Jewish legal works that occurred from mid-century and onward tell a different tale. The three central works written from circa 1250 until 1278, *Semag* of Moses of Coucy, *Kitsur semag* of Avraham ben Ephraim, and *Semak* of Isaac of Corbeil, each have a unique literary character, and each author alludes to a very different context for his work than the one that motivated Barukh. The two most influential books were Moses' *Semag* and Isaac's *Semak*, and it is these that I describe in brief, noting the distinctive character of each.

Moses of Coucy (active c. 1230–55), in addition to being a tosafist of good lineage, a student of Judah of Paris, and a grandson of Ḥayyim Ha-kohen, was unique among his peers as he was also an itinerant preacher. Sometime between the years 1236 and 1239, he traveled to various Jewish Diaspora communities, notably Christian Spain.[29] Upon returning to northern France from his preaching mission he seems to have settled in Paris or in its vicinity.[30] Between the years 1239 and 1247 he wrote his *Semag,* [31] a work heavily influenced by Maimonides' code but which was divided into two sections, negative and positive commandments.[32] A close reading of both of his introductions (each section has its own introduction) reveals that he wrote his work with two distinct goals in mind, to produce a code that summarized all of talmudic law and an aid for the preacher or the local rabbinic figure who wished to teach religious law to the people. This work, written in Hebrew, was the first true legal work produced by a northern French scholar; it was both comprehensive and sufficiently understandable for readers who were not scholars of Talmud.

In his introduction to the first section (the negative commandments), Moses placed his work within the context of the history of codification of talmudic law and presented his work as a superior version of Maimonides'

Mishneh Torah, a work that served as his model. The two key areas he felt needed improvement were the inclusion of French legal content (from the writings of Rashi and the tosafists) that Maimonides did not know, and the citation of the talmudic source of the laws that Maimonides decided not to include in his work. In short, his goal was to produce a comprehensive code of Judaic law that included even laws not relevant to a Jew residing in medieval Europe.[33]

Despite the changes wrought by its author, the book still remained simplified and structured enough to follow Maimonides' overall goal to reach out to a broader reading audience beyond the Talmud scholar and his students.[34] It is quite clear, however, that his work would not have appealed to someone with minimal education, such as a layman whose education was complete after he learned to study the Pentateuch together with the standard French rabbinic commentary of Rashi.[35] It would seem, then, that he had in mind a reader who had at least some talmudic training in addition to his knowledge of the Bible and its standard commentary. Being educated, such a person could have easily become involved in some aspect of commerce or worked as a clerk but would have still retained an interest in the law. Another potential reader of his book would have to belong to the "secondary elite," to use a phrase Ephraim Kanarfogel has made popular recently.[36] This group would include highly literate and intelligent individuals whose primary interest lay outside of advanced talmudic legal studies, such as those who specialized in liturgical poetry, biblical interpretation, science, medicine, storytelling and morality tales. Such a diverse group of people, who would have studied Talmud in their youth but were no longer engaged in its study,[37] would be very interested in an accessible summary of the law, written in relatively simple Hebrew, without too much Aramaic, the language of the Talmud.

From his second introduction (positive commandments) it emerged that Moses had another potential type of reader in mind: the preacher or local scholar who wished to educate and edify. The bulk of this prologue is theological and polemical, devoted to defending the Jewish faith from theological attacks by the rival religions who claimed that the law of Moses had been superseded. He also explains the religious goals of the Torah in terms of the battle between man's godly, or angelic, nature and his animalistic one.[38] He emphasized the need to devote all of one's physical drives and desires to the service of God. However, after concluding these non-legal remarks he writes: "This introduction I preached to the exiles of Jerusalem in Spain and to the other exiles in Christian Europe [lit., exiles of Edom] to draw their hearts to the service of the God of Israel, and afterward I would preach to them about the commandments."[39]

In other words, these words of introduction served a similar purpose in the book as they did during his preaching mission. Before teaching his audience the details of the law, Moses would begin with an inspiring religious sermon. By placing the sermon at the head of the second section of his work, before detailing the laws, he was in a sense recreating his public performance within a literary setting.

In addition to this structural move, there are a number of indications that the author envisioned his work as an extension of his activity as a preacher and as a tool for those who wished to continue the important work of inspiring religious observance and of teaching the law to the entire Jewish population as he had done.[40] Previous scholars have argued that Moses' *Semag* was a book of sermons or at least a collection of model sermons for the potential preacher.[41] Although such a classification is in my opinion erroneous, due to the very close literary association and borrowing of Maimonides' *Mishneh Torah*, there is still something redeemable from this assessment. Moses did see the book as a tool that could help the preacher or local rabbinic figure in preparing his sermons, just as he had prepared his own sermons in advance of his mission to the exiles of Spain and other exiles in Christian Europe.[42]

In short, the reading audience for whom Moses of Coucy wrote his two-volume code of law was a diverse one. It included the elite talmudic scholar and students, but was aimed as well at the potential preacher and teacher. In addition he targeted the secondary elite and the well-educated layman. It is doubtful, however, that he included the semi-educated layperson with his smattering of basic education (Pentateuch and Rashi's commentary) within the potential readers of his book.

Isaac of Corbeil (active c. 1250–80) studied in the study hall of the "Brothers of Evreux" and was the son-in-law of the famous leader of French Jewry, Yeḥiel of Paris.[43] Recent manuscript research by Simcha Emanuel has reinforced Norman Golb's position that the study hall of the brothers of Evreux was actually located in the vicinity of Paris.[44] Later Isaac settled in Corbeil, a town close to the French capital, and was recognized there as a rabbinic authority, although he does not seem to have been a teacher of Talmud for advanced students.[45] Not much else is known about Isaac other than that he wrote a legal handbook, *Semak*, devoted to summarizing only practical religious laws relevant for a medieval Jew, which he completed in 1276–77, a few years before his demise.[46] The book is presented as a book of commandments but is constructed very differently from Moses' work. It is divided into seven pillars, corresponding to the seven days of the week. With regard to its legal content, this portable and accessible religious law guide was an abridgment of Moses of Coucy's extensive code of law. However, despite the strong ties between these two works it is quite clear that Isaac's program was very different from that of his predecessor.

The distinctiveness of Isaac's work can be demonstrated from two features, one relating to the body of the work and the second to what initially seems to be its table of contents. Regarding the work we already noted that it is much shorter than Moses of Coucy's work. Laws not practiced by medieval European Jews were removed. More importantly, its legal content was simplified and made accessible by removing much of the talmudic sources and by limiting the amount of alternate legal opinions. In short, his work was much more appropriate for the lay educated audience, even those with limited exposure to serious Talmud study.

The second innovative element was the list of commandments that he appended to the head of his book. Although one may think that this list was merely a finding aid, this was not the case. An oral report dating from the early fourteenth century by students of Isaac reveals its true purpose. We are told that Isaac of Corbeil and his colleagues

> considered the fact that numerous commandments (written in the Torah) will never present themselves to a person to be fulfilled, and were a person to see them written before him in a book he would at least resolve to fulfill them, and our Rabbis of blessed memory said that the Holy One, blessed be He, combines good intentions with deed.
>
> Accordingly they recorded all the commandments that apply outside the Land [of Israel], and divided them into seven sections, so that a person should recite one section every day. They wrote in each section to recite the *mitsvot* that are fit to be written and recited on that day. . . . And they fasted several days so that a person should receive reward when he reads the daily section, as if he were reading from the book of Psalms.[47]

From the continuation of this report it emerges clearly that the above passage was referring to the list of commandments and not to the book itself, which is referred to as "explanations and rulings" (*perishah u-fesakim*).[48] Moreover, there is corroborative evidence for this report from one of the earliest surviving manuscripts of Isaac's work. In the Nimes 26 manuscript which I have dated to some time between the years 1286 and 1293,[49] one finds prefacing the list of commandments the following: "These are the commandments that our teacher Isaac ben Joseph has established (*tiken*) [to be recited] each day of the seven days of the week, suitably explained and in a clear language so that the reader may read them quickly."[50]

Apparently, Isaac of Corbeil was interested in a ritualistic recitation of the practical commandments, and possibly even including it in the daily liturgy, as if one was reading from the Psalms. One can surmise that what concerned him was that all his fellow Jews should be made cognizant of God's commandments. In fact, his motivation may have been that of making all Jews more aware of their distinctive religious tradition as a piety of commandments, not only of prayer.[51]

Isaac's program of religious reform, however, did not end with the daily recitation of the practical commandments. The second part of his program included daily communal study of his accessible legal work.[52] In the letter of introduction that he circulated together with his work, and that later was appended to some of the medieval copies of the book, Isaac wrote:

> Sometimes a commandment presents itself, and a person does not know what to do. Accordingly, every person must put it to heart, for if not now, when. . . . And the great one should also not abstain from teaching the lesser one. Therefore I ask that they should establish a "blessing" [communal sanction] to do this, so that we should form a single band (*agudah aḥat*), and in this way the servant might reconcile himself to his master. Whoever does more is praiseworthy, to study each day the commentary (*lilmod be-khol yom perush*) of two or three commandments, and all "according to the effort [so] is the reward."[53]

In contrast to the daily recitation of his list of commandments, Isaac realizes that when it comes to the study and understanding of the law, even a simplified work of law, he could not expect much from most laypeople without the assistance of the more learned members of the community. To overcome this, he suggested that every community utilize its authority to "band together" and create within the synagogue a confraternity of learning. Isaac wished to enforce study of his legal handbook and encourage the learned to help out those who were less adept than themselves.

Isaac's vision of religious piety was linked to an awareness of God's commandments and their application in the world through knowledge of the law. It was this vision that he hoped to impart to all segments of the Jewish population, learned and less than learned alike. The evidence of this letter together with the accessible nature of the book itself leads to the conclusion that the author was determined to write a work of religious law that could appeal to a the widest possible reading audience.[54] Despite all of the above, it is worth recalling that the majority of the Jewish population was not literate in the full sense of the word. There is evidence that many Jews in France and Germany were able to read their prayers, but this does not mean that they actually understood the Hebrew text.[55] As Paul Saenger has taught us, there is vast distance between "phonetic literacy" and "comprehension literacy."[56] Many synagogue-attending Jews may be able to read Isaac's list of commandments but would need help understanding his accessible handbook of religious law. Nevertheless, by producing a simple work he did widen the pool of potential readers.[57]

What accounts for the development of works such as these? We will consider internal Jewish as well as external French factors. I begin with the stimuli from within the Jewish community, especially from the class of rabbinic intellectuals, and then examine the impact of some of the broader social developments that took place in France at the time.

The Influence of Maimonides and of the German Pietists

In the introductory section of this study I noted that some have argued that Franco-Jewish, in contrast to German-Jewish culture, was heavily influenced by the cultures of the Geonim from the east and of Muslim Spain. An example of such influence was the development of the maḥzor literature from the eleventh and early twelfth centuries, which can be viewed as the beginning of accessible legal literature on religious law. During the bulk of the twelfth century, there was no further progress in this type of literature in France because all energy was directed toward the development of the tosafist dialectic revolution. However, toward the end of the twelfth century there was a major breakthrough that occurred outside of France that had a major impact on developments in France.

Sometime between 1177 and 1181 Maimonides, the famous Spanish legal scholar, philosopher, and physician, completed in Old Cairo his magisterial code of Jewish law, *Mishneh Torah*, and released it for copying.[58] It is not clear when his work first reached northern France, but it seems to have been some time around the year 1200.[59] By the year 1240 it began to have impact on French intellectuals, albeit the secondary elite.[60] The book, however, never became central in the study halls of the French tosafists. One is hard pressed to find any citations of the work within the entire Tosafot corpus.[61]

It would seem that exposure to Maimonides' accessible code of law and his program to popularize the law[62] awoke within the consciousness of some French scholars the wish to produce accessible works of their own. In addition, over a hundred years had passed since the last maḥzor was written and there was a dire need to update the literature of religious law according to all the legal innovations that had occurred. In short, one can see in the thirteenth-century French developments a similar movement to what had already occurred in the eleventh and early twelfth centuries. In that previous era it was the siddur of Amram from Babylon that served as the model, whereas in the thirteenth century it was Maimonides' *Mishneh Torah* that may have inspired the scholars and actually served as the model for at least one scholar, Moses of Coucy, in composing his own accessible work of law.[63] A second avenue that needs to be explored is the impact of Ḥasidei Ashkenaz, the German Pietists.

In recent years much has been written about the influence (or lack thereof) of Ḥasidei Ashkenaz, led by Judah the Pietist, on the French scholarly community.[64] The discussion has focused mainly upon the school of Evreux and their graduates.[65] And although the jury is still out regarding the extent of this influence, it is quite clear that Isaac of Corbeil admired the leaders of that movement and was reading some of their works, as Ephraim Kanarfogel has demonstrated.[66] This connection between the Pietists and Isaac of Corbeil leads us to consider its influence on Isaac's religious reform and popular handbook of religious law. Israel Ta-Shma, in a series of articles originally published in the late seventies, suggested that one could explain the development of all halakhic literature in both Germany and France as a result of the impact of the religious ideals of the German Pietists. This religious group downplayed the importance of tosafist dialectics and emphasized the study of simpler works of practical law, at least for those who were not capable of intense intellectual analysis.[67] Although this fascinating hypothesis was never really accepted by other scholars, as can be seen by Simcha Emanuel's comments in the introduction to his recent work on legal writing in Germany and France,[68] there is still a strong case for its validity regarding Isaac of Corbeil and his handbook of religious law.[69]

While these internal Jewish aspects are important in helping us to understand the divergence between France and Germany, there are additional broader historical factors that must be considered in order to fully appreciate these thirteenth-century developments.[70]

French Society and the Paris Book Trade During the Thirteenth Century

Laura Light, in her study of the individual and the "Paris Bible" of the thirteenth century, emphasized "the importance of Paris both as a large and vibrant urban center and, more particularly, as a center for commercial book production."[71] These two factors, Paris as a center for book production and as a vibrant urban center, may also help us explain the uniqueness of the French Jewish legal culture in contrast to that of Germany. To properly understand the relevance of these two features, I summarize what scholars have taught us about the Paris book trade and the various social developments that impacted upon this industry during the thirteenth century.[72]

Until the twelfth century, copying of manuscripts in northern France among Christians was carried out almost exclusively in the monasteries.[73] This began to change with the growth of the schools in Paris. Concurrent with their expansion and later with the consolidation of the various schools into a university structure, we find the development of a professional class of scribes and of workshops there (and in other centers as well).[74] In time (possibly as early as the mid-thirteenth century), these professionals supplied books to the monasteries in France.[75] In the Rhineland at this time there was no such parallel development and to a large extent the monasteries remained centers for study and for book production.

When one examines the output of the Paris workshops, other than the traditional books needed by the monasteries, one can identify three broad types of works that had a strong market during the course of thirteenth century. The first and most important type for the copyists was the books needed by the growing student body, whose demand was the engine that fueled the burgeoning book industry.[76] The area of the student's interest began with the arts, but for those who continued their studies it would then shift to more specialized areas of knowledge such as theology, law, and medicine.[77] Once the university structure was put in place, at the beginning of the century, these disciplines had to have well-defined curricula,[78] and the students needed textbooks, many of which were glossed works that combined texts and commentary.[79] The textbooks were usually of large format and not easily portable.[80]

There were, however, other types of works, with their own distinct readerships, which caused the industry to expand in other directions. Toward the end of the twelfth century there began a preaching revival in Paris within the circle of the moral theologian Peter the Chanter, his student Stephen Langton, and others.[81] The two most visible and effective preachers produced by this school were Fulk of Neuilly and Jacques de Vitry.[82]

This explains why already in the first quarter of the century we find the beginning of the production of various preaching aids.[83] However, it was only after Lateran Council IV (in 1215) and the growth of the preaching orders that one finds major growth in the number of people active in preaching to uproot heresy and raise the level of religiosity among the laypeople.[84] The Franciscans and Dominicans spearheaded this effort but were not the only ones active in the promotion of religious values.[85] In short, it would seem that a revival that had its roots in the late twelfth century became a major movement beginning around 1230 and gaining strength as the century progressed.[86]

The Dominicans arrived in Paris as early as 1217 and soon after established an educational institution there. The Franciscans arrived in 1219 and established their institution later, in the year 1228.[87] These "religious" and other clerics in the city had different needs from the student, which included the Bible and various liturgical works, such as Missals, Breviaries, and Psalters. However, in addition to these very traditional religious works it is worth noting a distinct thirteenth-century development: the proliferation of preaching aids and models sermons that were copied extensively during this time in Paris,[88] to the extent that David d'Avray likened Paris to a communication center for preaching literature.[89] In this context the appearance of the heavily copied, portable, one-volume "Paris Bible" starting about 1230 is telling as well.[90] In short, although members of the various religious orders themselves may have copied these works, the professional copyists were very active as well in supplying the demands of this growing market. In filling the various needs of the religious, especially those of the friars, they expanded their book trade alongside that of the students.[91]

The last significant market to appear was the demand for books by laypeople, both aristocrats and the financially comfortable. This market would have been limited during the thirteenth century and seems to have developed the latest, during the second half of the century. One can distinguish between two types of books ordered by laypeople, those written in the vernacular and those in Latin. In the first category there are the various romances (*Roman de la rose*, *Chanson de Roland*, and others) and texts of popular science and self-improvement.[92] In the second group there are basic devotional texts that were treasured by all walks of society, religious and lay alike. The primary text that fulfilled this purpose during this time was the Psalter; however, toward the end of the century the Book of Hours began to make inroads and with time even replaced it as the most popular text during the later Middle Ages.[93] This emerging market of lay readers, men and women, during the thirteenth century has been linked to the growth in lay literacy and lay piety,[94] two separate but interrelated phenomena that developed as the Middle Ages progressed.

In short, one can identify three distinct types of readers whose demand for the written word generated the burgeoning Paris book trade: students, the religious, and the laity. Both in importance and chronologically this industry began already in the twelfth century with the demand produced by the schools and later the university. Circa mid-century, the religious orders, especially the Franciscan and Dominican friars who had specific book needs relating to their preaching mission, beyond the traditional religious works, also created robust demand. And finally there were the needs of the lay population, in Latin and the vernacular, that developed at a more leisurely pace, and whose demand for diverse works gathered strength toward the end of the century, especially devotional works.

The French Rabbis and Their Readers

The three works of Jewish religious law of the thirteenth century described above run roughly parallel to the social developments in Christian society that were expressed in the changing Paris book trade. Barukh's *Sefer ha-terumah*, completed circa 1202, was basically a book for the Jewish intellectual elite, the tosafists and their students. It was a book of consolidation and summary that followed on the tails of an outburst of creativity. Its structure, practical focus, and most importantly its innovative table of contents, which doubled as an abridgment, made the work considerably more useful and accessible as a work of law than the standard Tosafot collection on a tractate of the Talmud. There would seem to be intent to produce a somewhat more practical learned textbook of religious law, albeit limited in scope. Its primary reading audience, however, remained those individuals with strong ties to the talmudic study hall.

Moses of Coucy's well-organized and all-encompassing *Semag* imitated the Maimonidean code of law and was relevant for a much broader reading audience than Barukh's work. Moses, like Maimonides, wished to spread the knowledge of Torah widely and wrote a work that was accessible not only for scholars but also for the secondary elite, the educated layperson, fluent in Hebrew and having some talmudic background. Moses, who was a preacher himself, also wished to produce a work that would assist any potential preacher or teacher in preparing his sermons, despite the fact that this book was neither compact nor portable.[95] The preacher's preparations would have to be carried out at home similar to the way Moses himself prepared his sermons before setting out on his mission. Moses' book meant different things to different people but it was also a preacher's aid for the ultimate goal of educating the laity in the ways of the law.

Isaac of Corbeil's *Semak*, a compact manual[96] or handbook of religious law relevant for all Jews living in medieval Europe, was completed in 1276–77. The author, like the German Pietists, seemed to have had a clear religious agenda of educating the laity, men and women, directly through his work.[97] He envisioned a dual program for the laity that would emphasize the unique brand of Jewish piety: a piety of *mitsvot*. The program consisted of daily ritualistic recitation or incantation of commandments in order to complete the entire list of relevant *mitsvot* once a week and daily study of part of his legal work, which was essentially a commentary to the *mitsvot* listed. His book was concise and portable.[98]

In discussing the three major Franco-Jewish legal works of the thirteenth century and their authors, one cannot but be struck that all of them had strong ties to Paris. At this time the city was not only the capital, it was the commercial center and it housed a flourishing university. All these factors made Paris the home of the most important commercial book trade in Europe in the thirteenth century.[99] Jews throughout the Middle Ages, gravitated to the urban centers, which were also the centers of commerce, and Paris was no exception.

Jews residing in Paris and its vicinity were able to observe up close the bustling activity that made up this city's life. It was in the urban center of Paris from the end of the twelfth century onward that Jews not only had the opportunity to converse with their Christian neighbors but could actually see, in real time, the various developments relating to their books. Even if Jews could not read the Latin content of these works, they would still be exposed to their various formats, layouts, shapes, and sizes.[100] Moreover, they could see and converse with the actual readers who were ordering or even buying prepared copies,[101] and thus could easily understand their purpose.

PART II

Secular and Religious Authorities

Chapter 5

The Madrasa and the Non-Muslims of Thirteenth-Century Egypt: A Reassessment

Luke Yarbrough

In the year 627 AH (1229–30 CE) the official Abu l-'Ala' Ibn al-Nabulusi regaled the Ayyubid sultan with the tale of a "strange and wondrous coincidence" that had befallen him long before.[1] We shall return to his story presently. We begin, however, with a different coincidence: the two men most closely associated with the introduction of the madrasa in Iraq and Egypt—Nizam al-Mulk (d. 485/1092) and al-Turtushi (d. 520/1126), respectively—were also the first two Muslims to write works of political counsel that sternly denounced non-Muslim state officials.[2] Nizam al-Mulk's famous *Siyasat nameh* (Book of Government), for example, makes much of a parable in which an unnamed Jewish official in Iraq is unceremoniously replaced by a Muslim, in spite of his superior skill.

The coincidence, and the connection it implies between the madrasa and dislike of non-Muslim officials, might be dismissed as less "strange and wondrous" than trivial if not for what happened in the centuries after the two works were written. The period from the mid-eleventh to the mid-fourteenth century saw a deterioration in the conditions under which Jewish and Christian communities existed in the central Islamicate lands, from Iraq to Egypt—what S. D. Goitein called "the catastrophic worsening of the legal and actual positions of non-Muslims in the late Middle Ages."[3] The deterioration proceeded unevenly, to be sure, across both space and time. Yet few historians fail to see a significant trend in the widespread waves of conversion to Islam, heightened tax pressures, mutual social antagonism and suspicion, and exclusion from prominent public roles that non-Muslim communities experienced in these centuries. The cumulative effect left those communities numerically diminished and socially isolated relative to their former condition. The attention that this trend has received from Middle East and Islamic historians hardly bears comparison, in quantity or sophistication, to that lavished on the "persecuting society" by historians of medieval Europe.[4]

Increased pressures on Jewish and Christian communities are often understood in relation to the Sunni turn of the eleventh to thirteenth centuries. This shift saw the eclipse of Shiʿite dynasties such as the Fatimids, Buyids, and Hamdanids by rulers, often ethnic Turks, who turned to Sunni ideologies (and ideologues) for legitimacy, with profound consequences for the long-term fortunes of those ideologues and their followers. According to this account, since Sunni law, much of it formulated during or after the centuries in question, expresses "intolerant" attitudes toward non-Muslims, the "Sunni revival" led quite naturally to the legal instantiation of that purported intolerance. Muslim responses to the Crusades and Mongol incursions are also frequently said to have stirred up animosity on the part of Muslim elites and non-elites alike toward non-Muslims, who might be accused of sympathy or even collusion with the invaders.

While these modern explanations contain a considerable measure of truth, our current understanding of the trend nonetheless remains a collaborative work in progress. The issue is occasionally oversimplified by treating (for example) instances of the trend, such as accusations of treason or Friday sermons inciting mob violence against churches and synagogues, as its final causes. We have a wealth of generalizations but a relative poverty of nuanced and compelling accounts of the subtler, locally conditioned social forces that must have been at work. Why was religious difference increasingly seized upon as a marker of social and political belonging during this period? More saliently, why did so many people come to see the inverse of belonging—social and political exclusion—as occasion for violence, both symbolic and physical?

One influential answer to this question has pointed to the madrasa, an institution that George Makdisi linked famously though still inconclusively to the European university.[5] Nearly three decades ago a widely cited article by Gary Leiser, a student of Makdisi and Goitein, drew a causal connection between the madrasa and the phenomenon of deepening religious antagonism. Leiser proposed that "Islamization" in Egypt was in large part a result of "the rise of the madrasa," itself by all accounts a strand woven deep into the fabric of the "Sunni revival."[6] In this chapter, I offer a new account of the causal link between the two phenomena. I contend that a general climate of competition, which formed as the advent of the madrasa in Egypt helped to forge a relationship of unprecedented interdependency between political elites and Sunni religious leaders (*'ulama'*) and raised *'ulama'* expectations of state patronage, catalyzed the animosity of some *'ulama'* toward non-Muslim officials, their competitors for certain kinds of state patronage. This pressure to dismiss non-Muslim officials, the secular elites of their own communities, brings us full circle to the works of political counsel by Nizam al-Mulk and al-Turtushi with which we began; these books were addressed to Muslim rulers at the very moment their authors were working, in their different ways, to establish madrasas in their adopted lands of Iraq and Egypt. The larger goal of the chapter is to achieve a more accurate understanding of the relationship between the rise of an educational institution and the marginalization of religious out-groups, in order thereby to see more clearly why the social position of Middle Eastern Jews and Christians might have deteriorated during and after the thirteenth century. Egyptian Jewish elites were doubly entangled in the larger political and institutional changes of the period, on the one hand forced to navigate a social landscape that was increasingly conditioned by the ideological preoccupations of Sunni *'ulama'*, and on the other caught up in the rivalry between those *'ulama'* and the elites of a fellow non-Muslim community, the Coptic Christians.

After introducing some of the key historical and terminological background to these developments, I summarize Leiser's three-tiered model of the causal relationship between the madrasa and the "Islamization of Egypt." I then draw on neglected primary sources and recent scholarship to revise this causal model. I conclude by gesturing to a point of potential comparison with scholarship on the experience of Jews in western Europe.

Madrasas and Non-Muslim Officials

The Madrasa

The character and function of the madrasa in twelfth- and thirteenth-century Egypt are the subjects of ongoing debate,[7] but the considerable body of existing scholarship (on which this account depends) has rendered the broad outlines clear enough to permit generalization.[8]

By all accounts, madrasas in Ayyubid and Mamluk Egypt were endowed institutions that supported instruction in Islamic jurisprudence (*fiqh*). Their endowments typically provided income and facilities for a teacher of law and his students to carry out the work of studying and elaborating upon Islamic jurisprudence according to a particular school of law (*madhhab*). Other subjects (e.g., Arabic grammar and Qur'anic exegesis) were also taught, to the extent that they contributed to the study of jurisprudence.

The endowments on which madrasas depended were constituted, according to a legal mechanism of immense historical importance, as charitable trusts (*waqf*s) that rendered private property inalienable. Such property might be agricultural land, of course, but also markets, bakeries, forges, mills, baths, houses, springs, urban buildings, shops, and so forth. A comparably wide range of charitable enterprises might receive the proceeds (e.g., Sufi lodges, mosques, drinking fountains, the poor, the Holy Cities, etc.). In most schools of Islamic law the founder of the *waqf* for a madrasa had wide latitude in planning its future (the Maliki school of law granted the least). He or she (for many madrasas and other endowments were founded by wealthy women)[9] could stipulate what school of law would be taught in the madrasa, how the proceeds of the endowment would be distributed, and even who would staff it. Not surprisingly, founders often designated their own descendants as beneficiaries. Because Islamic law places certain limits on bequests, *waqf*s were a way indirectly to benefit one's family with one's property and thus to perpetuate the social power of households.

The madrasa itself was usually a physical structure that might be attached to another kind of institution, such as a Sufi lodge, a mosque, or a tomb. Some were as simple as a converted house. Students did not matriculate in or graduate from a particular madrasa in quite the formal sense that one does now at college or university. Instead a student came primarily to study under a particular teacher, much as he might study with a teacher outside a madrasa. At the end of a course of study the student could receive from that teacher personally a kind of authorization to issue legal opinions and to teach law according to the doctrines of a particular school.

The function of the twelfth- and thirteenth-century Egyptian madrasa with respect to the state and society was quite complex. One still hears echoes of the thesis that the madrasa was a kind of service academy set up to supply the state with trained, loyal, and orthodox bureaucrats. Yet Makdisi, Michael

Chamberlain, and Daphne Ephrat have all shown that there is scant evidence for it. I return to this point below. The madrasa did, however, play an important (if subtler) role in the dialectic of power between military and religious elites in these centuries. Madrasas were a means by which political elites supported the preachers, judges, and jurisprudents who could confer or remove the state's legitimacy in the eyes of its subjects. We can also observe, especially in the late twelfth century as the Ayyubids took over former Fatimid and crusader possessions on a large scale, that captured properties were given as endowments to support madrasas and thus to deprive the state's enemies and its potential challengers of benefit from them.[10] Not coincidentally, the students who studied at these madrasas would be ideological advocates for the supremacy of traditionist-oriented Sunni law to which Ayyubid and Mamluk military elites paid lip service, at the very least.[11]

The complex relationship between state elites and the madrasa can in fact already be glimpsed at the institution's origins. Unlike the *waqf* on which it relied, the madrasa was not an ancient Islamic institution. In Egypt, one hears of madrasas for the first time in the early twelfth century.[12] The first evidence of the madrasa anywhere comes from western Persia in the late tenth and early eleventh centuries,[13] whence the model was adapted in eleventh-century Baghdad by the Saljuq vizier Nizam al-Mulk, whom we have already encountered as the author of a political manual and detractor of non-Muslim state officials. In Egypt, Salah al-Din and his servants and successors adopted many forms of Sunni governance that had been pioneered in the east under the Ghaznavid and Saljuq states. They established endowments that supported numerous madrasas, the numbers of which grew rapidly in Egypt during the late twelfth and thirteenth centuries.

The property that they used in order to make *waqf* endowments for madrasas was often that of which their official functions had given them control, notwithstanding the jurists' insistence that the property used for a *waqf* must be private (*milk*).[14] There existed, however, a commonly used if somewhat murky legal mechanism, the *irṣād*, for endowing state property. Muhammad Amin, the noted Egyptian historian of medieval endowments, argued that the bulk of Salah al-Din's pious endowments in Egypt were made with state property using this mechanism.[15] Thus powerful state agents were directly engaged in the founding and funding of madrasas, using state resources. The Ayyubids in Egypt tended at first to staff madrasas with foreign Sunni scholars who served as a kind of loyal ideological vanguard in a land that had until recently been under Fatimid Shiʿite control. By the Bahri Mamluk period that conventionally began in 1250, however, there was no longer any need to seek out foreign scholars. The patronage-driven prestige of Cairo was by then attracting Sunni scholars from all corners of the world.

The Leiser Paradigm

We have seen that madrasas fostered the study of Islamic jurisprudence, that their number was growing in Egypt in the late twelfth and thirteenth centuries, and that they enjoyed substantial patronage from the Ayyubid and Bahri Mamluk states. It is not obvious, however, that any of this should have affected the Jews and Christians of Egypt. The merit of proposing a plausible causal connection between the rise of the madrasa and the signs of growing pressure on non-Muslim populations belongs to Leiser's 1985 article.

Egypt's Fatimid period, according to Leiser, was a time of "great tolerance and prosperity" for non-Muslims (his focus is on Christians, but the arguments adduced are relevant to the smaller Jewish population). Non-Muslims "served as a counterweight to the Sunni community" for the Shi'ite Fatimids, and were thus preferred for public offices.[16] Indeed, Leiser sees in "the arrival of [the Armenian convert to Islam and powerful vizier] Badr al-Jamali in the Delta in 466/1073 . . . the beginning of increasing Christian involvement in Egyptian politics" that lasted until the fall of the Fatimids in 567/1171.[17] This involvement was at times so pronounced that Leiser was led to take Muslim fears of an outright Christian takeover at face value. It is this viewpoint that allows him to speak of the madrasa's function in rolling back the "aggression" of indigenous non-Muslims.[18]

The Fatimid period was, however, a kind of Indian summer for the non-Muslims of Egypt, according to Leiser, for in the Ayyubid and Mamluk periods their position "began its final decline and then was reduced to a shadow of its former glory." The same periods witnessed "the appearance, early development, and efflorescence of the madrasas."[19] Since "the greatest challenge that Sunnis faced in Egypt was . . . a large and powerful Christian community," the madrasa played a crucial role as it "strengthened Sunnism, that is, encouraged its militancy, contributed to its ideological defense, and trained a cadre of officials who promoted its interests and found their way to the highest posts in the government."[20] All of this, according to Leiser, came at the expense of Christian and Jewish communities in Egypt, beginning with their elites.

Leiser argued that this process proceeded in three principal ways. The first way involved Muslim group consciousness, which was strengthened by the more widespread study of Islamic jurisprudence (*fiqh*) in madrasas. *Fiqh*, for its part, was all encompassing; it "governed everything from brushing one's teeth to interfaith relations." In the latter case *fiqh* urged views that "emphasized the superiority of Islam to other religions," including discriminatory sumptuary regulations and, it might be added, opposition to non-Muslim state officials.[21] Since madrasas promoted *fiqh*, in other words, and since *fiqh* was, by Leiser's account, inherently supremacist and exclusionary, "the madrasa promoted the strict enforcement of the rules defining the social distance between Muslims and non-Muslims."[22]

The second way in which madrasas brought pressure to bear on non-Muslim communities, according to Leiser, appears to be closely related.[23] As Makdisi showed, public debate was central to the madrasa curriculum, as it was also to the contests for prestige among leading Muslim scholars. Students who had studied in madrasas emerged equipped for debate and proceeded aggressively to engage in it with non-Muslims (little evidence of this is given). His third way is of a rather different variety. Madrasas "trained a growing number of bureaucrats who competed with Christians for government positions." In fact, elites who endowed madrasas sought not only to "gain a certain patronage and influence over the religious class," but also to "create a cadre of officials whose loyalty was unquestioned."[24]

To recapitulate Leiser's account, then, a period of non-Muslim flourishing and influence under the later Fatimids gave way after 1171 to one of increasing exclusion under the Ayyubids and early Mamluks. This, in turn, coincided with the spread of madrasas in Egypt, a process that marginalized Christians and Jews by promoting an exclusionary legal system (the *sharīʿa*, undergirded by *fiqh*), equipping religious elites with the tools of formal debate, and creating a class of trained bureaucrats who vied to replace Christian and Jewish state officials. The latter half of Leiser's article traces the early history of the madrasa in Egypt in some detail, highlighting connections, documented and hypothetical, to the position of non-Muslims there. It adds invaluable narrative, documentation, and detail,[25] but no major new components, to Leiser's three-tiered account of how the founding of madrasas helped to cause the Islamization of Egypt. His account remains the latest word on the subject.

Ibn al-Nabulusi's "Strange and Wondrous Coincidence"

Among the many sources that Leiser drew from in his article is a short work of the mid-thirteenth century, the *Tajrid sayf al-himma li-stikhraj ma fi dhimmat al-dhimma* (Unsheathing Ambition's Sword to Take Back What the Dhimmis Hoard) of the sometime high finance official 'Uthman ibn Ibrahim al-Nabulusi (d. 660/1262).[26] In this section we examine sections of this work, using it as a heuristic lens through which to take a fresh look at the madrasa and its relation to processes of Islamization. The *Tajrid* was written around the year 640/1242, shortly following the issuance of a decree by the Ayyubid sultan al-Malik al-Salih (r. 637–47/1240–49) that imposed a number of discriminatory disabilities on non-Muslims in Egypt. The stated purpose of the work is to urge the sultan to dismiss non-Muslim (*al-dhimma*) state officials and to confiscate their allegedly embezzled wealth. While the quarter of the work that Claude Cahen transcribed for publication might justly be called a "diatribe against the Copts,"[27] the work also contains polemic against Jews, suggesting that the author also wrote against Jewish officials,[28] as well as, *inter alia*, lengthy sections of poetry and *bons mots* by state officials (*kuttāb*). Thus it was also meant to entertain the reader, to praise the Arabic scribal tradition, and to advertise the author's own administrative talents in contrast to those of incompetent pretenders (who also rate a section).[29]

A different part of the *Tajrid*, also edited by Cahen in the late 1950s, has been neglected by scholars since its publication.[30] The most likely reason for this neglect is that the section in question was attached as a poorly marked appendix to an edition of another work by the same author. This section, I argue, points to significant respects in which Leiser's arguments concerning the manner of the madrasa's effect on non-Muslim populations in Egypt should be revised.

The section occurs at a point in the work where the author, Ibn al-Nabulusi, has all but exhausted his direct arguments against non-Muslim officials. At this juncture he directs the reader's attention to a new villain: ignorant and incompetent Muslim officials from rural backgrounds. His chosen vehicle for this anti-rustic diatribe is a "strange and wondrous coincidence" with which, he informs the reader, he once regaled the Ayyubid sultan al-Malik al-Kamil (r. 615–35/1218–38). Ibn al-Nabulusi begins his tale by informing the reader that as a young man he was pious and utterly detached from the state: "Ever since I was quite small I was engaged in the study of religious subjects. As a young man I had nothing to do with the state administration."[31]

In the story, a young Ibn al-Nabulusi (he was about twenty-two at the time) is riding along a road when he encounters a graying, dark-skinned Egyptian man. The man greets him and then, unexpectedly, implores him to ignore any bad rumors he should happen to hear about him. Startled, Ibn al-Nabulusi replies that he does not know the man at all, adding, "And who am I that I should hear what your opponents say about you? That's the kind of talk one directs to powerful people. I am not one of them."

The "strange and wondrous coincidence," which does not emerge fully until the tale's end, begins with the older man's reply. Introducing himself as Ibn al-Sakhr, the man says that he has heard a rumor that Ibn al-Nabulusi plans to fine him seven thousand gold coins on behalf of the sultan. At this point the character Ibn al-Nabulusi, professing his ignorance of any such matter, gives a brief explanation that is of interest to us: "'I have no acquaintance with serving any sultan or vizier. Really I am one of these people who spends all his time in the madrasa, busy with religious subjects. And I know absolutely nothing about your situation, or anyone else's for that matter. I am not that type at all. Perhaps you have made some mistake about me!' I was quite astonished at what he had said." The story then leaps forward several years to narrate the manner in which Ibn al-Nabulusi became, in fact, a state official. After hearing him speak in a formal debate (*mubāḥatha*), the sultan al-Kamil commanded that he "be enrolled among the servants of the state"—a command, in fact, that he "take charge of the administrative bureaus in all the land of Egypt save for a few places." Ibn al-Nabulusi claims that at this point he attempted to demur. His account merits quotation in full.

> I replied in writing, informing the sultan that I had never worked in a bureau of any kind, nor did I know anything about the customs of the bureaus or their current conditions. I added that when the employees in the various towns found out that someone entirely ignorant of administration had been appointed over them, they would conspire with the supervising accountants and embezzle the funds. When the sultan . . . received my letter, he directed that I be excused. He also thanked me, saying, "How many of the men who beg to serve in some branch office, or of those whom we actually end up appointing, from Mecca . . . to Damietta, ask to be excused and say 'I have never so much as seen

> an administrative bureau'?" Then one of the attendants said, "Master, if this is so, then let the sultan appoint him over al-Sharqiyya and al-Gharbiyya. He will learn the customs of the administration in those places, then the sultan can transfer him to these central offices." He replied, "Let us not overburden him. We shall appoint him over al-Sharqiyya alone to learn the customs of administration, for it is a relatively minor district." Then the sultan . . . summoned me into his presence. He said to me, "I appoint you over the lands of Egypt and you refuse, saying, 'I'm not suitable'? I have here a recommendation from the judge Safi al-Dīn ibn Shukr that says you are qualified to run the whole state." I said, "Master, the judge Safi al-Din thinks too highly of me. I know myself better." "Do not try to dissuade me," he said. . . . So I blessed him and departed for al-Sharqiyya as he had commanded.

From that point forward Ibn al-Nabulusi served as a financial official in the administration of al-Malik al-Kamil. This experience formed the background to his later appointment by al-Malik al-Salih, shortly after the writing of the *Tajrid*, as a tax official in the Fayyūm. It was on the basis of this experience that he compiled the work for which he is best known in modern scholarship, a tax register of virtually unparalleled richness and detail.[32]

It was in the course of his service to al-Malik al-Kamil that the "strange and wondrous coincidence" came about. By some twist of fate, Ibn al-Nabulusi found himself in a position of authority over the very same Ibn al-Sakhr whom he had met on the road nearly two decades before. Due to the latter's incompetence, which the text ascribes to his "rural mind," he fell under suspicion of malfeasance and was eventually compelled to pay a fine. The job of determining its amount fell, as fate would have it, to Ibn al-Nabulusi himself. He recounted the story of his first meeting with Ibn al-Sakhr to the sultan, who set the sum at the very same seven thousand gold coins.

The fictionalized coincidence itself—the account's driving plot device—is of course as irrelevant to the madrasa as it is to the position of non-Muslims in Egyptian society, and a fortiori to any relationship between the two. The account does, however, deliver, in passing, evidence of the manner in which the madrasa was widely viewed in relation to state employment in the early thirteenth century, of how a man might move from a madrasa background to such employment, and of widespread attitudes toward those who made such a transition.

Ibn al-Nabulusi's tale strongly suggests that the madrasa, far from producing "an army of 'graduates' . . . who took positions . . . in the government,"[33] was on the contrary unrelated in the imagination of elite audiences to state employment. This is the force of Ibn al-Nabulusi's protest to Ibn al-Sakhr. He knows nothing about serving the state *precisely because* he is a madrasa student, occupied with learning (*'ilm*). The exchange makes little sense if the madrasa was acknowledged to be a kind of service academy for bureaucrats.

This impression is confirmed by the arguments adduced in Ibn al-Nabulusi's response to the sultan upon first being offered appointment. However artificial his demurral may have been, the reasons that he gave must still have possessed rhetorical validity, at the very least. The madrasa background that had prepared him to speak formally in the sultan's presence had evidently left him so unprepared to supervise an administrative bureau (*dīwān*) that he feared his inferiors would take advantage of his ignorance to defraud the state.

If the madrasa was not widely expected to prepare students for administrative employment, in financial record keeping, for instance (religiously significant offices such as *qāḍī*, *khaṭīb*, and even *muḥtasib*, as well as positions such as the epistolary scribes [*kuttāb al-inshā'*] that prioritized linguistic mastery are, of course, another matter), it is nevertheless obvious that men who had studied in madrasas did in fact occupy such positions in the early thirteenth century. What hints, then, can this account give us concerning how madrasa students eventually became finance officials? The hints we find are not surprising, but they do provide useful reminders about the culture of bureaucratic appointment at the time. The first is the importance of personal connections, in this case a written recommendation from a senior official to the sultan on behalf of Ibn al-Nabulusi. Similiarly, the historian Ibn Waṣil (d. 697/1298) joined the entourage of al-Malik al-Salih Ayyub (the patron for whom Ibn al-Nabulusi was writing), upon being "mentioned" to him in 644/1246.[34] Their cases were typical. There was of course no regularized route to state employment on par with the civil service examinations that were the ideal in premodern China. The madrasa as such did not issue a diploma, let alone certification to serve in state bureaus of finance or taxation. The ties of personal patronage and clientage (as distinct from their Weberian "rational" equivalents) that we observe here are of the normal variety that one expects to encounter in agrarian societies,[35] yet in this case their prevalence has further significance. To wit, it points to institutional inertia, inasmuch as powerful individuals themselves, not the educational institutions they founded, continued to function as the gatekeepers of direct access to state patronage. In other words, however many madrasas may have been established under early Ayyubid rule, if bureaucratic appointment was mediated largely by individuals already in positions of influence, then it was these individuals, and not the preparatory educational institutions, who provided access to appointment. Whatever state elites intended when founding madrasas, then, these institutions patently cannot have begun immediately supplying droves of officials. The process by which madrasa patronage networks became entangled with bureaucratic ones must have been protracted, stretching across generations in the twelfth and thirteenth centuries; this is one reason that we observe numerous non-Muslim officials throughout the Ayyubid period, the madrasa notwithstanding.

In addition, Ibn al-Nabulusi's account reminds us that a great many people sought state employment in the early thirteenth century. It is to their throngs that the sultan refers when remarking upon Ibn al-Nabulusi's self-effacement.[36] The account also shows that the general run of these applicants were considered to be unfit for employment. When the sultan accepts the suggestion that he hire Ibn al-Nabulusi, precisely because of his unusual candor in professing his ignorance of the job, it is implied that other candidates are also generally unqualified, their apparent confidence notwithstanding. Ibn al-Nabulusi is at least honest about his limitations. This obvious self-promotion on the part of the author (and protagonist) cannot be taken as a reliable statement of fact in any sense save one: in a work composed by a high official for a sultan, it must have resonated with views on the recruitment of state officials that were widely shared in their rarified milieus. It follows that madrasas were not producing a glut of candidates qualified, from an employer's standpoint, to assume the positions they sought. Here again the contrast to China, in this case under the Sung, is instructive; in the Chinese case many more candidates performed to a high level on the civil service examination than could be incorporated in the bureaucracy.[37] On this evidence, too, it is difficult to see the thirteenth-century Egyptian madrasa as an institution in which men prepared consciously for state employment other than as religious and legal specialists (which roles were, to be sure, significant, numerous, and unavailable to non-Muslims).

Fortunately, the autobiographical account of Ibn al-Nabulusi provides an answer—though not a novel one—to the question that naturally arises at this point: how then did men from a madrasa background acquire the skills they needed to discharge official assignments competently? In Ibn al-Nabulusi's case, as in that of virtually all premodern state officials in Islamicate societies, the answer lay in a combination of personalized transmission of knowledge and on-the-job training.[38] The text does not suggest that this arrangement was unusual, though it may well have been less common for men of his age than it was, for instance, for sons and nephews of officials. The strongest claim that we can make for the madrasa's connection to state employment on the basis of this account, then, is one that will sound familiar to humanities faculty in the early twenty-first century: the madrasa background that Ibn al-Nabulusi advertised gave him broadly applicable skills, including literacy, eloquence, and finely honed reasoning skills, that prepared him, albeit indirectly, to adapt to a new and unfamiliar career. But there is no suggestion that the versatility of this preparation was by design.

Ibn al-Nabulusi's account is obviously anecdotal. This is its advantage as a source. However exceptional and fictionalized the series of events it describes, the assumptions on which the narrative's literary coherence and persuasive potential depend reveal outlooks that must have been widely held in his circles. Yet the account is in other respects unexceptional and shot through with topoi. The upright scholar, wary of the sinful state and persuaded only reluctantly to associate with it, is only the most obvious. The evidence of this polemical work by Ibn al-Nabulusi does, however, furnish a lens through which to take a new look at the relationship between the madrasa, in which he received his formation, and the non-Muslim officials whose dismissal he ardently sought. In the next section I combine these observations about Ibn al-Nabulusi's work with the conclusions of recent scholarship on the madrasa and its milieu to offer a new account of that relationship.

The Madrasa and Islamization: An Alternative Paradigm

In Ibn al-Nabulusi's work we see a madrasa-trained scholar carefully selecting and crafting an argument that opposes the employment of Jewish and Christian state officials. Islamic jurisprudence as such (*fiqh*) plays only a minor role in that argument; historical anecdote and satire feature far more prominently. This fits poorly with Leiser's first explanation of the madrasa's contribution to Islamization, which, it will be recalled, proceeded thusly: since the madrasa taught Islamic *fiqh*, which governed all aspects of social life, and since "*fiqh* required the imposition of discriminatory measures . . . on non-Muslims," the madrasa indirectly promoted such measures and thus contributed to non-Muslims' marginalization or conversion. This argument is compelling to the extent that the madrasa, supported by the massive endowed resources placed at its disposal, infused the Sunni elites of Egypt with fresh group consciousness, confidence, and a reinforced ideological vanguard. In inverse fashion, the great conversion waves of the fourteenth century corresponded to the Coptic Church's loss of agricultural lands and revenues.[39] The madrasa's spread does in fact seem to have brought in its train the reassertion and, indeed, fresh formulation of Islamic law's exclusionary aspects.[40] Yet Leiser's explanation seems to posit too mechanical a model of the process by which this reassertion occurred.

In fact, the broad heritage of Islamic law did not necessarily militate against the employment of non-Muslim state officials, or require in practice that a particular dress code be maintained by non-Muslims at all times.[41] Instead, because the tradition was in fact rather equivocal on these matters, madrasa-trained jurists and officials like Ibn al-Nabulusi had consciously to choose the more restrictive positions they advocated. For example, a writer on the subject of "discriminatory measures" such as Ibn al-Nabulusi, an adherent of the Shafi'i school of law, might easily have turned to such prominent earlier authorities in his school of law as Abu al-Hasan al-Mawardi (d. 450/1058), whose widely acclaimed political treatise, *al-Ahkam al-sultaniya*, permitted non-Muslim officials to occupy official offices in which they discharged their superiors' orders (*tanfīdh*), rather than receiving the full delegated authority of those superiors (*tafwīḍ*). In al-Mawardi's view, a non-Muslim might be sent to collect the alms tax (*zakāt*) or even be appointed vizier to carry out the orders of the imam.[42] It seems safe to presume that most of the Jewish and Christian finance officials of the Ayyubid state occupied subordinate roles, and would thus have qualified for employment within al-Mawardi's scheme. Another Shafi'i jurist (and Ayyubid vizier) who wrote on politics in the mid-thirteenth century, Abu Salim Muhammad ibn Talha al-Nasibi (d. 652/1254), was content to restate al-Mawardi's position on the issue, as well as that of his critics, without expressing a preference.[43] Thus Ibn al-Nabulusi's position was not inevitable, even for a Shafi'i. For a jurist of the Hanafi school, meanwhile, it would be significant that the paradigmatic early work on taxation and administration by Abu Yusuf (d. 182/798), *Kitab al-kharaj*, was silent on the matter of non-Muslim state officials in an age when they were certainly common. The eponym Abu Hanifa (d. 150/767) seems to have had nothing to say concerning the issue.[44] A jurist of the Maliki school could invoke the example of the well-respected ninth-century paragon Isma'il ibn Makki al-Azdi

(d. 282/895), who publicly defended the validity of a Christian vizier, basing his argument on the Qur'an, while one of the Hanbali school could cite his eponym's view that Jews and Christians were not objectionable as state officials because they did not proselytize.[45] True, the legal tradition also provided ample precedent for opposing non-Muslim state officials on principled grounds.[46] However, the important point is that madrasa students and professors had decisions to make. If the drift of those decisions was ultimately detrimental to the fortunes of Egypt's non-Muslim communities, we must look to historical circumstances for the reasons rather than to the supposedly unified and inexorable force of the legal tradition itself.

To the extent that the spread of the madrasa did contribute to a legally motivated marginalization of non-Muslims in Egypt, then, this process must be acknowledged to have involved a great deal of intentionality and agency on the part of its chief actors, the Muslim religious scholars (*'ulamā'*). The legal doctrines that became prominent in this period had to be consciously selected and asserted; we do well to remember, too, that systems of law that sought to restrict the conduct of military rulers in agrarian societies, Islamic *fiqh* among them, were aspirational at best. Here the example of the *Tajrid* is again instructive. Even if we grant that in the mid-thirteenth century, when madrasas had flourished for more than a century in Egypt, they taught a strictly exclusionary subsection of *dhimmī* law, it is a noteworthy fact that a well connected scholar-official felt compelled to memorialize the sultan concerning his non-Muslim officials, who were evidently numerous and influential. If the fact that it was the madrasa product Ibn al-Nabulusi who undertook this assignment suggests that his educational background may have been instrumental, the contents of the work, which has little to say about *fiqh*, suggest that it may not have been the law as such that motivated his petition. In fact Ibn al-Nabulusi made his three motives for composing the work explicit in its final section. They were, he informed the sultan, his zeal for the money of the Muslim community (which non-Muslim officials were accused of stealing), his ardent love for the Ayyubid state, and (most importantly, one senses), his own pressing need for employment, due to the large number of his dependents and their lack of any reliable source of income.[47]

Ibn al-Nabulusi's tale of "a strange and wondrous coincidence" has indicated that the thirteenth-century madrasa was in fact probably not seen by its contemporaries as a training ground for state officials; if it were, what sense would his claims of ill preparedness make? This suggestion is confirmed by scholarship on the madrasa that has appeared in the last two decades. For Baghdad in the period of the madrasa's introduction there, despite the presence of the famed and in many ways trend-setting Nizamiyya madrasa established by Nizam al-Mulk himself, Daphna Ephrat concluded that "there is nothing to attest to the existence of any program for the training of potential bureaucrats."[48] If the *'ulama'* trained by teachers in madrasas later entered the bureaucracy, their routes thither were non-linear and independently plotted.

The work of Michael Chamberlain on twelfth- through fourteenth-century Ayyubid and Mamluk Damascus, too, indicates strongly that the madrasa was in no way an academy for state officials.[49] His broader conclusions concerning the madrasa in Syria are in all likelihood relevant to Egypt as well, which was usually under the same political regime and saw the importation of the madrasa at nearly the same time. Madrasa professors frequently moved back and forth between Syria and Egypt. Chamberlain denied that madrasas actually created what Leiser calls a "college-trained leadership" that provided stiff competition to Christian functionaries.[50] Rather, "there is no evidence that madrasas were ever intended to advance an ideological program or train state cadres."[51] In fact, "men did not acquire learning in order to gain professional knowledge or qualifications."[52] The madrasas "did not provide the a'yān [elites] with cultural distinction, specialized knowledge, or formal qualifications."[53] In sum, "there was no 'system' of education, patronage, appointment, or of government."[54]

Although Chamberlain probably goes too far in denying the madrasa curriculum any systematic quality, and while his conclusions regarding state appointment seem less definitive for religious or legal appointments than for secretarial or bureaucratic ones, the larger picture that he sketches of the madrasa in its social setting allows us to form a more nuanced conception of the madrasa's effect on non-Muslim communities, one that, moreover, fits more closely the evidence of such texts as Ibn al-Nabulusi's *Tajrid*. In short, the madrasa forged new ties between military elites and *'ulama'*, heightening both the scholars' expectations of appointments to salaried posts and the elites' expectation that the scholars would lend their overt support for the state. The result was unprecedented competition for state patronage among the *'ulama'*. In Chamberlain's words, "Where madrasas and dar al-hadiths [schools for the study of the Prophet's sayings] were founded as a means of attaching the prestige of 'ilm [religious knowledge] and the protection of waqf to the personal and political strategies of powerful households,[55] their effect was to transform the nature of competition among the a'yān [elites]. . . .

Struggles over manṣibs [salaried positions] were much like struggles for all the monetized honors of the city. This is why such struggles were so often referred to as fitna [civil discord]."[56]

Chamberlain's description of a culture marked by competition for status provides a more compelling motive for the opposition that high-status Jews and Christians weathered in Egypt in the thirteenth century. By reading, with Chamberlain, "law, institutions, even knowledge itself" as "simultaneously instruments and arenas of a never-ending struggle for social power and status,"[57] it appears that it was not the intrinsic force of *fiqh*'s content that dictated "discriminatory measures" for non-Muslims, but rather the need of the *'ulama'* to valorize the visible Sunni superiority on which they depended for their collective and individual status. They framed their competitive practices as legal norms: "the 'rules' they occasionally pointed to neither established nor described the terms of the competition. What we have interpreted in the sources as descriptions of rules was often part of the ordinance directed by one side against another in competitive struggle."[58] If *'ulama'* accused one another of "immorality, impiety, or unbelief"[59] in order to disqualify their competitors, for instance, it was not because a newly resurgent *fiqh* frowned on these moral failings, but because such accusations were newly incentivized by the virtual flood of patronage now available to the *'ulama'*.

Similarly, even if madrasas in the thirteenth century were neither intended nor perceived as academies for bureaucrats, it is at least clear that they redirected state resources to support the training of larger numbers of Sunni *'ulama'*. For *'ulama'* brought up through such a system, state elites were naturally viewed as the major potential patrons; if positions in the religious and legal hierarchies were unavailable or insufficiently remunerative, it is not surprising that madrasa-trained *'ulama'* accepted or even sought employment as officials (*kātib*, *'āmil*, *mushidd*, *nāẓir*, *mustawfī*, etc.). Here, despite the dubious relevance of their training, they competed with non-Muslim officials for appointments, giving them ample reason to highlight the more restrictive strains within the Islamic textual tradition and mobilize these in apostrophizing the military elite, as Ibn al-Nabulusi did in the *Tajrid*.

In sum, then, the refined account that we have outlined here of the relationship between the spread of the madrasa and the Islamization of Egypt stresses the new patronage culture that was fostered by the madrasa and other endowed institutions associated with the return of Sunni rule in the twelfth and thirteenth centuries.[60] The flood of patronage and accompanying creation of salaried posts raised *'ulama'* expectations of state support and created a culture of competition and mutual antagonism—what Chamberlain described using the indigenous term *fitna* (discord). Jewish and Christian officials, the non-clerical elite and pillars of their communities, became threats to the aspirations of the *'ulama'* within this culture and were targeted in polemical works such as Ibn al-Nabulusi's *Tajrid* and numerous others.[61] To the extent that these campaigns were successful, they undermined the political and social position of non-Muslims in Egypt and contributed to the marginalization and diminution of their communities.

Parallels to a "Persecuting Society"

Given the geographical foci of this volume, it is worth noting that the causational mechanism I have proposed to connect the madrasa and the increasingly straitened condition of Jews and Christians in Egypt finds a parallel in that proposed by R. I. Moore in his path-breaking work on the institutional developments that contributed to antipathy toward Jews, heretics, and lepers, among others, in northwestern Europe between the tenth and the thirteenth centuries, a phenomenon he called "the formation of a persecuting society."[62] No argument will here be made that Egyptian society in this period was becoming a "persecuting society"; if evidence for the widespread persecution of lepers in Ayyubid or Mamluk Egypt exists, for example, it has yet to emerge. Nor am I in a position to judge the historical accuracy of Moore's arguments.[63] My modest purpose in these brief concluding remarks instead uses the causal mechanisms that Moore proposed to highlight an apparent historical parallelism: in both Moore's account and the Egyptian case we have studied, for all their differences, the development of educational institutions that more closely connected political elites to religious scholars contributed to the marginalization of religious out-groups.

In Europe of the twelfth through fourteenth centuries, as in Egypt during the same period, we observe the growth of novel educational institutions, most obviously the universities that George Makdisi attempted to connect to the madrasa, as well as novel uses for old institutions like the cathedral schools. The same period also saw unprecedented interest in and codification of canon and Roman law both within and outside those new institutions, as well as opposition to non-Christian officials amid general pressures on non-Christian communities. Around roughly the twelfth century, historians are suddenly confronted with canonists, decretists, and decretalists, and with the clerks or *literati* who become increasingly common at court.

Within this setting, Moore concluded in 1987, "it is hard to evade the conclusion that the urgent and compelling reason for the persecution of Jews . . . was that they offered a real alternative, and therefore a real challenge, to Christian *literati* as the advisers of princes and the agents and beneficiaries of bureaucratic power."[64] Others followed Moore. Brigitte Bedos-Rezak suggested that "by the beginning of the twelfth century the written word . . . was in the hands of monks and clerics who competed with each other, and with the laity, for the maintenance of a scribal monopoly associated with control of the cultural and political arenas. Within this context, the traditionally available literacy of Northern French Jews made them appear as competitors. Jews were, in effect, challenging the hegemony of churchmen."[65]

Walter Pakter independently reached complementary conclusions after surveying canon legislation on the issue of Jews in public office: "At the end of the middle ages it was no longer the princes or even the councils which feared harm from granting Jews authority over Christians; it was the legal scholars. The ancient fear of Jews in public office had been replaced by self-interested professional elitism."[66] For Pakter, too, it was competition for resources mediated by an increasingly powerful state that catalyzed opposition to Jewish public officials among newly prominent legal scholars.

Moore retracted the strong version of his argument in the second edition (2007) of his study, admitting that there had been "no substantive evidence of ['direct competition for positions at court'] in northern Europe."[67] He retained a prominent explanatory role, however, for the more generally conceived

> anxieties of the clerks, who also lived in a condition of chronic insecurity, not only in their careers but in their identity and their position in society. . . . Their prospect of position and respect in the world, their claim to legitimacy in office and the exercise of authority which many of them could not assert by birth . . . hung ever more directly on their education. The status and authority of their education depended in turn on the position of the ablest and most respected among them as the unquestioned guardians and interpreters of the Christian faith. . . . Every alternative source of religious authority, real or potential . . . must therefore be denigrated

> and if necessary destroyed. . . . That is why it was necessary . . . to destroy the present identity of the Jews.[68]

Moore thus shifted the focus of the competition that he proposed from a bureaucratic to a religious arena. With little *mutatis mutandis* wizardry, both the original and revised versions of his model ring true for the *'ulama'* of Egypt in the early madrasa era. But in the Egyptian case, unlike the European, there exists copious evidence for direct professional competition between the swelling ranks of the literate majority jurists and their minority out-group contemporaries. Thus the model proposed in this chapter for the madrasa's effect on non-Muslim elites recalls Moore's central contention: "However the tremendous extension of the power and influence of the literate is described, the development of persecution in all its forms was part of it."[69] The Jews and Christians of thirteenth-century Egypt were comparatively fortunate that the persecution they suffered took fewer and less violent forms.

Chapter 6

Jews in and out of Latin Notarial Culture: Analyzing Hebrew Notations on Latin Contracts in Thirteenth-Century Perpignan and Barcelona

Rebecca Winer

On 12 August 1261, Jacob of Montpellier and his son Jucef, Jews of Perpignan, decided to cut their losses and not seek to reclaim money they were owed from the Christian debtor Bernat Boshom. Along with their Christian client they entered the office of the royally appointed notary, Pere Calvet, to have their settlement recorded. The Christian notary registered the transaction in Latin along with Boshom's release of his claim to any of the "usury" that Jacob and Jucef of Montpellier received from him, "with or without charter," or in "any other way."[1] Boshom declared that the father and son had fully satisfied his financial claim against them and stated he would seek nothing further.

Who owed what to whom had been in dispute. This is evident from the witness clauses: legal disputes between Jews and Christians required witnesses from both religious groups for resolution. In this case Ruben, son of Abram of Montpellier, and Mossé Samiel, two Jews of Perpignan, appeared on behalf of Jacob and Jucef de Montpellier; and two local Christians, Guillem de Tuïr (Thuir in French) and Guillem Vallespir, bore witness for Bernat Boshom.

The Christian Boshom had the upper hand over his Jewish creditors, because of ambivalent attitudes toward Jewish moneylending in this society. By royal decree it was legal for Jews to lend money at a rate of 20 percent interest annually in the Crown of Aragon, the realm where Perpignan was situated, and royal courts defended the rights of Jewish creditors. On the other hand, Canon 67 of the Fourth Lateran Council (1215) mandated that Christians eschew all contact with Jews who charged "oppressive and excessive interest."[2] Indeed, in the 1260s the Crown was increasingly becoming aware that although it explicitly allowed Jewish creditors to charge the rate of 20 percent interest, some of its Christian subjects viewed this as excessive and local Church authorities agreed with them. A contributing factor in shaping their opinion may have been that Christian moneylending was also royally regulated and the maximum interest set for a Christian creditor was the much lower rate of 12 percent. This contradictory situation enabled Christian debtors to evade Jewish creditors by suing them for usury in ecclesiastical courts, where they gained more favorable verdicts than in royal courts. After 1275 the Crown cracked down and a Christian debtor who behaved this way could face a truly crushing fine of 1,000 morabatins (around 9,000 sous or shillings), or sixteen times the median figure for a woman's dowry in the later thirteenth-century protocol books.[3] In the 1260s, however, the ecclesiastical loophole was not yet closed and Boshom was one of hundreds of Christian debtors in Perpignan who sought to take financial advantage—hence the references to "usury," as opposed to interest, in his declarations—in order to shortchange his Jewish creditors.[4]

The notary, Pere Calvet was supposed to be a neutral party; he accepted six pennies (*diners* in Catalan) in payment from each side. But this notary did something that revealed himself as not so equitable: he made Jacob and Jucef de Montpellier sign his register in their own hands and include declarations acknowledging that they no longer had any financial claim over Boshom. Calvet did not require this of his other client, their Christian opponent; indeed, no Christian ever signed his protocols (the official archive of the legal transactions that Calvet facilitated). This Jewish father and son were asked to sign and made an accompanying declaration in Hebrew, "Jacob de Montpellier acknowledges" and "Jucef, his son, acknowledges," in the same form as those of many other Jewish clients of Christian notaries in the 1260s.

In this essay I argue that not only was Calvet personally not a neutral party in the transactions of his Jewish clients, but that the institution the Christian and Latin notary represented was often an intrusion into the lives of Jews, even if, at other times, Jewish clients benefitted from access to Latin notarial legal expertise. The place of Jews within Christian, Latin notarial culture has already been the subject of some important work, but new discoveries in the area of Hebrew deeds (*shetarot*) and Jewish/Christian relations means it is a good time to revisit this issue in light of the concept of entanglement. Previous scholars have focused too much on the Latin documentation, particularly that in which Hebrew deeds are mentioned, because the Latin record in this region is so much more extensive. Some have seen Jewish notarial culture as only developing under Christian guidance in the late thirteenth and fourteenth centuries, and as only really existing to draft *ketubot* (marriage contracts), *gitei nashim* (divorce documents), and witness testimony relating to deathbed declarations, not wider commercial transactions.[5] I would argue instead that a developed and functioning Jewish system for the drafting of Jewish "notarial" documents/*shetarot* of many kinds was in existence well before the fourteenth century. The earlier system included documents drafted through less formal channels, since what mattered most in drafting contracts was the presence of two valid Jewish witnesses, but this did not necessarily mean Jews found the system markedly less efficient than the later one that was more carefully controlled by the Crown. The Crown harnessed, taxed, and regulated the Jewish system from the mid-thirteenth century on, as it encouraged the recourse of Jews to Latin notaries, to increase revenues and amplify royal control. I revisit the issue of how Jews figure in the Latin and Hebrew notarial records here by reflecting directly on what Hebrew notations and deeds imply about the status of Jewish legal culture in the mid-thirteenth century as the Crown increasingly sought to regulate matters and as royal legislation mandated that more and more of the transactions Jews made had to be conducted before Christian notaries. This in turn affected how Jewish notaries conducted their business, encouraging them to echo terms included in the majority legal system, for example, but it may have limited the power of Jewish notaries as much as it fostered it.

The transaction of Jacob and Jucef de Montpellier is one of eighteen bilingual exchanges I have found in the two earliest unedited and unindexed notarial protocols from Perpignan, from 1260–61 and 1266.[6] Only seventeen of these Latin registers currently survive, from between 1261 and 1287, out of a total of what Richard Emery has estimated as approximately a thousand.[7] The Hebrew signatures and declarations in particular have led me to revisit the position of Jews in Latin notarial culture in the Crown of Aragon during the mid-thirteenth century. Jews regularly hired Christian notaries to draft their contracts in Latin. Jewish notaries, or *sofrei hakahal* (lit., community scribes) as they are referred to in Hebrew sources, drafted contracts in Hebrew. Why would a Jewish client choose one over the other?

Recent historiography on medieval Jews who availed themselves of majority, non-Jewish legal systems has stressed the elective side of the phenomenon.[8] Medieval Jews, especially in the Islamic world, were integrated members of the broader society who understood the advantages of bringing certain suits to non-Jewish courts, even cases involving fellow Jews. In the medieval Crown of Aragon there were instances in which Jews sought the benefit from legal protections that existed in the well-developed majority Christian system of law. Local Jewish religious leaders objected to legal moves that ran directly counter to what they deemed permissible for Jews, but accepted the widespread use of Latin notaries as a fact of everyday Jewish life. Indeed, the facility with which some Jews navigated Latin notarial culture in the Crown of Aragon is striking. But the parallel between the earlier centuries of the *Dar al-Islam* and the thirteenth-century Crown of Aragon has its limits. Historians cannot ignore the differences in the linguistic situations in the two societies: Latin was the language of law in western Christendom but not of everyday life, and Jews there did not know it as well as Jews in the *Dar al-Islam* knew Arabic. There were also strong pressures on the Jews of the Crown of Aragon to conduct business before Christian notaries that had nothing to do with Jewish interests per se. In mandating that Jews use Christian notaries, the rulers of the Crown of Aragon sought to centralize their control, generate revenue, and appease Christian contingents, who often saw their commercial interests as at odds with those of Jews. In this chapter I contextualize the eighteen Hebrew statements made within Latin notarial register books in Perpignan and bring them to bear in sketching out the sometimes coercive and biased legal landscape a Jew navigated when s/he walked into the thirteenth-century Christian notary's office.

Bilingual intersections in the record are often studied for their sociolinguistic value.[9] However, the Hebrew signatures and notations in the Latin protocols from Perpignan are repetitive, terse, and formulaic, making analysis of these statements more conducive to helping answer questions about Jewish negotiation of Latin and Hebrew notarial culture than questions of language per se. In order to explain the legal work that this group of Hebrew declarations did and its ramifications for our understanding of Jewish/Christian entanglement, I draw on recent discoveries relating to medieval Hebrew deeds as well as Hebrew notations on Latin parchment charters from Barcelona. I argue that the Hebrew signatures and acknowledgments from Perpignan were not symbolic expressions of Jewish identity, as Juliette Sibon has deemed the brief and fleeting Hebrew interventions in the Latin notarial record for fourteenth-century Marseilles, and as Annliese Nef has those from fifteenth-century Sicily.[10] Rather, the short Hebrew notations in the Perpignan notarial record did real legal work. Their formulation validates the Latin contracts and echoes analogous situations in Latin parchment charters.

Latin Notaries and Their Craft

To bring the legal landscape of medieval Perpignan into focus we must first turn to an examination of Christian and Jewish public scribes, as well as the types of legal documents, parchment charters, and paper protocols they generated. Christian notaries writing in Latin worked throughout the western Mediterranean in the High Middle Ages. Their presence accompanied and facilitated the rise of commerce. They were analogous to lawyers, in particular to solicitors in the United Kingdom, since they drafted contracts and, generally, did not go to court unless required to testify about the transactions they validated. Clients who sought advice in urgent legal disputes, or needed an especially well-informed arbiter for an ad hoc arbitration, went to the expense of hiring even more specialized legal professionals with formal university training: the *iuris peritus,* or his senior colleague, the *legum doctor* schooled in the principles of the *ius commune* (Roman and canon law and their relation to quotidian legal matters).[11] In western Europe, notaries first became common in the towns of twelfth-century Italy. The ratio of notaries to the rest of the urban population in late thirteenth-century Genoa has been estimated at 1 to 500, similar to that of lawyers to citizens in the United States today. Robert I. Burns estimates that for the towns of the Crown of Aragon in the thirteenth century, notaries were only somewhat less common.[12]

In the Crown of Aragon, notaries received some formal training and were licensed by the Crown. They served as scribes in the royal chancery, the king's courts, and for the bailiffs and vicars representing the Crown in the urban centers and villages. Notaries like Pere Calvet, who registered the settlement with which this article began, were urban professionals. Throughout the towns and larger villages of the medieval Crown of Aragon, notaries were royally appointed as civil servants.[13] Although there were variations in notarial practice from place to place, rulers issued some uniform legislation concerning the trade, which was enforced throughout the Crown of Aragon. Most townspeople and villagers, other than the abject poor, sought out a notary at a certain point in their lives to draft marriage contracts, last wills and testaments, loans, investments, sales of real estate or goods, or rental contracts. Merchants and lenders must have visited the notary's office several times a month, or more.

The notary's charge was to draft contracts, for a fee, in his office workshop. His clients would take these charters away with them and the notary would retain a record of the contracts; or, the notary would register a contract only, without the client requiring the additional parchment charter. The notary might complete the work himself and/or could hire additional scribes whose work he supervised within his workshop. The notary guided his clients through a transaction by asking them a series of questions; he even kept a template for more complicated contracts, such as last wills. The notary or scribe wrote his initial notes on scraps of paper, then registered each transaction in an abbreviated form on paper in sequential entries grouped together by date. The notary was legally obligated to keep this summary of all the business that he drafted. If the clients requested and paid, he wrote out official parchment charters as well. Eventually the notary had the folios bound for safekeeping; this bound register survives as the protocol book.[14]

Sofrei Hakahal and Their *Shetarot*

The key obstacle to the study of Jewish notaries in the medieval Crown of Aragon is that their *shetarot* are rare, numbering in the dozens, while other sources in Hebrew and Aramaic, such as the responsa of famous authorities from this time and place, run into the tens of thousands. The evidence that does exist implies that there were many parallels between Christian notaries and Jewish public scribes, or *sofrei hakahal.* There is therefore a strong argument for referring to these Jewish public scribes as "Jewish notaries," as Kenneth Stow does the analogous *sofrei meta* (lit., town scribes) Leon and Isaac Piatelli, who generated the approximately 6,000 Hebrew documents that form the basis of his studies of the everyday lives of the Jews of the sixteenth-century Roman ghetto.[15]

Most of the information on the Jewish notaries in the Crown of Aragon comes from the fourteenth and fifteenth centuries when Crown authorities carefully oversaw the institution in relation to its Christian counterpart.[16] In the thirteenth-century Crown of Aragon, Jewish notaries were sometimes appointed by the king, in which case they often hired a staff to help them, or, more often, by the leaders of the prominent *aljames* (communities). Solomon ben Abraham ibn Adret (1235–1310), the great religious leader of Barcelona, the capital of Catalonia, the commercially dominant region within the thirteenth-century Crown of Aragon, refers to regulations concerning *sofrei hakahal* from different towns in his responsa. And Latin documents and registers from the royal chancery from the late thirteenth and fourteenth centuries allude to "Jewish notaries."[17] As their Christian counterparts did, Jewish notaries worked in various legal venues: *sofrei hakahal* kept *pinkasim* (community record books),[18] made transcripts for *batei din* (Jewish courts), and drafted *shetarot* for individuals, also presumably keeping their own registers/protocols of private documents in Hebrew, although these have not survived.[19] There was probably more overlap between the various positions of Jewish notaries, especially in the smaller Jewish communities, than their Christian counterparts. Still, Jewish notaries in the medieval Crown of Aragon were clearly more formal officials than the scribes that S. D. Goitein depicts working in medieval Cairo.[20] Although, as Malachi Beit Arié has shown, throughout the medieval Jewish world many adult men could work piecemeal as scribes for wealthier individuals interested in hiring them to copy books for their private collections,[21] the thirteenth-century *sofrei hakahal* who oversaw the drafting of Hebrew deeds were much more knowledgeable than the run of the mill piecemeal scribal worker. By the later thirteenth century and early fourteenth they gained some legal muscle in imitation of the Latin institution: for example, in some towns they were empowered to the degree that their signature on a *shetar* had the legal force of two valid Jewish witnesses, making *sofrei hakahal* analogous to Christian notaries in this regard.[22] Just as calligraphers were specialized scribes, so were Jewish notaries. Burns describes the Jewish notary as "a salaried bureaucrat in charge of both communal and private legal documents; he was a secretary to the community, presumably able to hire assistant scribes."[23]

Jewish notaries had extensive knowledge of the correct formulae to document different types of transactions between Jews. These individuals could draft documents like *ketubot,* deeds of divorce, and death-bed declarations, of course, but numerous property-related transactions, acknowledgments of debts or other legal responsibilities, or the taking up of offices, like that of guardianship, also survive. According to royal decree in the Crown of Aragon, documents drafted by Jewish notaries held the same validity as those written by Christian notaries.[24] The Jewish community of Barcelona had a well-developed tradition for the drafting of a great variety of legal deeds in Hebrew from the beginning of the twelfth century, at the latest. This tradition is evident from the normative guide to best scribal practice, the *Sefer ha-Shetarot,* of the great codifier Judah b. Barzillai Bartseloni, which dates from that period.[25]

Negotiating Notarial Culture and Hebrew Deeds: Legal Literacy Among Jews

One issue that influenced a Jewish client's choice between the two available types of notaries and their legal systems would have been the ability to understand what s/he was signing. Jews operated in three main languages in the north of the thirteenth-century Crown of Aragon (the main regions of Roussillon and Catalonia, and the major urban centers of Perpignan, Girona, and Barcelona): they spoke Catalan in their everyday pursuits (although some in Perpignan may have done so in Occitan accents since many descended from immigrants from southern France); they read Hebrew and some wrote in Hebrew cursive (or semi-cursive); and they went before notaries to have their contracts drafted in a specialized Latin. In the notary's office, Jews would have conversed with the Latin Christian notary about their transactions in Catalan. There were varying levels of Hebrew literacy within the Jewish community. Jewish boys learned to read Hebrew characters from childhood. And, as a reference to a *hekdesh*, or charitable trust, set up by Sara, widow of Daví de Cabestany, of Perpignan, in her Latin will of 1286, indicates, there was a communal expectation that Jewish men know how to read basic Hebrew texts. Sara bequeathed the income of several houses in Narbonne to be used for the education of poor Jewish boys, in Perpignan and Béziers, "in the knowledge of Hebrew"; and she donated two volumes "in which are contained the five books of the laws of Moses" and instructed that more Jewish books be bought for them with which the boys might study.[26] This education was not just about preparing these boys to follow the service in the synagogue; it was giving them the tools they needed to go into any kind of business that required record keeping or the ability to read Hebrew legal documents. If reading Hebrew was a skill most adult Jewish men possessed, however, fluid writing in cursive was only mastered by a smaller group, including scholars, merchants, and lenders.[27]

Still, it seems likely that many Jewish men knew how to sign their names in Hebrew, even if they could not write much more. Some could even sign in semi-cursive, perhaps as children with writing challenges in American schools today are increasingly required to learn to write only their own signatures in cursive, while completing the rest of their written work in print. All eighteen Hebrew notations in the Perpignan Latin protocols of 1260/1261 and 1266 are written by the individual Jewish men involved in the particular transactions. Three of the instances are only signatures, with names written in large and shaky semi-cursive letter forms.[28] The other fifteen signatures are accompanied by declarations of acknowledgment and most are written in slightly better semi-cursive hands, although the one by Jucef, son of Jacob of Montpellier, who was possibly a young teenager, is written in a square script.

Jewish merchants and financiers may have read a little Latin, but it is highly unlikely that they could write the Latin alphabet.[29] For his own convenience a Jew in possession of Latin charters notated them on the dorse (back) in Hebrew. Latin parchment charters pertaining to the Perpignan *aljama* (Jewish community) were filed in a communal chest; a group of four from 1408 have Hebrew notations written in the same place across the dorse, which would have made them easier to locate.[30] And Jewish businessmen, like Astrug Roven and his siblings, who lent money in mid-thirteenth-century Barcelona, also filed Latin charters away for safekeeping at home in their personal or familial strongboxes with Hebrew notations.[31] Joseph Shatzmiller rounds out the picture, based on his work on Jews of Manosque in Provence, and explains that "the Jews of the city must have kept in their shops registers written in Hebrew where operations were recorded as well as the [Hebrew] identifying notes that were attached to pawns."[32] Given their relative lack of Latin literacy, unlike their Judeo-Arabic-writing counterparts in the Islamic world, it is not surprising that the Jews of the Crown of Aragon would prefer *shetarot* when making many kinds of transactions with other Jews, not just in drafting a document that historians would expect to find in Hebrew characters, like a *ketubah*. Yet few *shetarot* survive from this region, while the Latin documentation is some of the richest for all of medieval Europe, making ironclad conclusions elusive. The thirteenth-century Hebrew deeds that are extant mostly involve real property transfers between Jews, a business matter that could have been covered by a Christian notary without legal complication, but often was not.[33] We should follow David Abulafia's assertion that, due to the dominance of the Latin documentation in the overall record, much of the commercial activities of the Jews of thirteenth-century Perpignan are lost to us;[34] certainly transactions between Jews are not adequately represented. One reason for the disappearance of a section of Jewish business is that *shetarot* have not been preserved in greater number.

Jew as Clients of Christian Notaries

The fit between a Christian notary and a Jewish client was not a perfect one. The position of the Jew vis-à-vis the Christian notary is in some ways analogous to that of a Christian woman. Jews, like Christian women, especially wives, had more legal hoops to jump through than Christian men, such as special oaths to take, and they both possessed less Latin literacy than elite Christian men. The most sophisticated Christian merchants probably understood notarial practice better than the most elite Jewish merchants and lenders. There were, however, many Jewish businessmen active in the credit sector who were more knowledgeable about the financial instruments that related to their work than their often rural, artisan or knightly, Christian clients were. Perpignan was a boomtown in great need of cash liquidity. Jewish lenders did frequent business with all and sundry and they conducted this before Christian notaries. To balance out this picture, it must be said that even if elite Christian men wielded the most economic and financial control in this town, there were others who left their marks. Some Jews were experts at navigating Latin notarial culture, but poorer Jews could find themselves at a disadvantage, for example, if asked to take additional oaths or add signatures, because they were Jews.

Given the possible disadvantages, and that Jewish notaries were active and legally recognized by the majority authorities, why would Jews choose Christians to draft their contracts at all? Earlier, in the eleventh century, it seems that they did not; in property transactions between Jews and Christians in Barcelona, bilingual documents were the norm, with the *shetar* of the Jewish party written in Hebrew directly below the Latin charter drafted for the Christian client.[35] By the thirteenth century this had changed, with Jews opting to have some documents drafted by Jewish notaries and others, especially those made with non-Jews, by Christian ones. Several factors contributed to Jewish use of Christian notaries, including Jews employing a defensive legal strategy against possible Christian opponents, especially converts from Judaism; a desire on the part of some Jews to avoid restrictive halakhic situations; and the fact that Christian notaries were simply more convenient or inexpensive.[36] These rationales are akin to the phenomenon of judicial "forum shopping" that has been documented in many societies for those not in power, from the Christians and Jews of the medieval Islamic world to the subjects of British rule in Colonial India.[37] If thirteenth-century Jews perceived a legal or financial matter as vulnerable to challenge from some member of the Christian community, they made a point of bolstering their positions by drafting their business before a Latin notary. So it was that in Castelló d'Empúries, on 28 June 1346, Duran de Sant Ponç, a childless Jewish physician, attempted to disinherit his estranged convert brother by leaving his goods to his Jewish wife and her relatives through a cleverly crafted Latin testament.[38] If a type of legal maneuver could be facilitated through the Christian's notary's formulae, but not those of the *sofer hakahal,* then Jews resorted to Christian notaries. So, on 19 June 1329, Bonadona, wife of Mossé Vives, whose husband was "mismanaging and wasting all of his goods," used a Latin legal contract to sequester her dowry, avoiding his creditors and keeping her family afloat, in spite of the fact that both Ibn Adret in Barcelona and Yom Tov ben Avraham al-Ishbili of Saragossa (1250–1330) wrote responsa prohibiting a wife from reclaiming her dowry while her husband was still alive.[39] Bonadona realized that a Christian notary could help her to do the medieval version of declaring bankruptcy when a *sofer hakahal* could not. There were dozens of Christian notaries in her town of Perpignan who were happy to take her business.

David Abulafia discusses the Hebrew notations in the Perpignan registers as an indication of the possible advantages to Jews of using this legal form: "The presence in the registers of signatures and annotations in Hebrew makes it plain that the Jews themselves valued recourse to a notary, which removed all doubt about the date and value of the transaction, crucial information in the money lending business."[40] There is truth to this; transactions between Jews and Christians had more potential for conflict than those between Jews. And loans from Jews to Christians which were supported by the Crown's own legal system were probably most likely to be repaid.

The issue of convenience, although real, can be overstated, however. An additional rationale behind the choice by Jewish clients to employ Christian notaries over Jewish ones cannot be ignored: compulsion by royal and urban authorities. In the mid-thirteenth century in the Crown of Aragon, if Jews lent money to Christians and they wanted a written contract, they were legally bound to transact that business in Latin and in front of a Christian notary. This had a knock-on effect of dragging transactions that might otherwise have been drafted by a *sofer hakahal* into the Latin legal realm. For example, if any business related to a marriage or inheritance involved promissory notes for debts owed by Christians, contracts surrounding the matter might well end up in Latin, often with technical Hebrew terms like "*aḥarayot*" (meaning a lien on property) quoting from and standing in for the Hebrew *shetarot* that had been drafted first.[41] This situation was set in motion by royal legislation and was part of a concerted effort by King Jaume I "the Conqueror" to forward his interests while managing the diverse population under his rule.

Royal and Urban Legislation on Jews, Lending, and Latin Notaries

Jaume—in English, James—I "the Conqueror" (1213–76), the ruler of the Crown of Aragon, used the law as a tool to bind, centralize, and govern his far-flung congeries of territories with their diverse inhabitants. By the middle of the thirteenth century, Jaume I had become king of Aragon, Valencia, and Majorca, count of Barcelona, Urgell, Roussillon, and Cerdanya, and lord of Montpellier and Carlat.[42] The Christians of these regions spoke different languages: Aragonese in Aragon, the western mountain upland; Catalan in Catalonia and Roussillon; a mix of the two (with Catalan ascendant) in Valencia and the Balearics; and Occitan in Montpellier and Carlat. The majority of the population in Valencia was newly colonized Muslims, and there was a sizeable Muslim population in Aragon as well, most of whose first language was Arabic. Jews lived throughout the Crown and spoke the language of the region where they resided. In addition to having some knowledge of Hebrew, some Jewish scholars were also Arabic specialists. In this varied cultural landscape, whose secular and ecclesiastical elite had a long memory for their Visigothic and Christianized Roman predecessors, the concepts of the *ius commune,* coming out of universities like the local one in Montpellier, found fertile ground. Jaume I also legislated and validated codes in this idiom for his separate realms, including mobilizing the team that authored the *Furs* ("law code") of Valencia. He fostered an efficient chancery by the mid-1250s, fueled by the paper mills of the Muslim town of Xativa in Valencia. Jaume I sought increased legal control of his vassals, and local noblemen struggled to preserve what they saw as their ancient privileges against royal encroachment. This count-king also restructured the government of his towns. Perceiving this as both opportunity and threat, Christian town fathers drafted their own codes and registered their own charters, jealously seeking royal recognition of their ancient liberties and rights against nobles, ecclesiastics, foreigners, and other outsiders, including the Jews of their own urban centers. Finally, Jewish *aljama* representatives (*secretarii* in Latin, *ne'emanim* in Hebrew) jockeyed with the other interest groups for official royal recognition of religious, legal, and commercial rights and privileges.

It is in this context that Jaume I's legislation concerning Jews and notaries must be understood. On 26 February 1241, Jaume met with his *Corts* (representative assembly of Catalonia) in Girona, halfway between Barcelona and Perpignan. Jaume I was in a somewhat vulnerable position, still at war in Valencia and maneuvering to take over in Roussillon, technically sharing power with his uncle Nunó Sanç, until the latter's death in December 1241. Jaume I approved a body of legislation regulating Jewish moneylending, which marked a partial defeat for him, an expression of mistrust of the Jews of his realms, and a qualified victory for the nobles, knights, and urban patricians. These Christian groups wanted clear legal controls placed upon the Crown's Jews, especially Jewish lenders. The king set the rates of interest for Jewish and Christian lenders (20 and 12 percent, respectively), not a prejudicial decision since it openly recognized that both Jews and Christians were lending money at interest. Less even-handedly, however, Jews were obligated to swear an oath before the local royal official (the vicar of Barcelona or of Roussillon) that they were abiding by the laws regarding interest and did not cheat their Christian clients in any way, including using false weights and measures for loans paid in kind. Christian creditors were not required to so swear. Lists of those Jews who had taken the oath were to be delivered to all notaries, who were not to draft loan contracts for those whose names were not found there.[43] In practice, this meant that all Jews who did business in that particular urban center needed to swear this oath so their names appeared on the notary's list.[44] Previously, in 1228, King Jaume had legislated that a Jewish lender taking a public oath concerning debts owed to him was insufficient proof to claim repayment without either a pawn, suitable witnesses, a mortgage, or a legally valid Latin contract.[45] Now the oath was required before a Jew could even engage in business, which, if related to moneylending by contract, always had to be transacted in Latin before a Christian notary.[46]

In addition to this legislation regulating the commerce of the Jews throughout the Crown of Aragon, Philip Daileader argues that there was a protracted battle waged between Jewish creditors and Christian debtors in Perpignan in particular. Daileader describes the first mention of the Jews of Perpignan in the great municipal legislation of 1243, the *Customs of Perpignan*, as a "preemptive strike." The Christian urban fathers decreed that "Jews have no privilege against the men of Perpignan through any [royal] concession made to them or in any other way."[47] The Christian urban leaders had two main goals; they were seeking moratoria on Christian debts to Jews and to keep Jewish commerce within the city limits to better profit from it. Daileader deems this struggle one sign of Jewish marginalization in medieval Perpignan and coercive policies relating to Jews and their use of Christian notaries as another. Increasingly, Christian notaries throughout the Crown of Aragon sought additional control over Jewish commerce by purchasing royal monopolies over Jewish credit transactions, which was to the disadvantage of Jewish lenders. Individual, or groups of notaries (depending on the size of their jurisdictions), purchased the royal privilege of drafting all contracts that related to Jews; their protocols are entitled *libri judeorum* (books of the Jews). In Perpignan during the reign of Jaume I, as a document of 1274 shows,[48] the Jews had pushed back against these pressures, acquiring the right to have loan contracts drawn up wherever they were transacted, something Jewish lenders found convenient since many of their clients dwelt in the villages of Roussillon and beyond. By 1326, however, the Jews of Perpignan had lost this right when twelve Christian notaries of the town banded together and purchased the monopoly on recording loans from Jews to Christians.[49]

These struggles had ramifications upon the everyday interactions between Christian notaries and Jewish clients. A suggestive, if partial, comparison between the character of relationships between a Christian notary and elite Jewish and Christian clients can be made. Two extant protocols are devoted primarily to two such businessmen: Jaffia Ravalla, Jewish moneylender of Castelló d'Empúries, and Arnau de Codalet, Christian financier of Perpignan. Jaffia Ravalla was the secretary of the *aljama* of Castelló d'Empúries from 1305 to 1315, the mid-sized medieval capital of Empordà in the Pyrenees, not far from the Mediterranean Sea and a southern neighbor of Perpignan's region of Roussillon. The Latin loan and investment contracts of Ravalla and his son, Vidal, big fishes from a middling pond, are all registered in a single notarial protocol from 1323 to 1331.[50] On the surface such a register is analogous to the notarial protocol from late thirteenth-century Perpignan, which is dedicated almost exclusively to the commercial activities of the rising Christian investor and financier Arnau de Codalet and his sons, Guillem and Arnau, from 1276 to 1287.[51] These two protocols could both be read as testimony to the wealth and influence of these businessmen and their close professional relationships to particular Latin notaries who accorded them the consideration of recording their portfolios in a convenient way. In fourteenth-century Castelló d'Empúries, however, the institution of the *liber judeorum* was in existence; notaries had paid money to the Crown for the right to force the Jews to conduct business only before them, not their competitors with more shallow pockets. Ravalla and his financial affairs were a moneymaking prospect, which is what made him a valued client. "His" register is filled with loans he made to Christian clients; it does not seem to include the records of the Ravalla family dowries, properties, and will-related transactions that characterize de Codalet's register alongside de Codalet's transactions as a Christian financier. Indeed, inside the cover of "Ravalla's" protocol is a Latin notation about the four evangelists, when commemorating the authors of the gospels was not something this Jewish client would have relished. Although Ravalla lived in a mid-sized community, possibly lacking the favorable proportion of Jewish notaries to prospective Jewish clients of a great urban center, Ravalla probably still sought Jewish notaries out. It seems likely that the Ravalla family's dowry and property contracts were not drafted by a Latin notary but by a *sofer hakahal*. Jaffia Ravalla would have kept Latin parchment charters in his home, after he annotated them in Hebrew, stored alongside the Hebrew documents his family acquired concerning their marriages and inheritances, and probably also *shetarot* relating to property and other transactions they had made with other Jews.

Latin Transactions Accompanied by Hebrew Notations in Perpignan

Whatever their reservations concerning Latin notarial culture, it was an everyday reality in the lives of the Jews of the Crown of Aragon in the 1260s. Approximately fifty different Jewish people appear in the forty folios of the earliest surviving Perpignan notarial protocol, ADPO 3E1 register 1 (1260–61), and they make over a hundred different transactions, mostly loans to Christian clients. That constitutes about an eighth of the members of this Jewish community of around 300–400 people.[52] Out of these one hundred transactions, only fifteen are accompanied by Hebrew notations. In the next register from 1266 there are only three Hebrew notations, and there are none in the one that follows from 1272 or any afterward.

Sibon sees the isolated Hebrew notations in the Marseilles notarial record as concerted assertions of Jewish identity. She envisages the person who would write in Hebrew as an educated, empowered member of the Jewish elite who lived alongside the Christian urban elite of Marseilles and, if discretely, still consciously expressed himself in Hebrew as a dignified assertion of his Jewish identity (in Latin he would attempt to control the discourse by referring to himself as "hebreus," not "judeus").[53] This interpretation of concerted self-assertion does not fit the body of Perpignan evidence. Hebrew declarations and signatures were made in Hebrew because Hebrew characters were the only ones these Jews knew how to write. Most importantly, they were written not because these people were proudly asserting their identities as Jews, but at the insistence of Christian notaries whose Jewish clients were in legal positions that obligated them to acquiesce. Notaries followed prescribed forms that mandated statements and oaths in certain cases, but they also drafted contracts called *pacta*, which they could improvise based on the situation. Notaries might also be creative in administering additional oaths if the parties involved asked. In the Crown of Aragon parties to transactions regularly made signed declarations if they owed money, were relinquishing a right, or were acknowledging or promising something. If the party they had borrowed from, or were quitclaiming to, did not feel that their promises and signatures were sufficient, he or she could ask that an oath accompany them.

Creditors required this of some clients to whom they lent money. In most instances when the Jewish clients signed the protocol books they owed money to Christians: in five cases they were taking out loans,[54] in two they bought cloth on credit,[55] in one grain on credit,[56] and in five Jewish lenders relinquished their rights to money owed or repaid by Christian borrowers.[57] None of the eighteen contracts were new loans from Jewish lenders to Christian borrowers. Lending money to others put the Jewish party in a position of legal strength; none of those who signed in Hebrew were in that position. Christians loaning money to Jews was a rather rare phenomenon on the ground: the entirety of the seventeen thirteenth-century registers from Perpignan only contains seventy-four acts where Jews contracted debts to Christians or purchased goods on credit from them, as compared to the 1,321 acts where Christians borrowed from Jews.[58] Hence these signatures and acknowledgments are also rare.

The three Jews who were made to swear an oath in addition to their signatures were likely the most vulnerable of the group, the greatest financial risks, or perhaps tradesmen guaranteeing their future return on large investments. The Jewish debtor, Mossé de Soal, for example, does not seem to have been an elite person. In one debt from 1260, for thirty-five sous, Mossé appeared as guarantor for his wife as borrower, making her dowry liable for repayment.[59] This may have been the action of a couple in real need of money; elite men avoided implicating their wives' assets in their debts, but Christian artisans, laborers, and peasants were often forced to go this route. There is not a lot of information about de Soal, and it is always dangerous to argue from silence; still, it should be noted that he never appears lending money to Christians, standing surety for fellow Jews outside his intimate family circle, or as a creditor in any capacity. De Soal appears in a total of three protocol entries borrowing, or helping his wife to borrow, from Christian lenders. Two of the transactions were for smaller, if significant sums: twenty-two and thirty-five sous, respectively, when another Jew is recorded as renting a small house in Perpignan that year for twenty-five sous per annum.[60] The last loan de Soal borrowed was for a substantial amount. On 24 June 1261, Mossé de Soal received sixteen pounds minus two sous, or 318 sous, from the Christian, Bernat Bendit.[61] De Soal signs his name in Hebrew to this contract but makes no declaration, simply writing his signature in a large and shaky hand.[62] It seems likely that de Soal knew how to sign his name but not to write fluid Hebrew cursive.

Although we know so little about Mossé de Soal himself, there are some clues as to the identity of another man who stood surety for de Soal for his 318 sous debt and acted as his witness to that transaction, Vidal Salamó. Vidal Salamó was married to the sister of the lender Bonjuses, son of Mossé Catalan, and seems to have held some loan contracts in his brother-in-law's name, probably assets belonging to Salamó's wife's dowry. Emery entertains the possibility that Vidal Salamó was an artisan. Information on Jewish artisans is notoriously difficult to come by for thirteenth-century Perpignan; almost no Jews are identified by their trades in the notarial record, although they can be found more frequently identified as such after 1348. Vidal Salamó appears often in the 1260s, never lending money, but once purchasing precious metals. Was he engaged in a trade that some later medieval Jews specialized in? Was he a silver or goldsmith?[63] If this was so, and if Mossé de Soal was an artisan too, this might explain why Salamó served as de Soal's guarantor; and de Soal's lower social rank could explain his level of literacy. His work as an artisan could explain the large loan as an investment, not written in the *commenda* form used among Christians because there was no need to hide the interest involved. It is interesting to speculate but impossible to be certain. What is clear is that in the extant notarial registers from the 1260s, Jews were required to sign their names when they were debtors and the notaries administered oaths to them if their Christian creditors required them.

Among the Latin protocol entries with Hebrew notations, there is only one transaction made between Jews alone, not between Jews and Christians:

a public acknowledgment to the *aljama* of Perpignan. On 5 August 1261, Bonjuses, son of Mosse Catalan (a.k.a. Yehudah Catalan), made a public declaration to Leo de Elna and Daví Bonet, two of the four secretaries, or representatives and financial trustees, of the *aljama* of Perpignan. Bonjuses acted on behalf of the men of his family, which included his brother Vidal, his nephew Mossé, and his brothers-in-law Vives Daví and Vidal Salamó.[64] The secretaries seemingly were concerned that Bonjuses and his relatives had not shouldered their full financial burden in terms of the annual tax owed the king, and for other *aljama* debts; and/or Bonjuses had sought a lessening of his tax assessment. Bonjuses declared that he had explained the extent of his family's assets to the secretaries without fraud. Bonjuses presented them with a signed list of all the debts owed to him and to his male relatives and swore that if any contracts had been omitted the interest now belonged to the king. Finally, Bonjuses swore an oath to this effect. One of the secretaries, Leo de Elna, confirmed Bonjuses's statements, returning his document.[65] Bonjuses Catalan's declaration had ramifications vis-à-vis his standing in the Jewish community; seemingly, an intracommunal matter like this would not appear in a Latin notarial protocol at all. However, related Crown legislation from Zaragoza in 1264 mandated that a Jew who maintained he was being overtaxed and sought to contest his assessment was required to make a sworn declaration in front of a Christian notary.[66] Moreover, Bonjuses's statement included an admission that he forfeited money to the king should he be found to have perjured himself. Thus, because of royal mandate in Perpignan, in accordance with legislation from before 1261 that is no longer extant, or through good sense concerning the safest way to conduct this affair when much of the Catalan's family's assets were in the form of promissory notes for money owed by Christians, the secretaries of the Perpignan *aljama* found it prudent to handle this intracommunal matter in the Christian, not the Jewish legal sphere.

Acknowledgments in Contemporary *Shetarot* and Bilingual Parchment Charters

Jews signed the Christian notary's protocol book under circumstances where Crown law placed them under the notary's authority and their Christian creditors insisted. They signed in Hebrew and most, the more literate, added an acknowledgment meaning that they understood the previous Latin document and agreed to its conditions—as Jacob and Yosef Montpellier did in their settlement discussed at the beginning of this chapter. The phrase they used to make this declaration (*modeh*) appears in contemporary *shetarot*. *Shetarot* acknowledged situations: debt, receipt of payment, and renunciation of rights that characterize the bilingual exchanges in the Perpignan protocols, and, understandably, employ the phrase "I acknowledge" or "he acknowledges." Three unedited *shetarot* from Perpignan, extant from the early 1400s, are promissory notes between Jews, written in Hebrew on small slips of paper, and all beginning with the phrase: "I, the undersigned, acknowledge."[67] José María Millás Vallicrosa edited a *shetar* from 1255 that he termed a *hoda'ah umeḥilah*, an acknowledgment and renunciation. Elka Klein has also edited examples of thirteenth-century acknowledgments from Barcelona: a 1235 receipt for payment in a property sale by Bonastruga, widow of R. Shmuel, son of R. Ezra to R. Yosef, son of R. Shelomoh; and another from 1262 from Cruxia, widow of R. Shemuel b. Yitzhak ha-Sardi, to Avraham Ascandrani.[68] Thus the Jewish clients of the notaries of Perpignan used a phrase they were familiar with from *shetarot*. Everyday legal practice encouraged the Jews of Perpignan to write "*modeh*" after a release or public acknowledgment of debt, since the impulse for this kind of validation existed in both legal systems and this phrase accompanied it in the Hebrew one.

Additional corroboration can be found in bilingual parchment charters. In the Crown of Aragon a parchment charter contained a fuller picture than the abbreviated entry of the same transaction in a notarial protocol. The purpose of the protocol was to register all of a notary's transactions as a fail-safe understandable to the notary should he need it, not reproduce them word for word. Thus an acknowledgment of payment in a parchment charter can reveal more about the parties' actions than an analogous notarial register entry. Latin loan charters with Hebrew notations are not extant from thirteenth-century Perpignan, but they are from thirteenth-century Barcelona. Ten small parchment charters in Latin, around nine by ten centimeters each, survive from between 1233 and 1256, belonging to the family of Astrug Roven of Barcelona.[69] The group includes seven loans written for Astrug Roven, one Latin loan contract made in the name of his brother Solomon, another made in the name of his sister Regina, and, most importantly, a final receipt of payment made out in Astrug's name and confirmed and signed by Astrug in Hebrew. Unlike the Perpignan protocols, where only Jews were made to sign, in the Barcelona charters Christian debtors also signed their names in Latin, apparently whenever they were able.[70] Two out of three Christian creditors in the Roven family charters signed for themselves; the last, who was a local knight, did not and presumably could not. Signing a parchment charter seems to have been standard practice for a debtor, or someone who relinquished rights to another.

The form of the acknowledgment that Astruc Roven made for repayment from his Christian client provides the closest parallel to the transaction of Jacob of Montpellier and his son Jucef, Jews of Perpignan, with which this essay begins. On 30 September 1239 Astrug Roven acknowledged that Guillem Eimeric paid back ninety sous of a 640 sous debt that he, his mother, and his wife jointly owed Astrug.[71] In Latin, the notary used the phrase "*profiteor et recognosco*" or "I acknowledge publically and recognize" for Astrug's acknowledgment of payment. This is the same phrase used in the Perpignan Latin acknowledgments of the Jewish Montpelliers. And when it came time for him to sign within the body of the charter, Astrug did so in Hebrew. He wrote "Astrug acknowledges (*modeh*)" on one line since he was acknowledging the repayment and thus relinquishing his rights as creditor over that money; on the next line, the signature of a Jewish witness appears in Hebrew.[72] Astrug Roven and the Jewish witness both wrote in their own hands.

Practice in Barcelona charters supports my conclusion that the Perpignan notaries, Pere Calvet and Arnau Miró, in 1261 and 1266, amplified the requirement for signatures on charters by asking their Jewish clients, when they were borrowing money, relinquishing their claims, or taking oaths, to essentially sign in duplicate. Their Jewish clients signed not only the parchment charters, which, judging from the Barcelona parallel, many Christians did also, but they signed the protocol books too, which Christians never did. The 1241 Crown legislation mandated that Jewish lenders with Christian clients had to take an oath before the local royal official, the vicar, and then have their names delivered to the notary, but it did not state that Jewish clients had to sign the notary's protocol. The Perpignan notaries decided individually to have Jews sign their registers as a safety measure. Calvet and Miró wanted additional legal protection for themselves and their clients in a legal environment in which Jews were suspect.

Conclusion

Jewish use of Latin notaries can be seen as an example of "entanglement," as Elisheva Baumgarten describes some Jewish/Christian interactions. That is to say, there was both attraction and coercion involved. On 12 August 1261, when Jacob of Montpellier and his son Jucef, Jews of Perpignan, settled with the Christian Bernat Boshom in the Latin notary's office, they may have gained some security by doing so in this legal venue, but in the end this was not why they were there. They went before the Christian, Latin notary because they were forced to. In mid-thirteenth-century Perpignan, business between Jews and Christians had to be transacted before Latin notaries by local interpretation of Crown fiat. Indeed, legal pressure mounted as the century progressed and more and more of Jewish commerce found its way into the Christian record. By the mid-fourteenth century a combination of legal pressure from the Crown (and the consuls of the towns) pushed Jews into transacting more types of business before Christian notaries with greater frequency than they might otherwise have done by choice, even though Jewish notaries continued to be active and available. The facility of Jewish businessmen in negotiating Latin legal culture is impressive, but this familiarity and astuteness cannot be interpreted as an unambiguous sign of positive interaction through self-determination. The situation was more tangled than that.

Chapter 7

From Christian Devotion to Jewish Sorcery: The Curious History of Wax Figurines in Medieval Europe

Kati Ihnat and Katelyn Mesler

Magicumne istud an sollemne et commune simulacrum est?

—Apuleius of Madura, *Apologia*, LXIII.6

Figurines and effigies of various kinds are well known cross-culturally and historically, but the remarkable way in which they functioned as a focal point for questions of Christian and Jewish practice in medieval Europe is a story that has yet to be told. Effigies were employed in a variety of contexts, both devotional and magical, in cultures with which Christians interacted from antiquity through the Middle Ages, but these objects were understood in new ways in their Christian context. At first proscribed as vestiges of pagan religion, statuettes—usually made of wax—that represented either the full body or just a particular limb went on to become an accepted form of votive offering left at saints' shrines in exchange for healing. This transformation in attitudes toward such images, though gradual, nevertheless made way for the possibility that the practice could be abused, that an effigy capable of mediating healing could likewise be exploited to cause harm.

Jews had been associated in the Christian legendary and historical traditions with iconoclasm and sacrilege against Christian objects since late antiquity, generally at times when Christians sought to justify their own use of icons and crucifixes for veneration. In the case of wax images, Jews became entangled once again in Christian fears that such objects could purposefully be abused either in acts of ritual desecration or in the pursuit of sorcery. The legends about Jewish misuse of wax images thus help us to understand how Christians sought to distinguish proper, Christian use of them from improper, "Jewish" use.[1] In effect, imagining Jewish practices of desecration and sorcery served as a hermeneutic tool for Christians in their attempt to define the boundaries of acceptable devotional practice, shaping the understanding of Jewish behavior along the way.

In this essay we explore how western Christians imagined the misuse of non-decorative wax figurines by Jews as a way of understanding the appropriate use of these objects in devotional practice.[2] The growing popularity of wax votives coincided with the emergence of two types of legend that Jews misused such objects. One type of abuse appeared in stories that depicted Jews fashioning wax figurines and crucifying them in scorn and mockery of Christ's Passion. The other type of abuse was a form of sympathetic magic, in which harm done to the figurine was believed to cause physical injury or to induce states such as love or madness in the person depicted; this activity was also associated with Jews in chronicles and in the evidence from legal trials.[3] While the use and various misuses of wax images are not new to scholars, they have mainly been treated phenomenologically, with little sense of historical development, and usually in isolation of each other. By treating first the history of wax images used in devotional practice, and then the history of each accusation of misuse in turn, we demonstrate that all three were deeply intertwined in the culture and history of the Latin West.

Ancient Roots

Our story has its roots in the Mediterranean and Near Eastern cultures of antiquity. Figurines of bronze, lead, clay, and wax are well attested in the textual and archeological records, and they filled a variety of functions in addition to decoration. Two of these functions resemble those found in the Middle Ages. Figurines depicting the person's body in full or just the injured member were often left at healing shrines. A remarkable number of eyes, heads, hands, feet, arms, legs, heads, breasts, and more have been recovered from these practices (Fig. 7.1).[4] Similar figurines were also used in binding spells, in which the statuette would be pricked, burned, buried, or have its

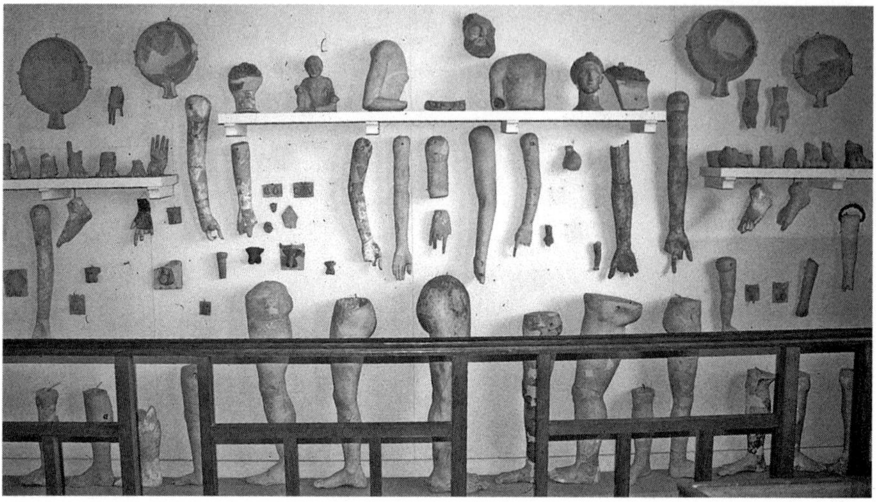

Figure 7.1. Terracotta anatomical votives from the Asklepieion in Corinth, circa fifth century BCE to fourth century CE. Archaeological Museum of Ancient Corinth. Photograph by Alexandra L. Lesk. Used by permission.

limbs bound in order to inflict injury or different states on the individual, such as love, illness, or madness (Fig. 7.2).[5]

According to Theodoret of Cyrrhus, some eastern Christians were using anatomical votives by the fifth century, and there is evidence that sorcery with figurines was familiar to Byzantine and Coptic Christians.[6] In contrast, Latin writers for several centuries only discussed figurines in the context of condemning pagan practices. As far as we can determine, Latin Christians did not begin to adopt the votive practice until around the ninth century. Furthermore, if they took any interest in sorcery with figurines, which they could have encountered in writers such as Virgil, Horace, Ovid, and Pseudo-Callisthenes, there is no clear indication of it prior to the twelfth century.[7]

For archeologists, it can be difficult to determine which purpose a figurine may have served, unless aided by additional clues of context. But this is not only a modern problem. When the second-century writer Apuleius of Madura was accused of performing magic with a statuette, he drew attention to the problematic versatility of these multipurpose objects, asking rhetorically: "Is this a magical statue, or an ordinary, ceremonial one?"[8] A similar problem underlay Christian ideas about figurines in the Middle Ages, and the

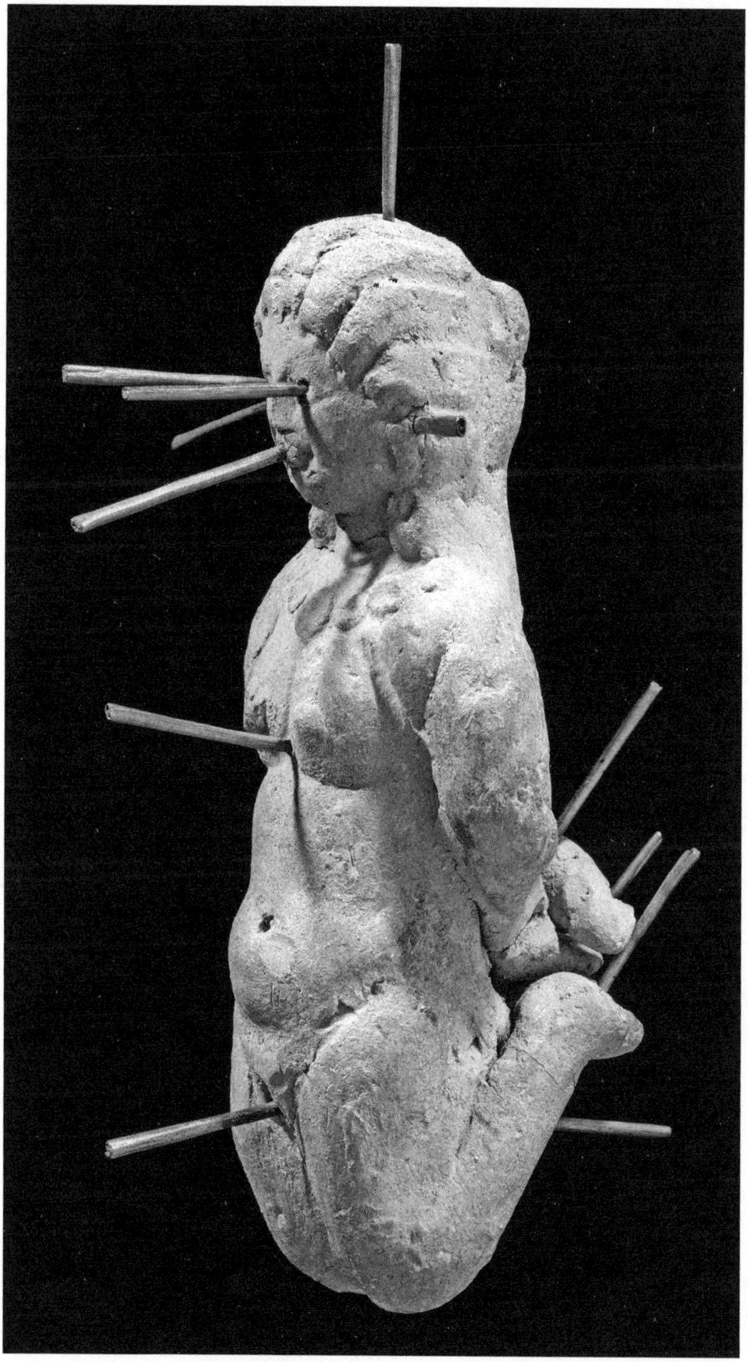

Figure 7.2. Egyptian clay figurine, discovered along with a lead curse tablet, circa second to fourth centuries CE. Musée du Louvre, Paris. Egyptian Antiquities, item E27145a. Photograph © Musée du Louvre, Dist. RMN-Grand Palais.

implications of the figurines' multiple roles will serve as a key to understanding the accusations and stories involving Jews.

Votives, Idolatry, and Representation in the Latin West

As early as the sixth century, we can detect a growing concern among church authorities with the use of figurines and anatomical votives, which they condemned as an idolatrous practice of the Germanic tribes. Perhaps the earliest reference is a canon from the Diocesan Synod of Auxerre (c. 561–605) that forbade making vows at pagan holy sites. It concludes: "Nor should anyone dare to make carvings of wooden feet or wooden men."[9] Around the same time, Gregory of Tours recounted in his *Life of the Fathers* (580s–590s) that his uncle had found a temple at Cologne where "barbarians . . . sculpted limbs from wood whenever one of them was afflicted with pain."[10] Dado of Rouen's *Life of Eligius of Noyon* (c. 660–86) includes a sermon attributed to Eligius, in which the faithful are enjoined not to make "likenesses (*similitudines*) of feet, which they [i.e., pagans] place at crossroads"[11] (Fig. 7.3). Likewise, Bishop Pirmin's catechetical and homiletic *Scarapsus* (c. 724–50) admonishes, "Do not make or place limbs of wood at crossroads, trees, or anywhere else, for they can offer you no healing."[12] Around the same time, the *Short List of Superstitions and Pagan Practices*, which seems to have been composed by the 740s, condemns a variety of likenesses (*simulacra*), including "wooden feet or hands in pagan ritual."[13]

During the same period in which these pagan practices were being condemned, Christian votive practices began to adopt aniconic methods of representing the specific person who sought or had received healing. Building on the data gathered by Anne-Marie Bautier, who surveyed the references to votive offerings in about 150 miracle collections from 800 to 1200, we can begin to reconstruct the historical development of votive practices.[14] The custom of leaving wax candles at saints' tombs dates back to at least the fourth century and remained common throughout the Middle Ages.[15] No later than the sixth century, there is evidence of the practice of measuring candles to the height (or sometimes circumference) of a person seeking healing, thus creating an identification between the person and the candle.[16] It is clear that churches benefited from votives made of wax, for we know that they were remade into church candles from at least the late eighth century. In fact, from the ninth century some votive offerings were no more than blocks of wax, which could be

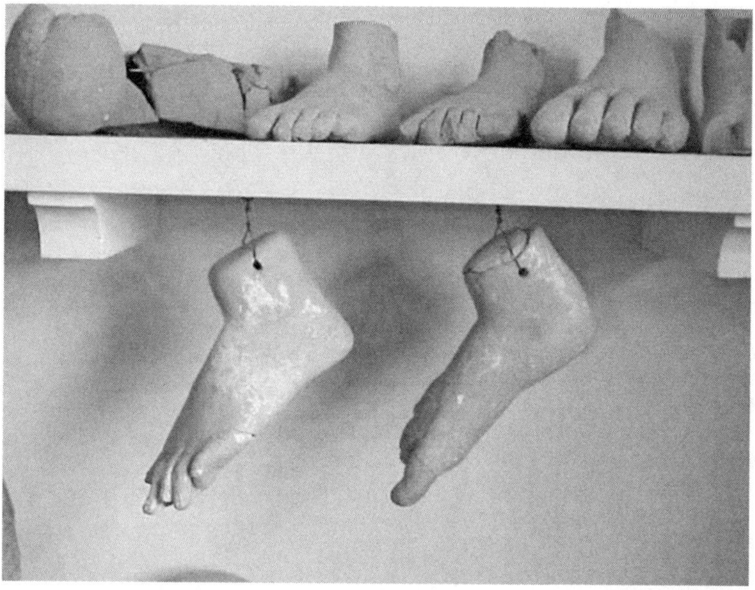

Figure 7.3. Terracotta votive feet from the Asklepieion in Corinth, circa fifth century BCE to fourth century CE. Archaeological Museum of Ancient Corinth. Photograph by Alexandra L. Lesk. Used by permission.

matched to the supplicant's weight instead of height.[17] By the ninth century, the practice of measured candles had been extended to sick animals.[18]

The ninth century is also the point at which the use of iconic, anatomical votives is first recorded as an accepted Christian practice. A miracle collection from Prüm, datable to around 845–60, tells of a woman with a deformed head who had a votive candle "in the shape of her own head" offered on her behalf.[19] Nevertheless, this practice does not seem to have become more popular until the end of the tenth century, when more accounts of anatomical votives began to appear and these votives had grown distinct from candles. In the *Life of Ida of Herzfeld* (c. 980–83), Uffingus of Werden recounted the story of Eggua, a woman suffering from a withered right hand, who received instructions in a dream "that she should depict a wax hand formed in the likeness of her half-dead one, and she should carry it to the tomb of St. Ida."[20] It is perhaps telling that the impetus is said not to come from Eggua herself but from the voice in the dream, which adds a hint of divine approbation to the practice. Another testimony comes from Gerhard of Augsburg's *Miracles of St. Ulrich* (c. 982–91), in which he describes the "many likenesses (*analogiae*)

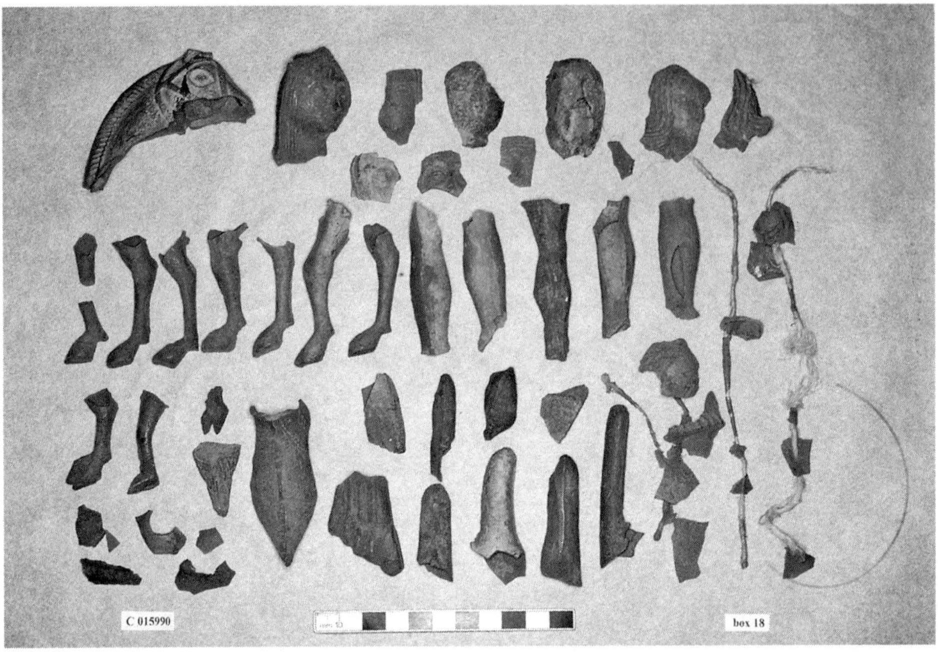

Figure 7.4. Anatomical votives from the tomb of bishop Edmund Lacey (d. 1455), circa 1455–1540. Exeter Cathedral. © Royal Albert Memorial Museum & Art Gallery, Exeter City Council.

fashioned according to the specific limbs of the debilitated."[21] Elsewhere in the text, we hear of a duke of the Vandals who was struck in the arm with an arrow and vowed to craft a silver arm in exchange for healing.[22] The use of full-bodied images is almost certainly confirmed shortly thereafter by the anonymous *Miracles of Firmin of Verdun* (c. 1000), which describes a votive offering: "He balanced the wax statue (*statuam*) with the weight of his body."[23] The object's considerable size reflects the growing sense of identity between the votive and its donor, here thought of in very literal terms, and the substantial cost it would have incurred suggests that the practice had been eagerly embraced. Indeed, it is also around the end of the tenth century when we find evidence of merchants who specialized in selling wax to pilgrims.[24]

Although the archeological evidence from medieval Europe is limited, we should imagine these objects as anthropomorphic figurines and individual limbs, most often made of beeswax (occasionally of various metals or other materials) (Fig. 7.4). Wax could offer a close approximation of the color and

Figure 7.5. Votive figurine from the tomb of bishop Edmund Lacey (d. 1455), circa 1455–1540. Exeter Cathedral. © Royal Albert Memorial Museum & Art Gallery, Exeter City Council.

texture of human skin, but it was also common to bleach the material.[25] In quality, the figurines ranged from crude forms to carefully sculpted statuettes, but those used for votives were frequently made from molds as well. In some cases they were made life-size—this was especially common for votives of limbs—or matched to the person's weight, but to judge by the few references offered in medieval sources, most figurines were smaller, weighing around one or two pounds.[26] The only medieval votive figurine that has been recovered intact was made from a mold, displays a caramel color, and measures eight inches in height (Fig. 7.5).[27]

From 1000 through 1200, the use of representational votives only continued to gain ground, with little evidence of ecclesiastical resistance. Bautier identified no fewer than fifty-three accounts of anthropomorphic or anatomical votives in this period.[28] While these votives were usually made by the petitioner, by the end of the eleventh century there were artisans who specialized in the sculpting of votives.[29] During the eleventh and twelfth centuries, the methods of establishing identity between votives and votaries also continued to expand. From the eleventh century, there are references to candles made to the length of individual limbs rather than the full height of the person, and the twelfth-century records attest to figurines of animals as well as objects such as ships.[30] These figurines were hung above the saint's tomb with string, placed directly on the tomb, or placed near it (Figs. 7.6–7.11). In a study of votive offerings from the twelfth to the fifteenth century, Pierre André Sigal found 224 instances of anatomical votives and more than 100 anthropomorphic statuettes.[31] A few sources offer even more impressive numbers. When a papal commission made an inventory of the votives at the tomb of Thomas de Cantilupe in 1307, they recorded 436 wax figurines, 1,200 wax limbs ("and an uncountable quantity of eyes, breasts, teeth, ears"), and 129 silver replicas of bodies or limbs.[32] Such examples could be multiplied with ease.[33]

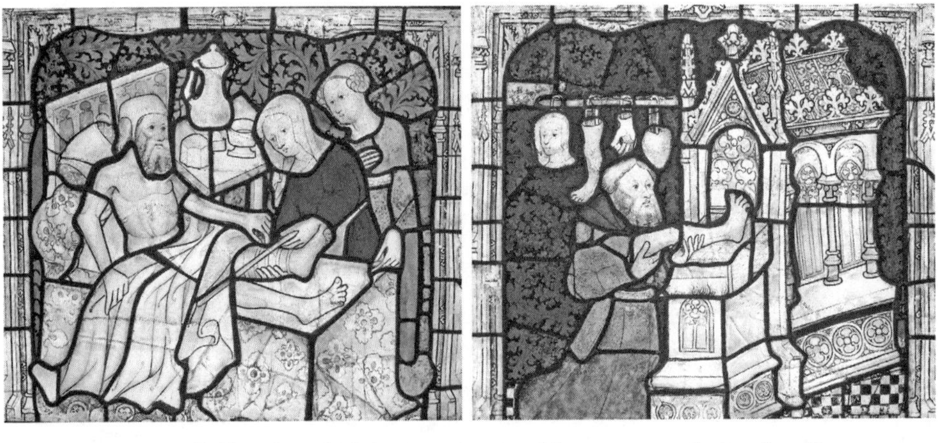

Figures 7.6 (left) and 7.7 (right). A man's injured leg is measured, then he offers a votive leg at the shrine of William of York, with a votive head, leg, hand, and heart hanging above, circa 1414. St. William Window, north choir (CVMA nVII, panels 22a, 22b), York Minster. Left image: The York Glaziers Trust. Right image: By courtesy of Roger Rosewell. Both images are reproduced by the kind permission of the Chapter of York.

Figure 7.8. Votive heads, thigh, breasts, foot, leg, arm, and hand at the tomb of St. Margaret of Antioch, circa 1420. Turino Vanni, Altarpiece depicting the Life of St. Margherita (detail). Pinacoteca Vaticana. Photo © Vatican Museums. All rights reserved.

Figure 7.9. Pilgrims offer anatomical votives to St. Mary. Arms, legs, and figurines hang above. Jakob Issickemer, *Das Buchlein der Zuflucht zu Maria der muter gottes in alten Oding* (Nuremberg, circa 1497), title page. The Pierpont Morgan Library, PML 36051. Photographic credit: The Pierpont Morgan Library, New York.

Figure 7.10. Votive arms, leg, figurine, and other objects at the tomb of St. Wolfgang, circa 1480. St. Wolfgang Altarpiece (detail), attributed to the workshop of Jan Polack. St. Wolfgang in Pipping, Munich. Photograph by Sarah Blick. Used by permission.

Figure 7.11. Pilgrims at the tomb of Simon of Trent. A votive figurine and limbs hang nearby. Johannes Matthias Tiberinus, *An Senat und Bürgerschaft von Brixen* (Nuremberg, after 4 April 1475). Bayerische Staatsbibliothek München, Rar. 338, fols. 6v and 7r. Used by permission.

Despite the ubiquity of representational votives in the late Middle Ages, there was also a resurgence of the association of the practice with idolatry, which continued into the Reformation.[34] For example, the Florentine satirist Franco Sacchetti added the following comment to one of his *Three Hundred Stories* (c. 1392–1400): "These ex-votos and similar things are offered every day and they are more a form of idolatry than of Christian faith. And I, the writer, have actually seen someone who had lost a cat vow that if he should find it, he would bring a wax one to [the image of] Our Lady of Orsanmichele [in Florence], and so he did. . . . [God] wants our hearts and our minds; he doesn't go searching for images of wax, nor for this pride and vanity."[35] Whatever their source, however, Christian anxieties over the acceptance of the practice came to be reflected in two particular types of imagined abuse: mock crucifixion and sorcery. Both types of misappropriation were predicated on the fundamental principal of identity that underlay the object's perceived effectiveness in religious practice. The votives functioned not merely as likenesses or representations but as sympathetic substitutes for the individual that remained in the physical presence of the saint in place of the votary.[36] The sense of identity is strengthened by the material and the form of the figures. Not only does beeswax offer a good approximation of human skin, but Megan Holmes has also pointed out that it had long been associated with seals and impressions, and that medieval Aristotelians frequently cited wax as a prime example of the hylomorphic impressing of form onto matter.[37] The use of wax thus reinforced the possibility of conferring identity on a representation.

The identification between object and votary helps to clarify the connection been votives and the imagined misuse of wax figurines through mock crucifixions and sorcery. For, if the accepted devotional use of such figurines leaves the proxy under the protection of the saint, the same logic suggests that such a proxy could also fall into—or worse, be created by—the wrong hands. And while the accepted use of wax figurines presumes a salutary outcome for the votary, the misuse of such a figurine logically carries with it the risk of injury.[38] Medieval Christians imagined this injury as an inversion of both the Christian ritual and its goal, that is, as an injury to the faith in the form of an anti-Christian sacrilegious ritual and as an injury to the individual by turning a source of healing into a method for harming. It is just as the practice of leaving wax votives seems to have become increasingly widespread that we begin to see accounts of both types of misuse, which appear almost simultaneously in the 1130s. This is where Jews enter our story.

The Abuse of Wax Figurines: Mock Crucifixions and Sorcery

Mock Crucifixions and Jewish Desecration of Christian Objects

The idea that Jews represented a risk to Christians by expressly seeking to defile, desecrate, and even destroy Christian sacred images and objects, which eventually came to include wax figurines, was an old one. From late antiquity, Jews had been imagined to carry out violent acts in contempt of Christian symbols, generally in an effort to define proper Christian approaches to devotional objects. The burning of effigies of Haman during the Jewish festival of Purim, for example, was forbidden in the Theodosian Code of 438 for fear it could also function as an expression of contempt for the cross, although recent analysis has underlined that the legislators sought primarily to separate Christian from Jewish practices.[39] Fear of Jewish antagonism toward images intensified especially during the iconoclastic controversy of the eighth and ninth centuries in the East, when Jews became a primary target for iconophiles.[40] Although the Jewish threat to icons was largely a rhetorical device to counter Christian iconoclasts, it was nevertheless transmitted in vivid narratives that ensured its longevity and impact. Already in the sixth century, a tale recorded in Gregory of Tours's *On the Glory of the Martyrs* (c. 588) and attributed in a longer eighth-century version to the patriarch Athanasius of Alexandria (d. 373) describes one particular image of Christ found by a Jew on the wall of a house. Gregory had the man attack the image himself, whereas Pseudo-Athanasius described how a group of the man's co-religionists spat on it and pierced it with a lance, with the words, "Whatever our fathers did to him, let us all do the same to this image," at which point the image emitted blood and water.[41] The Pseudo-Athanasian story went on to become the basis of a widespread liturgical celebration in most of western Europe by the eleventh and twelfth centuries.[42] The idea that Jews did not just refuse to venerate icons, but actively sought to destroy them, therefore became cultural capital as such stories became part of the Christian devotional tradition in the East and West.

The incorporation of the Pseudo-Athanasian tale into the liturgical celebration of the Exaltation of the Cross in some places may have caused western Christians to envision the desecration not of an eastern-style icon, but of another type of image that was gaining in popularity around the turn of the millennium: the crucifix itself.[43] The anniversaries of Christ's birth and death around the year 1000 marked a significant surge in veneration of the cross, driven by fears and hopes for the coming apocalypse.[44] As depictions of the crucified Christ shifted to emphasize his suffering and death, chroniclers recorded miraculous incidents that included the appearance of fiery crucifixes in the sky and the sudden profuse weeping of a figure of Christ on the cross.[45] Around this time, abuse of crosses was imputed to dissenting groups, such as the accused heretic Leutard, active around Orleans.[46] Jews were also the target of such accusations.[47] Ademar of Chabannes, for example, blamed the Jewish community of Rome for causing an earthquake in 1020/21 by mocking a crucifix in their synagogue, although his account may have been inspired by the Pseudo-Athanasian tale, which Ademar incorporated into one of his sermons.[48] By the end of the century, the outbreaks of religious violence committed against Jews in northern France and the Rhineland by those embarking on the First Crusade may well have triggered the acts of defiance, including spitting on the cross, attributed in later sources to Jews faced with forced baptism.[49] Whatever the extent to which Jews actually committed such acts, increased devotional emphasis on the cross explains the anxiety Christian authors felt about its misappropriation at the hands of non-believers.

The legendary and historical accounts of Jewish desecration gave way in the early twelfth century to a new way of imagining the behavior of Jews toward Christian figures. The rise of devotion to the Virgin Mary as figure of the church and universal intercessor with Christ was expressed perhaps most vividly in new collections of Marian miracles that emerged in the 1130s.[50] A considerable number of these stories depict Jews in various guises, but always as enemies of the Virgin and her followers.[51] While many of the tales were merely extracted from older sources, including Byzantine stories about miraculous icons, some of them appeared for the first time in the twelfth-century collections, such as the story of the Jews of Toledo.[52] The very popular Latin version relates that on the feast day of the Assumption, as the archbishop of Toledo was performing the mass, a voice called out from the heavens, wailing, "Woe, woe, how monstrous and vain has the perfidy of the Jewish people proven to be, woe what a terrible injury that the insanity of the Jewish people persists and prospers . . . and is taunting a second time my only son, light and salvation of the faithful, and is trying to inflict on him the suffering of the cross."[53] The Christians, puzzled by the message, searched the houses of the Jews, and in the synagogue discovered them subjecting what is described as "a waxen image that looked as if it were alive (*imago quam quasi viventem*)" to "torments by means of thorns [i.e., crowning with thorns], slaps and death" in order to disgrace the Christian faith.[54] In a version reworked by the monk William of Malmesbury between 1134 and 1138, he added that the image was pierced with a lance, and that it was made "for the mockery of our lord Jesus" (*ad domini Jesu ludibrium*).[55] The Christians immediately fell upon the Jews and murdered them on the spot. In some versions, they also destroyed the "offense and perfidy of the false Jews" (*dolum et perfidiam Judaeorum fraudulentorum*).[56] The story was no doubt influenced by the Byzantine stories of Jewish violence against icons, but the change to the nature of the image is highly significant.[57] The story came to include the unprecedented idea that the Jews themselves fabricated the image they abused, whereas earlier stories of desecration involved objects produced by Christians.

The story of the Jews of Toledo captured the Christian imagination throughout western Europe in the twelfth and thirteenth centuries; it was put into verse and translated into various vernaculars as miracle volumes spread for use in meditative reading, liturgical practice, and performance in courtly contexts.[58] It also began to transcend the boundaries of legend. In the *Chronicle of Saint-Maixent*, written around 1140, the brief entry for 1123 states that the Jews of Rouen did "something terrible" to a waxen image.[59] An account preserved only in a seventeenth-century chronicle describes how the Jews of Pescara were accused in 1062 of piercing a waxen image of Christ with a lance, in imitation of the Passion.[60] A more detailed incident is recorded in the *Chronicle of the Slavs* by Arnold of Lübeck (c. 1210) as having taken place in Cologne during the archiepiscopate of Philipp of Heinsberg (1167–91).[61] A certain Jew of the city is said to have had a vision of the Holy Spirit on the Easter Vigil, which he mulled over until the following Good Friday, when it was the custom for Jews to crucify a waxen image in mockery of Christ. After having subjected the image to all kinds of abuse, including whippings, slaps, spitting, and nailing to the cross, they pierced the side with a lance, upon which blood and water poured out.[62] The Jew recognized the miracle and ran to the archbishop, denouncing the actions of his fellow Jews, and accepted baptism at the Vigil. The text is explicit in affirming that through this mock crucifixion Jews were fulfilling the blood guilt of Matthew 27:25. Although there is to our knowledge no historical record of Jews being persecuted for abusing wax effigies in this period, the chronicle sources suggest that the once legendary accusation was gaining traction. Like the Toledo story, the chronicles portray the tendency for Jews to create and desecrate wax images as a desire to mock the Passion through reenactment of the crucifixion. The *Chronicle* of Arnold of Lübeck is nevertheless explicit that this is a *ritual* act (*consuetudo*), one committed every year on Good Friday. This aspect is significant because it echoes the emergence during this period of the claim that Jews annually crucified Christian children in derision of Christ's death. The first formulation of the charge, in the *Life and Miracles of William of Norwich* (c. 1150) of Thomas of Monmouth, describes how William was kidnapped by the Jews "to be mocked and put to death by the Jews in scorn of the Lord's passion," an act described later in the text as one the Jews committed every year.[63] The charge surfaced many times in subsequent centuries, eventually producing the blood libel, in which Jews were thought to require the blood of their victims, often for Passover rites. Later, after 1290, host desecration accusations would offer yet another way in which Jews were seen as attacking the literal body of Christ.[64] The fear that Jews were intent on mocking the Passion by replicating it in ritualized fashion, either with waxen or human stand-ins, was made explicit in the law code (1256–65) of Alfonso X of Castile (d. 1284), the *Siete Partidas*: "We have heard it said that in some places Jews celebrated, and still celebrate Good Friday, which commemorates the Passion of Our Lord Jesus Christ, by way of contempt: stealing children and fastening them to crosses, and making images of wax and crucifying them, when they cannot obtain children."[65] It is no coincidence that Alfonso's most prized cultural achievement, the monumental *Cantigas de Santa Maria*—a collection of over 400 Marian miracle stories in Galician-Portuguese, richly illuminated and set to music—includes the Toledo story. The corresponding image shows a child-sized waxen figure being tortured by Jews (Fig. 7.12).[66] The

Figure 7.12. The Jews of Toledo are caught in the act of crucifying a wax figurine. Biblioteca del Monasterio de El Escorial, MS T.I.*1*, fol. 20v. Copyright © Patrimonio Nacional.

thirteenth century thus saw the culmination of the legends developed in previous centuries into a powerful new understanding of Jewish danger not just to representations of Christ in wax but in the flesh.

The interchangeability of wax images and human bodies in the Alfonsine law code is revealing of the dynamics at play in accusations of Jewish mistreatment of both. By the thirteenth century, the iconoclastic assault on images of earlier centuries had evolved to include the active creation and abuse of figures made to represent the intended victim. The notion of sympathetic identification between the wax symbol and its signifier, such that the wax image was thought to replace an actual individual, is very reminiscent of the principle behind the use of wax votives; the image took the place of Christ just as the votive stood in for the votary. The emergence and spread of the idea that Jews caused harm to wax images in parallel with the rise of wax votives therefore echoes the process by which allegations of Jewish desecration of icons and crucifixes arose in periods when these objects increasingly became the object of veneration. At a time in the twelfth century when votive figurines appear increasingly in the sources as accepted objects of religious practice, the emergence of stories about Jewish mistreatment of them legitimized and supported their use in the correct way. These tales reinforced the power inherent in the objects themselves, while at the same time providing medieval Christians with a useful counterexample of what not to do with religious objects. Pinning misuse on Jews was thus an effective way for Christians to establish the efficacy of these objects when used correctly, with the result of additionally underlining the sharp distinction between proper Christian and improper "Jewish" behavior. The shift from the domain of legend to history, as chronicles and law codes expressed assumptions that Jews really did subject wax figures to abuse, marks a crucial step in the evolution of the idea.

Wax Figurines and Sorcery in the Middle Ages

At the same time that stories of desecration were beginning to circulate, another means by which Jews were thought to abuse wax images emerged, this time in connection with magic. The magical use of figurines was well known in antiquity and remained accessible throughout the early Middle Ages in the descriptions of Horace, Ovid, and Virgil; yet the practice seems to have disappeared from Latin and vernacular writings from the late fifth century until the early twelfth. If any awareness of the practice persisted during these centuries, it is surprising that it has not been found mentioned in any of the legal, moral, and penitential literature that describes a wide range of forbidden magical and superstitious practices.[67] The notion seems to reappear only in the twelfth-century *Laws of Henry I* (1114–18), in which one canon addresses murder by potion, spell, sorcery, and *invultuatio*.[68] It remains a mystery why this term, based on the Latin *vultus* (face, image, statue), suddenly appears without an explanatory gloss. Nevertheless, the etymology and the context point toward some form of sorcery with images, and the word in its various forms—including the French *voult*, *envoulter*, and *envoultement*—became a technical term for sorcery with figurines.

The renewed interest in classical literature in the twelfth century played a role in incorporating sorcery with figurines into moral and theological discussions of magic, especially among scholars associated with Paris. The first such reference comes from the *Policraticus* (c. 1159), where John of Salisbury explicitly referred to Virgil's *Eclogues* and Ovid's *Heroides* when describing practitioners of magic who "fashion in a somewhat soft substance (as wax or clay) images of those whose natures they are striving to distort."[69] After John, authors of the twelfth and thirteenth centuries such as Peter of Blois, Hélinand of Froidmont, and William of Auvergne also looked to classical sources when discussing figurines.[70] If we were to rely on these sources alone, we might be tempted to interpret the twelfth-century appearance of figurines for sorcery as merely a classical revival. Other accounts, first dating from before John of Salisbury, nevertheless demonstrate how deeply the medieval understanding of these figurines was tied up with the contemporary use of votive figurines.

A twelfth-century chronicle provides evidence of the link between the magical abuse of wax images and the abuse of Christian practices, and it implicates Jews in a surprising way. In the *Deeds of the Treveri*, a chronicle of Trier, we are told that bishop Eberhard died in the sanctuary on Holy Saturday in 1066, after the conclusion of the divine office.[71] By around 1132, a set of expansions and continuations were added to the text, which fashioned Eberhard's end into a martyr's death.[72] According to this version, Eberhard had decreed that the Jews were to be expelled from the city, unless they converted by Holy Saturday: "And so, certain ones of that wicked race, after fashioning a wax image (*imaginem*) in likeness of the bishop, which they placed among the candles (*lichnis*), bribed a certain cleric of the monastery of Saint Paul, a Christian in name but not in deed, to baptize it. On that Saturday, after the bishop had already prepared for the solemn celebrations of baptism, they lit it on fire. Once half of it had burned, the bishop, who was presiding over the holy offices at the [baptismal] font . . . fell gravely ill and . . . died."[73]

Since the aforementioned *Laws of Henry I* do not actually describe the practice of *invultuatio*, this passage offers the earliest known description of a magical figurine in the medieval West. The placement of the figurine among the candles suggests a connection to Christian votive practices, but the most striking aspect of this account is the significance of baptism, in which the baptism of the figurine stands in sharp contrast to the bishop-martyr's administration of baptism on the Easter Vigil. The notion that Jews would believe such an image had to be baptized, and that they would seek out a Christian cleric to perform it, demonstrates that the depiction of Jews and of alleged Jewish practices was strongly influenced by Christian conceptions of figurines and the ways in which they were meant to function. For Christians, the sacrament of baptism conferred both a name and a Christian identity, and baptizing the figurine would thus have resonated as a means to establish the connection between the image and the person it was meant to represent (especially since the figurine was created by a third party without the knowledge or physical contact of the person represented).[74] But the baptism also plays another role in the story. The misuse of baptism for a magical purpose, much like the use of chrism or consecrated hosts in magic, would have been considered superstitious, idolatrous, and even demonic.[75] The baptism of the figurine, which turns a potential devotional object into a magical one, highlights the parallel between misusing the sacrament of baptism and misusing a (votive) figurine.

Not all medieval accounts of figurines involved baptism, but this act of sacramental abuse became a particular concern of canonists and inquisitors in the thirteenth and fourteenth centuries, who often condemned it alongside theft and abuse of the Host.[76] Nor were Jews the only ones accused of the practice, as they were in the case of mock crucifixions, since Christian women as well as men of political significance were too, but the cases in which Jews were implicated are particularly revealing. Two prominent cases among the growing numbers of sorcery trials demonstrate the persistence of an imagined connection between Jews and sorcery with figurines. The first case is that of Guichard, bishop of Troyes, who stood trial from 1308 until his acquittal in 1313.[77] Among other charges, he was suspected of having murdered Joan I of Navarre (d. 1305), the queen consort of France. In the trial, one witness testified that a Jew named Hagin from Troyes had assisted Guichard by preparing "a certain image" (*quandam ymaginem*) from wax.[78] Presumably this image was a figurine of the kind Guichard allegedly had a sorcerer use against Joan.[79]

The second case involved Hugues Géraud, the bishop of Cahors, who came into conflict with Pope John XXII (r. 1316–34) from the very outset of the latter's pontificate.[80] Hugues was first put on trial for misconduct as a bishop, but then charges arose that he had led two groups of conspirators in several failed attempts to assassinate the pope and three cardinals. One of these groups, based in Toulouse, procured wax figurines of the pope and two cardinals from a "baptized Jew" called Bernard Jourdain, who made the figurines from molds. The figurines were "blessed" (*benedicere*) in a church ceremony, but they were then intercepted en route to Avignon. The second group, based in Avignon, was led by Hugues himself, who tried to acquire figurines from several sources. At one point, he is said to have written to his brother: "Go quickly to Limoges, and take some of your pure wax, and have an image (*ymaginem*) made, and send it quickly with a trustworthy messenger, so that I can have it by the Feast of the Purification of Blessed Mary, so that I can offer it to Blessed Mary of Valvert."[81] According to this testimony, Hugues feigned his intention to offer a votive in order to obtain a figurine for sorcery. It is an extraordinary piece of evidence that explicitly connects votives and sorcery in Christian thought. After this too failed, Hugues sent his treasurer, Aymeric de Belvèze, to procure a figurine in Toulouse. The inconsistent testimony of the witnesses implicated either one or several Jews (or none in one version) in providing the wax figurine. Then, a Jew either from Toulouse or Avignon instructed Hugues and an accomplice in use of the image. He told them to baptize it, to recite certain words, and he taught them how and when to prick it. Here is just one way the incident is described:

> And the aforementioned bishop [Hugues] revealed the image in the presence of the witness [Pierre Fouquier] and a Jew who had come from Toulouse, a teacher of this art; he [Hugues] baptized it, sprinkling holy water on it and anointing it with chrism, reciting prayers and words written in a book he was holding. Afterward, according to the instructions of the Jew, the aforementioned bishop pierced it in the stomach with a stylus, and the witness pierced it in the side with a needle, saying *May those who persecute me be thwarted*, etc. (Jer. 17:18), *May his days be few*, etc. (Ps. 108:8), and the remaining verses of that Psalm. Having done this, they placed the aforementioned image as though it were dead on its back, in a chest of the aforementioned bishop.[82]

As other testimonies make clear, even the method of baptism was supposedly taught by the Jew.

Given the various conflicting details in these two trials, it is very likely that the Jews and their roles were largely fabricated. The Jews mentioned in these records were never interrogated or even identified, whereas most of the secondary figures in the stories were questioned if not arrested. Repeated instances of torture and interrogation shaped the witnesses' accounts in Hugues Géraud's trial, pointing to an active contribution by the papal commissioners and witnesses themselves in ascribing a meaningful role to the Jews. Here, the context is important. Both trials reveal hostility toward Jewish presence that was undoubtedly shaped by their expulsion from France (and accompanying refuge in Provence) during the years 1306–15, as well as anxiety about relations between bishops and Jews.[83] In fact, Hugues and Aymeric argued throughout the trial over which one of them knew the Toulousain Jew personally, both trying to distance themselves from him. The hermeneutically constructed Jews in this trial were the purveyors of sorcery with figurines. Association with Jews emphasized the non-Christian—technically, idolatrous—behavior of Hugues and his co-conspirators, while providing a template for the improper use of objects meant for devotional practice.

Conclusion: Drawing Together Use and Abuse

So far, our evidence in this study has been limited to Christian texts and Christian perspectives on wax figurines. Yet there is also one particularly enlightening Hebrew account, written at some point between the twelfth and early fourteenth centuries, which offers a Jewish perspective on the accusations concerning figurines. The anonymous narrative recounts events that allegedly occurred to a French community in 992. The text tells the story of a convert's attempt to destroy the Jewish community by hiding a wax figurine in the synagogue and reporting that the Jews were using it to try to kill the ruler. The convert explains to the ruler: "They made a wax image in your likeness and they crucify it, [sticking] a goad in it, each year at the three pilgrimage festivals [Sukkot, Passover, Shavuot] in order to destroy you from the face of the earth. This is what their ancestors did to your god."[84]

The ritual element and the imitation of the Passion seem taken directly from the Christian legendary tradition. The fact that the figure is not of Christ but of a living human being, the abuse of which is intended to harm him, is nevertheless more reminiscent of magic than of mock crucifixion. There is an inconsistency in the text, for the figurine is later found not as the convert described but rather in a position consistent with magical use: "its hands on its loins, nails between its knees, and its feet severed."[85]

Such a conflation of mock crucifixion and sorcery does not appear in any of our Christian sources, where these contexts are distinguished by precise theological concerns: the former is seen as a sacrilegious mockery of

Christianity and the latter as idolatrous sorcery and superstitious misuse of a sacrament. These borders occasionally reveal themselves in the sources through juxtaposition. The *Siete Partidas*, for example, describes the use of wax images in successive chapters on sorcery and on Jews—the latter touching on desecration of images—using the same terminology for both (*imagines de cera*) without crossing the topics in either account.[86] The anonymous Hebrew account is undoubtedly the exception that proves the rule, for it is the only account written by a Jew, and it is the only one that conflates mock crucifixion and sorcery. While the Jewish author was aware of both kinds of Christian accusation, he did not understand how Christians conceived of the boundaries that separated mock crucifixion and sorcery. In this Jewish account, unlike Christian ones, there is slippage between the two types of abuse.

* * *

Votive practices serve as the basis for understanding the connection between wax and identity that lay at the heart of the accusations against Jews in cases of mock crucifixions and sorcery. Wax was the dominant material not just in use but also in imagination; when medieval Christians thought about figurines for any of the purposes described in this essay, they most often thought of them specifically as wax. Wax, as we have noted, was also a material with strong conceptual connections to the notion of identity. In the Marian stories, the figure was identified as Jesus, and when it came to sorcery, figurines represented the intended victim, a connection often strengthened by baptism as an additional way to establish an unambiguous bond between the two. This is what allowed votives to be imagined as the object of abuse. As the trial of Hugues Géraud reveals, medieval Christians were aware that a wax figurine made for pilgrimage could be used instead for sorcery. The use of votives and their imagined misuse through mock crucifixion and sorcery, though distinct in the minds of medieval Christians, are related precisely because the same material object, with the same sympathetic link of identity understood between wax figure and individual, could be employed in any or all of them.

The spread of wax votive figurines from around the year 1000 paved the way materially and ideologically for the accusations of mock crucifixion and the fears of sorcery. As anthropomorphic figurines came to be accepted and even promoted, having previously been condemned as idols, narratives of abuse helped illustrate forms of improper use while simultaneously affirming the representational efficacy of wax figurines. There is certainly no reason to assume that Christian representations of these Jewish practices, whether mock crucifixions or sorcery, were based on observed acts of Jews. Rather, the depiction of Jews served a specific hermeneutic function. The Jewish use of the figurines highlighted both the efficacy—attested by the Jews, just as stories of host desecration would later attest to the reality of transubstantiation—and potential danger of devotional objects. The notion that Jews would have figurines baptized for their own use is quite absurd if taken literally but makes sense within this hermeneutic framework: for Christians, baptizing a figurine is mockery and abuse of both devotional effigies and the sacrament of baptism. It is a Christian conception of an attack on Christianity, and it makes most sense as a product of the Christian imagination. Narratives of Jews then came to stand as boundary markers, separating the uses that were appropriate for Christians from those that were not. By imagining Jewish practices, Christians thus clarified their understanding of their own.

Chapter 8

Nicolas Donin, the Talmud Trial of 1240, and the Struggles Between Church and State in Medieval Europe

Piero Capelli

On 25 June 1240 in Paris, the Babylonian Talmud was put on trial before a jury of bishops, other clerics, and university scholars commissioned by Pope Gregory IX, convened by King Louis IX, and chaired by the queen mother, Blanche of Castile. The jury and judges found the Talmud guilty of several charges leveled against it and, after a delay of one or two years, the king implemented the sentence with the burning of a huge number of copies of the Talmud in the main square of Paris.

This is the second securely documented burning of Jewish books by Christians in the history of medieval Europe, and the first to take place after a regular trial and not at the hands of a raging mob (as had happened only four years earlier in Brittany).[1] The whole procedure of the trial is attested in a collection of Latin documents and in a literary account in Hebrew, the *Vikuaḥ rabenu Yeḥi'el* (The Disputation of Our Rabbi Yeḥiel), composed by Yosef Official, a student of the main Jewish defendant in the trial, Rabbi Yeḥiel of Paris.[2]

Some of the historical questions surrounding the Paris trial still await deeper understanding. Which institutions were involved in the event? What were their respective agendas as represented not just in the trial but in the intense succession of events involving the French and German Jewish communities in the 1230s and 1240s? And what was the role of Nicolas Donin, the convert from Judaism who prompted the trial, not only in the trial itself but in the other events of his time—particularly the struggles between the church and the state? In this essay I focus on Nicolas Donin, highlighting his background and his connection to contemporary events, in order to understand the role of a convert who became a central figure in the changing relations between Jews and Christians in the thirteenth century.

The main events we know of Nicolas Donin's life unfolded during the 1230s and 1240s, a period that marked a turning point in the web of relationships between the church, the various states of Europe, and the Jews. The German empire granted the Jews the protected status of *servi camerae regis*, "serfs of the imperial treasury," so that, in theory, anyone who caused them harm caused harm to the emperor himself. In France, however, the local barons exerted constant financial pressure on the Jews—particularly violently in the first half of the thirteenth century when the lords grew severely indebted from answering the call to the crusades—and the attendant hostility culminated in 1306 in Philip the Fair's expulsion of the Jews. In Aragon, during the expansion of the kingdom under James I, the monarchy granted the Jews some protection and privileges, while at the same time promoting the mendicant orders' missionizing activity, including forced attendance at Christian preaching.[3]

These new relationships had both theological and institutional consequences. The Christian perception of the Jews shifted from the traditional Augustinian category of preservers of Scripture to that of heretics;[4] these were also the years of the crusade against the Cathars and the fall of Montségur, 1244, and of the great Inquisition of the Lauragais, 1245–46.[5] In sum, the church turned with new aggressiveness toward non-conformists; but it would not have done so without competition with the states and could not have done so without the state's help. A series of events during this nearly two-decade period reconfigured the relationships among church, state, and Jews. Nicolas Donin, a convert who turned against his former co-religionists, was deeply entangled with all of these events, whether through direct involvement, influence, or alleged association:

1230–35 Outburst of polemics in Provence on Maimonides' thought and philosophical rationalism versus rabbinic tradition ("Maimonidean controversy").

1235 Blood libel in Fulda.

1236 Frederick II decrees investigations about the Fulda libel in Hagenau and Augsburg. In his *constitutio* of July 1236, he states that he was immediately convinced that the Jews were innocent of the crime of ritual murder, but he nonetheless convened an assembly of converts from Judaism for the benefit of the people and of the law; among them were experts in Jewish law sent by "all the kings of the west." These experts, being apostates, would have had every reason to expose the Jewish atrocities, including ritual murder, of which they had wished to liberate themselves by converting. On the basis of Scripture and the Talmud, the assembly deems the accusation devoid of truth, and the emperor decrees the statutory protection of the Jews as *servi camerae regis*.[6]

1236 The convert Nicolas Donin from northern France brings to Pope Gregory IX a list of thirty-five charges against the Talmud.

1239 Pope Gregory IX (in the bull *Si vera sunt*) prompts the Christian kings of western Europe to investigate the Talmud according to Donin's accusations.

1240 Talmud trial in Paris.

1241 Probable date of the burning of the Talmud in Paris.[7]

1244 Pope Innocent IV (in the bull *Impia iudaeorum perfidia*) prompts a new inquisition, and the confiscation and burning of the Talmud in France.[8]

1247 The Jews of France appeal to Innocent IV for restitution of the Talmud; tense exchange of letters between the pope and his legate in France, Odo of Châteauroux.

1248 "Sentence"[9] of Odo of Châteauroux: no restitution of the Talmud to the Jews.

While previous historians have connected many of these events, to the best of my knowledge no one has yet considered the entire succession and its implications, let alone the significance with respect to the activities of Nicolas Donin.

The Life and Career of Nicolas Donin

Nicolas Donin Before the Talmud Trial of 1240

Who was Nicolas Donin? His name was a diminutive of Dedon, in its turn a diminutive of Dieudonné, and therefore the French etymological equivalent of the Hebrew name Matatyah or Matityahu, "given by God as a gift"; according to Henri Gross, it was a fairly common name among Jews from northern France.[10] As for Donin's provenance, according to the Latin Christian materials about the Paris trial of 1240 that are contained in MS Lat. 16558 of the Bibliothèque nationale de France, he was born in La Rochelle (*Rupella*):

> Around the year 1236 of the Incarnation of the Lord, the Merciful Father called to the faith [i.e., baptized] a certain Jew whose name was Nicholas Donin of La Rochelle, purportedly of immense erudition in Hebrew even according to the testimony of the Jews themselves, to the point that one could hardly find his equal in the characteristics and rules of the Hebrew language. He went to the Apostolic See and, in the twelfth year of the pontificate of Pope Gregory IX of blessed memory, he revealed the unspeakable malice of the aforementioned books. He selected some sections in particular and begged the Pope to send an apostolic letter about them to the kings of France, England, and Spain, with the aim that, if they happened to find such things in those books, they should have them burnt.

In the *Vikuaḥ rabenu Yeḥi'el* according to the Paris manuscript (the oldest witness preserved and the basis of Samuel Grünbaum's standard but faulty edition),[11] Rabbi Yeḥiel twice mentions the fact that Donin was expelled or estranged from the Jewish community:

> What did you find against us, that you brought us here to defend our lives and fight for our Torah against that sinner, *who already fifteen years ago ceased to believe in the words of the sages*—according to whom the Talmud is one thousand five hundred years old—and believed only in what is written in the Torah of Moses without

> interpretation? You know that every word needs commentary. This is why *we separated him from ourselves and excommunicated him.* And since that moment, he has conspired to harm us in order to destroy everything; but in vain. [12]
>
> From the day *you separated yourself from us, fifteen years ago,* you have been looking for a pretext against us in order to attack [us] with false and unjust accusations, but you will not succeed! [13]

According to the Hebrew source, thus, Donin was expelled from the Jewish community in 1225, or rather walked out of it; the same date is confirmed in the Moscow manuscript (the other main witness of the *Vikuaḥ*).[14] The Latin source says that he was baptized only eleven years later, in 1236. If this is true, Donin's criticisms of Judaism preceded his conversion to Christianity. We cannot confidently say the same about other converts who engaged in anti-Talmud polemics, such as Peter Alfonsi, author of the influential *Dialogue Against the Jews* (written around 1109), one of the sources for Donin's polemical arguments. In sum, Donin was critical of rabbinic texts long before he criticized them on behalf of the church: not in every case did anti-talmudic criticism imply straightforward conversion to Christianity.

Another source for Donin's biography is the letter of one Ya'akov ben Eliyah to Pablo Christiani, which Robert Chazan believes was written in Spain shortly before 1263:[15]

> Do you not know, or have you not heard, what happened to *Donin the apostate, who became a convert from the laws of God and his Torah, and did not even believe in the Roman religion?* The saintly Rabbi Yeḥiel, moved by the honor of the God of Heaven, pushed him aside with both hands, and separated him for evil to the sound of the *shofar* [ram's horn] and the *teru'ah* [blast of war] because there was no truth in his mouth, faith had been cut out of his heart, and he became a root productive of gall and wormwood. *This apostate went before the king superior to all kings in name and honor, and spoke lies and made false accusations that on Passover nights we slaughter young boys still accustomed to their mothers' breasts, and that the Jews had adopted this custom, and that the hands of merciful women cook the children and we eat their flesh and drink their blood. . . .*

> This wicked man sought to destroy us, and gave a sword in the hands of the king to kill us. He lied to him. But God returned his iniquity to him twofold. . . . The honored king, in his piety and cleanness of hands, did not believe his words, and paid no heed to him, knowing that they are folly and nonsense and vanity. Nor did all the kings of the world and the inhabitants of earth believe that anything other than a learned wild-man was speaking. . . . *And our God sent one of his bears* [Elisha and the two bears, *2 Kings* 2], *and he returned his reward upon his head because he had rebelled . . . , and the day of misfortune came upon him because he had sent forth his tongue against the wise men. He was struck and he died and there was none to avenge. . . .* So may perish all Thine enemies, Lord; and His lovers [be] like the going forth of the Sun in its strength.[16]

After other scholars had variously attempted to identify the "king superior to all kings in name and honor" as Gregory IX[17] or Louis IX,[18] Solomon Grayzel convincingly proposed that what was being discussed was the council of Hagenau-Augsburg, and that the king was therefore Frederick II.[19] It is debated, though, whether Ya'akov's accusation that Donin supported the blood libel is reliable or not. The *Vikuaḥ* provides a clue on the issue *ex silentio*, in that it never says that Donin perpetrated the blood libel: it is unlikely that such a polemical text would have missed an opportunity to put some more blame on Donin. Nor is the blood libel mentioned in any of the sources directly related to the Talmud trial.

In addition to Frederick II's *constitutio* of 1236, which recounts that he consulted converts about the blood libel, the other sources that might connect Donin to the emergence of the blood libel are a passage from Thomas of Cantimpré's *Bonum universale de proprietatibus apum*, whose Dominican author had resided in the monastery of Saint-Jacques in Paris in 1237–40 and composed his work in 1256–63,[20] and another from Yosef ben Natan Official's *Sefer Yosef ha-Mekane'*, an anti-Christian Jewish polemical work composed in Paris only a few years after the Talmud trial. The first passage reads:

> Further, I have heard an extremely learned Jew—who converted to Christianity in our days—saying that a certain person, who was almost a prophet, prophesied in his last moment to the Jews: "We know absolutely certainly that there is no other way for us to be

> healed from the most shameful torture by which we are punished than by Christian blood." The blind, haughty and impious Jews seized these words and inferred from them that Christian blood should be shed every year in every region, so that they could be healed by virtue of it. And that Jew added: "They misunderstood those words as meaning 'the blood of any Christian'; whereas it means that blood that is poured daily on the altar for salvation from sin. Each of you who converts to the Christian faith and properly takes such blood is immediately healed from the curse of his fathers."[21]

In the *Bonum universale* this passage is immediately preceded by an account of the Pforzheim blood libel of 1261, so here Thomas of Cantimpré might be referring to an episode related to that case, or else attesting the existence of the blood libel in the region (possibly Brabant) where he was composing his work between the 1250s and 1260s, rather than in Paris (or northern France) in the years around the Talmud trial.[22] What remains of interest, though, is his claim that his source on the matter was a learned convert from Judaism to Christianity (who espoused the view that the need to sacrifice Christian children was a misunderstanding on the part of the Jews). That doesn't mean that this convert was Donin himself, but if it wasn't, it was undoubtedly someone like him.

The passage from Yosef Official suggests that in these early days of the blood libel, not all the rabbis were already acquainted with a repertoire of apologetic counterarguments against Christian accusations:

> *Until it has drunk the blood of the slain* (Num. 23:24). Rabbi Avigdor, the son of Rabbi Yitsḥak, told me that in his presence the chancellor of Paris said to Rabbi Yeḥiel and Rabbi Yitsḥak: "You eat the blood of the uncircumcised, since thus prophesied Balaam: *Until it has drunk the blood of the slain.*" They stood still and did not answer. About them I quoted the verse: *I turn back the wise* (Isa. 44:25), as they should have answered that this "blood of the slain" refers to the beginning of the verse: *Look, a people rising up like a lioness, and rousing itself like a lion! It does not lie down until it has eaten the prey and drunk the blood of the slain* (Num. 23:24), that is, it refers to the "lion" or the "lioness," which both metaphorically indicate the "people."[23]

The chancellor, that is, Odo of Chateauroux (see below), quotes Numbers 23:24 (Balaam's prophecy about Israel) as a prooftext for the blood libel; the rabbis do not answer; the narrator complains that they should have counter-quoted the first half of the same verse in order to demonstrate that the drinking of blood cannot be understood literally.[24]

Neither Thomas of Cantimpré nor Yosef Official provides us with positive evidence for Donin's connection to the blood libel. What seems to be beyond doubt is the identification of the "chancellor from Paris" of the *Mekane'* with the aforementioned Odo of Châteauroux, who was the chancellor of the University of Paris from 1238 to 1244 and would become Innocent IV's legate to France and have a crucial role in the aftermath of the Talmud affair in the late 1240s. For the rest, we cannot precisely identify the Rabbi Yitsḥak and his son Rabbi Avigdor mentioned by Yosef Official, nor can we by any means be assured that the erudite convert who informed Thomas of Cantimpré of the activities of the Jews was Donin rather than Thibaut de Sézanne—the Dominican convert who possibly directed the editing of the *Extractiones de Talmut*, including the Latin sources about the Paris trial of 1240—or some of the latter's colleagues.[25] However, we can conclude that even though the blood libel was not formulated during the Paris trial, and though there is no way to unmistakably connect Donin's thought and activity with it, it is nonetheless very likely to have been a present concern in Jewish-Christian polemics in Paris in the years around the trial and in its milieu—much as it was at almost the same time in the German empire after the Fulda case.[26]

Donin and the Trial of the Talmud

In 1236, not long after his conversion, Donin took it upon himself to write to Pope Gregory IX with a list of thirty-five charges against the Talmud. Although Petrus Alfonsi and Peter the Venerable had written about the Talmud, Donin's charges went far beyond these earlier criticisms, asserting the Talmud posed a threat to Christianity and should be unlawful for Jews. Gregory responded by issuing the bull *Si vera sunt* (9 June 1239), which called upon the kings of western Europe to investigate Donin's claims. King Louis IX of France offered the most enthusiastic reaction, ordering the mendicants to assist in the confiscation of Jews' books. In 1240, the Talmud trial, a disputation on the legitimacy and contents of the Talmud between Donin and Rabbi Yeḥiel of Paris, took place at the royal court in Paris. The following year the

Talmud was burned in Paris.[27] These events surrounding the trial are only the beginning of a program of opposition to the Talmud that would last for centuries.

The trial against the Talmud is the best-documented event in Donin's life and career. In the wake of the trial, someone close to the events—possibly the converted Dominican Thibaut de Sézanne—compiled a dossier known as the *Extractiones de Talmut*, a vast collection of passages from the Talmud (including hundreds of glosses from Rashi)[28] translated into Latin and organized for reference. The oldest manuscript of the *Extractiones* is Lat. 16558 of the Bibliothèque nationale de France, compiled soon after 1248.[29] In addition to the talmudic passages and the list of Donin's charges (fols. 211vb–217ra), the manuscript also contains two chancery abstracts of the responses given by the Rabbis Yeḥiel of Paris (*Vivo Meldensis*) and Yehudah of Melun (*Magister Iudas*) to the tribunal that asked them whether Donin's accusations were actually supported by the Talmud (fols. 230va–231ra): as recounted in the *Vikuaḥ*, Yeḥiel refused to respond under oath, but both rabbis apparently admitted to almost every article of the case for prosecution.[30] There follows (fols. 224va–230rb) a separate dossier of 160 additional glosses of Rashi on the Bible (*De glosis Salomonis Trecensis*), accurately translated into Latin and placed under accusation for their content on the same grounds on which the Talmud was also accused.[31] All of the material in this manuscript shares an underlying categorization scheme with Donin's original charges, thereby suggesting that Donin's charges formed the basis for it, even though there are significant differences.

Donin's Thirty-Five Charges Against the Talmud

The thirty-five charges leveled against the Talmud by Donin are supported with prooftexts translated from the Talmud itself and from Rashi's commentaries. Following Robert Chazan's recent reappraisal, they can be categorized as follows:

Articles 1 through 9: Jewish claims about the Talmud, presented from rabbinic sources but formulated to prove that the Talmud is a human contrivance and that the Jews favor it over the genuine Torah.

Articles 10 through 14: Talmudic teachings condoning or even requiring anti-Christian behaviors, including extensive arrangements for the breaking of oaths, making Jews untrustworthy in their relations with Christians.

Articles 15 through 25: Talmudic teachings about God that are blasphemous in their inanity.

Articles 26 and 27: Talmudic teachings that blaspheme Jesus and Mary.

Articles 28 through 30: Talmudic teaching about the Church and its leaders that are likewise blasphemous.

Articles 31 through 33: Talmudic teachings that promise blessings to Jews and the opposite to Christians in the world to come.

Articles 34 and 35: Talmudic teachings that say foolish things about key biblical figures.[32]

The typology of these charges against the Talmud corresponds very precisely to the categories of both the anthologies of Rashi's commentaries and of the *Extractiones*, thereby demonstrating that Donin's charges became an important basis for categorizing criticisms of the Talmud. We can thus further group all these texts translated into Latin according to three more general categories:

1. Absurdities or profanities, i.e., passages that fail to conform to the new standards of rationality in European culture and theology.
2. Passages legitimating the doctrine of the dual Torah, rabbinic tradition, and their authoritativeness.
3. Anti-Christian passages that are blasphemous according to Christian standards.

Gilbert Dahan has observed that at least in the dossier of Rashi's glosses, the category most abundantly represented is the absurdities or profanities; also well represented are texts that emphasize the authority of the Talmud and the rabbis,[33] thus exemplifying the shift in the Christian perception of the Jews from keepers of Scripture to followers of a different, potentially heretical source of authority. (The emphasis on the legitimacy of rabbinic authority further explains why a dossier of glosses to the Bible should be included in a plaidoyer devoted to the Talmud controversy of 1240.) The third type of accusation, texts blasphemous according to Christian standards, is historically important because church censors and Jewish printers removed many of the passages and glosses against the *nationes* from the later recensions or editions of both the Talmud and Rashi.[34]

The Latin Dossier and the Hebrew Account: A Comparison

Reconstructing what Nicolas Donin and Rabbi Yeḥiel actually discussed in Paris is not easy. The Latin list of accusations and the Hebrew account do not coincide on the subject of the talmudic passages that were discussed in Paris (see Table 8.1).

The overlap between the two sources is only thirteen prooftexts, roughly a quarter of the material. Thus the Hebrew and the Latin materials tell different stories about the Paris trial. The part of the Latin manuscript related to the debate is, in the main, a chancery document, also relating the questioning of the two rabbis (with a certain bias)[35] and the sentence condemning the Talmud to the flames. The Hebrew *Vikuaḥ* is a literary reworking or rewriting whose author and agenda are on the whole clear: the author is in all likelihood Yosef ben Natan Official, the author of the *Sefer Yosef ha-Mekane'*, because at the end of the *Vikuaḥ* in the Paris manuscript we find an acrostic in a poem that reads "*ben ha-rav Natan Ofitsial,*" and also because the same manuscript contains the *Mekane'* itself in the same hand as the copy of the *Vikuaḥ*—which suggests that the Paris manuscript might even be the autograph. The text celebrates Yeḥiel as the champion of the faith of Israel and

Table 8.1. Prooftexts in MS Paris Lat. 16558 and Paris Hébr. 712

Latin dossier	*Hebrew account*
52 prooftexts	54 prooftexts
50 from the Talmud	46 from the Talmud
13 with Rashi	none with Rashi
	5 from the Mishnah
	1 from the Minor Tractates
2 from Rashi to the Bible	1 from Rashi to the Bible
	1 of uncertain provenance
(+ 160 glosses of Rashi to the Bible)	

exhorts the Jews to resist Christian proselytizing and persecution, celebrating the purported Jewish dialectical victory in the disputation, and completely omitting the actual sentence. I find myself convinced by Joseph Shatzmiller's contention that the Paris Hebrew manuscript is a plaidoyer prepared by the Jewish representatives on the eve of the second disputation held in Paris in 1269,[36] because it also includes, in a different hand, a short list of New Testament passages in Latin written in Hebrew letters with Tiberian vocalization, to serve as a tool in future disputations.[37]

In sum, the portrait of Donin that emerges from the Paris trial is one of a convert who had not only embraced wholeheartedly the church's previous criticisms of rabbinic authority and rabbinic literature (inclusive of both the Talmud and Rashi on the Bible and the Talmud) but also developed new foundations for criticizing rabbinic literature, which ultimately justified the church's unprecedented intrusion into internal Jewish affairs; and as we have seen above, he seems to have done so even before his conversion to Christianity.

Donin After Paris 1240

The evidence about what became of Donin after the Paris trial is scanty. The last mention made of him appears in the Hebrew account of the second disputation held in Paris in 1269, but no further biographical information is to be found there. Here the narrator states that Pablo Christiani "resumed part of the arguments of the earlier apostate (*min*) from Yeḥiel's time."[38] One of these arguments must have been the late dating of the Talmud, since the Jewish disputant, the otherwise unknown Rabbi Abraham ben Samuel of Rouen, starts the discussion by stressing—as Yeḥiel had done "around twenty years earlier"[39]—the antiquity of the Talmud and the fact that no one until now had ever criticized it. The account acknowledges that Donin's knowledge of the Torah was not utterly irrelevant as Christiani's: "You should have followed the ancient example and cursed this apostate, whose words are pointless. And the little finger of the earlier apostate was thicker than the loins of this one, who by comparison is not even worth a garlic-skin,[40] since his whole life he never really knew what to say."[41]

A long-standing tradition in modern secondary literature, dating from the *Histoire littéraire de la France* (1847), has it that Donin might have become a Franciscan, and identified him with one Nicolas "who, in 1279, wrote a pamphlet against Pope Nicolas III for having changed the rule of the Friars

Minor, and who was therefore condemned in 1287 by Matthew of Acquasparta, Minister General of the order."[42] However, Franciscan sources from the fourteenth century (the *Chronicon XIV vel XV Generalium* and the slightly later *Chronica XXIV Generalium Ordinis Minorum*) show that the "frater Nicolaus," who had written a commentary on the Franciscan Rule against Nicholas III's prohibition, was officially condemned for it by the Franciscan general Matthew of Acquasparta in 1287 or 1288, and was himself at the time the Minister for the Franciscan region of France: he can therefore be safely identified with Nicholas of Ghistelle (near Ostende), provincial of France from 1285 to 1289, who is known from archival sources.[43] If Donin did eventually become a Franciscan (or a Dominican),[44] there is simply no known evidence of it or of any of his other activities after the trial.

A Social, Religious, and Intellectual Profile of Nicolas Donin

Donin as an Intellectual: The Question of the Talmud's Antiquity

Donin served along with the Friars as one of the most important chess pieces in no fewer than two games developing on the chessboard of *Realpolitik* in Europe: Frederick II versus Pope Gregory IX (if Donin was really involved with the investigation about the Fulda blood libel) and Louis IX versus the Counts of Toulouse. Frederick II used his protection of the Jews as *servi camerae regiae* against papal incursions into his realm. Louis IX, for his part, used the Jews as sources of income, and heretics—talmudic Jews being increasingly perceived as such—as a means of earning the pope's support and the Dominicans' help in expanding into what would soon become southern France. Donin is thus the earliest well-documented example of how the church, the empire, and the rising national states exploited Jewish intellectuals converted to Christianity in their policy of expanding their jurisdiction on the Jews.

Donin's religious identity before conversion does not neatly fit in any of the best-known rubrics of his age. As we saw, in the *Vikuaḥ* Yeḥiel calls him simply *kofer divrei ḥakhamim*, "one who ceased to believe in the words of the sages." Several scholars have claimed or suggested that he was a Karaite, in generic intellectual inclination if not in group adherence.[45] Others are rightly more cautious: opposition to the Talmud is not enough to make one a Karaite.[46] Further, there is no evidence of Karaite groups in northern France in the thirteenth century.

Nor can we define Donin as a full-fledged, philosophically aware "rationalist" on the basis of his accusations against the Talmud. It has been suggested, speculatively, that he *might* have been involved in the translation of the *Guide of the Perplexed* into Latin, which *might* have taken place in Paris in the 1240s.[47] One element of philosophical rationalism clearly underlies at least one category of charge he brought, that of absurdity (a charge that included anthropomorphic representations of God: Donin may well have taken from Alfonsi the criticism of God wearing phylacteries [BT Berakhot 3a]). But Donin does not articulate this rationalism in philosophical arguments; he merely says that these things are absurd and offend reason. He was certainly influenced by rationalism and the fiery intellectual climate of the Maimonidean controversy in Provence[48]—but only indirectly, as far as our evidence enables us to conclude. We have no evidence that he ever spent any time in southern France, or that he maintained connections with rationalist Jewish intellectuals in Sepharad and Provence, or that he became a friar, or that he contributed to the translation of the *Guide* into Latin.

More plausibly, though this is a point limited to the intra-Jewish context, we can define Donin as someone who opposed classical rabbinic literature as the justification for contemporary rabbinic leadership (as we saw in the case of Donin's seventh charge). Milan Žonca has suggested a parallel with the *sola scriptura* movements that were agitating the masses in Christian societies of the twelfth and thirteenth centuries, such as the Waldensians in Bourgogne;[49] John Baldwin has suggested to me another parallel, with the aversion to patristic tradition as manifested in the twelfth century by Peter Cantor.[50]

In order to understand how far Donin's scripturalism went, let us examine the passage of the *Vikuaḥ* on the dating of the Talmud according to the Paris manuscript:

> The Rock of the faithful girded himself with strength and said to the apostate: "Why do you want to dispute with me? And about what are you planning to interrogate me?"
>
> The apostate replied: "I will interrogate you about an ancient question: in this respect, I cannot deny[51] that *the Talmud dates from four hundred years ago*."
>
> The rabbi said: "*From more than one thousand five hundred years ago!*" Then, turning to the Queen: "I pray you, my Lady, do not force me to respond to his words, since he himself admitted

> that the Talmud is extremely ancient. And until now, no one has found anything to say against it. Indeed, Saint Jerome the priest was acquainted with our entire Torah, that is, the Talmud, as all the clergy knows: had there been anything blameworthy in it, [t]he[y] would not have let it alone thus far. Furthermore, haven't there existed prior to now priests and apostates as important as these here? [Yet] for one thousand five hundred years, not a sentence or even a single word has been heard [against the Talmud]."[52]

According to Israel Ta-Shma,[53] the fact that for Donin the Babylonian Talmud was 400 years old does not mean that he did not know his tannaitic and amoraic chronology (an accusation that was actually leveled against him at the dawn of modern research),[54] but that for him the Talmud dated to the middle of the ninth century, "an era presumed—or traditionally acknowledged—for the arrival of the Talmud in Christian Europe." It is seductive, if speculative, to think that Donin could have been referring to the diffusion of rabbinic tradition in Europe—including Ashkenaz—after Paltoy Gaon in the mid-ninth century, his responsum to an Iberian Jewish community against the use of *halakhot ketu'ot* ("decided laws" or "fragmentary *halakhot*"), and the copy of the Talmud he then sent to al-Andalus.[55] (I discuss Yeḥiel's early date below.)

The question of the dating of the Talmud is clearly related to that of its real or proclaimed authoritativeness. Donin's revision of the traditional date for the Talmud might also indicate that he opposed a particular aspect of early Ashkenazic rabbinic culture, what Talya Fishman calls the "textualization in written form" of talmudic lore, and the institutionalization of the whole of rabbinic literature as the main text for teaching and legal adjudication, a process that had taken place over the course of the previous two or three centuries in the Rhineland and in northern France (Rashi and tosafists).[56] Donin and maybe others could perceive this development as a betrayal of the *oral* origin and transmission of rabbinic culture throughout late antiquity and the geonic era. The accusations against the Talmud thus would attest not only to the church's recent awareness of the authoritativeness of the Talmud in Jewish life, but perhaps also to a new form and role the text had taken among Jews themselves.

The dating of the Talmud is more complicated in the account of the discussion according to the Moscow manuscript (Byzantine, fifteenth century).[57] First, Yeḥiel dates the committing of the Talmud to writing to fifteen hundred years earlier, which he says was the age of Ravina and Rav Ashi.[58] Here Yeḥiel refers to the talmudic statement that "Rav Ashi and Ravina represent the end of the oral teaching of the law" (*Rav Ashi ve-Ravina sof hora'a* [BT Bava Metsi'a 86a]). Then, Donin argues that the Talmud was burnt in the age of emperor Vespasian (an argument that would establish a precedent in Roman law that Christian sovereigns should reenact).[59] Yeḥiel replies that in Vespasian's time "they did not burn the Talmud as such, but the whole Bible, since the Talmud was written only a certain number of years later, in the age of Ravina and Rav Ashi" (thus invalidating Donin's suggested precedent, since Christian monarchs could no longer burn the Bible).[60] Lastly, at the conclusion of the debate Yeḥiel makes the same point as in the Paris manuscript, that is, the Talmud is "very ancient, more than a thousand years old, and no one has argued anything bad against it till now."[61] Yeḥiel's first dating to fifteen hundred years is incompatible with a dating after Vespasian and to the age of Ravina and Rav Ashi, following BT Bava Metsi'a 86a;[62] some editor or copyist seems to have noticed the inconsistency and corrected it to a more moderate "more than a thousand years" earlier.[63]

The question of the Talmud's antiquity was a significant point in medieval polemic because it supported the arguments on behalf of rabbinic authority or against it. Indeed, it wasn't just the Talmud that went on trial in Paris, but rabbinic tradition as a whole, including the midrashim and Rashi: in the discussion in Paris, according to both the Latin and the Hebrew accounts, Rashi got as much conceptual weight as the Talmud itself. We saw this in the prooftexts (the disputants discuss Rashi as a source even independently of the Talmud). As early as 1963, Herman Hailperin observed, "For the Christians of the *later* Middle Ages, the 'Talmud' of the Jews meant the totality of rabbinic literature—including the Midrash (halakhic and aggadic), what *we* know to be the Talmud, and Rashi's commentaries."[64]

Donin as a Borderline Jew

At the risk of sliding into dime-store psychohistory, one has to take into consideration the eleven years between 1225 and 1236 that Donin would have spent both as an ex-Jew and a not-yet Christian in a society in which identity and sociability were defined mainly by religious belonging.[65] Living, as Shlomo Simonsohn put it, "in a sort of religious no-man's-land (no mean feat in the Europe of his age)"[66] was exceptional and also exceedingly difficult. It was about precisely this state of mind that another convert, Herman of

Cologne, had written at length around 1150 in his *Opusculum de conversione sua*, expressing his terror of being expelled from the synagogue, or of "being confined," or of being persecuted by his former co-religionists.[67] Both Herman's writing and Donin's biography exemplify what Caroline W. Bynum defined as the new religious concern of the twelfth century (the thirteenth in Donin's case) with "how groups are formed and differentiated from each other, how roles are defined and evaluated, how behavior is conformed to models."[68] In a different, more contrastive, and quite lachrymose perspective, Kurt Schubert used the Eriksonian category of "identity crisis" to explain Donin's conversion to Christianity: "The impression is that he did so more out of conflict (*Auseinandersetzung*) with his own Judaism than out of belief in Christian teaching. Thus Donin became a typical example of any Jew *who, because of inner instability, becomes an outspoken enemy.*"[69]

Schubert's conclusion is similar to Judah Rosenthal's, that Donin "was basically a rationalist who never became a good Christian":[70] a dismissive evaluation, but again a correct one in the main, all the more so if we accept what the Moscow manuscript says in its opening about Donin's fate ("He was eventually killed in his church")[71] and Ya'akov ben Eliyah apparently confirms in his letter ("He did not even believe in the religion of Rome" and "He was struck and died and no one avenged his blood").[72] This agreement among sources grants important confirmation to the possibility that Donin was heterodox by the standards of Judaism and Christianity alike.

In an insightful essay on Jewish intellectuals converting to Christianity in the Middle Ages, Yossef Schwartz distinguishes between communities of knowledge and communities of discourse: a community of knowledge is the wider frame of communication and transmission of culture across boundaries and ages, while a community of discourse involves interpersonal communication within a circumscribed sociological context. The Jewish apostates of the Middle Ages—Donin among them, I would add—"created a new community of knowledge separated from all their former surroundings, yet at the same time they were involved in a variety of discourse communities, one of which was the inner discursive circle they themselves had formed."[73] One must, then, consider Donin's inner discursive circles both before and after he converted.

As for Donin's community of knowledge, I would suggest that it may be a mistake to class him under the same rubric as the Hispano-Provençal converts who preceded and followed him—Alfonsi, Christiani, Abner of Burgos, Pablo de Santa Maria, etc.: their intellectual roots were different, as were their polemical agendas, and Donin's philosophical and exegetical instruments were more circumscribed than theirs. His realms of action and propaganda were always confined to Capetian France and possibly the German empire, realms in which there would not be important cases of educated Jews converting and remaining active as "public intellectuals" after the conversion, as far as I know, until much later.[74] But the cultural distance between Sepharad and Ashkenaz would be bridged only slightly after Donin by Pablo Christiani—the convert who became a Dominican and the Christian representative in the most famous of medieval disputations, that of 1263 in Barcelona—who was from Montpellier and whose preaching activity emerged under the sponsorship of the church in Provence, Catalonia, and ultimately northern France too, as in the second disputation in Paris in 1269. As the Hebrew account of Barcelona has it, Donin really was different from his successors. It is also certain that he belonged to a "community of discourse" *distinct* from that of the Sephardic converts. His hometown (La Rochelle) in Poitou was governed for the entire twelfth and thirteenth centuries by a local aristocracy in perennial rebellion against distant rulers, first the Plantagenets, then the Capetians. Among these aristocrats was the duke of Brittany, Pierre de Dreux, who for almost two decades had been conducting his own fight for suzerain rights, at times against his own vassals when they became excessively independent, at others against the bishops who had suzerainty over the Jews and therefore over the assets of Jewish moneylenders. In his oscillating politics, the duke alternately pursued help from the king against the bishops or help from the pope against the barons. One finds a similar convergence of aims and efforts—both political and military—in the *moyenne durée*, from 1215 to the 1250s, between the church, which aimed at repressing the Albigensian heresy, and the Capetian monarchy under Louis VIII and Louis IX, which aimed at expanding into the duchy of Toulouse and Provence. There is also another relevant parallel between Louis IX's politics toward the Jews around the Paris trial—using them as a tool to please and accommodate the pope's political theology—and their exploitation by Pierre de Dreux (and eventually by other suzerains and the Capetian kings themselves) as a financial resource to fund participation in the crusade that Gregory IX had proclaimed in 1234, to which Pierre adhered in 1236.[75] It thus happened that in 1236, participants in the crusade massacred the Jews of Poitou along with those of Anjou and Brittany. Pierre's son, Jean le Roux, eventually expelled the Jews from Brittany in April 1240, thus wiping out the huge debts his father and his vassals had incurred in order to fund their participation in the crusade. Donin's stance on the massacres of 1236 appears in the *Vikuaḥ*: "The villain said: 'How many myriads of you fell by the sword in Brittany, Anjou and Poitou? Where are the portents and the signs that your God wrought for you, if you—as you say—are the chosen people?'"[76]

One can even explain how Donin might have adopted such a position given the status and treatment of the Jews in the region from which he came. In the bull *Lacrimabilem iudeorum in regno Francie commorantium* (5 September 1236)[77] to all the bishops of northern and western France, Gregory IX admitted that his earlier bull of 7 November 1234 proclaiming the crusade (*Rachel suum videns*) might have been misunderstood, in that the Jews at home had been inadvertently subsumed into the same category of the "enemies of Christ" that the Pope had meant to define only as the Saracens abroad. In the *Lacrimabilem* Gregory graphically describes the massacres, quantifies the loss of Jewish lives as 2,500, and mentions in passing the first securely attested burning of Jewish books by Christian hands in medieval history (the one in which Maimonides' works were burnt in Montpellier in 1233 seems to have been invented for propaganda by the Maimonidean party).[78] Such, then, was the condition of the Jews in northern and western France on the eve of the Paris trial and Donin's participation in it.

Conclusion

The fact that both Donin and Thibaut de Sézanne, the probable editor of the Latin materials on the Talmud trial of 1240 (MS Paris Lat. 16558), were converts from Judaism and extremely well versed in rabbinic tradition, attests to the existence of intra-Jewish polemics about rabbinic authority—polemics that only at a later stage developed into Jewish-Christian disputations.[79] The trial attests to the growing importance of rabbinic literature for both the church and for Ashkenazic Jews themselves—as does Donin's resistance to that literature. The trial should be understood as directed not merely against the Talmud as we know it, but against all of rabbinic literature and against its authoritativeness as a corpus—a corpus comprising the Talmud, the main midrashim, and Rashi's commentaries both to the Bible and the Talmud, which for both the prosecutors and the defendants were of a piece with the rabbinic corpus and one of its main vehicles. Whatever the truth about Donin's involvement in fabricating or justifying blood libels, his dissatisfaction with rabbinic Judaism started long before he took it to the extreme of converting to Christianity. Although not explicitly related to a philosophical stance, his criticism of talmudic tradition is best explained when seen against the background of Jewish and Christian polemics about rationalism and Aristotelianism in the 1220s and 1230s. Only after a long period when Donin seemingly did not deem it necessary to go to the extreme of becoming a Christian in order to voice his dissent did he ultimately convert and thus become the deepest, most articulate Christian critic of talmudic tradition before the modern age.

PART III

Translations and Transmissions of Texts and Knowledge

Chapter 9

Cultural Identity in Transmission: Language, Science, and the Medical Profession in Thirteenth-Century Italy

Yossef Schwartz

The "entangled histories" that stand in the midst of the this volume present an essential feature of Jewish daily reality during the late Middle Ages. Beyond any normative divergence and ideological interreligious conflicts, Jews shared with their Christian and Muslim neighbors identical social, intellectual, and economic infrastructures. At the same time, the intellectual and religious identities provided each community with a natural locus of self-definition, in which it was precisely the role of the intellectuals to provide a distinct religious and philosophic narrative. In this chapter I would like to use a unique testimony in order to demonstrate how two Jewish intellectuals could differ from each other, despite sharing the same geographic environment, the same language of communication, the same professional occupation, and seemingly the same ideological position. I would like to claim that this significant moment of alienation between members of the Jewish European intellectual community is but another indirect reflection of the same basic phenomenon: the commitment of our protagonists to their basic larger cultural frameworks, such as Arabic against Latin.

Two letters sent by Zeraḥyah ben Isaac ben She'alti'el Ḥen (Gracián) from Rome to his colleague Hillel ben Samuel (ben Elazar of Verona), in Ferrara, contains Zeraḥyah's response to two (non-preserved) letters written to him by Hillel.[1] This partially conserved correspondence, dated to the year

1289–90, stands at the immediate focal point of the present chapter. Zeraḥyah, a physician, philosopher, and translator of scientific and philosophic texts from Arabic into Hebrew, corresponds here with another physician, philosopher, and translator of scientific and philosophic texts from Latin into Hebrew. Although we do not possess Hillel's two letters to Zeraḥyah, significant parts of them are quoted by Zeraḥyah in his responses, which enable us to reconstruct a whole segment of dialogue between them.

These letters, two outstanding documents of late medieval Jewish intellectual history, reveal the depth of hostility between the two protagonists. Although Zeraḥyah's tone is polite and friendly in his first letter, in which he responds rather laconically to a set of questions posed by Hillel about Moses Maimonides' *Guide of the Perplexed*, even here one can sense a certain amount of tension. In this rather short first letter Zeraḥyah avoids a full discussion of the questions posed by Hillel and takes a critical tone concerning what seems to him to be a problematic influence of Nahmanides' thought (whom Zeraḥyah admires as talmudic authority but whom he rejects as philosophic authority) underlying some of Hillel's assumptions. Zeraḥyah's second letter, written a few months later in response to Hillel's second letter, is much more hostile and aggressive in tone and discusses a set of theological controversies that had been raised in Hillel's letter, from which Zeraḥyah quotes at length. According to Zeraḥyah, Hillel's positions are not only totally erroneous but also ridiculous and absurd. Besides the detailed refutation of the discussed opinions, the letter also includes a long personal attack on Hillel himself.

The second letter of Zeraḥyah to Hillel, on which the large part of my discussion is based, opens with a massive personal attack on Hillel. Zeraḥyah mentions their long friendship and his favorable attitude toward Hillel, who, without any justification, responded to Zeraḥyah's friendly comments with a public attack. Emphasizing the public character of their debate, Zeraḥyah continues to argue that every person who was exposed to Hillel's questions and to Zeraḥyah's response was absolutely satisfied by Zeraḥyah's answers. At the same time, everyone who read Hillel's attack agreed that Hillel exposed himself as a complete dilettante. Moreover, not only did Hillel expose himself in his arguments as a premature scientific mind, but his style, according to Zeraḥyah, reflected a harsh and careless mind, whereas Zeraḥyah's arguments were carefully constructed after much consideration. While reading Hillel's observations, Zeraḥyah could only regret the fact that he shared with him so openly his thought, a consideration Hillel apparently did not deserve. Later he was astonished by the great absurdities conveyed by Hillel and wondered from what strange sources such ludicrous opinions might have been derived. Whoever believes in such strange ideas must be considered as a practitioner of the lowest forms of magic and superstition, and, most importantly, such false opinions should never be mentioned as belonging to the thought of Maimonides. After this general remark Zeraḥyah proceeds to quote a long commentary of Hillel dedicated to Jacob's nightly encounter with the angel (Gen. 32:24–25) and to Balaam's she-ass (Num. 22:28), which he then systematically refutes as a legitimate interpretation of Maimonides. According to Zeraḥyah, Hillel connected his ridiculous interpretation with a more general critique regarding Zeraḥyah's understanding of the basic elements of Maimonides' hermeneutic method, which Zeraḥyah answers with a detailed outline of Maimonidean biblical hermeneutics followed by interpretation of another biblical passage that involves angelic figures (Gen. 18:1–15). From here the discussion moves to a different topic, confronting Hillel's notion of Hebrew as a natural language, including a version of the famous infant language experiment reported by Hillel, to which Zeraḥyah responds with a sharp denial based on the understanding of language, including Hebrew, as the mere result of human convention. Zeraḥyah then briefly evokes a series of additional issues brought by Hillel that he does not find worthy of detailed and systematic refutation, simply repeating his derogatory statements regarding Hillel's peculiar method of argumentation. According to Zeraḥyah, regarding all those elementary questions, Hillel fails to meet any basic scholarly requirements and proves himself to be one of the ignorant Ashkenazic scholars. After discussing some further Genesis episodes and their true interpretation, Zeraḥyah ends his letter with another massive personal attack on Hillel, quoting in his support some of Rome's leading intellectuals, calling Hillel to withdraw into his true Ashkenazic "homeland," and raising serious doubts also regarding Hillel's quality as physician.

Hence for the sake of the present discussion one can summarize the content of this debate as related to different interpretations of Maimonides' *Guide*, a major canonical philosophic-theological work among Jewish intellectuals. Since Hillel and Zeraḥyah were among the most prolific Jewish authors of their time, it is relatively easy to fit their positions in this debate into a broader set of ideas conditioned by the specific social and cultural context in which they were prevalent.[2] Fitting the correspondents' positions into this larger context will provide us with a unique opportunity to explore the relationship between the social and the intellectual among different medieval European Jewish communities. Accordingly, I observe this local struggle between two Italian intellectuals in the last quarter of the thirteenth century from a comprehensive approach, one that evokes a series of directly related issues. The first part of this essay explores the basic conditions that made such a controversy possible, perhaps almost inevitable. In order to do so, I portray the development of philosophy and science written in Hebrew since the mid-twelfth century and the two parallel translation movements that were included in it: from Arabic into Hebrew and from Latin into Hebrew. In the second part I analyze the case study presented above, trying to unpack the different motivations of the two protagonists. Again, I do not concentrate primarily on the personal psychological level—as we shall see, our knowledge of both persons is rather limited and makes such assumptions highly speculative—but on different social and cultural frameworks that might have contributed to this interpersonal crisis. This controversy depicts the emerging cultural gap between Jewish European Arabophones and those who were closer to the Latin scholastic European tradition. I emphasize the role medicine as an occupation and an intellectual superstructure played among western European Jewish intellectuals and, finally, follow the changing relations between medicine, natural philosophy, and theology. Through this act of reconstruction I attempt to portray a larger picture of thirteenth-century Jewish European intellectual history, one that can give an account of both the linguistic affinities and the deep barriers so forcefully revealed in our debate. I strongly believe that such a descriptive method can reveal a social universe that has escaped the attention of most modern scholars who have tried to deal with the controversy because of disciplinary barriers.

Migration of Knowledge: The Peculiar Case of Medieval Hebrew

Let us begin with the linguistic medium of communication as a minimal condition necessary for the existence of any controversy: in the case of this particular debate it is the Hebrew language used by the two interlocutors. Contrary to the intuitive feeling a contemporary reader might have, before the twelfth century, Hebrew was not a natural choice for a medieval Jew speculating about cosmology, or about any other "scientific" issues. The few exceptions only confirm this general rule. Hellenistic Jews around the Mediterranean and eastward conducted their affairs and inquiries in Greek, and later Arabic became the main language of communication both in daily life and for more literary purposes. Hebrew works such as *The Book of Creation* (*Sefer yetsirah*) or *The Book of Asaph the Physician* (*Sefer Asaf ha-rofe'*) remained isolated, deprived of immediate cultural context and therefore, especially in the case of *Sefer yetsirah*, exposed to different and often contradictory readings. It is mostly during the twelfth century that one can point to a change in the status of Hebrew as it began to encompass a whole scientific-philosophic speculative horizon. This shift seems to have occurred in al-Andalus and the Christianized parts of the Iberian Peninsula and the Christian areas of southern France, Provence, Italy, and England. The best-known early pioneers of this new use of Hebrew were the two Abrahams, Bar Ḥiyya and Ibn Ezra, and—shortly after—the founder of the Tibbonid dynasty, Judah ibn Tibbon.

Two points must be emphasized regarding this unique form of intellectual migration. First, it was preceded by a process in which eastern Judaism fully adopted, integrated in, and participated in the Arabization of all branches of knowledge. Without leaving their homelands, Jewish intellectuals living in Arabic-Islamic domains migrated into an entirely new cultural sphere. Second, in the time period discussed here, representatives of this Jewish-Arabic culture were in the process of a geographical migration into new territories, especially the southern parts of Christian Europe. While migrating into these new areas, they became involved in a process of cultural metamorphosis, developing new linguistic strategies in order to preserve and further advance the intellectual life they had had back in their Arabic homeland. Their own transformation and the transformation of communities that received them were two essential parts of the same process.

European Jews, although assimilated into the spoken vernacular,[3] could not adopt Latin as their literary language. Without exception they chose Hebrew as their sole language of literary communication. As Cyril Aslanov defines it, "Medieval Jews relied on a Hebrew superstrate, rather than a Latin one."[4] Meanwhile the Arabic-into-Hebrew translation movement, just like its parallel Arabic-into-Latin movement, gave birth to a political and social phenomenon in which new social groups that identified with the new intellectual horizon opened by the translated materials developed cultural frameworks for the absorption of those materials. The members of this new intellectual group were of course the main beneficiaries as well, enjoying the privileged status gained by their expertise as authorized teachers of the new knowledge. As a result of the reproduction of new texts and their organization into a whole new system of knowledge, there emerged a new society of letters, engaged in defining the social, political, and cultural context of this knowledge. Such social and intellectual revolution necessarily provoked social conflict whose outcome determined the place of the new learning within the broader cultural framework of medieval Christian and Jewish communities.

Regarding the Jewish intellectual community, I would like to reemphasize what was said at the beginning of this section: as much as one can underline the significant differences between two different cultural orientations, Arabic versus Latin, at the end of the day they both merged into one literary corpus. The new Hebrew science was composed of a combination of original works written in Hebrew and myriad translations into Hebrew, which themselves can be divided in three major categories:[5] (1) Judaeo-Arabic "classic" writings (Sa'adia, Ibn Paquda, Halevi, Maimonides) that were normally among the first to be translated into Hebrew and constitute the main corpus of the Hebrew philosophic canon; (2) Arabic-Muslim texts (Alfarabi, Avicenna, Averroes) or Arabic translations of classic texts (Aristotle, Euclid) that were translated in order to provide the new Hebrew scholars with the basics of the great Arabic library (which in the East was an integral part of the typical Judaeo-Arabic curriculum);[6] (3) Latin sources, either part of the Latin Christian tradition or translations of Greek and Arabic texts.

These three separate streams merged into one Hebrew philosophical/scientific tradition, with varying consequences for Jews of different regions and backgrounds. In order to enable a Hebrew reader who had never before been exposed to such material to be able to follow and grasp the new literature, there was a desperate need to create a whole set of bibliographic tools—translations, compilations, encyclopedias, and paraphrases. The effort to fulfill this need constitutes a unique moment in Jewish intellectual history. It signifies a radical project to establish a universal discourse of philosophy and science (not liturgy, not *halakhah*, not talmudic learning, nor midrash) within the boundaries of the Hebrew language as well as an ambitious attempt to constitute Hebrew as a language of science and philosophy on an equal footing with Arabic and Latin. This new Hebrew, like its medieval Latin counterpart, always functioned within a diglossic framework, together with at least one European vernacular. The medical works in Hebrew were part of a larger move in Christian Europe in which Jews played a significant role: the medicalization of life and professionalization of medical praxis through standardization, licensing, and control procedures.[7]

Indeed, when observed as a broad cultural-linguistic phenomenon, Hebrew science and philosophy can easily be compared with other Hebrew genres of the same period, such as Jewish esotericism and Kabbalah. The geographical and chronological framework for the development of Hebrew scientific/philosophical scholarship and Kabbalah is very similar, emerging in southern France, northern Spain, and Italy in the thirteenth century. Both literary streams were made possible by and took place within the Hebrew language, and both absorbed external influences—either Christian or Muslim or both.[8]

However, unlike kabbalistic literature, whose references were mostly to ancient Jewish sources, in the case of the new Jewish philosophers/scientists we witness a unique phenomenon of self-Orientalizing Jews who lived under Christian cultural hegemony but chose to define themselves in accord with a faraway culture. How striking such a situation is becomes apparent if one considers the fact that, while the first Jewish immigrants from Muslim al-Andalus to Christian Spain and Provence during the twelfth century were Arabophones, later, any real knowledge of Arabic was rare among their descendants, not to mention their local followers in the Jewish communities that received them.[9] On the other hand, while their level of formal Latin learning was certainly very limited, they freely conversed in the local vernacular, and the usage of *le'azim*, transliterated Latin or vernacular words, in the Hebrew scientific texts reveals a certain fluidity, typical of the intellectual situation of the time, among high Latin, "Latinized Vulgar," and "vulgarized Latin."[10]

When Gad Freudenthal considers the cultural integration or disintegration of European Jews in their Christian environment, he begins with a quantitative comparison that demonstrates that Jewish intellectuals were oriented toward Arabic literary sources and not toward Latin-Christian ones.[11] Indeed, according to their writings, Provençal Jews were much less interested in scholastic thought than their contemporaries in Italy. Similarly, it is clear that physicians were more involved with Latin-Christian literature than other Jewish intellectuals were. Such a quantitative comparison aiming to calculate whether Jews were more receptive to Arab or to Latin ideas fails to give an account of the significant fact that some Jewish and some Christian intellectuals were (simultaneously) engaged with the same enthusiastic reception of the same Arabic sources. This is precisely the lesson to be drawn from the scene provided to us by our two protagonists, Hillel and Zeraḥyah. The former translated from Latin, the latter from Arabic. But all the Latin texts translated by Hillel were themselves the product of the Arabic-into-Latin translation movement. In that sense, the Christian-oriented Hillel can see himself as belonging to the same tradition of translation from Arabic into Hebrew. This state of affairs becomes even more apparent when it comes to the addressees of the translated texts. In most cases the reader of the Hebrew translation could no longer recognize its exact linguistic origins.[12] Moreover, essential portions of the total sum of Arab-Muslim philosophic texts translated into Hebrew are various texts written by two authors: Alfarabi (c. 870–ca.950) and Averroes (c. 1126–98).[13] Interestingly enough, these two Arabic authorities were the same pillars that constituted the Latin scholastic reception of Arabic thought. The choice of Averroes as a central philosophic authority is not more natural than the strange inversion of Algazali (ca. 1058–1111), the big opponent of the *falsafa* movement, into a loyal pupil of Avicenna, thanks to the fact that during the thirteenth century his philosophic encyclopedia (*Maqāsid al-falāsifa*; *Intentions of the Philosophers*) was translated into Latin and Hebrew, but none of his mature critical anti-philosophic polemic.[14] Once again, how peculiar that the same strategic decision was taken by the scholastic and the Hebrew translators!

Avicenna as a philosophic and medical authority seems to offer an exception to this general affinity between the Hebrew and the Latin translation projects. His philosophic texts were widely translated into Latin and had great impact on early scholastic thought but were not translated into Hebrew (though Avicenna's thought was influential in many indirect ways).[15] His medical work was translated into Latin rather early and into Hebrew only a century later. However, I would like to assert that this exception only proves the rule: Avicenna's *Qānūn fil-ṭibb* as well as his *Kitāb al-Shifa'* were both translated in Toledo in the mid-twelfth century by Gerard of Cremona and Dominicus Gundissalinus, respectively,[16] but the two works subsequently had very different fates within Latin scholastic circles. While the philosophic work had an immediate impact on the early scholastics of the late twelfth and early thirteenth century,[17] the medical work became canonical only during the first half of the thirteenth century when it was integrated into the academic curricula.[18] This state of affairs finds its exact parallel in the Hebrew reception. The impact of scholastic thought on Jewish intellectuals during the early period was very limited, hence also the limited reception of Avicenna's philosophic writings.[19] The translation of Avicenna's medical work was done directly from the Arabic, but only after its integration into the scholastic medical curriculum and, as David Wirmer demonstrates in yet unpublished research, with clear emphasis on the parts that were crucial for university study.[20]

Finally, although the study of medicine, which attests to significant cross-cultural exchange, might present us with an exception to the other intellectual spheres, we must remember that disciplinary borders are not at all decisive, especially not among Jewish physicians.[21] Medical praxis and medical theory surely established their own defined areas, especially in European society, but they had a great impact on other fields as well. The materials we examine below demonstrate that point very clearly. They demonstrate another point as well: while different areas shaped distinct intellectual cultures, late medieval society created manifold ways for the diffusion and circulation of ideas. For Jews and Christians alike, "Italy," "France," "Midi/Provence/Languedoc," "Germany/Ashkenaz," "Aragon," and "Castile" remain important signifiers that retain their distinctive character while at the same time functioning as home base for all kinds of cultural vagabonds migrating between them.

With all that in mind, let us turn now to one of the finest historical examples of a direct interpersonal confrontation, which involved all the above-mentioned elements.

The Inner Maimonidean Controversy

Hillel ben Samuel ben El'azar of Verona, a Jewish Italian physician, translator, and philosopher, was, during the late 1280s, already a man in his late sixties or early seventies, living in northern Italy (Ferrara, Forlì, Bologna). The reconstruction of his early life is based mostly on his own biographical remarks, together with some external evidence, which, often erroneously interpreted, has led scholars to some significant confusion. It is clear that he spent many years in the Jewish centers of Rome and southern Italy, and also a few years in Barcelona.[22]

The main point of confusion regarding Hillel's biography has to do with the episode of his early legal education in the circle of R. Jonah Girondi in Barcelona. Our information on this matter comes exclusively from Hillel's own notes, especially a statement in his letter to Maestro Gaio ("Isaac the physician," court physician of Pope Boniface VIII in Rome). A major ambiguity derives first from the fact that many scholars doubt Hillel's credibility on that subject and tend to dismiss the entire description as fictitious.[23] The second problem is that since the mid-nineteenth century scholars have misunderstood Hillel's words and therefore wrongly dated his stay in Barcelona to the early 1260s. In fact, Hillel's testimony should be trusted and the period of his stay in Barcelona must be predated to the late 1240s or early 1250s.[24]

Our ability to date Hillel's studies in Barcelona to the early 1250s brings much coherency to the fragments of his documented biography. Returning to southern Italy sometime before 1255, Hillel started to build his career as legal leader and physician. In 1255 he was active in a legal case involving the Tibbonid family in Marseilles and Naples.[25] At the same time he also emerged as a translator of Latin medical texts. In the 1260s he is reported by the famous kabbalist Abraham Abulafia to be his teacher of Maimonides' *Guide*, which they read together in Capua.[26] If we can deduce from his remarks to Maestro Gaio and to Zeraḥyah that he spent time with both of them in Rome, then this was most likely in the 1270s. Whether he moved to the north from Rome or from the south seems to be impossible to determine.

Thus, it is clear that Hillel acquired his professional *Bildung* in some of the most important contemporary centers of Jewish learning, but developed his own creative intellectual activity as an independent scholar very late, while dwelling in northern Italy, far from the traditional southern Italian centers of learning. Besides some translations of medical works, Hillel's most important works are his commentary on Maimonides' twenty-five metaphysical premises, his *Book of the Rewards of the Soul,* and some short treatises composed in the form of scholastic disputations.[27] All the works were written after 1290, including the translation of Galen's *Ars parva* with the commentary of Ali ibn Ridwan.

During the Maimonidean controversies of the 1280s, Hillel took a clear position on the side of the Maimonideans. However, his intense debate with Zeraḥyah demonstrates the extent to which his interpretation of Maimonides differed from that of other Maimonideans. As we shall see, Zeraḥyah himself draws our attention to another essential point by accusing Hillel of being influenced by alien wisdom, referring to Hillel's many encounters both with non-Jewish authors and with Jewish mystical and magical Ashkenazic circles.

Zeraḥyah ben She'alti'el Ḥen (Gracián) was born in Barcelona, where he probably started his scholarly career.[28] He arrived at Rome during the 1270s and it was while dwelling in Rome that he composed all of his writings and translations that are known to us.[29] He translated four works of Aristotle from Arabic, pseudo-Aristotle's *Book of Causes*, three of Averroes' middle commentaries, the philosophic works of Alfarabi and Themistius, and parts of the medical works of Galen, Avicenna, and Maimonides. At the same time he left us his own writings in the typical style of the Maimonideans: he composed a commentary on the *Guide* and further commentaries on the more "philosophic" parts of the Bible (Proverbs, Job). He was also a practicing physician and he taught in Rome, where he concentrated on the teaching of Maimonides' writings and (philosophic-allegorical) biblical hermeneutics. His last work is dated to 1291.

Based on Zeraḥyah's existing correspondence, it is possible to reconstruct some of his social network. It includes Maestro Gaio as well as R. Shabtai ben Solomon and Immanuel ben Salomon, both from Rome, and Judah ben Solomon, Zeraḥyah's relative from Barcelona.[30] In his letter to Judah,[31] Zeraḥyah mentions his commentary to Maimonides' *Guide* as the direct outcome of his intensive teaching activity in Rome.

According to these descriptions, Barcelona and Rome were the places where our two authors spent time together. While there is no doubt that they became acquainted in Rome during the 1270s, one cannot rule out the possibility that they may have known each other already from their early period of study in Barcelona. It is from their short quarrel the following year that we derive most of our information about them, as if momentarily the two figures were caught in a light before disappearing again from sight. The dates of their respective deaths, probably just a few years later, remain unknown in both cases.

Areas of Competition and Rivalry

It is now time to turn our gaze to the polemical correspondence between our two scholars. Already in the nineteenth century the extremely violent tone used by Zeraḥyah drew much attention from scholars.[32] It is most puzzling in light of the fact that according to established dichotomies the two rivals belonged to the same camp, that of the Maimonideans. Moreover, they seemed to have been acquainted with each other for decades and there is no previous indication of any tension existing between them.[33] What could have been the cause for such a sudden break?

Though a definitive answer is beyond the reach of the information provided by the present documents, I would like to offer here five potential reasons for the falling out:

1. *"Inner Maimonidean Controversy": The Inner Struggle over the True Interpretation of Maimonides*

Maimonides, more than any other single author, symbolized the possibilities and risks of the cultural turn imposed on European Jewry by a determined intellectual elite. His philosophic writings were promoted and popularized by a whole group of intellectuals, starting in Provence with the Lunel circle of R. Meshulam ben Jacob, who had direct contact with Maimonides, and Samuel ibn Tibbon, the first translator of *The Guide of the Perplexed* into Hebrew. It continued in southern Italy with Samuel's student and son-in-law, Jacob Anatoli.[34] The elite group promoting the status of Maimonides and the intellectual ideal he stood for were simultaneously promoting themselves as the qualified teachers and interpreters of this new content and perhaps even as an alternative leadership for the Jewish community. This is the immediate historical context of the debate, a competition between two would-be Maimonidean authorities.

At the same time it would be a mistake to reduce the debate solely to a conflict between personal aspirations. Personal hostilities were rooted in different approaches toward the legacy of Maimonides and his work. As Deleuze and Guattari have phrased it, philosophers' names can easily become "conceptual personae," philosophic concepts in themselves.[35] Platonists, Aristotelians, and Spinozists are well-known cases[36] in which the names of individuals are assigned a value by specific followers (or opponents) that is sometimes almost entirely independent of the original philosophic content found in their writings. Indeed, our two protagonists are totally committed to the nominal value attached to the name "Maimonides," although the real components of their philosophic thought derived from other sources: Zeraḥyah follows Arabic philosophy as formulated by Alfarabi and Averroes, and Hillel is mostly inspired by the Latin Aristotelianism and its Scholastic proponents, from Dominicus Gundissalinus to Thomas Aquinas.

Based on their own assertions as well as on their literary production, it is clear that both authors saw themselves as great authorities in matters related to the interpretation of Maimonides' philosophic writings. Both wrote commentaries on Maimonides' *Guide.*[37] Hillel claimed for himself the status of an expert on Maimonides' *Guide* in his letter to his Roman friend Maestro Gaio.[38] Zeraḥyah asserted the same in his response to Hillel's first letter, placing it within a broader correspondence in which people sought his guidance regarding Maimonides' ideas. It seems reasonable that Zeraḥyah interpreted

Hillel's first letter precisely in this light: as a request for magisterial guidance, to which the former responded in a firm but polite tone. However, Hillel's second letter made it clear that he was not writing as a pupil addressing his master but that he viewed himself as a participant in a critical dialogue between two independent scholars of equal authority. In that sense Zeraḥyah's aggressive response was intended to put things back into their right order.

The debate itself seems to have had three main foci, which at first sight appear to be rather idiosyncratic; yet, when organized around basic principles of Maimonidean hermeneutics, they begin to become much more coherent. The first issue is clearly exegetical: namely, a dispute over how much space Maimonides leaves in his hermeneutics of biblical esotericism as allegorical philosophy (*sitrei tora*) for the traditional reading of its literal sense. Zeraḥyah positions himself here as a radical Averroist who turns the distinction between the two interpretive levels into a social one between two "textual communities": simple-minded believers against sophisticated philosophers, who accurately understand that the "mystery" of the Torah refers only to the fact that beyond its apparent mythical vocabulary there is hidden reference to scientific truth. Hillel, on the other hand, takes a position that is much closer to Christian scholastic theology. Unwilling to give up the literal meaning of Scripture, Hillel strongly asserts that the mysteries of the Mosaic Scriptures cannot be reduced to scientific truisms of profane knowledge that would be apparent to any of his contemporary university scholars.

The second point of polemic can be taken as a specific case of the general exegetical debate. Here both authors disagree regarding angelology, the interpretation of biblical description of celestial spiritual entities. Again, Zeraḥyah, as a radical Maimonidean deeply oriented toward Averroes, denies the possibility of any corporeal appearance of angels. Any biblical description of angels in human shape and with bodily organs must be systematically interpreted (away) as a dream, vision, or parabolic speech. Hillel, in contrast, seems to make great though rather unconvincing intellectual efforts in order to save the literal meaning of the biblical narrative without giving up basic Maimonidean principles. As quoted by Zeraḥyah, his explanations make little sense. The angel himself cannot be a creature equipped with bodily organs, but he was able to miraculously affect the air surrounding Jacob (Gen. 32:25–31) or Balaam's she-ass (Num. 22:22–33), creating a physical phantom that includes bodily effects. As strange as that might sound, this explanation not only saves the biblical narrative but also is consistent with Hillel's Avicennean reading of Maimonides, as clearly developed at the same period in the second part of his

Rewards of the Soul. In the context of Hillel's main topic of discussion in this work—the nature of human soul and intellect and their perfection—his general attitude is unique; although writing during the last decades of the thirteenth century, in an era totally dominated by Averroes' commentaries on Aristotle, he insists on remaining faithful to some of Avicenna's ontological principles. Hence, in the second part of his work he adheres to an Avicennian definition of the soul as separate substance attached to the body. He attributes to Maimonides the opinion that the perfected human being, after reaching the level of moral and intellectual perfection, "has returned, even in his lifetime to be at the level of the highest angels and even high above them."[39] Here Hillel goes beyond the limits of many of the rationalists—surely beyond the limits of Maimonides himself—when he claims:

> While being at that level he can work all the miracles that we find by the prophets and the sages of the Talmud, that they were raising the dead back to life through prayer, and bringing a sudden death on the living as punishment. And they would create human beings and animals, and make the rain fall or stop it from falling down, and they would have done all this great miracles while being alive, in one single moment, as pure act of their will, without any usage of holy names, simply by arriving at that angelic level of existence. . . . And blessed is the one who has reached that level [of perfection], because the angels and all the heavenly bodies are standing to his command, without any usage of holy names.[40]

Hillel puts here as the final goal of philosophic contemplation a perfect act of will that subdues the powers of nature. The closest possible source for that would be a rather well-known passage of Avicenna's *De anima*[41] in which Avicenna defines one of three sorts of prophecy: the first leads the prophet to the knowledge of the future contingent events;[42] the second leads to an intuitive grasp (*ḥads*) of general principles of thought and especially of the middle terms of syllogism; and the third leads the prophet's will to reach out beyond the subjective realm of the individual and gives him power over material objects.[43] The implementation of the same principle for angels seems very natural. Not less evident is its vehement denial by Zeraḥyah.

Zeraḥyah's attack on Hillel's concept of natural language, forming the third issue of their controversy, shall be viewed as part of the very same debate on thc realm of the supra-natural, this time vis-à-vis language. Regarding the nature of human language, and against Zeraḥyah's pure conventionalism,[44] Hillel propagates here the well-known Renaissance concept of Hebrew as a natural language,[45] the language of creation, which became the true language of nature, and as such elevates the natural capacities of human speech to the level of magical speech-act.

Hillel is one of the only Jewish authors to use the historic anecdote normally attributed in its medieval version to Frederick II, who allegedly experimented with babies raised without contact with any human tongue in order to perceive what would be their natural primary tones.[46] Zeraḥyah mocks the legend and insists that such a hypothetical situation would lead to the death of the experiment's subjects or else cause them to utter in meaningless voices. Irene Zwiep, who thoroughly discusses this debate,[47] describes it as the first case of systematic scholarly debate in Jewish thought regarding such linguistic theorems. But far more than an abstract dispute about the nature of language, it is the nature and status of the *Hebrew* language that is the focus of the debate. Unlike Judah ha-Levi, who, like Hillel, argues in favor of the ontological superiority of Hebrew but does so in Arabic, Zeraḥyah denies any such status for Hebrew language but does it in Hebrew. This linguistic formal change encapsulates the cultural metamorphosis that the Hebrew language went through between the mid-twelfth and mid-thirteenth centuries. Hillel's position locates him not only closer to magical speculations but also to kabbalistic theories, especially to those of Abraham Abulafia, Hillel's companion in the study of Maimonides' *Guide*.

When the debate took place, Zeraḥyah could not yet have been acquainted with Hillel's major philosophic work, but his suspicion toward the mystical and magical tendencies he identified in his rival and their different possible kabbalistic and Christian sources were quite accurate. Zeraḥyah seems to be completely aware of these elements in Hillel's thought—and also of their potential sources. Already in his first letter he points to Hillel's affinity with the teaching of Nahmanides, whom he respects as a spiritual leader but not as a philosophic authority. In the second letter he blames Hillel because of his attraction to mystical and kabbalistic traditions, explicitly referring to Ḥasidei Ashkenaz and Nahmanides, and to the foreign doctrines of Christian scholastic teachings.

2. *Two Competitive Translation Projects*

As James Robinson claims,[48] in the multicultural reality of the Middle Ages, the translator is a significant and distinct cultural type. Medieval translators developed different methods in order to establish their intellectual authority and legacy. This might be a proactive method of translation, in which the translator inserts his own commentary, usually with the phrase "the translator says" (*amar ha-ma'atik*), a practice used by Hillel in some of his translations and much less by Zeraḥyah. In other cases the translator might be involved in oral teaching of the translated materials, a practice used by Zeraḥyah in Rome but not by Hillel. Finally, the translator might turn to write his own independent tractates, putting into use the new concepts and methods acquired by his own translations. Zeraḥyah and Hillel both composed their own writings, albeit using starkly different approaches. Zeraḥyah was more faithful to the traditional commentary genre commonly used among the Maimonideans, while Hillel developed new literary forms under Christian scholastic influence: he wrote a systematic treatise on the soul and added to it three queries (*mevukashim*) written in the form of scholastic dialectic discussions (*disputationes*).

Beyond this general observation on translation methods, the striking parallel between the two contemporary intellectuals relates to the list of texts each of them chose to translate. In fact, there are a few cases in which both translated the same authors, though of course from two different source languages. Both authors translated the *Book of Causes*, and both translated medical writings of similar authors. The proximity of place, patronage, and works make it into what can be easily conceived as competing translation projects.[49]

Hillel's most popular translation, transmitted in fifteen manuscripts, was of Bruno da Longobucco's (or "di Lungoburgo") *Chirurgia magna*,[50] written in Padua in 1252. Moritz Steinschneider claimed thet Hillel's translation was produced almost immediately after the composition of Master Bruno's work, perhaps even in the same year.[51] This seems to be hardly probable considering Hillel's biography. Most probably the translation of the *Chirurgia* reflects Hillel's acquaintance with teaching materials of the northern Italian universities after he moved to the north during the 1280s. If this is the case then his earlier translations must be dated to the late 1270s, perhaps Hippocrates' *Aphorisms* with Galen's commentary, dated to 1278.[52] It is precisely during that period, after 1275, that Zeraḥyah began his activity as translator in Rome, and among his first translation efforts were Galen and Hippocrates. Galen's *Book on Illnesses and Their Accidents* (*De causis et symptomatibus*) is dated to 1275 and the *Chapters of Hippocrates* to 1279. Needless to say, Zeraḥyah did not have any parallel translation to Bruno's work, originally written in Latin.

In 1277 Zeraḥyah translated another central Judeo-Arabic medical text—the medical treatises of Maimonides. Parallel to that we find a letter, written from Hillel to Rome, ordering a translation of the very same work, but from the hands of another translator. In this letter, sent by Hillel in 1279 to Maestro Gaio, Hillel shows his great regard for Maimonides' *Medical Aphorisms* and commentary on Hippocrates' *Aphorisms*. Hillel considers the Judeo-Arabic Maimonides alongside the Greek Galen and his different Arab and Latin commentators as a most important resource:

> Although I already have the commentaries of the Pisan [Burgundius of Pisa] I still have more than a hundred severe queries on Galen's explanations according to this translation, while the ones made by Constantine [the African] are totally corrupted. Perhaps the wise speculations of our teacher [Maimonides] will solve the burden of these questions, which is why my soul desires them so much. Further on I beg you for the 25 comments of our teacher to Galen's work. Therefore brother, do not neglect me and do not care about the cost, and make a scribe copy them, and send them with R. Daniel *and I shall immediately send you the scribe's salary and [the price] of the paper and the corrections, as much as demanded. Even if it turns out to be a substantial expenditure it will become smaller [in my mind] when considering how much I love them [the books]*, since it is for many years that I heard about these compendium to Galen made by our teacher, and I have always desired it. [emphasis mine][53]

So in 1289, Hillel developed an urgent interest in Maimonides' medical writings. Keeping in mind the different possible uses of the word "copyist" (*ma'atik*), both as translator and as scribe, one can speculate whether Hillel here acted simply as the one ordering a scribe's copy of an existing translation or whether he in fact initiated the act of translation itself. Indeed, one gets the impression from Hillel's repeated emphasis on his willingness to accept any necessary costs that Hillel presented himself here as a rich and powerful person who could act as a patron, much like his Roman friend, Maestro

Gaio.[54] A short time later, Hillel himself translated Galen's *Ars parva / Microtechne / Tegni* with the commentary of the Egyptian physician Ali ibn Ridwan, from the Latin translation of Gerard of Cremona.[55]

Finally, another work was translated into Hebrew for the first time simultaneously by both authors: The *Book of Causes* (Arab. *Kitāb al-iḍāḥ fil-khayr al-maḥḍ*; Lat. *Liber de causis*; Heb. *Sefer ha-sibot*).[56] Here again Hillel translated into Hebrew from the Latin translation prepared by Gerard of Cremona in Toledo while Zeraḥyah translated directly from the Arabic. It is hard to decide which of them was the first and whether one of them was motivated or provoked by the other. Hillel's translation is dated by Mauro Zonta to circa 1260. If this is the case, then Hillel was certainly the first to translate the work and Zeraḥyah might have reacted by translating from the Arabic during the mid-1280s. However, here again I would suspect a much later date for Hillel's translation, probably close to the composition of his own theological works during the late 1280s. If this is the case, then we are dealing (once again) with parallel translations.

As Jean-Pierre Rothschild clearly demonstrated, the *Book of Causes* entailed some important psychological ideas that influenced scholastic discourse on the soul.[57] The debate on the soul and the intellect was a major topic in the universities, culminating in the 1270s.[58] It should not surprise us, therefore, that both our authors turn their attention from the 1280s onward toward psychology. Zeraḥyah translated (Pseudo-) Alfarabi's *On the Soul* and Aristotle's *De anima* (1284),[59] and Hillel composed his own treatise on the soul. We consider these writings below.

Could it be that this repeated parallelism regarding translation materials led to a sense of competition that in its turn created the enmity evident in our correspondence? I have not found any literary evidence in order to prove a causal relationship, but I would suggest it must be taken seriously into account, as part of the larger framework of a developing conflict.

3. "Professional" Controversy Between Two Physicians

As I have demonstrated, Hillel and Zeraḥyah were leading two parallel and competitive translation projects, primarily within the medical realm. But because the debate in the letters concentrates on purely theological and exegetical matters, it is too easy to ignore the medical context. In fact, the medical background of Jewish (and Muslim) authors is normally ignored when discussing their non-medical writings. This is perhaps due to the fact that, in the absence of intellectual establishments like an academic faculty of medicine to anchor the class-identity of its members, medicine was accepted mostly as a practical occupation and not as a distinguished branch of scientific education.[60]

In spite of all that, I would like to insist that medical identity is an important component for both our interlocutors and seems to underlie the entire debate, even though it suddenly and explicitly comes to the fore only toward the end of their correspondence. In the last part of his second letter Zeraḥyah suddenly changes the course of his attack. No longer a Sephardic anti-Ashkenazic rhetoric, no longer Arabic-oriented anti-Christian or rationalist anti-mystical, the debate has become now a professional quarrel between two practitioners of medicine, as Zeraḥyah adds a denunciation pointed directly to Hillel's medical knowledge and perhaps even to his medical praxis:

> Answer me, have you studied the books of Hippocrates and Galen, who rise above the mountains of Ararat? Have you observed and investigated [Galen's] *The Use of Members* [*De usu partium*] and the *Book on Illnesses and Their Accidents* [*De causis et symptomatibus*] and the book on the methods of cures in wounds and infections [*De methodo medendi*]: have the chapters of *Epidemics* [Galen's commentaries to Hippocrates' *Epidemics*] been revealed to you and his six [sixteen?] major works and the book on ten categories [*De compositione medicamentorum secundum locos*], or is it enough for you to observe your patients and diagnose [their illness] examining urine and consulting [al-Rāzī's] *Kitāb al-Manṣūrī*; and if you even consulted Ibn al-Jazzār's *Provisions for the Traveller* [*Zād al-musāfir / Sefer Tsedat ha-Derakhim*][61] then you shall be admired by the people of the place who will call you Tsafnat-paneaḥ [Gen. 41:45]; and if you further added Isaac Israeli's *Book of Famine* and *Book of Urine* you certainly become a tail among lions and head to foxes [Avot 4:20].[62]

Zeraḥyah's critique here seems to go in two different directions. On the one hand, he mocks Hillel for deriving his medical knowledge from popular books of secondary importance, or even more, for practicing a very low level of theoretical medicine, perhaps directly related to his poor level of philosophical speculation as demonstrated in previous parts of his letter. On the other hand, he asserts that Hillel is taking advantage of the poor state of knowledge in his local environment in order to become "a head for foxes." Our own evaluation of Hillel's intellectual achievements might be more generous, in the realms of both philosophic speculation and medical translation. As for Zeraḥyah's low estimation of Hillel's intellectual environment, again the modern scholar will note that northern Italian faculties of medicine during the late thirteenth century were much more developed than what might have been known to Zeraḥyah. In fact, Hillel represents a more progressive attitude that would subsequently gain popularity among Jewish physicians all over Europe, as reflected in the wide circulation of his translation of Bruno. But even here one can assume that the translation of works like the *Chirurgia* reflects a more practical orientation. Bruno's work is rooted completely in Arabic knowledge but the work is organized and written primarily for practical needs,[63] not as a basic theoretical-medical discussion.

In sum, it is clear that in both authors' writings, medical knowledge is fully integrated within the general philosophical and theological discourse. The ease with which Zeraḥyah moves between the two spheres parallels the way in which Hillel moves among philosophy, theology, and medicine in his different writings. Their parallel theoretical-medical careers reveal enough reasons for conflict, and the theological aspects of their quarrel do not contradict its medical subtext.

4. Heading Toward New Writings— A Debate Between Two Independent Philosophers?

The lack of biographical documentation and the inaccurate narratives often ascribed to our protagonists have made it all too easy to ignore a rather astonishing feature of their careers. While the overall picture of our authors shows their successful careers as scholars, physicians, and translators, it is only during a very short period in their lives, very late and roughly simultaneous to their controversy, that both of them experimented with producing their own independent philosophic-theological works. All of their mature independent writings must be dated to the years 1289–91, after which we have no more written evidence regarding them, although the assumption concerning both is that they lived until about 1295.

In their own literary production each of them chose a very different genre. As mentioned above, Hillel attempted to write the first systematic tract in Hebrew on the human soul and its intellectual potential and spiritual rewards, a discussion to which he added three scholastic disputations on typical theological questions (free choice, Original Sin, fall of angels). Hence in those later works he implemented two typical writing methods of Latin scholastic literature, that in their turn reflect two forms of his contemporary university discourse.

Zeraḥyah, on the other hand, having composed commentaries on the biblical "Books of Wisdom," first on Ecclesiastes and then on Job, was following the intellectual legacy of Maimonides as understood by his followers, similar to Samuel ibn Tibbon with his Ecclesiastes commentary[64] and to Moses ibn Tibbon with his commentary on the Song of Songs.[65]

Beyond this important variation in their style and method of writing, I would like to reemphasize the crucial point made above: for many decades Hillel and Zeraḥyah acted as two leading intellectuals, physicians, teachers, spiritual leaders, and translators of medical and philosophic texts without composing any original works of their own. This state of affairs changed only during the very last period of their public lives. Taken from this perspective, the letter exchange between them marks a kind of late rite of passage, leading them to the new and final intellectual phases of their careers.

The fact that the correspondence survived and was transmitted in five manuscripts, from Spanish to Byzantine lands, demonstrates the wide range of the debate, which transcended its original personal context to become representative of a moment of deep controversy within the Maimonidean camp.[66]

5. "Return to Your Father's Homeland": Intra-Jewish Cultural Hostility

At the end of his letter, Zeraḥyah addresses Hillel in a typically sarcastic tone: "You revealed yourself in those things [you have written] as one of the Germans who have never seen the heavenly light."[67] Accordingly, he orders him: "Return to your father's land and summon your *ḥashmalim* that require purification, and dwell in *talit* and in prayer, and read in the Book of Creation [*Sefer yetsirah*] and *Sefer ben Sira,* and study *Sefer shi'ur komah* and *Sefer ha-razim* and abandon the books of nature and the wisdom of (mathematical) arts."[68] Emanuel of Rome joined Zeraḥyah in his attack on Hillel. In a letter he sent to Hillel he wrote: "He [Hillel] profaned the holiness of the Lord which he loved, and he had the daughter of a strange god [Mal. 2:11] . . . and he abandoned the faith of the Hebrews and desired the foreigner's seed . . . and spoke aliens' words."[69]

One might wonder what exactly was this land to which Hillel needed to return, given that, at the time of the correspondence, Hillel lived in northern

Italy, the same land where his father and his famous grandfather had lived before him. It is important to note, however, that the geography used by Zeraḥyah and Hillel is, more than anything else, mental and cultural. Hillel himself experienced his place of living as a "foreign land" or even a land of exile (*erets nod*), compared to the flourishing cultural centers of southern Italy and Rome, where he had dwelled for many years. Zeraḥyah, on the other hand, himself a "new immigrant" from Barcelona to Rome, who in his first letter to Hillel expressed his wish to "travel back to my homeland and lie down with my ancestors,"[70] is using the vocative form "return to your father's land" in a purely metaphorical sense. Hillel's "homeland" is the bookshelf of the magical and mystical Ashkenazic literature and the rituals related to it. In the first letter Zeraḥyah rightly identified Hillel's speculation with the teaching of Nahmanides, and Hillel himself proudly declared himself to be a direct disciple of Rabbi Jonah Girondi. Nahmanides and Jonah were central figures of Aragonese Jewry, but at the same time, in heritage and cultural lineage they remained within Ashkenazic framework. Hence Ashkenaz here is not a geographic denominator but a cultural one.

Moreover, as Bernard Septimus has powerfully argued, the Catalan spiritual conflicts in which Jonah Girondi and Nahmanides were so deeply involved were above all social tensions between old aristocratic elites, who cultivated secular learning, and a new dynamic communal leadership, who challenged their authority.[71] When Zeraḥyah, originating from one of the most aristocratic families in Barcelona, blames Hillel for being Ashkenazic and identifying his spiritual positioning with Nahmanides, Zeraḥyah clearly tags Hillel as belonging to the social faction of his enemies.

Concluding Remark: An Italian Aftermath of the Toledo Project?

The *Liber de causis* was one of the typical products of the Jewish-Christian coproduction of Toledo. It seems that it was the Judeo-Arabic heritage of the work that shaped its later special reception among European Jews. Among the four Hebrew translations of this work made in the thirteenth to fifteenth centuries, two were made in Italy, by our two authors, at approximately the same time: Hillel of Verona from the Latin, and Zeraḥyah, directly from the original Arabic version. This episode frames the intimate space in which our two rivals found themselves, sharing the same Arabic-Latin-Hebrew superstructure while differing radically from each other in their sources of immediate authority.

Indeed, the final result of our analysis is a picture of two intellectuals who, though belonging to the same confession and sharing the same scholarly language and even the same intellectual ideology ("Maimonidean"), were part of two different intellectual frameworks, in a way that precluded any significant dialogue between them. Their conflicts transcended most of the common classifications used by modern scholars. Being both "Jewish Italian physicians" and followers of Maimonides, they did share the same new language of science and philosophy and yet, within that joint project, they oriented themselves toward different Arabic philosophic sources (Avicenna versus Averroes), different medical traditions, different Jewish spiritual paths, and different general cultural environments. Their public debate reflects much more than a unique personal antagonism and might serve as a warning against too strict a reliance on conventional classification as the only legitimate tool for framing the existential reality of an intellectual persona.

Chapter 10

Matter, Meaning, and Maimonides: The Material Text as an Early Modern Map of Thirteenth-Century Debates on Translation

S. J. Pearce

A sixteenth-century manuscript copy of a Hebrew-language life of Alexander the Great, the only text in an aesthetically unremarkable codex copied in a square Franco-Spanish hand with no illuminations, significant water damage at the top edge of its Italian-manufactured paper, and a modern binding, sold at auction at Christie's in New York in 1999, bringing in well over six times the expected hammer price. It was the first time that the manuscript had formally come on the market and just over a century since the last time it had changed hands. The exceptionally high final bid for the manuscript—which would subsequently be sold twice more, again doubling its price, before its accession to Yale University's Beinecke Rare Book and Manuscript Library in 2006—is just one of a series of peculiar features of the ownership history of this book. That history begins with a scribe copying the book to be sold through a dealer with a particular set of intellectual interests and, perhaps to add to the monetary value of his work, adding a fantasist's colophon[1] that made this life of Alexander the Great the site for debating and perpetuating the legacy of another figure who loomed large over the textual history of the Middle Ages: Moses Maimonides. After the first, every subsequent owner who bought or traded or donated the book and scrawled or stamped his name and initials onto its pages left a trail that can be traced as a map of its

Mediterranean origins and relocation into the Jewish communities in northern and central Europe. The seeming lack of coherence between the content of the body of the text and that of its imaginative colophon is the feature that makes this otherwise unremarkable book particularly worthy of study: it is no longer just a life of Alexander the Great in which any reader might see some aspect of himself as any reader of any life of Alexander the Great is wont to do.[2] Rather, this book's cartography of interested readers speaks to an early modern resurgence of a thirteenth-century debate, namely that over how best to transmit, disseminate, and translate the religious and philosophical works of Maimonides.

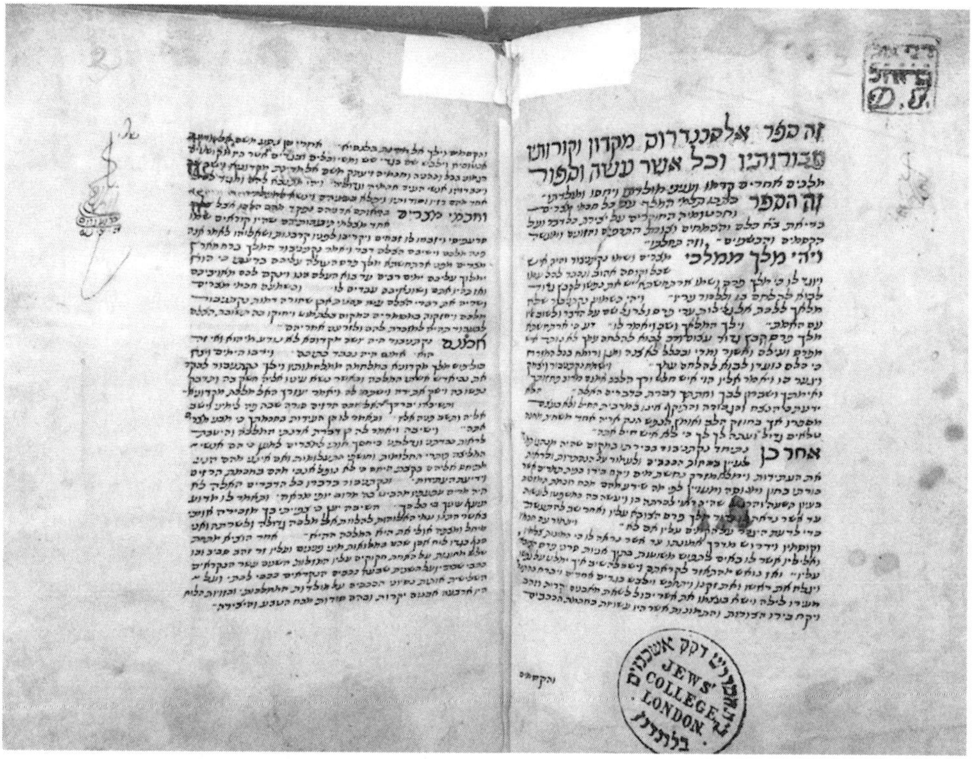

Figure 10.1 This opening bifolium (folios 2r–3v) of the Hebrew life of Alexander the Great (Beinecke Heb. Suppl. MS 103) shows the first two pages of the text, the signed owner's mark of the earliest identifiable owner, Isaac bar Menaḥem of Narbonne, and the stamped owners' marks of Daniel Itzig and Jews' College London. Courtesy of the Beinecke Rare Book and Manuscript Library, Yale University.

The single text contained within this codex is typically studied as a relatively insignificant part of the long literary tradition of lives of Alexander the Great. However, this present study is less interested in the body of the text and more in the extraordinary claims about its creation made from within the colophon appended to its end and the role those claims play in the ownership and readership history of the book. They place this particular version of the life of Alexander the Great within a wholly distinct textual tradition, namely that of the Arabic-language religious, philosophical, and scientific texts translated by some of the most prominent Hebrew translators of the twelfth and thirteenth centuries, the textual tradition that saw the translation of Moses Maimonides' *Guide of the Perplexed* into Hebrew for distribution to a wider audience of non-Arabophone Jewish readers in Europe.[3] The five owners' marks drawn and stamped into its pages, three of which have not been previously deciphered or identified, along with the unreal creation narrative of the text, situate this book within the early modern reemergence of debates over the transmission and translation of Maimonides' work. The entanglement of the Beinecke codex, with its unusual and partially falsified authorship history, and with the lives of Ashkenazic Jewish readers who were revisiting questions that originated in Sepharad, shows the book to be as much a referendum on the translation of the *Guide of the Perplexed* as a history of Hellenistic conquest in the Mediterranean.

Both methodologically and theoretically, literary and historical studies owe much to the broad field of anthropology and its various subdisciplines; one common borrowing from the critical equipment of the latter into the work of the former is the examination of phenomena, behaviors, objects, events, and texts alongside and within their cultural contexts rather than alone, a type of reading known as thick description, pioneered by Clifford Geertz in the 1973 monograph *The Interpretation of Cultures* and borne out in later studies, such as *Islam Observed*.[4] The peculiar colophon of the manuscript under discussion, traced along the line of travel of its codex through different private and institutional library collections, is perhaps best explained by another theoretical framework that comes to literary study from anthropology, and more specifically from archaeology. The key term that unifies all the studies in this present volume is "entanglement"; and while most of my coauthors are using it as a way to frame the ways in which members of different religious and cultural groups of the long thirteenth century interacted in organic ways, both productive and destructive, I have chosen instead to frame my "entanglement" within the anthropological framework of actor-network theory in which that very term presumes a mutual dependence between people and objects that emphasizes the impact of things upon people rather than focusing solely on the impact of people on the world around them, centering the material object as itself a social agent.[5] "Entanglement," the archaeologist Ian Hodder writes, "is a mix of humans and things, culture and matter, society and technology."[6] This definition forms the foundation of the present study concerning the entanglement of the material text with the lives of its readers set into its contexts, thickly described.

The Manuscript, the Fictive Translator, and the Colophon

The Hebrew Alexander codex, now known as Beinecke Hebrew Supplemental MS 103 and identified as Jews' College London MS 145 in scholarship published prior to the year 2000, contains a single text, a Hebrew Alexander romance based upon a now-lost Arabic translation of *Historia de proeliis*, the Latin translation of the authoritative Greek-language novelistic biography written by the author identified as Pseudo-Callisthenes, with other Alexander source material drawn in throughout.[7] This version of Alexander's life was adapted to appeal to a Jewish readership, eliminating some, though not all, of its protagonist's attributes and practices that would mark him as pagan; he is also explicitly Judaized in an episode that reconstructs his visit to Jerusalem through various turns of phrase, through mentions of Jewish practice in Alexander's realm, and through the representation of Alexander's prostration before the *kohen* in the Jerusalem temple, which is explained away as an adoration of the divine name and not of the *kohen* himself, so as not to make Alexander seem too much like a pagan.[8] It also pays particular attention to astronomical knowledge, tying it in with rabbinic ideas about that set of practices.[9]

What makes the work particularly significant and gives it a reach beyond the historiography of the Alexander romance is the colophon, which falsely attributes the Hebrew translation to Samuel ibn Tibbon (c. 1160–1232), the translator best known for his Hebrew version of Maimonides' *Guide of the Perplexed*. He adhered to a word-for-word method of translation that reproduces texts almost exactly in the target language, preserving the syntax and diction of the source language as much as possible, rather than the more holistic and readable sense-for-sense method that had been in vogue since the ninth century and that was favored by Maimonides himself; because of this, Samuel was not the creator of the only, or even the most easily readable,

Hebrew translation of the *Guide*. However, Samuel's epistolary correspondence with Maimonides ensured his place in the collective imagination as the authorized, and therefore the best, translator of the *Guide*, despite his disregard for Maimonides' explicit admonition to translate sense-for-sense.[10]

Word-for-word rendering as a translation method presents significant difficulties with respect to intelligibility because it preserves even the highly idiomatic aspects of the source language, thereby creating a text that is difficult to use for readers who are not equally familiar with the source and target languages. Conversely, it has certain advantages in that "such a translation, in as far as it succeeds in being an entirely exact reflection of the original, would give the reader the possibility of appreciating Maimonides's method of exposition and all that is involved therein."[11] Samuel, following his father's lead, believed that this was the correct way to transmit the esoterica in Maimonides' writing. Conversely, Judah al-Ḥarizi, a competing translator and *adīb*, a kind of Arabized literary jack-of-all-trades, based in the Castilian city of Toledo, created a Hebrew-language translation of the *Guide* that more closely conformed to Maimonides' preferences about how it should be translated, that is, sense-for-sense. The two translators found themselves on opposite sides of a newly reemerging late antique debate about the role of the translator and about what constituted a reliable translation:[12] was it one that replicated the words and syntax of the source language exactly or one that clearly transmitted the ideas of the text in the target language?

The colophon of the aforementioned Hebrew Alexander romance adds itself to the list of those commonly and (for the most part)[13] more securely attributed to Samuel ibn Tibbon and, furthermore, implicates the text in that same debate over word-for-word and sense-for-sense translation and whose translation of the *Guide* should be considered the best. The colophon reads:[14]

> נשלם זה הספר והעתיקו החכם החוקר על סודות המציאות והחכמה באמת ר'
> שמואל ב"ר יהודה אבן תבון ז"צ"ל מרמון ספרד והעתיקו בזמן אשר העתיק ספר
> המורה אשר לא יסולה בכתם אופיר וזה הספר נמצא ביד קצת אנשים בהעתקת אל
> חריזי והוא משובש מאד כי הוא העתיקו מלשון והמעתיק השלם הנזכר העתיקו
> מלשון הגרי ללשון עברי תהי משכורתו שלימה.

> This book was completed, having been translated by the sage and the true investigator of the secrets of life and wisdom, R. Samuel bar Judah ibn Tibbon (of blessed memory) of Rimon-Sefarad

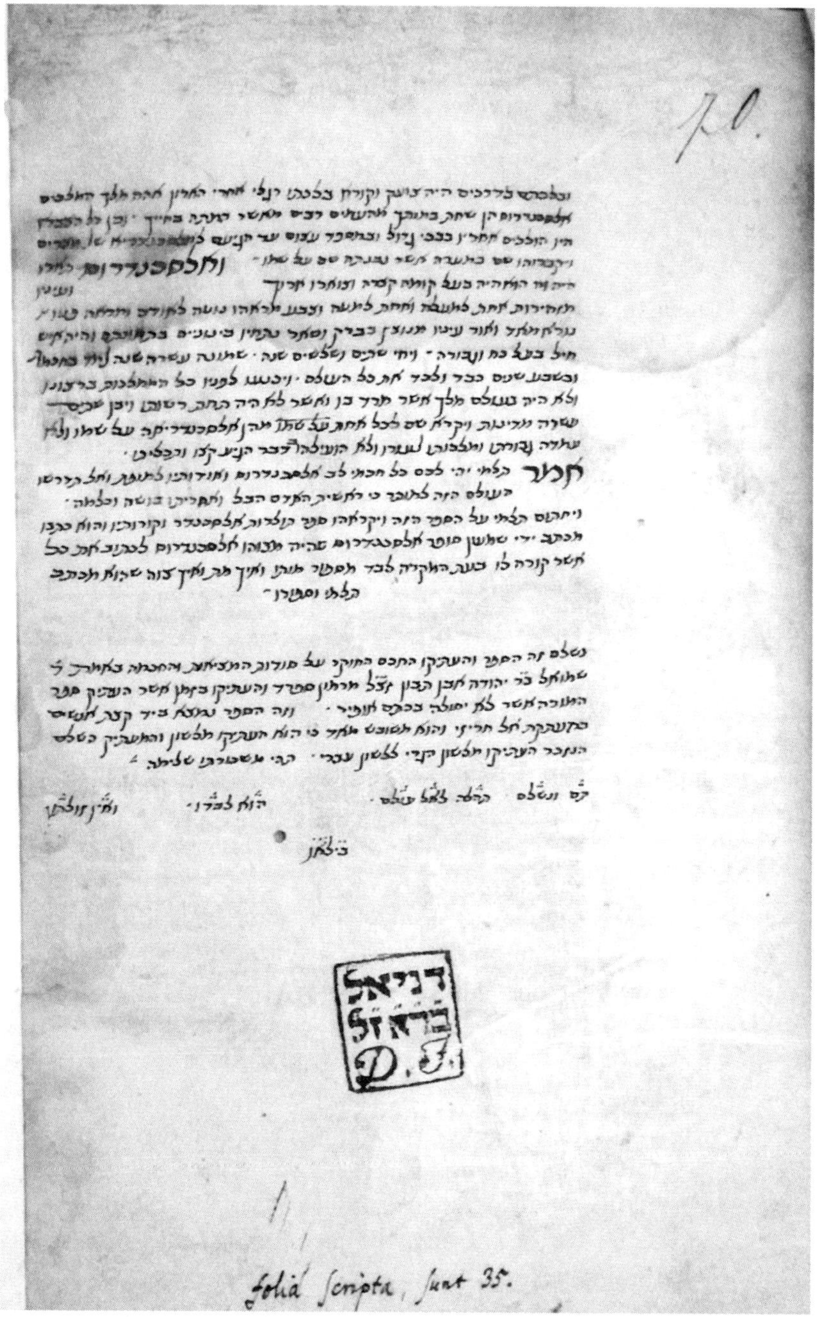

Figure 10.2. Folio 35v of the manuscript contains the final lines of the text and the colophon that incorrectly identifies the Hebrew translation as the work of Samuel Ibn Tibbon. It also shows Daniel Itzig's stamped owner's mark and the Latin note "Folia scripta sunt 35" in Solomon Hirschell's hand. Courtesy of the Beinecke Rare Book and Manuscript Library, Yale University.

> [Granada]; he translated it at the same time as he translated *The Guide*, which cannot even be valued by the gold of Ofir. This book is found in the hands of few people in the translation of al-Ḥarizi, which is very error-ridden because *he adapted it from its language*, but the excellent above-mentioned translator (let his recompense be complete!) translated it from Arabic[15] into Hebrew. Perfected and completed, praise be to the Lord of the Worlds. He alone is God and there is no other.[16]

Despite the unreliability of the colophon's statements about its own creation, the Arabizing features of the Alexander romance's Hebrew make it quite likely that this text was in fact translated from a now-lost Arabic version, as the text itself claims. They are not as rigidly Arabizing as we would expect properly Tibbonid Hebrew to be, however. And furthermore, the chronology of texts upon which this version draws makes it all but impossible for Samuel ibn Tibbon to have been the translator.[17] The reader is faced with a counterfactual but not totally implausible statement that attempts to accrete some of the prestige of a famous translator to itself and makes the Hebrew Alexander romance a site for continued debate over who created the best translation of the *Guide* and how. The present section examines the fictional character of the colophon and its implications for interpreting the text as a whole, as well as various scholarly responses to what is, on the face of it, a puzzling bit of text.

One particular infelicity in the phrasing of the colophon has been responsible for many of the interpretive difficulties that this text poses, and has typically been interpreted as some kind of scribal error. However, I intend to argue that it is not an error at all but a subtle salvo into the debate over which translation of the *Guide* is superior. The colophon explains that Judah's version is "*meshubash me'od*" (very error-ridden) because al-Ḥarizi "*he'etiko me-lashon*" whereas Samuel "*he'etiko mi-leshon hagari*." This distinction, apparently between "translation from [lacuna?] language" and "translation from the Arabic language," is unexpected and initially points to a copyist's omission of an additional adjective. However, a more detailed linguistic and historicizing reading of this colophon begins to suggest that this phrase represents, rather than a mistake, a clear assertion of the stylistic stakes of the question about the transmission of the *Guide* in Hebrew. The sense of this phrase, which has fortuitously been the subject of a variety of attempts to parse it, hangs upon the multivalent sense of the verb *he'etik*[18] and reveals a very sensitive understanding of the distinctions between Samuel and Judah's versions of the *Guide*.

A reconsideration of this phrase requires that we begin at the historiographic beginning: Moritz Steinschneider initially dismissed the value of this brief paratext on the basis of it seeming garbled: "This confusing epigraph appears completely worthless."[19] Subsequently Adolf Neubauer grappled more purposefully and seriously with the challenging phrasing of the colophon as he catalogued the original Jews' College manuscript collection,[20] suggesting in subsequent publications that the first instance of the word *lashon* was a misrendering of *laṭin*, and that the colophon should be understood to be accusing al-Ḥarizi of not having translated from the Arabic original but rather from a Latin translation made from Ibn Tibbon's Hebrew one.[21] This interpretation was rejected almost immediately by Israel Levi on the grounds that al-Ḥarizi was working from the same Arabic as Ibn Tibbon and because Levi could not establish that al-Ḥarizi knew enough Latin to give the author of the colophon any idea that this might have been plausible,[22] regardless of how plausible a scribal error it might be (particularly given the similarities between the letters *ṭet* and *shin* in the scribal hand). Linguistic evidence further troubles Neubauer's reading, with *laṭin* appearing in Hebrew to describe Latin or the Romance vernaculars only very uncommonly prior to the copying of this manuscript. Some scholars do, in fact, claim that al-Ḥarizi's translation of the *Guide* was derivative, either coming from a Latin version or a more readable Hebrew adaptation of the Ibn Tibbon translation. We shall see in the following section that late medieval authors had no trouble at all concocting fantastical back-and-forth accounts of texts' translation histories; and so, inaccurate and inelegant though this solution may be in absolute historical terms, it comports with the literary imagination of writers in that time and place with respect to the transmission and translation of Maimonidean material. Perhaps we should be less hasty to dismiss Neubauer's suggestion.

The most common explanation for this infelicity has been the assumption that the awkwardness is the result of the scribal omission of an adjective that would distinguish the language from which Samuel translated the *Guide* from the language from which Judah translated it, despite the usual care of the scribe to correct his own few errors. We do not know at what point in time the colophon was added to this text. It is not included in a related but unidentical Hebrew translation of *Historia de proeliis* that also came through a now-lost Arabic version, nor do we yet know of a *Vorlage* from which the scribe might have been working where the error might have been introduced if it was not our scribe's. However, because both Judah and Samuel were translating from the same Arabic version of the *Guide*, as Levi noted, there is no word that could sensibly fill the lacuna and distinguish between the text from which Samuel translated and the identical text from which Judah translated because both men worked from the same source. A solution that proposes a dropped word would have to presume a certain degree of ignorance or willful confusion on the part of the colophon's author about the Maimonidean sources from which Samuel and Judah worked.

The editor of the text, Wout van Bekkum, moved generally, if tentatively, toward a different solution that could explain the text as it is received, without any emendation, writing in the notes to the text: "A deliberate omission?"[23] In other words, while van Bekkum does not propose an alternative reading, he opens the door to the possibility that such an alternative ought to come from what is on the page rather than from an addition or emendation to it; and it is upon the foundation of his suggestion that I would like to build one final proposal for reading the text of this colophon. As noted above, the verb *he'etik* has an unusually wide and flexible semantic range and is sometimes even used with different meanings within the same text or even the same paragraph.[24] It is this suggestion that I would like to draw out further in my own reading of the colophon, resolving (at least to a great extent) the apparent awkwardness in the language and also explaining the colophon author's choice not only to implicate Samuel ibn Tibbon in the creation of the Alexander romance but also to stand him in sharp contrast to Judah al-Ḥarizi.

Bearing the flexibility of the word and its multifarious definitions in mind, it is possible to understand the first occurrence of the word, the one that describes Samuel's work, as meaning he translated, while simultaneously understanding the second occurrence of the word, the one used with respect to Judah's, to mean *he adapted*. This contrast draws upon the distinctions between the task of the translator and the task of the author that were current in discussions about the translation of Maimonides' work and that the Ibn Tibbon family members themselves set out. In other words, the sense of the colophon takes advantage of the many possibilities of a single lexical item in order to create a salient and realistic distinction between the two translators of the *Guide*, to articulate the terms of the existing debate over the two modes of translation, and to take sides in that debate by claiming that Samuel's method of translation (that is, word-for-word translation) is better than Judah's method of adaptation (that is, sense-for-sense translation). This solution retains the slight awkwardness of the phrasing but keeps the meaning of the text in line with the rest of the details drawn into this made-up history of the text. And regardless of whether a reader chooses to return more seriously to Neubauer's suggestion, rejecting Levi's rejection of his substitution of *laṭin* for *lashon* as illustrative of an additional twist in the fictive premise, or whether that reader chooses to accept the proposal that I have made here that hinges upon the fungible semantic range of the verb in question as encoding a criticism of sense-for-sense translation, the colophon clearly embraces its own embellishment of the history of the Alexander romance and Samuel ibn Tibbon's professional record as the prime way to comment upon translating and transmitting in the Maimonidean context. Either reading offers up an invented translation history that calls attention to and engages with the thirteenth-century debates over translation and highlights the extent to which literary creation played a role in teasing apart the dilemmas that those debates presented.

The relationship between the colophon and the text fortifies reading of the colophon as a referendum on the two different styles of translation. Connections exist between the text and the colophon in two major categories: first, the fact that both Alexander and Maimonides bore a close intellectual relationship to the work of Aristotle, and second, through the question of this Alexander's interest in esoterica and Samuel's insistence upon literal translation as the best way to translate the esoterica in the *Guide*. Shamma Boyarin, the scholar to have most recently contended with this codex, has delineated these connections in some detail:

> The colophon places the work of perhaps the most influential Jewish medieval neo-Aristotelian, Maimonides, next to the ostensible biography of a man whom many considered one of the greatest students of Aristotle: Alexander the Great. Samuel ibn Tibbon's translation project might be described as the importation of Aristotelian and neo-Aristotelian works into Hebrew, and some, obviously including the colophon's author, might have viewed the Alexander romance as a natural component of such a project. . . .
>
> The colophon describes Ibn Tibbon as the "learned investigator into the true secrets of existence" because of his inquiry into, and exposition of, Maimonides' esoteric teachings. The colophon's author is simply making an easy connection between Maimonides' (neo)-Aristotelian esoteric writings and another group of esoteric teachings that present themselves and were accepted by some as written by Aristotle. . . . And studying the Alexander Romance 'at

> the same time as' the *Guide* makes sense if one views Alexander's relationship to the knowledge transmitted via this relationship, as part of "the enhancement and intensification" of the philosophical inquiry that led both to the original writing of, and Ibn Tibbon's deciphering of, the *Guide* . . . even the incidental information contained in the colophon of Beinecke Heb. Suppl. 103 is important to its meaning.[25]

As noted at the outset, the Alexander romance as a genre can produce stories that serve the interest of any audience. The colophon of Beinecke Hebrew Suppl. 103 is what gives this Alexander romance yet another cultural function, arguing, in effect, that an Alexander romance is the appropriate place for an Arabized Jew to expound upon Maimonideanism because of the Aristotelian substrates in both, a connection that is amplified by this Alexander's interest in the pursuit of scientific and philosophical knowledge;[26] and it further contends that Alexander's interest in esoterica demands Samuel ibn Tibbon's literal approach to translation in the same way that Maimonides' esoteric work does.

By disregarding Maimonides' own ideas about translation in the interest of Samuel ibn Tibbon's method and his Maimonideanism, the colophon goes farther than commenting upon the text, placing it firmly in the realm of its readership history. The specific ownership and readership history of the codex can then play a role in helping modern readers to understand the post-thirteenth-century reception of Maimonides' work and the results of the Maimonidean controversies. The codex represents a significant metric for the reception of the *Guide of the Perplexed* among European readers in the early modern period. In the following section, we see that this discussion of the transmission of Maimonides' work in translation was of considerable and self-evident interest to readers in early modern Europe; and on that basis, I argue that precisely in the locations where the debate over the translation of the *Guide* was resurgent, the colophon and the phrase distinguishing between Ibn Tibbon's and al-Ḥarizi's methods of translation is the most significant element of the book.

The Ownership History of Beinecke Hebrew Suppl. MS 103

The history of the ownership of the book traces the map of interest because it traces out a cartography of readers who were prepared to purchase a book that deliberately draws itself into controversies over how best to translate Maimonides' work; as it happens, this path tracks cleanly along the lines of the resurgence of those debates in the early modern world. The readers who owned this book were themselves members of communities that were grappling with the modes of reading and disseminating the *Guide* and its brand of rationalism. By reconstructing the ownership history of the book, we are better able to gauge the constituency of this non-sequitur of a colophon.

The first identifiable owner is a certain Isaac bar Menaḥem of Narbonne, who was active in the decades following the copying of the manuscript around 1520. Based on Malachi Beit-Arié's typology of the language of colophons, there is no reason to believe that the book was copied for Isaac specifically.[27] Little is known about his life other than that he was a business confederate of the only marginally better documented Pinḥas of Narbonne, a book dealer who traded principally between the south of France and communities in and around Berlin and who had particular interest in the trade of works by Moses Maimonides and those subsequent works by later authors that commented on them.[28] Isaac's signature appears on folio 3r: *"Sheli. Yitsḥak bar Menaḥem ha-Ts[arfati] N[afsho bi-] 'E[den]"* (This belongs to me, Isaac, the son of Menaḥem the F[renchman whose] s[oul is in] E[den]) (Fig. 10.3).[29] Notable is the form of the signature, which appears to take the shape of a tughra, a highly stylized signature design used by Ottoman officials, a practice that is not yet well documented among rank-and-file populations in the Mediterranean during the Ottoman period.

A significant caveat is in order with respect to this identification, though: identifying this mark as the signature of a known bookseller from Narbonne is not without problems, chief among them being the Italianate character of the Hebrew script he used to sign his name. Particularly striking is the Italianate letter *kuf* at the end of his given name and the Italian paper on which the book was copied: these were local features rather than luxurious and exoticizing imports, and the suggested Oriental character of the Hebrew script perhaps takes precedence over the ostensibly but not perfectly French character of the letters that constitute the body of the text. Two possibilities present themselves: on the one hand, the use of a more Italian script may simply be in keeping with the Orientalizing features of the tughra-style signature and the pan-Mediterranean outlook of someone buying paper and books in Italy and reading Andalusi and Egyptian philosophy. On the other hand, this identification may be incorrect and the book might have belonged to the Italian Isaac bar Menaḥem ha-Tsa'ir (with the ts- in the abbreviation standing for

Figure 10.3A. Detail of Isaac bar Menaḥem of Narbonne's signature. Courtesy of the Beinecke Rare Book and Manuscript Library, Yale University.

Figure 10.3B. Line drawing of Isaac bar Menaḥem of Narbonne's signature.

tsa'ir, the younger, instead of for *tsarfati*, French), an individual who may or may not have existed and who has certainly not been identified at this time. Furthermore, while I have read the first name in this very highly stylized signature as Yitsḥak (Fig. 10.3C), the alternative reading of Yish'ayahu has also been suggested to me (Fig. 10.3D). My proposed solution makes good contextual sense in terms of what we can read in the signature and what little we know about Isaac of Narbonne's particular intellectual and business interests, but it is also undeniably speculative: a preliminary proposal in a forward-backward take on the academic tradition of the *Wissenschaft*—putting my first

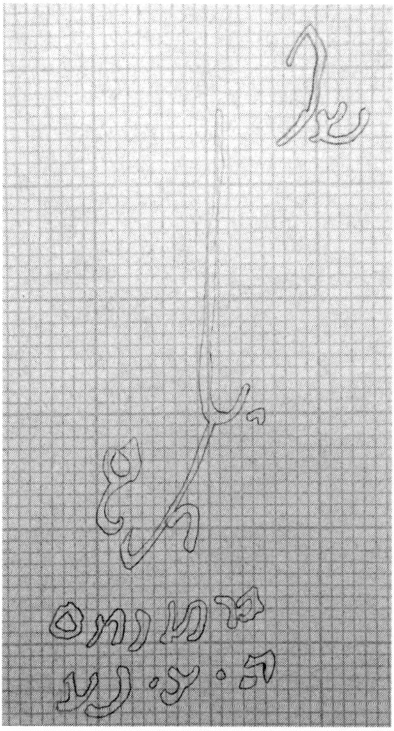

Figure 10.3C. Partial line drawing of Isaac bar Menaḥem of Narbonne's signature showing only the onomastic and not the decorative elements.

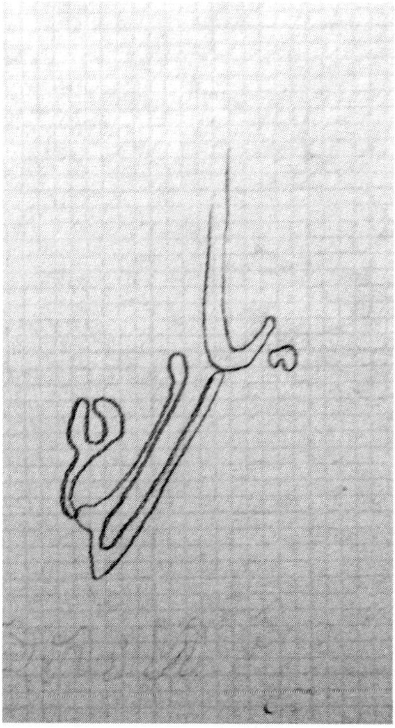

Figure 10.3D. Partial line drawing of the same signature, showing how a reading of the name Isaiah could be arrived at instead of Isaac, based on Malachi Beit-Arié's proposed reading.

steps toward identifying this individual out in the light in the hope that later scholarship may be able to build upon them.

After a gap of somewhat more than a century, the book reappears in one of the commercial centers where Isaac and Pinḥas did business, namely Berlin, in the personal collection of Daniel Itzig, also known as Daniel Berlin, an educational reformer who had made his name and fortune in the banking circles of his eponymous city.[30] He was among the first Jews to be granted rights as full citizens of Prussia; and Itzig himself held the title of Court Jew during the reign of William Frederick II. Itzig was an avid collector of Hebrew incunabula and manuscripts. Upon Itzig's death, the majority of his library collection came into the hands of Solomon Hirschell, a German Jew who would become the chief rabbi of London. Hirschell's signature (Fig. 10.4) appears on the flyleaf beneath a line of undeciphered text (Fig. 10.5). His patronymic surname, which refers to his lineage through his father, Hirsch (the German word for gazelle), appears in German (*Hirschell*) and, alongside it, a calque into Hebrew (*Ben-Tsvi*). The owner's mark as a whole reads: *Zeh ha-sefer shayakh li-Hirschell ben-Tsvi* (this book belongs to Hirschell/Ben Tsvi). Although fewer than half of them are identified as such in Neubauer's catalogue,[31] fully 20 percent of the manuscripts that ultimately formed part of Hirschell's collection, and later Jews' College's collections, were previously owned by Itzig, who identified his manuscripts with a stamped owner's mark (Fig. 10.6) and sometimes with a signature as well. The damage that created the water tide line that now appears at the top of the manuscript most likely occurred while it was in Itzig's possession. Additional manuscripts acquired by Hirschell from Itzig, such as the University of Pennsylvania's LJS 311 and LJS 453, contain the same tide line, as do manuscripts owned by Itzig that were never part of Hirschell's or JCL's collections, such as LJS 312. Upon Hirschell's death, his collection came to form the core of the Hebrew manuscript collection of the Beit Din of London placed on deposit at Jews' College London (Fig. 10.7), a degree-granting college that was originally a part of the University of London but now operates a separate institution for community study; it is now called the London School of Jewish Studies and has new and limited degree-granting powers authorized by the University of Manchester.

The governors of JCL decided in 1999 to divest the college of its manuscripts because of the poor state of the library (then as now),[32] and the collection was broken up and sold at auction at Christie's in New York. The Alexander manuscript sold for $12,560[33] after the auction house expected it to sell for between $1,000 and $2,000.[34] The Schoenberg Database of

Figure 10.4A. Solomon Hirschell's signature located on the flyleaf of the codex: "This book belongs to Solomon Hirschell [=] ben-Ẓvi." Courtesy of the Beinecke Rare Book and Manuscript Library, Yale University.

Figure 10.4B. Line drawing of Solomon Hirschell's signature.

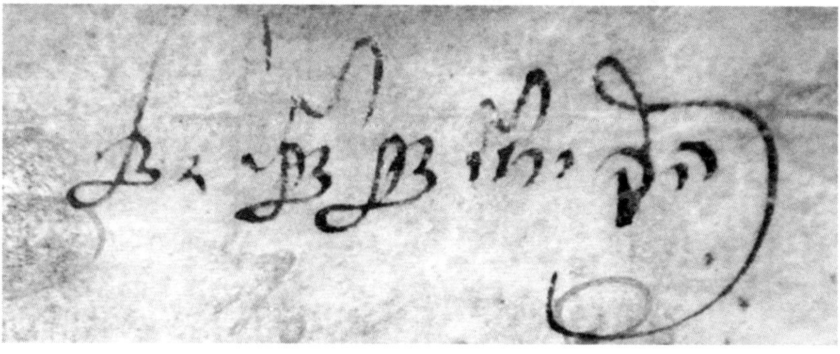

Figure 10.5. As-yet-undeciphered signature below Hirschell's on the flyleaf.

Figure 10.6. The stamped owner's mark of Daniel Itzig, giving his first name in Hebrew and his initials in Latin letters. Courtesy of the Beinecke Rare Book and Manuscript Library, Yale University.

Figure 10.7. The stamped owner's mark of Jews' College London. Courtesy of the Beinecke Rare Book and Manuscript Library, Yale University.

Manuscripts further records a sale of the manuscript, through a gallery called Les Enlumineurs based in Chicago, for $35,000. Les Enlumineurs, which acquired the manuscript not directly from the Christie's auction but rather through a London dealer, Samuel Fogg, Ltd.,[35] retains a catalogue entry online for the manuscript.[36] The Schoenberg Database (at the time of this writing) conflates two records for this manuscript (Schoenberg 30976 and Schoenberg 66773) with a third record (Schoenberg 48385) for another life of Alexander the Great, also dating from the early sixteenth century and also re-bound in modern red leather, but distinct in that it is written in German, printed rather than in manuscript, and had, until around the same time as the Christie's sale, been held in the library collection of the Earls of Macclesfield at Shiburn Castle, near Oxford.[37] What is interesting about this conflation is that holdings of the library of the Earls of Macclesfield were, until the collection was broken up and sold, particularly strong in works on Arabic, translation out of Arabic (particularly in Spain), and Spanish languages and literatures.[38] This error may have been introduced through simple sloppiness, but the contents and histories of these two very different books are closely enough related that it is not an error that jumped out and begged for correction. The Alexander manuscript with the colophon that makes a point about the Iberian translations of an Arabic work of religious law and philosophy has come to be associated, even by modern cataloguers and even through erroneous cataloging, with the loss of Sepharad and its Arabic literary culture. The Schoenberg Database notes a sale of the manuscript by Les Enlumineurs in September 2005, with Yale's catalogue dating formal acquisition of the book, purchased with monies from the Albert Childs fund (Fig. 10.8), to 23 November 2005.[39] I draw attention to these inconsistencies, discrepancies, and errors not in any way to find fault with the cataloguers but rather to demonstrate that, even in the space of the last fifteen years, one encounters considerable difficulty in keeping track of a clean provenance for this manuscript; and with that kind of confusion appearing within the most recent fifteen-year period, the loss that occurred over the course of five hundred becomes more tangibly comprehensible.[40]

The material history of this book, then, offers us a way into the historical provenance of the book, the concrete path traveled by a Hebrew-language Alexander romance with a falsified textual history, thereby raising questions about the interest of such a text for the readers through whose hands it passed and for their readership communities at large. Shortly after the copying of this book, of Isaac's ownership of it, and the period when it would have been

Figure 10.8. Bookplate added after the accession of the codex to the Beinecke Rare Book and Manuscript Library collection. Courtesy of the Beinecke Rare Book and Manuscript Library, Yale University.

traded up into historic greater Germany, certain aspects of the Maimonidean controversies reemerged as present, current, and terribly important. Chief among these was the debate over which Hebrew translation was best. And so this manuscript becomes a lens through which we must see a crashing together of intellectual trends from Sepharad and Ashkenaz and the way readers accounted for it.

In *Entangled*, his monograph expanding upon actor-network theory and deploying entanglement theory in the context of his archaeological work at the Turkish site of Çatal-Huyuk, Ian Hodder proposes a thought experiment in which he posits superimposing a concert grand piano on a hypothetical reconstruction of a scene from daily life at the Serbian Mesolithic-era site of Lepenski Vir. The purpose is to force the viewer to focus neither upon the overall scene nor upon the human actors alone, but rather on all the objects suddenly brought into high relief by the presence of this piano and the ways in which the humans are interacting—that is, entangled—with them:

> We can do something subversive—put in an object that does not fit. This is absurd. A concert piano? Suddenly the things, including the piano, force us to look at them more carefully. Why is a piano so absurdly out of place in Lepenski Vir? We look at the piano. It looks like those played in the symphony halls, it requires highly specialized skills to play, it is based on a specific western 12-tonal system, it uses a cast iron frame and high-tension wire that only became available in the Industrial Revolution. The grand piano needs symphony halls, it needs years of practice by trained musicians, it needs the system of tones in music, it needs factories able to pour precision iron. The people in the image could not understand, hear, make a grand piano. They did not have the factories, ships to import the materials, the imperial reach, the organization of labor, or the ideas about music that made the piano possible. So, subversively and subtly, the focus has changed from how things make society possible to the thing itself and its multiple connections. The gaze shifts to look more closely, harder at the thing, to explore how society and thing are co-entangled.[41]

Isaac's signature in Beinecke Heb. Suppl. MS 103 is the theoretical concert piano at Lepenski Vir. The tughra-as-piano is so strange, so difficult to disentangle, and so seemingly out of place in the manuscript that it compels us to ask questions about the cultural environment that valued the cultural prestige of the Ottoman and wider Islamicate worlds, that was clearly concerned with the transmission of Maimonideanism in Hebrew, and that was simultaneously firmly grounded in the separate Jewish culture of northern Europe. It is the thing that looks so indecipherable and seems so out of place in its context that it forces us to examine the relationships between all other elements in the mise-en-page and to delineate a context in which such a mark in such a book makes sense. It speaks both to the impact of the cultural context on the creation of the object and the impact of the object upon the lives of its owners—the mutual entanglement of matter and meaning, human and thing, and text and context. As we see in the following section, that context for a codex which needs books and a pan-Mediterranean trade in luxury goods and prestigious ideas in order to make sense turns out to be the renewed sixteenth-century interest in aspects of the Maimonidean controversies and the translation of Maimonides' work into Hebrew.

Translating the Interest in Translation

Diana Lobel opens her book *A Sufi-Jewish Dialogue*—the scope of which is medieval and deals largely with Sufi influence upon Andalusi Jewish philosophers and writers, and upon the work of Baḥya ibn Paquda (born c. 1040, died after 1090) in particular—with an anecdote told about one of the founders of the modern Ashkenazic pietist movement known as *ḥasidut*.[42] Lobel quotes a version of the anecdote, in which an eighteenth-century *ḥasid* tells some soldiers that, having won the battle they had just fought, they had to prepare for a greater, internal struggle; she then comments:

> The source of this anecdote is the Hebrew translation of Baḥya ibn Paqūda's *Duties of the Heart*, written in Arabic—more precisely, in Judeo-Arabic—in eleventh-century Spain, but translated in 1161 into Hebrew and a favorite of Jewish devotion down to this day. What the eighteenth-century Hasidic master no doubt did not realize is that the origin of the anecdote is the Islamic tradition of *ḥadīth* and that the *ḥasid* about whom it is told is the founder of Islam, the prophet Muḥammad. . . . Readers of the work in Hebrew translation might also be surprised that Baḥya's term for both the external battle and the greater, internal struggle is *jihād*.[43]

What Lobel signals here as important and, perhaps, surprising, is the notion of early modern Ashkenazim not only subscribing to, but building their entire pietistic mythology around, a worldview circumscribed by an Islamicate notion of greater *jihad*, or personal struggle, preserved in an Andalusi text written by a Jewish author not at all troubled by the Arabic terminology that was his native philosophical language, and translated out of Arabic and into Hebrew (by no less than Samuel's father, Judah ibn Tibbon, incidentally). Yet this phenomenon is less unusual than this registered note of surprise would seem to indicate. Both knowingly and unwittingly, early modern Ashkenazic readers accessed and valued Arabo-Islamicate Andalusi literary traditions through their textual canon, their intellectual debates, and the persistent memories that they adopted to give shape to their historical narrative. It is in this context of dependencies between imported ideas and material texts that the strange colophon and widely varied ownership history of Beinecke Hebrew Supplemental MS 103 truly begins to make sense.

The preponderance of *Guide* translations in Europe—indeed, in existence—are Samuel ibn Tibbon's.[44] However, the *Guide* as translated by Judah al-Ḥarizi and the fact of its use in certain circles was by no means unknown. Jewish readers as early as the middle of the fourteenth century were aware of the tensions inherent in the liminal space between the two translations and fiction became one of the modes through which those tensions could be explored. Another hotly contested work by Maimonides, his *Treatise on the Doctrine of Resurrection*,[45] is associated with a fictional paratextual element, in this case a preface, written no later than the middle of the fourteenth century but copied and recopied through the sixteenth.[46] The character of the preface has, like the Alexander colophon, been debated and dismissed as confusingly counterfactual, but a reading of the text less obsessed with the truth of it clearly yields a sense of the text as a work in line with other great prefaces attached to Hebrew-language Arabizing literary works, and even the literary prefaces attached to works of philosophy and theology. The preface, narrated in the voice of an otherwise unidentified Joseph ben Joel, recounts the narrator's efforts to find a copy of the *Treatise*, and the necessity that these efforts provoked to seek various translations back and forth between Hebrew and Arabic; the preface ultimately enumerates five translations and retranslations. This text, like the Alexander colophon, suggests an understanding on the part of readers of the fraught and complex history of translating the Maimonidean corpus. These literary counterfactuals further reflect a tendency, from the late Middle Ages moving forward, of its readers to use fiction and paratext as a way of grappling with that complexity. Nevertheless, they reflect the state of affairs in many Ashkenazic yeshivot around the time when these texts were copied in the sixteen century, which saw renewed interest in the *Guide* and a revisiting of many of the issues surrounding Maimonides' work that cropped up as it was being written and in the thirteenth century, in the wake of Maimonides' death, including those surrounding translation and transmission as well as those that attempted to reconcile religious belief and philosophical reason. In *The Historian's Craft*, the founder of the *Annales* school, Marc Bloch, writes: "Above all, a fraud is, in its way, a piece of evidence. Merely to prove that [it] . . . is not authentic is to avoid error, but not to acquire knowledge."[47] These fictions of Maimonideanism are more than error or even fraud, representing a medium through which Ashkenazic pietists could puzzle through knowledge to a broader historical and spiritual truth.

Ashkenazic *ḥasidut* was aware of Maimonides' work and the controversies it engendered from its earliest days, and there have been connections between the pietist movement and the nascent, competing Maimonidean movement at least as early as the end of Samuel ibn Tibbon's lifetime and the Maimonidean controversies of 1230–32,[48] largely those that were apparently designed, if unsuccessfully, to quell tensions between rationalists and kabbalists.[49] Ashkenazic reception of the Judaeo-Arabic philosophical corpus has, necessarily and from the outset, been colored by the types of translations that were available to readers and their awareness and knowledge of other translations; and much of that came through the Tibbonid project.[50] Two compelling examples in his overview of the response of Ashkenazic pietism to the Maimonidean controversies as they occurred in Aragon, Catalonia, and Provence illustrate this phenomenon. In one case, Joseph Dan writes about the extent to which Sa'adia Gaon was accepted into anti-rationalist kabbalistic tradition because such a tradition, explicitly in the absence of access to Judah ibn Tibbon's word-for-word translation and related lexicographic study, could accept Sa'adia as a compiler of tradition rather than as the author of Greek-style "dialectics," a term used pejoratively to refer to philosophical reasoning.[51] Another, and very early, example comes in the thirteenth-century reworking by one of the founders of the pietist movement, Judah of Regensburg, of another work of Andalusi theology, *Kitāb al-Radd wa-l-dalīl fi-l-dīn al-dhalīl,* written by Judah ha-Levi around 1140, translated into Hebrew by Judah ibn Tibbon, and commonly known as the *Kuzari*. The work is a philosophically informed dialogue between a central Asian king and a philosopher and Christian and Muslim clerics; when those three fail to satisfy the king's curiosity about how he might behave in a way that is pleasing to God, he deigns to consult with a Jewish interlocutor and is ultimately so compelled by the interlocutor's answers that he and all his subjects convert to Judaism. In Judah of Regensburg's version, three Jewish scholars present their perspectives—one Saadianic, one Maimonidean, and one based in the thinking of Abraham ibn Ezra—to an individual described as an Arab king of Spain who, by the end, converts to Judaism.[52] Fiction was comfortably one of the textual modes through which contemporaneous Ashkenazic thinkers reckoned with the Maimonidean controversies, and through which even the usually anti-rationalist pietists could assimilate philosophical thinking. As we see, only shortly after Samuel ibn Tibbon and Judah al-Ḥarizi created their respective translations of the *Guide*, Ashkenazic thinkers were participating in the debates over how best to understand and transmit Maimonides' work on completely different terms, ones that were ambivalent, at best, in their approach to philosophy and that did not yet account for differences in translation style but that did utilize fiction and error as a means to do so.[53]

The interface between Maimonideanism and *ḥasidut* had largely died down by the period that we identify in Europe as the Middle Ages but was then renewed and continued to develop in early modernity. Elchanan Reiner has documented a variety of sixteenth-century debates and disputations about Maimonideanism, the dissemination of esoteric ideas, and the methods of understanding the *Guide* in Hebrew. For example, he describes two related disagreements over Maimonideanism that took place in the Polish city of Poznan in the latter half of the 1550s. Those two debates staked out terrain that will be immediately recognizable to students of twelfth-century debates over the role of rationalism in religion and the thirteenth-century ones that followed, having to do with the dissemination of esoterica: in the first instance, one young yeshiva student argued that philosophical pursuits were tantamount to heresy, but the defenders of Maimonides among the student's peer group prevailed to the point that he was ultimately gagged and prohibited from expressing his view. In the second instance a rabbi delivered sermons to defend himself against charges made by his son-in-law in mishnaic terms that he, the rabbi, was reliant on "Homeric books"—yet another derogatory term for works of Greek philosophical reasoning—in explicating text and extrapolating theological positions.[54] Reiner distinguishes between the thirteenth- and sixteenth-century iterations of these debates: "I am not arguing that nothing happened in Ashkenazic Jews' intellectual world in the sixteenth century, or that their culture was a direct continuation of that of medieval tradition, without change. Far from it."[55] Nevertheless, the terms upon which they took place bear a striking resemblance to one another and thus the rhetoric and material supports are likewise similar.

Conclusion

The strange nature of the colophon of MS Heb. Suppl. 103, a seeming complete non-sequitur with respect to the text to which it was attached and the cultural-historical context in which it appears, in fact speaks directly to the renewed interest across the board in issues of *Guide* dissemination and interpretation, with translation and the interpretive tension between word-for-word and sense-for-sense techniques standing as synecdoche for the broader issues at stake, three hundred years apart. The circumstances that spurred interest in the issues that were tackled during the thirteenth-century Maimonidean controversies in Spain and France were, by the sixteenth century in Ashkenaz, distinct, even if they took place on similar terms and produced similar outcomes. One of these outcomes was the rise of fictional paratexts implicated in the dissemination of the work of Maimonides and the desirability of codices containing these elements. This codex that troubles with its paratextual elements—the colophon read in conjunction with the owners' marks—requires Sepharad, the prestige of Arabic and of Islamicate culture, knowledge of the debates over rationalism, and a keen ability to participate in the international book trade and finds them entangled together and with readers' lives in an Ashkenazic readership that, mutually entangled, requires the foundations of a library culture that allows it to engage with Andalusi intellectual tradition in a palatable way.

Chapter 11

Pollution and Purity in Near Eastern Jewish, Christian, and Muslim Crusading Rhetoric

Uri Shachar

Following the work of Mary Douglas and Jonathan Z. Smith, modern scholars often see systems of ritual purity as symbolic structures that mark and regulate communal boundaries.[1] Communities are thought to employ purity laws so as to map notions of "self" and "other" on spatial, cultural, and bodily borders. But idioms of purity/impurity also employ a curious dialectic, in which the very means of separation emerges as the one that facilitates inclusion;[2] sources of pollution, that is, also function as agents of ablution.[3] Blood, to take a prime example, circumscribes communities by separating them from the polluted "other," but also connects individuals and peoples.[4] Purity laws achieve this dialectic of separation and inclusion by building on the transmutable nature of key substances.

The example of the crusading Near East shows that not only laws but purity rhetoric itself works the very same dialectic, by capitalizing on the potent multifarious nature, not of substances, but rather of tropes and symbolic gestures. Indeed, many authors in the Near East deemed the notion of impurity helpful in establishing wars as mandated by God for the purification of His sacred places from defilement. Instead of assuming, however, that ideas about impurity were cultivated in isolation, this essay suggests that these very idioms were shaped through a complicated dynamic of exchange and entanglement between neighboring cultures. Claims for purity and charges of contamination became vehicles of interdependence, not only carrying messages of hostility but also marking the intercommunal space from which they derived meaning and to which they contributed.

The Impurity of Saracens in Early Frankish Literature

Notions of pollution, as many historians of the Latin East have noted, played an important role in Christian crusade rhetoric.[5] Consistent with the general tendency of early commentators and crusade ideologues to admonish Islam as a pagan heresy and to vilify Muslims as dangerous idolaters, time and again authors announced and condemned the impurity of the Saracens.[6] Nevertheless, over the course of the twelfth and thirteenth centuries Frankish purification rhetoric increased both in volume and sophistication. Authors came to employ a more abstract impurity idiom to serve a spatial terminology that conveyed theodicic claims regarding the territories of the Latin Kingdom of Jerusalem.

In most early crusade chronicles authors invoked the charge of pollution quite simply to convey a degree of hostility or a measure of erroneousness that was attributed to the Saracen foe. Raymond of Aguilers, for example, a participant in the First Crusade, chronicled the sentiments of the Franks upon their arrival to the foothills of Jerusalem in 1099: "We pray that the Lord may . . . exact judgment on His enemies, who obtained unjustly the places of his Passion and burial, and *defiled* [contaminant] them."[7] In a similar fashion, Robert the Monk[8] maintained that "the Holy Sepulcher of the Lord our Savior, [had been] in the possession of an *impure people* [immundis gentibus]."[9] What is more, in his account of Pope Urban II's speech, Robert describes the wretched state of the Eastern church by stating that Muslims dismantled altars after soiling them with their own filth and that they were polluting Christian churches by smearing the blood of circumcision on the walls.[10]

Early chroniclers, in other words, tended to concentrate on the insulting practices that Muslims were said to have performed in sites that were considered holy to Christianity, and on a sense in which Muslims were, in themselves, inherently impure. Accounts of pollution in early Frankish chronicles furthermore carried an implicit assumption that the contamination that Muslims were thought to effect was one that could be rectified immediately by expulsion of the wrongdoers and the repossession of the sites in Christian hands. The second half of the twelfth century, however, saw a shift in the way Frankish authors employed the theme of purity in depicting Muslims and conceptualizing the consequence of their presence in Palestine. Beginning with William of Tyre's (d. 1184) highly influential chronicle we find a more subtle attempt to map events onto historical and biblical frameworks, such that the very unbelieving presence of Muslims was thought to have a contaminating influence that both evoked and defined abstract spatial categories.[11]

William's intervention on Muslim impurity begins by invoking the generic trope of churches-turned-to-stables.[12] His account of Pope Urban II's famous Claremont address begins by stating,[13] "The revered places . . . have been made sheepfolds and stables for cattle";[14] but he quickly moves on to invert this trope: "The Church of the Holy Resurrection, the resting place of the dormant Lord, endures the rule [of the Muslims], and is desecrated by the filth of those who have no part in the resurrection, but are destined to burn forever, as straw [*stipula*] for everlasting flames."[15] Building on an image from Obadiah 1:18, William suggests that it is rather the Muslims, not the symbolic livestock, who are the cause for pollution. They turned the church into a stable and consequently they will, themselves, burn like the straw they fed the beasts. William's argument continues to employ a rhetorical symmetry: "The impious Saracens, heretical devotees [*sectatrix*] of a defiled religion, have pressed for a long time with tyrannical violence the holy places, where the feet of the Lord had stood."[16] Instead of worshipping Christ in the very place where his own blood was spilled for the sake of humanity, Muslims slay those Christians who refuse to "serve the impurity of the [Saracen] people, to deny the name of the living God, and to blaspheme with sacrilegious lips."[17]

For William, then, Muslim impurity is tied to the refusal, or inability, to recognize the soteriology that imbues space with meaning: the place not only where Christ, the historical figure, is "dormant" and will become resurrect, but also where he is believed to have stood, where he "spilled his blood," and where his name bears a living presence. Muslims, in other words, are thought to defile this space, but at the same time they *are* defiled *because* of this space; as a result, that is, of the sacred history that is encapsulated in it. What is more, the impurity that William attributes to this "defiled tradition" is not one that can be reversed merely by the expulsion of the Saracens from the Holy City. The faithlessness of the Muslim occupants of the sacred sites, in their refusal to accept the soteriological vision which renders that very space sacred, demands a full ritual purification, which is indeed how William portrays the Frankish conquest of the city in 1099. But before we look at how William of Tyre and successive Frankish authors contemplated the notion of purifying Muslim superstition, a theme to which we return in the second half of this essay, we first turn to notions of impurity in jihad poetry.

Ayyubid Literature: Faith, Pollution, Space Purification

It is hard to overemphasize the centrality of impurity and ritual purification in Ayyubid jihad literature from its birth in the second half of the twelfth century.[18] Much like its Frankish counterpart, Ayyubid purification rhetoric gradually came to revolve around a highly charged and historically pregnant spatial terminology that used categories of impurity to convey theodicic claims regarding contested territories.

The first half of the century saw surprisingly few reactions by Near Eastern Muslim authors to the Frankish conquest of Syria and Palestine, much less voices calling for jihad against the invaders.[19] This, however, began to change around the time of the Second Crusade and especially after Nur al-Din seized Damascus in 1154. With the rise of the Zengid dynasty to power, consolidating much of northern Syria and the *Jazirah* under one rule, there emerged a widespread interest in waging jihad to drive out the Franks from the Near East. In the 1150s, religious authorities in Damascus and Cairo began systematically to erect a corpus of literature that articulated an ideology on Holy War against the heretics and unbelievers, arguing for the centrality of this rite as an expression of spiritual commitment.[20] Subsequently, the region saw a flood of prose and verse attacks on the Franks, condemning their presence in the Near East, celebrating their few defeats, and calling for a full-fledged war to drive them out.

As part of this polemical stance toward the Franks, there emerged an increased desire to amplify claims regarding the sanctity of the land, on behalf of which Muslims advocated Holy War. Authors invoked, and at times revived, various genres and rhetorical traditions that sought to transform the space and its symbolic dimensions by relocating it within the broader framework of Islamic sacred history and culture.[21] The middle decades of the twelfth century, for example, saw a sharp rise in the number of compositions celebrating the merits and sacred history of cities in the region.[22] Particularly significant were *Faḍā'il al-Quds* (Praise of Jerusalem) treatises, which sought to cement the sacral status of Jerusalem, and especially of the al-Aqsa Mosque, vis-à-vis the other sites considered sacred to Islam.[23] The notion of ritual purification played an important role in these theological and rhetorical efforts to ground the sanctity of lands under Frankish control, which Muslim regimes hoped to repossess.[24] Mid-twelfth-century Ayyubid authors drew heavily on the foundations that generations of exegetes and poets had established in the Arabic tradition of purity rhetoric.[25] They put these traditional motifs to new uses, however, and introduced important changes: one of the most noticeable features in Ayyubid purity rhetoric has to do with the fact that it employed a more abstract notion of space, which authors imagined needed to be cleansed from Christian presence, and the means through which it was thought to be cleansed. Mid-twelfth-century accounts featured a distinct focus on the idea that the presence of unbelievers carried consequences for the sanctity of the land, and on the performance of purification rituals whose purpose was to rehabilitate the defiled space into its former sacred, Muslim status.

A telling example is to be found in the Diwan of Ibn al-Munir, a poet who early in life had fled his native Tripoli which was conquered by the Franks in 1102. He then joined the Zengid court of Damascus and composed numerous poems encouraging jihad against the infidels. Ibn al-Munir dedicated a panegyric to Nur al-Din, following the short-lived conquest of Tortosa in 1152. The poet was taken mostly by Nur al-Din's ability quickly to reintroduce Islam into a space that had become "infected" by disbelief:

> The land in the villages [around Tortosa] bore infidelity.[26]
> On the day before [i.e., during the conquest], Nur al-Din treated the fortification [*'awāṣim*] to a ritual cleansing [*ghasala*], [purifying it] from its filths [*adrānihim*].
> [As a result,] on the day after, the coastal plains were destroyed
> Such that [Nur al-Din] did not leave in all the land between *'al-Ḥawlatayn'* and *'al-Amid'*
> A cushion for the vengeful or blood-thirsty man.
> And [Nur al-Din] has removed the idols from the region and turned the trinity into negation.[27]

Significantly, it is from the contamination of *adrān*, a filth associated with disbelief, that Nur al-Din is said to cleanse the land. Ibn Munir, furthermore, portrays the return of Islam to the castle and its surroundings by having the Zengid Prince figuratively subject the space to the ritual bath (*ghusl*) which pious worshipers are obligated to undergo before prayer in order to cleanse from major pollution.[28] Nor is the choice of words in defining the space in which this ritual is thought to have taken place by any means incidental. By invoking the term *'awāṣim* Ibn Munir echoes a charged chapter in the history of the contact between Christianity and Islam.[29] For the castle of Tortosa was, in fact, the starting point of a fortress line, called *al-'awāṣim*, which stretched across the frontier between the early Islamic state and the Byzantine Empire in the eighth and ninth centuries.[30] This period, characterized by periodic raids and recurrent acts of militant heroism, was inscribed in Muslim history as a time of heightened spiritual virtuosity, to which Muslim authors often turn as a literary trope.[31] Ibn al-Munir, in other words, ties his verse to an illustrious tradition of war poetry and establishes Nur al-Din's act of figurative purification as one whose rehabilitating effect conveys a powerful claim about the spirituality and history of the region.

Metaphorical figurations of ritually purifying spatial units, such as the *'awāṣim*, was part of the Ayyubid response to crusading rhetoric in an attempt to articulate a spatial terminology that conveyed spiritual claims with regard to the territories of the Latin Kingdom of Jerusalem. The category of "Holy Land," however, did not carry the same soteriological and geographic meaning for Muslim rhetoricians as it did for their Christian contemporaries.[32] Ibn al-Munir's verse, therefore, is an early example of an attempt to apply classical Islamic tropes of pollution and purification on historically loaded spatial categories with the purpose of tracing putative boundaries of territorial sanctity.

Subsequent authors applied this trope to a variety of political contexts. Ibn Nabih (d. 1222), for example, in a panegyric to his patron al-Malik al-Ashraf (d. 1237), celebrated the return of Damietta to Muslim hands after it had been under Frankish control for a little under two years (November 1219 to September 1221), during the Fifth Crusade:

> He fills the land [*arḍ*] with justice [*'adl*] after it was occupied [by the Franks]
> The swords of [al-Malik al-Ashraf] expose the rapacity that used to be inside it.
> Oh conquest of Damietta, what dignity is left
> Of he who was [there] before; you are his destroyer.
> . . . You cleansed [*ṭahharta*] its high *miḥrab* and its *minbar*
> From their pollution, after you shook its pillars.

You shattered the idol [*timthal*] of the messiah
Despite those who mistake it for the divine.
Your diligence [*jiddak*] resembled that of Abraham
Your sublime intention agreed with his.[33]

In describing al-Ashraf's conquest of Damietta, the author is quite obviously invoking a highly loaded Qur'anic episode, that of Abraham destroying the idols (Q 21:51–70). Many commentators view this scene as one of the most powerful, if enigmatic, articulations of the nascence of monotheism in the Qur'an, and Ibn Nabih ties the two stories together in an interesting way.[34] For Abraham, who is said to have grown anxious about the cult of idols among his kinsmen, decides to shatter all but the largest one. When asked if he was responsible for the destruction he replies: "No, it was done by this one, the largest of them all; ask them, if they can speak [Q 21:63]." Abraham, as al-Tabari glosses, was hoping that the idolaters would recognize that their gods can neither speak nor defend themselves, and consequently would turn to worship the one God.[35] Ibn Nabih insists that al-Ashraf shared with Abraham both superior qualities and good intentions. But instead of trying to instruct the wrongdoers on the erroneousness of their belief, he has the Ayyubid prince demolish the Christological presence, represented by the one messianic idol. Rather than hoping to amend their incredulity, in other words, al-Ashraf is seen to cleanse the pollution of Christian disbelief after which justice spills into the land. Finally, with the notion of the eschatological trembling pillars (e.g., Q 56:4), the purification of Damietta places it on a soteriological plane that begins with the advent of monotheism and ends with the return of Islam, and ascribes al-Ashraf a powerful role in this drama of sacred history.

If in the verses of Ibn al-Munir and Ibn Nabih the association between purifying the land and the spilling of Christian blood is understated, for some subsequent poets this motif lies proudly at the very center of the conquest narrative. In fact, numerous authors in the second half of the twelfth century and onward penned versified figurations of conquest narratives, in which Christian blood was taken figuratively to be the cleansing agent with which the ritual purification of rehabilitated land is performed. 'Imad al-Din al-Iṣfahani, one of the most eloquent and popular poets of the Ayyubid period, employed this notion in several of his most moving verses celebrating Saladin's victories. In 1174, he composed a poem praising Saladin's political triumphs in Egypt, in which he alluded to the descent to Egypt of the biblical/

Qur'anic Joseph, with whom the sultan shared a first name.[36] The poet, then, asks that the sultan channel his success to attain a further victory:

> Go and conquer Jerusalem [*al-Quds*], and shed upon it
> Blood, the flow of which would cleanse [*yanẓufī*] it.[37]
> Lead the Hospitallers [*al-Isbitār*] to damnation
> And collapse the ceilings on the bishop [*al-usquf*].
> Clean that land from the presence of the infidels
> And Allah will reward you with a cleansing in the Mawqif [place of gathering associated with the Day of Judgment].[38]

Al-Iṣfahani recited this poem on the occasion of his entrance to the Holy City in 1187—after, that is, it was established that the conquest of Jerusalem had not, in fact, involved any bloodshed at all. After Balian of Ibelin had famously negotiated the terms with Saladin, the Franks handed over the city peacefully and ransomed themselves in exchange for safe passage.[39] Nevertheless, the poet chose to revive this image, where rivers of blood bring about the ritual cleansing of the city as well as a spiritual purification of the celebrated sultan-warrior. The context in which the poem was composed, in 1174, capitalizes on the conflation between Saladin and his biblical namesake, Joseph, in order to wish that the descent to Egypt might be followed by a return to Jerusalem. In 1187, however, it is the cleansing motif that helps al-Iṣfahani convey a measure of irony in how the blood that had been placed maliciously on Joseph's garment was, finally, the blood through which Saladin drove the pollution of the enemy away.[40] Reminiscent of Qur'an 16:26 ("Allah struck at the foundation of their [the unbelievers'] building, and then the roof fell down upon them"), the flow of blood is thought not only to cleanse the contamination of disbelief, but also to demolish the structural and symbolic presence of the Christian faith and its militant manifestation in the form of the Hospitaller Order.

Another Ayyubid poem provides a particularly striking example of how Muslim authors charged the technical terminology of ritual purification with political and spatial meanings. The following verse by al-Qaysarani, whose family too was driven away from Acre and Caesarea in the beginning of the twelfth century, conceptualizes Holy War as involving an act of purification whose purpose is to restore the sanctity of conquered lands and to rehabilitate them as Muslim space. The poet enlists the notion of ritual purification in order to ground a claim about the sanctity of the "coastal plain" to Islam.[41]

Al-Qaysarani penned a panegyric to Nur al-Din, calling on him to carry out jihad to conquer Jerusalem and reappropriate the coast:

Go and fill the earth with beauty and light
. . . Let there be no end to this attack
whose end in al-Aqsa has been decreed.
Let the Temple [*bayt al-maqdis*] be purified [*tāhir*]
By nothing but the stream of their blood.
If he performs ablution-by-sand [*tatayammam*] on the coastal plain
[*sāhil al-baḥr*]
Then, undoubtedly, he will reign over it.

As in the previous examples, this excerpt too is saturated with Qur'anic language that alludes to the laws of ritual purification. The verses draw metaphorically on the procedures of preparation for prayer, which Qur'an 5:6 lays out. First, the author suggests that Nur al-Din should perform a ritual cleansing of the Temple, but instead of water he should apply the blood of the defeated Franks. Next, al-Qaysarani refers to a procedure of purification through the use of sand, designed for those who are not in the vicinity of a water source. In discussing the rehabilitation of Jerusalem and the coast on the basis of these two purification rites, al-Qaysarani is in fact suggesting that the subject undergoing ablution—the land—is in a state of *major* pollution. Furthermore, this poem echoes another Qur'anic notion, which involves preparing not only the body of the pious for prayer, but also the ground upon which the ceremony is to take place: "And We charged Ibrahim and Isma'il, [saying] Purify [*ṭahhira'*] My House for those who perform *ṭawaf* [circumambulate] and those who are staying [there] for worship and those who bow and prostrate [in prayer]."[42] In keeping with this scriptural proof text, the poet, in other words, calls the sultan to perform an act of ritual purification in order to render the space fit and adequate for prayer. By applying Christian blood on its own soil, the land metaphorically rids itself from the contamination of the Franks and is made worthy of religious ceremony. Al-Qaysarani, therefore, utilizes the theme of purification in order to give account to the sacral dimension of the land that is to be redeemed by holy war.

Throughout the thirteenth century, generations of Ayyubid authors, too, integrated this motif into their literary repertoire. They both embedded into their compositions verses that drew continuity between defining acts of ritual ablution, and reproduced verses that by the beginning of the century had become canonical. The Damascene Ayyubid chronicler and poet Ibn Waṣil, for example, reflected on a short episode in which al-Malik al-Nasir Da'ud, the ruler of Karak, raided Jerusalem in 1239.[43] Nasir Da'ud, we are told, laid a surprise siege to the Frankish citadel in Jerusalem. After gaining control over the castle, the Ayyubid ruler demolished it and took down the Tower of David: "He took hold of Jerusalem and purified it from Christians, driving the Franks, who survived the attack, back to their cities."[44] Ibn Waṣil continues to report that an envoy of the Abbasid caliph arrived and praised Nasir Da'ud, pointing to the similarities between him and his uncle, the late Saladin:

> Al-Aqsa Mosque maintains a traditional custom
> If it is inhabited [by unbelievers]
> The Lord sets victory on the blood of the unbelievers
> While al-Nasir [Salah al-Din] purified it the first time
> al-Nasir [Da'ud] purified it for the last time.

The author, to be sure, employs the metaphorical power of the enemy's blood as an agent of ritual purification in conflating two scenes of conquest that, in fact, did not involve any bloodshed. As mentioned above, in the summer of 1187 the Frankish inhabitants of Jerusalem opted to pay a ransom and to evacuate the city peacefully. In 1239 the majority of the inhabitants fled, hearing that the Ayyubid prince was nearing the city with siege equipment, before al-Nasir arrived. A small group took shelter in the Tower of David, but they too surrendered a week later. This rendering of the events, in other words, demonstrates the symbolic power that literary accounts of militant purification came to hold in late Ayyubid culture. The fantasy that conquest of Frankish territories culminates in a figurative purification of the land involving the use of water, soil, or the very blood of the enemy came to occupy an important part in the rhetorical repertoire of Ayyubid authors in their efforts to put forth political, spiritual, and literary claims of ownership over contested space.

Cleansing Sacred Space in Frankish Literature

This trope, apparently, traveled to Near Eastern Frankish and Jewish literatures as well, where it took on some new meanings and usages, leaving others behind. The trajectory with which part one of this essay was occupied traced the emergence of a notion in Frankish literature that tied Muslim impurity with a hermeneutical misapprehension regarding the sanctity of space. For William of Tyre, an act of figurative purification was necessary in order to cleanse sacred spaces from the presence of a Muslim refusal to accept the soteriology that brought about the sanctity of that very space. It is to William of Tyre's chronicle that we now return, for it is here that for the first time in Frankish literature the notion of Muslim blood cleansing the Holy City is introduced.

Most early accounts of the First Crusade famously feature vivid images of the massacre that the crusading army witnessed upon entering the city in 1099. Chroniclers provided enthusiastic descriptions of the blood-soaked streets: the anonymous author of the *Gesta Francorum*, for example, reported that the Temple had "streamed with the blood of the slain,"[45] and Fulcher of Chartres further specified that the blood rose ankle-high. Raimond of Aguiler similarly recounted that "in the Temple of Solomon and the portico crusaders blood rose to the knees and bridles of the horses."[46] However, none of these authors, even those who showed concerned about the contaminating influence of the Muslims, insinuated that the massacre itself carried a purifying function. Robert the Monk, in fact, goes further in the opposite direction, suggesting that the bloodshed itself had an added contaminating effect: "The streets of the city were dyed with rivers of blood and strewn with corpses of the dead. . . . There was not a place in the whole city and no ditch which was not defiled with their corpses or blood."[47] Not only, in other words, does the blood in Robert's account not have a purifying effect, but it is said to have further contaminated the city.

In contrast to these early accounts, William of Tyre turns the episode of bloody conquest into a moment of purification. The portrayal of the scene builds on a passage found in Raymond of Aguilers' account, which William altered in a telling manner. Witnessing the Muslim bloodshed in the Temple, Raymond commented on the reestablishment of divine order through the collocation of sin and punishment: "I believe that it is by just judgment, that the same place spilled [*exciperet*] their blood, which had borne for such a long time their blasphemies of God."[48] William, in his turn, dwells on the connection between the nature of the sins the Muslims perpetrated against the Holy City, and the spilling of their blood there: "Certainly by the just judgment of God it came to be, that those who had profaned the sanctuary of the Lord through superstitious rites, and had rendered [it] alien to the faithful, should wash the sins of their disgrace by the spilling of blood there and die, [thereby] cleansing it [the Temple]."[49] William's use of Raymond's phrase brings his symmetrical rhetoric of impurity, which he had employed to introduce the crusade in Urban II's speech, to a closure. The blood that was spilled in the same place where the Saracens had diffused their false beliefs also helped to cleanse the contaminating effect of their very sins.

Sometime during the first half of the thirteenth century, William of Tyre's chronicle, originally composed in Latin, was translated into Old French.[50] With subtle changes, the anonymous translator infused his version with the sensibilities and ambitions of his own time. The translator, then, rendered the above mentioned passage: "It was indeed appropriate, that the faithless unbelievers, who had debased the sacred Temple of our Lord, and defiled it with mosques and false Muslim faith, would pay the same price there; and that [by] their blood they [the holy places] would be washed [*respanduz*], where they spilled [*espandues*] the defilements of their unbelief."[51] This rendering features a growing emphasis on the sense that the sins of the Muslims lay also in their unbelieving presence in a space that is considered holy to Christianity. It furthermore draws a link between the diffusion of sins and the ritualized washing of the space with expiatory blood. The blood of the Saracens, therefore, is felt as if wiping away the stains of their contaminating presence, and its spilling is part of the ritual that was necessary to restore the holy city to its original owners and sanctity.

William of Tyre died before the fall of Jerusalem to Ayyubid hands in 1187, but subsequent Frankish authors lived to see and portray this dramatic event. The shift in Frankish purification rhetoric, which began with William of Tyre and continued into the thirteenth century, is particularly telling precisely due to the difference in circumstances between both conquests of the city, in 1099 and 1187. Although early crusade historians were ostensibly occupied with questions of impurity, none of them explicitly developed the notion of the conquest as an act of purification or of the Muslim bloodbath as a metaphorical process of ritual cleansing. In contrast, after 1187 both Muslim and Frankish authors repeatedly invoked images of a ritually purifying bloodbath, although the Ayyubid conquest of Jerusalem did not actually involve any bloodshed. Late twelfth-century Frankish purification rhetoric, in other words, came to share with its contemporaneous Ayyubid accounts some key elements. Authors of Arabic, Old French, and Latin accounts entertained the idea that contamination of unbelief is not remedied by mere expulsion, but rather demands an act of metaphorical ritual purity with water or blood. Two short narratives demonstrate that Frankish authors were well aware of the fact that these ideas had become widespread among their Muslim contemporaries.

Several versions of an Old French narrative survive in local historiographic traditions relating how Saladin took possession of the holy sites after conquering Jerusalem. The sultan, one chronicler relates, "did not want to depart the city before performing worship there, and before *Christianity* is driven out." He is said to have asked his sister to join him in carrying out a prayer in the Temple. When she heard this request, "she packed twenty camels with *rose water* [*yaue/eve/aigue rose*]" and headed to Jerusalem. When Saladin and his sister entered the temple, they "saw to the cleansing [*laver*] of the grounds in the same way that prelates rehabilitated churches that had been violated. For Saracens believe that pork, or men who eat pork, must not enter into that Temple."[52]

This account demonstrates the author's familiarity with the Muslim trope: namely, the desire to convert and reappropriate a space that was contaminated by the presence of Christian faith, by invoking the framework of ritual purification. The narrative appears to be well founded, as numerous Arabic accounts of this same episode also celebrate the use of "rose water [*ma' al-ward*]."[53] Medieval Muslim traditions invoke the use of rose water—in preparation for prayer, or sprinkling on the Ka'bah—in celebratory occasions that feature an unusually heightened spiritual elevation. The Frankish author, however, does not only portray sympathetically the Muslim wish to cleanse the sacred precinct, for which the sultan brought special means; he seems to take advantage of the fact that in Old French "*aigue rose*" could designate either rose water or *red* water. The French-speaking readers, therefore, were likely to appreciate this double entendre, in which the rose water used by Saladin to cleanse the Temple is also reminiscent of the red water (blood) that the Franks had used to do the same, eighty-eight years earlier.

The anonymous author of a text written after the Third Crusade, probably an eyewitness Templar or Hospitaller, engages with the religious and doctrinal investments that were involved in the Muslim desire to purify the Holy City. *De Expugnatione terrae sanctae per saladinum libellus* relates the negotiations between the Franks and Saladin that preceded the Ayyubid conquest of Jerusalem and their immediate aftermath. In the first encounter with the Frankish delegation, the sultan puts forth a firm position that he grounds on the authority of the religious establishment: "Verily, I heard frequently from our scholars [*sapientibus*] *al-faqihs* [*alphachinis*][54] that Jerusalem cannot be purified [*mundari*] unless it is cleansed [*lavetur*] with the blood of Christians;

and I wish to take their counsel on that matter."[55] In face of the sultan's refusal to negotiate an agreement that could save the loss of more lives, the second Frankish delegation reciprocates with an equally belligerent statement, declaring that if an agreement cannot be reached "they would remain [to fight over the city] until their own fall."[56] Both sides, however, end up retracting from their original positions, and adopt a compromise that—in the eyes of the author—is disgraceful from the point of view of *both* traditions.

Instead of waging war in defense of the city, the Franks agree on the amount to be paid in return for the ransom of each Christian inhabitant. Rather than pious warriors, they have become, in the mind of the author, "the worst of merchants." Like "that vile merchant" Judas, the author explains, the inhabitants "sold Christ and the Holy City."[57] Judas, however, was punished for his crime: with the money he received for "selling" Christ, he purchased a field where he "burst in the middle . . . and all his entrails of malignity gushed out," which is why it became known as "the field of blood."[58] There is, therefore, no precedent for the Franks' decision to abandon the city: "Nowhere have we read [in Scripture] that the Jews had deserted the holy of holies without the *spilling of blood* and hard struggle; never had they turned it over willingly."[59] Jerusalem, the author admonishes, "was turned over to the hands of the impious [Muslims] by the impious [Franks],"[60] immersed as it was "in ashes, and in the pollution of [the Franks'] crimes."[61]

When the Ayyubid army finally marched into Jerusalem, the Muslims found a city contaminated with Christian crimes. But the agreement between Saladin and the Franks to avoid an armed clash meant that Christian blood was not available for use in cleansing. According to the Muslim's own perspective, therefore, they were unable to perform ritual purification. Instead—the author explains in an account that, again, stresses the role of religious authorities and demonstrates his familiarity with the Muslim rites and terminology—they exacerbate the state of the city's contamination:

> The Faqihs [*alfachini*] and Qaḍis [*cassini*]—ministers of the obviously impious error, bishops and priests according to the opinion of the Saracens—first ascended to the *Templum Domini*—which they call "The House of God,"[62] and in which they have great trust of salvation—as if to pray and for religious [purposes], believing to purify [*mundare*] it. But with unclean [*spurticiis*] and horrifying [*horribilibus*] growls, they polluted [*polluerent*] it [the Temple] by

> bawling with polluted lips [*pollutis labiis*] the Law of Muhammad: 'Allah Akbar [*halla haucaber, halla haucaber*].'[63]

The Muslims proceeded to "contaminate [*coinquinaverunt*] all the places that surround the Temple."[64] Saladin's brother, furthermore, was responsible for invading the sanctified space on the other side of Mount Zion and polluting it through their "drinking, feasting, and exuberance."[65] The reluctance of the Franks to shed their own blood in protection of the city, in other words, frustrated the desire of Muslims to use that very blood for their purification ritual. In the absence of Christian blood, the Ayyubid clerics, like makeshift muezzins who symbolize Muslim "soundscape," reappropriated the holy city by pronouncing publicly the supremacy and return of Allah. Finally, in the eyes of the anonymous author, the city remained polluted both by the crimes of the Franks against its sanctity and by the Ayyubids' clamorous adherence to the Muslim faith.

De Expugnatione terrae is a prime example of how Frankish authors aligned their notions of Muslim pollution on the Ayyubid trope of using the blood of Christians to cleanse conquered territory. But more generally, the many examples in Arabic, Latin, and old French, of authors who articulated a language of spatial sacrality that is predicated on categories of impurity, and who put forth conquest narratives which culminate in an allegorical cleansing of an unbelieving pollution, are a testimony to the intertwined literary culture that emerged in the crusading Near East. Both Frankish and Ayyubid authors utilized pollution rhetoric to think about the sanctity of land as well as of personal and spatial purification *through* each other. What is more, their rhetorical conventions came to denote not only notions of hostility and exclusion but also of the desire to take part in an intertwined literary space of co-production. Ritual purification of conquered territories, that is, became a rhetorical gesture that, hostile as much as it was in character, also encoded the self-conscious use of what emerged as a shared literary tradition. The fact that Jews who immigrated to Palestine in the thirteenth century chose also to frame their ideas about the Holy Land in terms of cleansing the land from major pollution caused by the presence of Christians and Muslims provides further evidence of the interconnected way in which authors put to use this motif.[66]

Purification and Conquest in Jewish Messianic Homilies

Over the course of the thirteenth century, Jewish scholars of French descent who immigrated to Acre as well as their successors established a rich corpus of messianic homilies.[67] Although unarmed and entertaining no immediate political ambitions, authors imagined the purpose of their passage to the Near East by drawing on a messianic framework. Sermons that constitute part of this corpus ascribed to the community of French émigrés the task of creating the circumstances necessary for the appearance of the messiah among them. After his arrival the émigrés are then imagined to partake in several cycles of triumph and defeat in which they eventually conquer Palestine and set in motion a series of eschatological events that bring about the end of time. The choice to utilize the framework of Holy War to discuss problems of spirituality and identity provided authors an opportunity to think about those questions through intellectual and rhetorical contacts both with their neighbors and with their own tradition.

One central motif that runs through this corpus has to do with the notion that, under Christian or Muslim rule, the Holy Land and the holy city of Jerusalem are in a state of pollution. As a result, the conquest of the land is thought to include several acts of ritual purification, with varying degrees of efficacy. In a way that seems to echo some of the motifs discussed above from Ayyubid and Frankish literatures, Jewish authors portrayed a personified figure of the Holy Land as undergoing a ritual bath, whose ablution also brings about the purification of the warriors involved in these messianic episodes.

The author of the "Homily on King Messiah," for example, who apparently participated in the largest of the thirteenth-century waves of immigration, in 1211, ends the introduction to his composition as follows: "Let no-one take it upon himself to say that the King Messiah will be revealed on an impure Land. . . . And let no one err to say that [the Messiah] will be revealed in the Land of Israel amid the Gentiles. Whoever makes this mistake and does not rush to make this happen, is disrespectful toward the King Messiah."[68] The task of the immigrants, in other words, is to prepare the Holy Land for the arrival of the messiah. The desired condition for this is one in which the land contains only "'practitioners of Torah [Jer. 2:8]' and 'the pious and men of deeds,' . . . and all whose hearts were stirred [Exod. 35:21, 29] and in whose soul was a spirit of purity and love of holiness." The author portrays this "Jewish Crusade" as one whose purpose is to prepare both the land and the spirits of the participants for messianic times. This marks the point in the narrative in which the author introduces the messiah, and begins to relate both the wars that he wages and the crucial participation of the émigrés. The messianic drama unfolds in several "acts" that revolve around the attempt, which at first fails and finally succeeds, to purify the Land of Israel.

Throughout this treatise, the author frames his desire to expel the foreigners from the land through the charge that they are unclean. Messiah-son-of-Jacob and the Israelite army, for example, are imagined to "'beat the King of Edom and the garrisons of Ishmael [1 Sam. 13:3]' who are in Jerusalem; and they will expel all of the uncircumcised, and 'the uncircumcised and the unclean shall never enter [it] again [Isa. 52:1].'" News about this initial success in subduing the polluted enemy spreads and draws additional members to join the army: "Israel will hear that the King Messiah will *putrefy* [cf. 1 Sam. 13:4] the uncircumcised, and [Israelites] from the four corners of the world will join him."[69] As if to exacerbate the decay that lies at the bottom of the heathens' corruption, the Israelites turn the impurity of the Christians against them, and use it to drive them away from the land of Israel.

The author of the *Homily on King Messiah* as well as his successors drew both on biblical and post-biblical categories of pollution, which are found ubiquitously in the early rabbinical halakhic, homiletic, and exegetical corpora.[70] However, these thirteenth-century messianic accounts creatively embedded them in new narrative frameworks and charged them with meanings that pertained directly to the spiritual and political experience of the Jews in the crusading Near East.

Nahmanides (d. 1270), for example, the renowned exegete and mystic who fled Iberia in 1267, invoked categories of impurity and sexual immorality in referring to the attitude of the Holy Land toward its foreign inhabitants.[71] Glossing Leviticus 26:32, Nahmanides famously maintained that "during all of our exiles our Land will not accept our enemies. . . . Since the time that we left it, it has not accepted any nation or people, and they all try to settle it, but to no avail."[72] Following Numbers 18:25, he further clarifies that "the land, which is the inheritance of God, will vomit whoever defiles it, and will not tolerate idolaters and those who practice incest [*'arayot*]."[73] A mid-century homily, paraphrasing the earlier "Vision of Daniel," seems to reframe Nahmanides' categories in a messianic narrative. This passage draws a connection between the polluting sins of the enemies and the measures that the Israelite army takes in order to restore a state of ritual purity: "A sinful ruler will emerge from the North, and will rule for three and a half years; he will commit a sin unlike any other from the creation of the world until its end; involving the copulation of sons with their mothers, and brothers with sisters and daughters with their fathers; and the impurity will be greater and more severe than any other described in the Torah. . . . The Lord will direct his fury against them, and he will spill his fire, and shower his water on them, and he will shake the seas and boil the waves [until Rome and Ishmael are obliterated]."[74] The King Messiah and God, in other words, are imagined to administer a metaphorical ritual immersion (*tevilah*) of the land in fire and water, in order to cleanse it from the state of impurity caused by the transgressions of the uncircumcised. Like their Muslim and Christian neighbors, therefore, Jewish authors invoked liturgical and legal categories that regulate the use of water in acts of moral and physical cleansing, and charged them with political, territorial meanings.

Furthermore, Jewish authors of messianic homiletic literature also entertained the use of blood as a means of purifying the land and its inhabitants. The author of a thirteenth-century version of the popular Ten Signs tradition, for example, enumerates the events that precede the arrival of the messiah. According to the second sign, God sends three "false messiahs" whose purpose is to attract followers from both the Israelite and the foreign communities, resulting in a dangerous cultural mix. Signs Four and Five describe how this is resolved: "Sign Four: The Lord sends rain from the heavens, for three days and three nights. But this will not be a rain of water, but rather of blood. Those who wrongfully followed the false messiahs [שלוחי שקר] drink from the blood and die. . . . Sign Five: The Lord then sends dew from the heavens for three days and three nights, which cleanses [מנקה] the blood that had descended upon the earth. This [dew] revives the grains, and the nations and [speakers of] tongues think that it is rain. But, in fact, it is dew."[75] The blood, in other words, helps identify the true believers from those who came to follow an erroneous faith. After the blood helps obliterate the wrongdoers—that is, to reach once again a state of social and religious purity—reviving dew is sent to cleanse the blood and restore the purity of the land.

Conclusion

The fantastical vision that blood kills, vacates, and cleanses the Holy Land from the defiled presence of the unbelieving enemy could be taken as a generic gesture of hostility. But an examination of the local rhetorical context in which it was put to use reveals that this and the other purification gestures were born out of a continuous intercultural dialectic between literary traditions that shared a tendency to take hold of opposite typologies and reorient them within new symbolic and political frameworks. Like their Christian and Muslim counterparts, thirteenth-century Jewish authors produced narratives about the purification of Jerusalem and of the Holy Land, and portrayed the conquest of the land as an act of ablution that was expected to cleanse the space from the presence of their impure neighbors. But the choice to frame their disposition toward the Holy Land through the vehicle of ritual purity was rhetorical rather than concrete. This rhetorical strategy put their corpus in contact not only with a long history of Jewish engagement with ideas of purity and warfare, but also with local living traditions of Ayyubid and Frankish literatures in which ideas on purity regularly breached and destabilized linguistic and cultural boundaries. Notions of contamination and ritual purification traveled within and across traditions and languages, taking on in the process some new meanings and usages, and leaving others behind.

Purification rhetoric, in other words, bears witness to a way in which these three neighboring cultures became meaningful to each other. Living side by side, occasionally in violent conflict and usually in a dialectic of suspicious and curious neighborliness, these cultures came to occupy a space of co-production, in which their very proximity shaped the language they used for thinking about their shared boundaries and entangled spiritualities. What is more, narratives about the impurity of the "enemy" provided authors with opportunities to mobilize a language that, in fact, took shape through the intellectual and cultural proximity to the very communities they, on the face of it, sought to exclude. Purification idioms that Frankish, Ayyubid, and Jewish authors employed, in other words, possessed the same multifarious quality as purity laws: they were born out of a highly refined intercultural dialectic that implemented strategies of exclusion, but also enabled acts of linguistic, political, and religious transgression, regularly breaching and destabilized cultural boundaries.

Chapter 12

Adoption and Adaptation: Judah ha-Levi's ציון הלא תשאלי לשלום אסיריך in Its Ashkenazic Environment

Elisabeth Hollender

Dedicated to the memory of Angel Sáenz-Badillos (1940–2013)

The existence of pervasive differences between Europe's two major medieval Jewish communities, usually summarized by the oversimplified pairing "Ashkenaz and Sepharad," has been among the basic assumptions of modern Jewish historiography, at least since the founding of *Wissenschaft des Judentums*.[1] This dichotomous model provided the underpinning for the notion that shares of Jewish culture were divided between Ashkenaz (Talmud study, piety, martyrdom) and Sepharad (rationalism, sciences, philosophy, aesthetics), and the corollary "myth of Sephardic supremacy"[2] that has long determined the attitudes toward medieval Judaism held by scholars and broader audiences. Contemporary scholarship has begun to argue that an approach is necessary and possible that does not contrast Sephardic rationality and Ashkenazic piety but aims at differentiated descriptions of the Jewish communities within their respective environments—as exemplified by the intellectual versatility of the tosafists in Ashkenaz and Tsarfat.[3] It has now been demonstrated that the communities of Ashkenaz and Sepharad were constantly in contact, despite the differences in their traditions, their environments, and the non-Jewish cultures in which they were embedded.

Recent studies trace the transmission of texts and ideas between medieval Jewish communities and their subsequent adaptation and incorporation into regional Jewish cultures.[4] In this context, "transmission" (and "transfer") refers to the intricate processes of choice and rejection, adoption and adaptation, change and reconstruction.[5] "Adaptation" is a key concept in intra-Jewish cultural transfer during the Middle Ages: even though Hebrew was the common language among Jewish communities, Hebrew texts (usually transmitted via standard travel routes) often arrived without the cultural and textual systems in which they had been embedded; the receiving community therefore needed to assign these imported cultural objects to existing slots in its cultural system or to create new positions for them. Thus, in their new settings, imported texts might not fulfill the same functions that they initially served.[6]

The example I discuss here is a poem by the prominent medieval Andalusian-Hebrew poet Judah ben Samuel ha-Levi, ציון הלא תשאלי לשלום אסיריך, "Zion, Will You Not Inquire After the Well-Being of Your Captive Ones?"[7] which was adopted as a liturgical lament (*kinna*) in the Ashkenazic liturgical rites and subsequently became the model for numerous Ashkenazic adaptations. The Ashkenazic rites effectively constructed a new environment for the Sephardic poem and assigned to it a role in a system that was quite distinct from the one for which it was composed.

From Sepharad to Ashkenaz

Manuscript evidence and the dating of some of the numerous Ashkenazic poets who composed *kinnot* following the model of Judah ha-Levi's "Zion, Will You Not Inquire" show that the poem must have reached Ashkenaz and become part of its liturgy for the Ninth of Av relatively soon after its composition, which according to Ezra Fleischer probably took place during Judah ha-Levi's stay in Egypt (September 1140 to May 1141).[8] Its ready adoption into Ashkenazic liturgy attests to the ease with which cultural objects traveled between medieval Jewish communities, including those without access to the Mediterranean and its (at least partially) shared cultural space, for example Ashkenaz.

Although we cannot fully map the (physical) transfer of Judah ha-Levi's poem and its introduction into Ashkenazic liturgy, aspects of this process can be retraced.[9] During the second half of the twelfth century, it seems that Sephardic *piyyutim* (liturgical poetry) were brought—probably through

Provence—to Tsarfat (northern France) and Ashkenaz. The agents of this transfer were most likely either young scholars who, having traveled to study with known sages, may have become interested in local liturgical texts and copied selected texts or unique collections, or well-read traders who heard texts performed in the synagogues that they visited and acquired copies of individual texts.[10] The insertion of such "imported" *piyyutim* would have followed the same processes that were applied to new Ashkenazic *piyyutim*: first precentors would add them into their repertoires, presumably monitoring their audiences' reactions; subsequently, the educated elite might have become involved before "successful" *piyyutim* were formally included in liturgical manuscripts, especially in the expensive grand manuscripts that have been preserved.[11] Therefore, in a given location, transfer of a text could have preceded its first transmission in a manuscript by a significant margin, especially since liturgical manuscripts were not commissioned on a regular basis, unless a new community was being founded or a long-standing community needed to replace its existing manuscripts, due for example to damage.[12] Since most extant medieval Ashkenazic liturgical manuscripts were exquisitely crafted for synagogue use, it is impossible to reconstruct the earliest reception of Sephardic *piyyutim* in Ashkenaz. That is to say, these Sephardic texts would have been well integrated in the local liturgies of their new cultural spheres by the time they were copied in these manuscripts, where we see them having been inserted in well-established liturgical slots as well as in collections of *piyyutim* that do not necessarily follow a set liturgical order. A substantial portion of these "imports" represented minor genres that were uncommon in Ashkenaz, like *piyyutim* that introduce liturgical stations such as *Barkhu* or *Kaddish*, but some belonged to familiar genres, like *ofanim* (embellishing the benediction before the *Shema Israel* in morning services) or *kinnot*. Especially with respect to lesser-known poetic styles, Tsarfatic and Ashkenazic poets used Sephardic *piyyutim* as models for their own production, thus augmenting the collections available in Ashkenazic communities.

On the other hand, twelfth-century Ashkenazic poets also began experimenting with quantitative meter—a feature of Hebrew poetry that developed in Sepharad—in *piyyutim* that otherwise follow Ashkenazic or even classical poetic traditions, surely as an outcome of their exposure to Sephardic poetry.[13] This trend further illustrates the receptivity of Ashkenazic liturgy to Sephardic texts that made possible the inclusion of Judah ha-Levi's lament, although those compositions differed in form and context from Ashkenazic *kinnot* of that time. It appears that certain formal aspects of that poem especially appealed to Ashkenazic liturgists and their communities, namely monorhyme on *-raykh*, quantitative meter, and a pronounced dialogical structure where a clearly identifiable first-person speaker addresses a second-person feminine singular subject (Zion).

A New Textual Environment: Ashkenazic Zionides

The reception of this singular cultural object, Judah ha-Levi's "Zion, Will You Not Inquire," which was assigned a new function that suited its new cultural context, led to the development of a new genre of cultural objects in the accepting culture, specifically within the Ashkenazic *kinnot* collections. Since the late twelfth century, Ashkenazic poets had composed *kinnot* that followed the formal model of "Zion, Will You Not Inquire" and had adapted its contents for an Ashkenazic audience. Both in liturgy and in research these *kinnot* are treated as a special subgroup of *kinnot*, usually referred to as "Zionides," since all (but one) of the Ashkenazic adaptations, in addition to using the same rhyme scheme and meter, also begin with the first word of the Sephardic lament, "Zion."

Twelve of these adaptations appear in printed editions of the western Ashkenazic prayer rite (*minhag* Ashkenaz) and eight in printed editions of the eastern Ashkenazic rite (*minhag* Polin).[14] A number of additional *kinnot* informed by that Sephardic model have been transmitted in manuscripts but are not included in printed editions, bringing the count of identified Ashkenazic Zionides to at least twenty-nine. Nineteen of them were likely composed during the "long thirteenth century,"[15] that is, within 150 years after Judah ha-Levi composed his lament. They form the textual environment in which Judah ha-Levi's lament was transmitted (and interpreted) in Ashkenaz since the thirteenth century.

We have sufficient evidence to offer a partial reconstruction of how the new environment for "Zion, Will You Not Inquire" emerged and how Ashkenazic Zionides became linked with that Sephardic lament, creating a distinct unit in the morning service on the Ninth of Av. Approximately 85 percent of the Ashkenazic manuscripts that transmit *kinnot* include Zionides. The remainder seem to have been copied in the early thirteenth century, when "Zion, Will You Not Inquire" may not yet have become part of the Ashkenazic liturgy for the Ninth of Av. Less than 25 percent of the known corpus of thirteenth- and early fourteenth-century Ashkenazic manuscripts include

Judah ha-Levi's "Zion, Will You Not Inquire" alone (ten manuscripts);[16] thus, a significant majority of *kinnot* collections transmit this Sephardic lament with at least one Ashkenazic Zionide. From that genre, the anonymous ציון קחי כל צרי גלעד, "Zion, Were You to Take All the Balms of Gilead," appears most frequently with Judah ha-Levi's composition (at least twenty-one manuscripts); the second most common is ציון הלא תשאלי לשלום עלוביך, "Zion, Will You Not Inquire After the Well-Being of Your Miserable Ones?" by El'azar ben Judah of Worms (at least twelve manuscripts). Each occurs sometimes as the sole Ashkenazic Zionide to accompany the Sephardic "Zion, Will You Not Inquire;"[17] five manuscripts transmit Judah ha-Levi's lament with both of these early Ashkenazic Zionides.[18] The next stage in the growth of Ashkenazic Zionides is less uniform: manuscripts with four to six Zionides all include the three laments mentioned here, but their complement varies widely. Not until the fifteenth century did some manuscripts present eight Zionides. The current norm—Judah ha-Levi's lament plus eight or twelve Ashkenazic Zionides—is a product of early modern changes in Jewish liturgy, when editors made choices from the available Ashkenazic Zionides based on contemporary taste as well as on the need to sell the printed collections to a variety of communities.[19] This process stands in contrast to the gradual mechanisms of liturgical development represented by medieval manuscripts, where each community would decide which *kinnot* and *seliḥot* to include in its local rite, with a tacit agreement that Judah ha-Levi's lament should be accompanied by similarly structured Ashkenazic *kinnot*. Proof for this agreement are the comparatively early acceptance of two Ashkenazic Zionides in western Ashkenazic and one in eastern Ashkenazic rites, and the continuous creativity of Ashkenazic liturgical poets who were drawn to this form of *kinna*.

Several of the Ashkenazic Zionides had likely been composed before the Sephardic model was accepted by the majority of Ashkenazic communities, yet clearly in response to Judah ha-Levi's lament. Both the desire to imitate a well-received and aesthetically appealing model and the need to enhance a popular but "deficient" text could have motivated the adoption and adaptation of this Sephardic model for Ashkenazic *kinnot*. The scholars in Ashkenaz who were responsible for liturgical choices did not subscribe to the "myth of Sephardic supremacy"; neither the embrace of Sephardic *piyyutim* nor the composition of *piyyutim* that draw from Sephardic models were prompted by a posture of inferiority vis-à-vis Sephardic poetry.[20] R. Judah the Castilian (ר' יהודה קשטלין), as Judah ha-Levi is often designated in Ashkenazic liturgical manuscripts, was regarded as an esteemed poet, but there is no indication that he and his oeuvre were elevated above the paragons of classical or Ashkenazic Hebrew poetry. To the contrary, several of the Ashkenazic Zionides that copy the form yet change the content of Judah ha-Levi's lament could aptly be described as *fartaysht un farbessert* ("translated and improved"), meaning that Ashkenazic scholars and poets retained its appealing elements and omitted whatever was "overly Sephardic."

The metrical aspect of Judah ha-Levi's lament may have been one of the unusual and aesthetically inviting elements for Ashkenazic scholars and poets who had already composed monorhymed poetry but had not previously employed the Sephardic *ha-mitpashet* meter, in which Judah ha-Levi's Zionide is composed.[21] For liturgical poetry, an advantage of meter is the musical quality that it adds, which may have proven particularly attractive, as select rubrics instruct for certain Ashkenazic *piyyutim* to be recited in a—or perhaps the—Sephardic *niggun*.[22] The rhyme on the closing syllable *-aykh* (or *-raykh*) would have been considered appropriate for the Ninth of Av since it phonetically resembles not only איכה (*ekha*), the opening word (and Hebrew title) of the Book of Lamentations, but also the mournful German sigh "ach."[23] With respect to poetic devices that were well-established Ashkenazic standards—such as acrostics, the use of biblical verses as a frame or to close a stanza, and the construction of elaborate structures within lines and stanzas—Judah ha-Levi's lament is artless. The Ashkenazic authors of *kinnot* experienced no technical difficulties in this regard. Given the taste of their audience, some Ashkenazic authors did try to "improve" upon the Sephardic model by using at least acrostics. The integration of biblical allusions was familiar to Ashkenazic poets, but the Sephardic use of biblical language rather than the poetic idioms that typified Ashkenazic *piyyut* offered a minor challenge that most authors of Zionides accepted.[24]

By definition, the overall message of "Zion, Will You Not Inquire" must have been considered fitting for the Ninth of Av for it to have been accepted as a *kinna*. Although it depicts themes such as the destruction of Jerusalem and the Temple in a fresh light, this lament also conveys highly familiar elements, like the image of Israel as prisoners who yearn for Zion and bow toward her gates, and biblical quotes that could be easily recognized. Furthermore, "Zion, Will You Not Inquire," like many thirteenth-century Ashkenazic *kinnot*, refers to future redemption without explicitly saying that its author or his audience will live to see it.[25] But the content of Judah ha-Levi's lament only partially matched the mood and message of the Ashkenazic morning service on the Ninth of Av. Some of his tropes are not featured in

Ashkenazic poetry, but neither would they be inconsistent with Ashkenazic understandings of Judaism, such as an emphasis on Israel as the land of prophecy. However, his personal lament makes no mention of several subjects that an Ashkenazic audience would find essential, namely descriptions of the Temple's role and of the destruction of Zion as well as Israel's culpability for the Temple's demise. Other elements in this Sephardic composition are more difficult to reconcile with Ashkenazic concepts of the Ninth of Av: Judah ha-Levi's intensely personal tone[26] would not have been deemed suitable for a communal service, especially given the Ashkenazic practice of reciting *kinnot* together in synagogue;[27] his poem also relates to the "real" Jerusalem of his time and advocates emigration to Israel, an aspiration that was not being promoted in Ashkenaz.[28]

"Zion, Were You to Take All the Balms of Gilead"

The Ashkenazic precentors who included "Zion, Will You Not Inquire" into the liturgies on the Ninth of Av and the intellectual elite that discussed and decided on liturgical changes apparently reacted to both the assets and deficits in this Sephardic poem. They positioned it with *kinnot* that would reinforce its aesthetic virtues but also alleviate its weaknesses, supplying its missing content while following its form, including meter and rhyme. Interestingly, their first choice was the anonymous Zionide whose features have led medieval and modern authors alike to mistake it for a Sephardic composition, ציון קחי כל צרי גלעד, "Zion, Were You to Take All the Balms of Gilead."

Many of the medieval manuscripts that include this anonymous *kinna* credit it to Abraham the Astrologer (אברהם החוזה), Solomon ibn Gabirol, or Elijah the Elder of Le Mans. Each of these ascriptions has been accepted by at least one modern editor of a liturgical collection of *kinnot*, though none of them can be accepted by contemporary scholarship. Modern scholars have attempted to identify Abraham the Astrologer as Abraham ibn Ezra, since El'azar of Worms occasionally refers to him using this name.[29] However, this identification cannot apply to the author of the anonymous Zionide, who was surely exposed to Judah ha-Levi's lament in a liturgical role and who adhered to certain Ashkenazic poetic conventions, such as references to rabbinic literature. The medieval ascriptions to (different) Sephardic authors mirror the confusion that "Zion, Were You to Take All the Balms of Gilead" creates through its combination of features that are often considered Sephardic with characteristics associated with Ashkenazic Hebrew poetry. Beyond the formal elements that it shares with all Zionides, this anonymous lament is dominated by biblical language, lacks any mention of Israel's sins as the main catalyst for the destruction of Zion, seems to follow Ibn Ezra's interpretation that the land of Israel is surrounded by the four rivers that flow from Eden, and asserts (in a relatively elaborate passage) that the intercalation of the Jewish year is conducted in Zion:

> Through you the thread of time was balanced with a perfect line:
> Through your doubling of the month of Adar the years were determined throughout the generations.
> The new moon (was fixed) according to your longitude, and its (first) appearance was determined according to your latitude, and through (her) light she revealed (the accuracy of) your secret knowledge.
> Orion rises and is visible by you (only) in (the month of) Tammuz, but in all other months is (hidden) in your chambers.[30]

Ibn Ezra identifies the "chambers" in Job 37:9 as the "chambers of the South," probably stellar constellations. The numerous astronomical studies by medieval Sephardic Jews justify a tendency to associate this passage with Sephardic traditions, but it should be noted that many of these references can be found in rabbinic sources: כסיל appears as a term for Orion (e.g., BT Berakhot 58b); the presumed system of determination of the new moon according to the testimony of witnesses by the Sanhedrin in Jerusalem during the Second Temple period is described in the Mishnah (M Rosh Hashanah 2:5); the option that a Sanhedrin in the Galilee might intercalate is explicitly ruled out (T Sanhedrin 2:13);[31] several rabbinic texts state that only a second Adar can be intercalated (T Sanhedrin 2:8 and 2:11; *Mekhilta de-Rabbi Yishma'el*, Bo 2 [ed. Horovitz-Rabin, p. 8]; BT Sanhedrin 12b);[32] and the rabbinic *molad* was calculated based on a longitude eastward of Alexandria, perhaps that of Jerusalem.[33] An Ashkenazic author who sought to establish Jerusalem as center of the Jewish world, including its critical role for determining the calendar for the Diaspora, had no formal need to probe post-rabbinic sources since he could have gathered this information and composed the passage cited above without access to astronomical treatises.[34]

Nor can the claim that the line "and from Eden, the source of all splendor, your rivers streamed forth" (verse 2)[35] be used to identify the author as

Abraham ibn Ezra. Ibn Ezra posited that Israel is surrounded by the four rivers that originate in paradise. However, this interpretation would have been available to any Ashkenazic scholar who had access to the explanation of Genesis 2:14 in *Bereshit Rabbah* 16.3, which states that the Euphrates "flows on its way and encompasses Eretz Israel."[36] Although neither of the other rivers is mentioned in this midrash, the lament also uses an unqualified plural form, נהריך. While familiarity with Ibn Ezra's commentary would adequately explain this piyyutic line, it is not a necessary condition; conversance in rabbinic literature, which was widespread in Ashkenaz, could have inspired the line as well.

Other components of "Zion, Were You to Take All the Balms of Gilead" also point to an Ashkenazic author. It is rich in references to rabbinic literature, among them the statement "Your people had a league of peace with the venomous serpent,"[37] which alludes to a passage in BT Yoma 21a, and the episode of R. Pinḥas ben Ya'ir's ass, that applied stricter rules of tithing than its owner (BT Ḥullin 7a; BT Shabbat 112b; Avot de-Rabbi Nathan 8; *Bereshit rabah* 46). This *kinna* highlights the miraculous qualities of the land of Israel (i.e., the healing power of its waters and the value of its dust and stones) and mentions the roles that the Temple had served, including during pilgrimage festivals. Further, this is one of the few Zionides that refrains from using the first-person singular voice that characterizes Judah ha-Levi's poem. Whereas Sephardic poetry regularly uses both the first person singular and plural forms to articulate individual and communal sentiments,[38] Ashkenazic *piyyutim* limit the first-person singular to the opening lines of *reshuyot* (poems in which an individual requests permission to speak for the community), introducing the precentor who would speak for the community. Thus the ubiquitous first-person voice in "Zion, Will You Not Inquire" presented a problem for Ashkenazic authors interested in experimenting with this style of composition.

Instead of reading "Zion, Were You to Take All the Balms of Gilead" as a hybrid of Ashkenazic and Sephardic content presented in a Sephardic format, I suggest that we view it as an Ashkenazic adaptation of Sephardic conventions, retaining deeply rooted Ashkenazic norms while displaying openness to new ideas. This reading is based on the assumption that Ashkenazic and Sephardic tradition are both complex and ever-dynamic constructions. Contact between these systems, for example through the dissemination of Sephardic poetry, instigated processes of cultural negotiations, in this case within the creative work of Ashkenazic poets as cultural agents who would each seek a balance between these two bodies of intricate rules and models. The new cultural objects that resulted from this process would logically be rooted in local tradition, like their authors and audiences. These objects would also integrate elements of the other culture—here Sepharad—that the local actors selected, thereby modifying their own cultural portfolios.

In this instance, "Zion, Were You to Take All the Balms of Gilead" may have been chosen as the ideal companion piece for "Zion, Will You Not Inquire," which was therefore copied most often, not (only) because it was an early response to "Zion, Will You Not Inquire" but because its anonymous author successfully crafted an Ashkenazic Zionide that captured what Ashkenazic audiences might have regarded as the essence of the Sephardic lament and re-created it in a text that was firmly anchored in the Ashkenazic tradition.[39] Once the pairing of these poems became widely accepted, the Ashkenazic components of "Zion, Were You to Take All the Balms of Gilead" effectively grounded this unit in Ashkenaz and neutralized the Sephardic—and thereby foreign—aspects of the imported text, thus combining the "exotic" attraction of the Sephardic poem with the familiarity of the Zionide.

"Zion, Will You Not Inquire After the Well-Being of Your Miserable Ones?"

The second most prevalent Ashkenazic choice to be transmitted alongside "Zion, Will You Not Inquire" by Judah ha-Levi was "Zion, Will You Not Inquire After the Well-Being of Your Miserable Ones?" by El'azar ben Judah of Worms. In two manuscripts it appears as the sole Ashkenazic Zionide and in three others as one of two Ashkenazic *kinnot* that complement the Sephardic "original." As one of the earliest poets to use the Sephardic model in Ashkenaz, El'azar ben Judah is best known for his *seliḥot* and *kinnot* that describe the contemporaneous suffering experienced by Jews in the Rhineland.[40] In his Zionide, he chose a different approach to Judah ha-Levi's "Zion, Will You Not Inquire"; he accepted the Sephardic form only, and even added a few typical Ashkenazic formal features, like an alphabetic and name acrostic and a stress on the word "Zion" by adding additional lines in the alphabetic acrostic that start with this word. Only part of his *kinna* addresses Zion, while the remainder is directed to God in the form of several long passages that use personal pronouns and the second-person masculine singular suffix. The thematic progression of his Zionide typifies Ashkenazic *kinnot* and *seliḥot*. After an introduction that calls on Zion to cry out to God, the text depicts the shame that Israel brought on itself, culminating in the destruction of the Temple and Jerusalem; it offers a petition to God for salvation; enumerates the persecutions and sufferings of Israel during the destruction; requests divine deliverance and retribution; then concludes by detailing the effects that salvation will bring upon Jerusalem. Ashkenazic *kinnot* usually combine hopes for redemption with succinct requests for divine retaliation against forces that threaten Israel, and El'azar ben Judah follows this pattern. In an allusion to Isaiah 63:1–4 he also refers to God's robe of revenge, dyed with the blood of Israel's martyrs, that will be used as evidence against Israel's enemies in the last judgment, an image that is often used in laments of the 1096 persecutions and martyrdom.[41] Only as it closes does this Zionide portray the beauty of Zion's with visions of the land, having been redeemed.[42] The inclusion of direct references to poems that memorialize the persecutions of 1096 link this Zionide to Ashkenazic *kinnot* such as "O That My Head Were Water" and "I Said, 'Look Away from Me'" by Qalonymos ben Judah, which precede the Zionides in both the western and eastern Ashkenazic rites.

Similar to the way he embedded his Zionide into the Ashkenazic piyyutic culture, El'azar ben Judah of Worms adeptly incorporates references to Judah ha-Levi's lament into his *kinna*, working mostly on a lexical level, sometimes alluding to full phrases from the Sephardic poem. He quotes the first hemistich of "Zion, Will You Not Inquire" almost in its entirety, only substituting its rhyme-word for one that is semantically close; he recalls the opening phrase of that first line in his final verse, answering the introductory question "Zion, will you not ask?" with an affirmation, "Then, Zion, you will ask."[43] Like Judah ha-Levi, who repeats the root *sh-l-m* four times in his first three verses (though they are translated as "well-being," "welfare," "peace," and "greetings," respectively), El'azar ben Judah uses this root twice in his first verse, the second time as a name of Jerusalem ("Zion, will you not inquire after the well-being of your miserable ones? Shalem, cry 'Oy' and 'Vey' for the devastation of your loving ones."). Throughout its fifty-three verses, the particle הלא (is it not?, surely), used to introduce established facts by means of a question, appears twelve times in this Zionide, transforming its assertive question into a motif that stresses the urgency of its plea. El'azar of Worms draws other phrases and images from his Sephardic source, but places them in different contexts. Where Judah ha-Levi describes the glory of God as the only light in Jerusalem "and no sun nor moon nor stars were (needed as) your luminaries,"[44] El'azar of Worms bemoans how the sun and moon were eclipsed and the stars were all extinguished when God ceased to protect Israel (verse 16). Judah ha-Levi inquires, "To whom are your anointed ones to be compared, to whom your prophets, and to whom shall your Levites and choristers (be likened)?"[45] which El'azar ben Judah reworks to ask, "Zion and Shalem, cry, where are the elders, and also the princes, prophets, and people? Your sharp blade made childless. Zion, where are Aaron's sons, the Levites with the song of the pilgrimage, where are the old ones and your young ones?" The use of the term שרים by both Judah ha-Levi and El'azar of Worms, translated here according to their contexts as "choristers" and "princes," conveys that the similarity between these texts is even more pronounced in the consonantal text of their Hebrew originals. These examples demonstrate that El'azar ben Judah consciously referred to the Sephardic model, but, since his understanding of what constituted an Ashkenazic *kinna* seems to have been informed by those *kinnot* by the seventh-century Byzantine Hebrew poet El'azar birabbi Qillir and earlier Ashkenazic *kinnot* that constituted most *kinnot* collections in his time, the aspects of the Sephardic model that he wove into his composition differ greatly from those selected by the anonymous author of "Zion, Were You to Take All the Balms of Gilead."

Common Features in Ashkenazic Zionides

While the individual choices for adapting Judah ha-Levi's lament by the authors of the two most popular thirteenth-century Ashkenazic Zionides differ meaningfully, their approach to the imported text was remarkably similar. Both maintained the formal characteristics of the Sephardic original, namely meter, verse length, and rhyme. They also employed a similar register of language, inspired by the biblical vocabulary that Judah ha-Levi favored. They also kept (at least to a certain extent) the address to Zion as a focus, locating the rhyme syllable on second-person singular feminine suffix (*-aykh*), which made possible a performance of the Ashkenazic laments that closely resembled the Sephardic model, with the exception of its precise wording. If we assume an audience whose members partially lacked fluency in Hebrew, which seems plausible for many who attended synagogue on the Ninth of Av in thirteenth-century Ashkenaz, the distinctions between Judah ha-Levi's lament and the Ashkenazic Zionides might not have been perceptible to all recipients.[46] Even for those with a moderate Hebrew level who did not attend to the details, the links between the Sephardic original and Ashkenazic adaptations could conceivably outbalance the contrasts, given their thematic resonance (mainly the prominence of Zion/Jerusalem, the description of her beauty and destruction, and the hope for redemption). These commonalities provide the nucleus from which the cluster of Zionides could be expanded until the emergence of printed volumes in the early modern period.

On the other hand, both poets "improved" the Sephardic original by applying poetic techniques that had been used since the inception of Ashkenazic *piyyut*, such as biblical and rabbinic allusions, acrostics, and structural techniques (for example, composing multiple lines that open with the same word). These characteristics tied Zionides to the broader poetic fabric of the Ashkenazic service on the morning of the Ninth of Av through echoes of firmly established liturgical texts and similarities that cast *kinnot* as an organic and coherent collection. The most noticeable discontinuity related to content, the shift from a personal lament by a poet who hoped to reach Jerusalem, the unrivaled city in the land of revelation and prophecy, to a series of collective laments that mirrored Ashkenazic intellectual tastes and expectations toward liturgical poetry, bemoaning the destruction of the Temple and Jerusalem that was caused by Israel's transgressions as well as the insurmountable chasm between Jerusalem's (and therefore Israel's) past glory, present destruction, and future redemption. The novel subjects in these Zionides provided a new set of references in their performative textual environment. Audience members who carefully read these *kinnot* could recognize these additional inflections in the service, relating the destruction of the Temple and providing a glimpse of the future, of Zion redeemed.

The reactions to "Zion, Will You Not Inquire" transmitted in the anonymous "Zion, Were You to Take All the Balms of Gilead" and in El'azar of Worms's "Zion, Will You Not Inquire After the Well-Being of Your Miserable Ones?" are representative examples of the processes of selection, evaluation, and adaptation of Sephardic culture in medieval Ashkenaz, but they are unusual with respect to the transfer of liturgical texts between these Jewish cultures. Among the numerous poems by Judah ha-Levi that reached Ashkenaz, some of which became permanent elements in its liturgies, this is the only one that was assigned an entirely new purpose,[47] and it is also the most frequently and obviously copied and adapted of his poems. Despite the differences between the Sephardic and Ashkenazic rites, liturgy is counted among the uniting elements in Jewish tradition. Transfer of liturgical texts among cultural spheres was possible and rarely caused more than aesthetic and stylistic developments, as with the adoption of quantitative meter by some

Ashkenazic poets. Medieval scholars, poets, and communities considered liturgical similarities to be sufficiently robust to allow for the transfer of liturgical texts that corresponded to existing slots or related to well-established liturgical stations. This process did not necessitate changes or disruptions of the basic structures; further, these cultural imports were perceived as natural additions to their new environment, as with *me'orot* (embellishing the benediction "creator of the lights" before the *Shema Yisrael* in the morning service) and *reshuyot* for *Kaddish.* "Zion, Will You Not Inquire" prompted more of a reaction and led to more visible adaptation of the system that adopted it because, in this case, the transfer included the assignment of a new position to the original text, which was not composed as a liturgical work. It needed to be enveloped in an environment that was designed to support both the text and its new position. But even under these conditions, where symmetry of function was absent, transfer of texts between Sepharad and Ashkenaz was successful, attesting to the ongoing contact, mutual interest, and identification with a unifying strand of Jewish culture that was shared by Jewish communities in Europe during the thirteenth century.

Sepharad in Ashkenaz

Although contacts and cultural transfers changed in early modern Judaism, the fascination of Judah ha-Levi's "Zion, Will You Not Inquire" and its outstanding Sephardic beauty, completely embedded in an Ashkenazic environment, continued for many centuries. This can be seen in one of the most famous translations of Judah ha-Levi's Zionide, that by the renowned eighteenth-century German Jewish philosopher Moses Mendelssohn,[48] which was reprinted often, including in popular bilingual Rödelheim editions of *kinnot* for the Ninth of Av (until the 1911 edition, which published new translations throughout). Certain aspects of Mendelssohn's work differ from the Hebrew original, reflecting his effort to bridge the gap between this medieval Andalusian text and his eighteenth-century German readership, attending to their tastes by romanticizing the ruins of Jerusalem and to their theological positions, recognizing their disinterest in pilgrimage to Jerusalem/Israel by shying away from portrayals of Israel as the seat of divine revelation in favor of descriptions of Jerusalem as the locus of the Temple, and by succinctly stating that not Israel ("jener unschuldigen Heerde") but God was to blame ("Dahin sie ihr Treiber zerstreuet?") for its destruction and their dispersion.[49] Given that Mendelssohn's Hebrew source was a liturgical volume of *kinnot*, probably the Frankfurt 1696 edition,[50] it is likely that he associated Judah ha-Levi's famous ode to Zion with the many laments about the destruction of the Temple that were also recited on the Ninth of Av, and especially with the texts immediately adjacent to it, namely the Ashkenazic Zionides. The Ashkenazic liturgical tradition had successfully integrated Judah ha-Levi's poem and made its reinterpretation possible and plausible.

Notes

INTRODUCTION

1. See Yeḥiel ben Judah, *Vikuaḥ R. Yeḥi'el mi-Paris, me-ba'alei ha-tosafot*, ed. Reuven Margaliyot (Jerusalem, 1938), 21. The two manuscripts differ on this sentence. We have used Paris, Bibliothèque nationale, héb. 712, fol. 51a, as did Margaliyot. Moscow, Russian State Library, Günzburg 1390, fol. 94v reads, "Go now to the Jews' street and see how many take interest (*noshim beribit*) even on the holiday itself." For a thorough discussion of these manuscripts, see Judah D. Galinsky, "The Different Hebrew Versions of the 'Talmud Trial' of 1240 in Paris," in *New Perspectives on Jewish-Christian Relations: In Honor of David Berger*, ed. Elisheva Carlebach and Jacob J. Schacter (Leiden, 2011), 109–40; Joseph Shatzmiller, *La deuxième controverse de Paris: Un chapitre dans la polémique entre chrétiens et juifs au moyen âge* (Paris, 1994); and the introduction in John Friedman, "The Disputation of Rabbi Yehiel of Paris," in *The Trial of the Talmud Paris, 1240* (Toronto, 2012). For this quote, see Friedman, "Disputation," 151. Our translation differs slightly from that of Friedman. We have provided references to his translation as it is the only extant English translation of the entire text.

2. Friedman, "Disputation," 145.

3. Ibid., 151.

4. For background to this debate, see Jeremy Cohen, *Living Letters of the Law* (Berkeley, Calif., 1999), 317–42. Robert Chazan brings a full survey of the literature in his recent "Trial, Condemnation and Censorship," in *The Trial of the Talmud Paris, 1240*, 1–92, at 3n.1. Piero Capelli addresses this event in his chapter.

5. Once again, we have slightly emended Friedman's translation. See Friedman, "Disputation," 151.

6. For discussions of business contacts, see Haym Soloveitchik, *Pawnbroking: A Study in the Inter-Relationship Between Halakhah, Economic Activity and Communal Self Image* (Hebrew; Jerusalem, 1985); idem, *Wine in Ashkenaz in the Middle Ages: Yeyn nesekh—A Study in the History of Halakhah* (Hebrew; Jerusalem, 2008), 276–304; Victoria Hoyle, "The Bonds That Bind: Money Lending Between Anglo-Jewish and Christian Women in the Plea Rolls of the Exchequer of the Jews, 1218–1280," *Journal of Medieval History* 34.2 (2008): 119–29; Joseph Shatzmiller, *Cultural Exchange: Jews, Christians and Art in the Medieval Marketplace* (Princeton, N.J., 2013), 5–58, 141–57; for domestic arrangements, see Jacob Katz, *The Shabbes Goy: A Study in Halakhic Flexibility*, trans. Joel Lerner (Philadelphia, 1989); Simcha Emanuel, "The Christian Wet Nurse During the Middle Ages: Halakhah and History" (Hebrew), *Zion* 73.1 (2008): 21–40; Elisheva

Baumgarten, *Mothers and Children: Jewish Family Life in Medieval Europe* (Princeton, N.J., 2004), 126–44.

7. See, e.g., Elazar Touitou, *Exegesis in Perpetual Motion: Studies in the Pentateuchal Commentary of Rabbi Samuel Ben Meir* (Hebrew; Ramat Gan, 2003), 11–45; Aryeh Grabois, "The Hebraica veritas and Jewish-Christian Intellectual Relations in the Twelfth Century," *Speculum* 50.4 (1975): 613–34.

8. Friedman, "Disputation," 133.

9. See Hanne Trautner-Kromann, *Shield and Sword: Jewish Polemics Against Christianity and the Christians in France and Spain from 1100–1500* (Tübingen, 1993); Daniel J. Lasker, *Jewish Philosophical Polemics Against Christianity in the Middle Ages* (2nd ed.; Oxford, 2007); Israel Jacob Yuval, *Two Nations in Your Womb: Perceptions of Jews and Christians in Late Antiquity and the Middle Ages,* trans. Barbara Harshav and Jonathan Chipman (Berkeley, Calif., 2006); Jonathan Elukin, *Living Together, Living Apart* (Princeton, N.J., 2007); David Berger, "Introduction," in *The Jewish-Christian Debate in the High Middle Ages: A Critical Edition of the Nizzahon Vetus with an Introduction, Translation and Commentary* (Philadelphia, 1979), reprinted in Berger, *Persecution, Polemic, and Dialogue: Essays in Jewish-Christian Relations* (Boston, 2010), 75–108; idem, "Jewish-Christian Polemics," in *The Encyclopedia of Religion*, ed. Mircea Eliade (New York, 1987), 11:389–95; idem, "Mission to the Jews and Jewish-Christian Contacts in the Polemical Literature of the High Middle Ages," *American Historical Review* 91.3 (1986): 576–91, reprinted in *Persecution, Polemic and Dialogue,* 177–98.

10. See n. 7 above.

11. See Kenneth R. Stow, *Alienated Minority: The Jews of Medieval Latin Europe* (Cambridge, Mass., 1992), 1–5; David Biale, ed., *Cultures of the Jews: A New History* (New York, 2002), xvii–xxiii, addresses these issues in an even broader framework.

12. Baumgarten, *Mothers and Children*, 134–44; William Chester Jordan, *Women and Credit in Pre-Industrial and Developing Societies* (Philadelphia, 1993), 20–38; idem, "Jews on Top: Women and the Availability of Consumption Loans in Northern France in the Mid-Thirteenth Century," *Journal of Jewish Studies* 29.1 (1978): 39–56.

13. Besides Baumgarten, *Mothers and Children*, see idem, "'A Separate People'? Some Directions for Comparative Research on Medieval Women," *Journal of Medieval History* 34.2 (2008): 212–28, and the other articles in the same issue, especially Monica H. Green, "Conversing with the Minority: Relations Among Christian, Jewish, and Muslim Women in the High Middle Ages," 105–18, Rebecca Lynn Winer, "Conscripting the Breast: Lactation, Slavery and Salvation in the Realms of Aragon and Kingdom of Majorca, c. 1250–1300," 164–84, and Hoyle, "The Bonds That Bind."

14. Although several of the chapters here deal with the Islamicate world, none addresses Jewish-Christian relations in the Byzantine lands. This has been discussed, however, in Joshua Holo, *Byzantine Jewry in the Mediterranean Economy* (Cambridge, 2009); Steven B. Bowman, *The Jews of Byzantium (1204–1453)* (Tuscaloosa, Ala., 1985); Linda Safran, *The Medieval Salento: Art and Identity in Southern Italy* (Philadelphia, 2014); and Robert Bonfil, Oded Irshai, Guy G. Stroumsa, and Rina Talgam, eds., *Jews in Byzantium: Dialectics of Minority and Majority Cultures* (Leiden, 2012).

15. See, e.g., Jürgen Kocka, "Comparison and Beyond," *History and Theory* 42.1 (2003): 39–44; Jürgen Kocka, and Heinz Gerhard Haupt, "Comparison and Beyond: Traditions, Scope and Perspectives of Comparative History," in *Comparison and Transnational History: Central European Approaches and New Perspectives*, ed. Kocka and Haupt (New York, 2009), 1–32.

16. For a discussion of these terms, see Ivan G. Marcus, *Rituals of Childhood: Jewish Accul-*

turation in Medieval Europe (New Haven, Conn., 1996), 9–13; Elukin, *Living Together*, 1–11; Elisheva Baumgarten, *Practicing Piety in Medieval Ashkenaz: Men, Women and Everyday Religious Observance* (Philadelphia, 2014), 5–9.

17. See David Berger's cogent summary of these matters, "A Generation of Scholarship on Jewish-Christian Interaction in the Medieval World," *Tradition* 38.2 (2004): 4–14, reprinted in Berger, *Persecution, Polemic, and Dialogue*, 40–50.

18. Natalie Davis suggests similar metaphors; see her *Trickster Travels: A Sixteenth-Century Muslim Between Worlds* (New York, 2006).

19. Quantum entanglement involves tiny particles that affect each other even at huge distances; the metaphor here extends only so far. See David Kaiser, "Is Quantum Entanglement Real?," *New York Times*, 16 November 2014, p. SR10, for a brief summary of the fifty-year history of the concept.

20. Itamar Even-Zohar, "The Making of Culture Repertoire and the Role of Transfer," *Target* 9.2 (1997): 373–81; idem, "Culture Repertoire and Transfer," in *Translation Translation*, ed. Susan Petrilli (Amsterdam, 2003), 425–31.

21. See n. 1 above.

22. For a survey of medieval Jewish communities in Europe at this time, see Stow, *Alienated Minority*; Robert Chazan, *The Jews of Medieval Western Christendom, 1000–1500* (Cambridge, 2007).

23. On varieties of Jewish cultures in different regions, and how scholars have envisioned them, see David Malkiel, *Reconstructing Ashkenaz: The Human Face of Franco-German Jewry, 1000–1250* (Stanford, 2009), 1–43.

24. See the chapter by Yossef Schwartz in this volume.

25. See the chapter by Ephraim Kanarfogel in this volume.

26. For a description of these circumstances, see Avraham Grossman, *Pious and Rebellious: Jewish Women in Medieval Europe* (Hanover, N.H., 2004), 33–48; Judith Baskin, "Jewish Traditions About Women and Gender Roles: From Rabbinic Teaching to Medieval Practice," in *Oxford Handbook of Women and Gender in Medieval Europe*, ed. Judith Bennett and Ruth Mazo Karras (Oxford, 2012), 41–43.

27. See also Michael Signer, "Rabbi and Magister: Overlapping Intellectual Models of Twelfth Century Renaissance," *Jewish History* 22.1/2 (2008): 115–37.

28. See the chapter by Rebecca Winer in this volume.

29. George Makdisi, *The Rise of Colleges: Institutions of Learning in Islam and the West* (Edinburgh, 1981), 224–91.

30. Ephraim Kanarfogel, *Jewish Education and Society in the High Middle Ages* (Detroit, 1992), 55–65.

31. Leonard E. Boyle, "The *Summa Confessorum* of John of Freiburg and the Popularization of the Moral Teaching of St. Thomas and some of his Contemporaries," in *St. Thomas Aquinas, 1274–1974: Commemorative Studies*, 2 vols. (Toronto, 1974), 2:245–68, reprinted in Leonard E. Boyle, *Pastoral Care, Clerical Education and Canon Law, 1200–1400* (London, 1981), chap. 3. See, for instance, D. L. D'Avray, "Philosophy in Preaching: The Case of a Franciscan Based in Thirteenth-Century Florence (Servasanto da Faenza)," in *Literature and Religion in the Later Middle Ages: Philological Studies in Honor of Siegfried Wenzel*, ed. Richard G. Newhauser and John A. Alford (Binghamton, N.Y., 1995), 263–73, esp. 263n.1.

32. See, among others, Baumgarten, *Mothers and Children*; Elka Klein, *Jews, Christian Society, and Royal Power in Medieval Barcelona* (Ann Arbor, Mich., 2006); Elisheva Carlebach and Jacob J. Schacter, eds., *New Perspectives on Jewish-Christian Relations: In Honor of David*

Berger (Leiden, 2012); David Engel, Lawrence Schiffmann, and Elliot Wolfson, eds., *Studies in Medieval Jewish Intellectual and Social History: Festschrift in Honor of Robert Chazan* (Leiden, 2012); Marcus, *Rituals of Childhood.*

33. Jeremy Cohen, *The Friars and the Jews: The Evolution of Medieval Anti-Judaism* (Ithaca, N.Y., 1982), 33–76.

34. R. I. Moore, *The Formation of a Persecuting Society: Authority and Deviance in Western Europe 950–1250* (2nd ed.; Oxford, 2007), gives an overview, and includes a chapter updating the work and responding to those who have attacked the book for eliding differences across different groups and across geographies. While the study of individual places and times brings more nuance than could appear in what is essentially an extended interpretive essay (see, e.g., David Nirenberg, *Communities of Violence: Persecution of Minorities in the Middle Ages* [Princeton, N.J., 1996], 241–43, for a critique of the first edition), Moore's point that political and religious authorities often used power simply to demonstrate that they had it retains a great deal of validity.

35. Moore, *Formation of a Persecuting Society*, 37–42.

36. See J. H. Burns, *The Cambridge History of Medieval Political Thought, c. 350–c. 1450* (Cambridge, 1988), 339–648; Antony Black, *Political Thought in Europe 1250–1450* (Cambridge, 1992), 162–78; Antonio Marongiu, *Medieval Parliaments: A Comparative Study*, trans. S. J. Woolf (London, 1968), 19–131.

37. Joseph Goering, "The Changing Face of the Village Parish, II: The Thirteenth Century," in *Pathways to Medieval Peasants*, ed. J. A. Raftis (Toronto, 1981), 328–30; Theo Clemens and Wim Janse, eds., *The Pastor Bonus: Papers Read at the British-Dutch Colloquium at Utrecht, 18–21 September 2002* (Leiden, 2004); Jeffery H. Denton, "The Competence of the Parish Clergy in Thirteenth-Century England," in *The Church and Learning in Later Medieval Society: Essays in Honour of R. B. Dobson. Proceedings of the 1999 Harlaxton Symposium*, ed. Caroline M. Barron and Jenny Stratford (Donington, 2002), 273–85; M. R. Génestal, *Le procès sur l'état de clerc aux XIIIe et XIVe siècles* (Paris, 1909).

38. R. I. Moore, *The First European Revolution, c. 970–1215* (Oxford, 2000), 160–80, quotation at 174.

39. William C. Jordan, *The French Monarchy and the Jews: From Philip Augustus to the Last Capetians* (Philadelphia, 1989), 105–27; R. I. Moore, *The War on Heresy* (Cambridge, 2012), 1–10, 329–31.

40. See esp. Solomon Grayzel, *The Church and the Jews in the XIIIth Century* (New York, 1966), 1:49–51; Walter Pakter, *Medieval Canon Law and the Jews* (Ebelsbach, 1988), 44–67.

41. Miri Rubin, *Gentile Tales: The Narrative Assault on Late Medieval Jews* (New Haven, Conn., 1999), 93–103; on the emphasis on transubstantiation more generally, see Miri Rubin, *Corpus Christi: The Eucharist in Late Medieval Culture* (Cambridge, 1991).

42. On Paris, see the chapter by Capelli in this volume; see also Benjamin Kedar, "Canon Law and the Burning of the Talmud," *Bulletin of Medieval Canon Law*, n.s., 9 (1979): 79–82; Cohen, *Living Letters of the Law*, 328–29.

43. Yossef Schwartz made this point in "Authority, Control, and Conflict in Thirteenth-Century Paris: Contextualizing the Talmud Trial," in *Jews and Christians in Thirteenth Century France*, ed. Elisheva Baumgarten and Judah Galinsky (New York, 2015), 93–110.

44. See esp. Jan A. Aertsen, Kent Emery, and Andreas Speer, eds., *Nach der Verurteilung von 1277: Philosophie und Theologie an der Universität von Paris im letzen Viertel des 13. Jahrhunderts. Studien und Texte* (Berlin, 2001).

45. Görge K. Hasselhoff, *Dicit Rabbi Moyses: Studien zum Bild von Moses Maimonides im lateinischen Westen vom 13. bis zum 15. Jahrhundert* (2nd ed.; Würzburg, 2005).

46. Sarah Strousma, "The Muslim Context," in *The Cambridge History of Jewish Philosophy*, vol. 1, ed. Steven Nadler and T. M. Rudavsky (Cambridge, 2008), 41; David Berger, "Judaism and General Culture in Medieval and Early Modern Times," in *Judaism's Encounter with Other Cultures: Rejection or Integration?*, ed. Jacob J. Schacter (New York, 1997), 57–141, reprinted in David Berger, *Cultures in Collision and Conversation: Essays in Intellectual History of the Jews* (Boston, 2011), 21–116, esp. 51–78.

47. Yossef Schwartz, "Images of Revelation and Spaces of Discourse: The Cross-Cultural Journeys of Iberian Jewry," in *Christlicher Norden – Muslimischer Süden: Ansprüche und Wirklichkeiten von Christen, Juden und Muslimen auf der Iberischen Halbinsel im Hoch- und Spätmittelalter*, ed. M. Tischler and A. Fidora (Münster, 2011), 267–87, here 270–76.

48. See Charles Homer Haskins, *Studies in the History of Mediaeval Science* (2nd ed.; Cambridge, 1927); Charles Burnett, ed., *Adelard of Bath: An English Scientist and Arabist of the Early Twelfth Century* (London, 1987); Biancamaria Scarcia Amoretti, ed., *La diffusione delle scienze islamiche nel medio evo europeo* (Rome, 1987); Colette Sirat, "Les traducteurs juifs à la cour des rois de Sicile et de Naples," in *Traduction et traducteurs au Moyen Âge*, ed. Geneviève Contamine (Paris, 1989), 169–91; Norman Roth, "Jewish Collaborators in Alfonso's Scientific Work," in *Emperor of Culture: Alfonso X the Learned of Castile and His Thirteenth-Century Renaissance*, ed. Robert I. Burns (Philadelphia, 1990), 59–71; Marie-Thérèse d'Alverny, *La transmission des textes philosophiques et scientifiques au Moyen Âge*, ed. Charles Burnett (Aldershot, 1994); Charles Burnett, *Arabic into Latin in the Middle Ages: The Translators and Their Intellectual and Social Context* (Aldershot, 2009).

49. See esp. Gad Freudenthal, "Arabic into Hebrew: The Emergence of the Translation Movement in Twelfth-Century Provence and Jewish-Christian Polemic," in *Border Crossings: Interreligious Interaction and the Exchange of Ideas in the Islamic Middle Ages*, ed. David Freidenreich and Miriam Goldstein (Philadelphia, 2011), 124–43; Mauro Zonta, "Medieval Hebrew Translations of Philosophical and Scientific Texts: A Chronological Table," in *Science in Medieval Jewish Cultures*, ed. Gad Freudenthal (Cambridge, 2011), 17–73.

50. In addition to Zonta, "Medieval Hebrew Translations," see Gad Freudenthal, "Arabic and Latin Cultures as Resources for the Hebrew Translation Movement: Comparative Considerations, Both Quantitative and Qualitative," in his *Science in Medieval Jewish Cultures*, 74–105; Alexander Fidora, Resianne Fontaine, Gad Freudenthal, Harvey J. Hames, and Yossef Schwartz, eds., *Latin-into-Hebrew: Texts and Studies* (Leiden, 2013).

51. And, according to S. J. Pearce's chapter in this volume, perhaps also because it excluded the less learned.

52. Joseph Shatzmiller, "Contacts et échanges entre savants juifs et chrétiens à Montpellier vers 1300," in *Juifs et judaïsme de Languedoc* (Cahiers de Fanjeaux 12) (Toulouse, 1977), 337–44.

53. See the chapters by Rami Reiner and Luke Yarbrough in this volume.

CHAPTER 1. RABBINIC CONCEPTIONS OF MARRIAGE AND MATCHMAKING IN CHRISTIAN EUROPE

1. See, e.g., Avraham Grossman, *Ḥasidot u-mordot* (Jerusalem, 2001), 88–117; idem, *Ve-hu yimshol bakh? Ha-Ishah be-mishnatam shel ḥakhmei yisra'el bimei ha-benayim* (Jerusalem, 2011),

59–61, 193–96, 268–72, 329–31; Simcha Emanuel, "Bitul shidukhin," *Meḥkarim be-toledot yehudei Ashkenaz*, ed. G. Bacon et al. (Ramat Gan, 2008), 157–202.

2. I am grateful to Elisheva Baumgarten, David Berger, Judah Galinsky, and Ronnie Warburg for commenting on an earlier draft of this study.

3. See Shmuel Shilo, "Ha-Shadkhan ba-mishpat ha-'ivri," in *Law, Morals, and Equity in the Jewish Legal System*, ed. B. Lifshitz et al. (Hebrew; Jerusalem, 2006), 361–63; A. A. Neuman, *The Jews in Spain: Their Social, Political, and Cultural Life During the Middle Ages* (Philadelphia, 1944), 2:25 (cited in Grossman, *Ḥasidot u-mordot*, 111n.86). Neuman (2:282n.37) mentions the appearance of a *shadkhan* in a late fourteenth-century responsum by Isaac ben Sheshet Barfat (Rivash, no. 193), but notes that this responsum deals with a German community. In one of Rashba's response (2:79), the questioner refers to an agent (*sarsur*) for both business and *shidukhim* purposes; and see also *Teshuvot ha-Rashba*, 4:258. Cf. Asher ben Yeḥiel (Rosh), *Piskei ha-Rosh 'al masekhet Kidushin* 2:4; and Isadore Epstein, *Studies in the Communal Life of the Jews in Spain as Reflected in the Respona of Rashba* (New York, 1968), 79–82. Rosh's responsum about the *shadkhan*'s role (below, n. 19) composed in Spain after 1305, cites (only) his Ashkenazic teachers.

4. See Isaac ben Moses, *Sefer Or Zarua', piskei Bava Kama* (Jerusalem, 2010), sec. 457, vol. 3, fol. 151a.

5. See ibid., fol. 151b.

6. See *Sefer Mordekhai 'al masekhet Bava Kama*, ed. A. Halpern (Jerusalem, 1992), sec. 172, pp. 213–14; *Teshuvot Mahram defus Prague*, #706; A. Grossman, *Ḥasidot u-mordot*, 111–12; cf. S. Emanuel, *Shivrei luḥot* (Jerusalem, 2006), 128n.110, 137n.149.

7. See *Sefer Ḥasidim* (Parma) [hereafter: *SHP*], ed. J. Wistinetski (Frankfurt, 1924), sec. 1131, p. 286. Cf. *SHP*, secs. 1890–91, p. 458.

8. See *Teshuvot Maharam defus Prague*, #952, which mentions the Erfurt incident but does not describe it. This ruling is also cited at the beginning of Meir ha-Kohen's *Teshuvot Maimuniyot le-Sefer Nezikin*, #22, based on Maharam's talmudic writings. Cf. A. Grossman, *Ḥasidot u-mordot*, 112 (end).

9. See *Sefer Mordekhai 'al masekhet Bava Kama*, ed. Halpern, sec. 172, pp. 212–13 (and note that R"I was the teacher of Samson of Sens). R. Judah Sirleon's formulation is cited by his student, Moses of Coucy, in *Sefer mitsvot gadol* (Venice, 1547), *'aseh* 74, fol. 153a. See also *Teshuvot Maimuniyot le-sefer Nezikin*, #22; *Sefer tashbets* (Jerusalem, 2011), 319 (sec. 583). Although Maharam was made aware of the full extent of R"I's allowances, he did not modify his view, even as the Tosafot of Joel ben Isaac ha-Levi of Bonn (d. c. 1200) also reflect the position of R"I and Simḥah of Speyer; see S. Emanuel, *Shivrei luḥot*, 82 (n. 140), and 84 (n. 149).

10. See *Sefer Mordekhai*, ed. Halpern, sec. 173, pp. 214–15. Cf. S. Shilo, "Ha-Shadkhan ba-mishpat ha-'ivri," 362n.11. On Joseph ben Abraham and his writings in *Sefer Mordekhai*, see S. Emanuel, *Shivrei luḥot*, 215–18.

11. See *Teshuvot Maharah Or Zarua'*, ed. M. Abittan (Jerusalem, 2002), no. 3, pp. 3–5. See also I. A. Agus, *Teshuvot ba'alei ha-tosafot* (New York, 1954), nos. 123–24, pp. 226–30.

12. See Grossman, *Ḥasidot u-mordot*, 113.

13. See above, n. 3.

14. See *Teshuvot ha-Rashba*, 1:1219. The desire of parents and other family members to control the choice of a husband is also evident in *Teshuvot ha-Rashba*, 1:549. See also S. D. Goitein, *A Mediterranean Society: The Jewish Communities of the Arab World as Portrayed in the Documents of the Cairo Geniza* (Berkeley, Calif., 1978), 3:79.

15. See *Teshuvot ha-Rashba*, 3:211. See also *Teshuvot ha-Rashba*, 1:771, 2:35, and *Ḥidushei*

ha-Ritva 'al masekhet Gitin, ed. A. Lichtenstein (Jerusalem, 1979), 1:185 (end, 30a), citing Nahmanides. Cf. *Teshuvot ha-Rashba*, 1:550, 1:1206, 4:314; *Teshuvot ha-Rosh*, 35:1; *Teshuvot zikhron yehudah le-R. Yehudah ben ha-Rosh*, ed. A. Y. Havazelet (Jerusalem, 2005), no. 81, fol. 78a; *Teshuvot ha-Rashba* 4:174, discussed below in n. 22.

16. See Yom Tov Assis, *The Golden Age of Aragonese Jewry* (London, 1997), 255–59.

17. See A. A. Neuman, *The Jews in Spain*, 2:24–27.

18. See *Ḥidushei ha-Ritva* to BT Yevamot 106a, ed. R. A. Jofen (Jerusalem, 1989), 2:1476; *Ḥidushei ha-Ramban*, ed. S. Dickman (Jerusalem, 1987), 352–53. Ritva demurs, since a doctor is required to share his knowledge to save lives without receiving significant compensation, but he agrees that payment may be warranted because medical knowledge is an invaluable form of wisdom. See also *Ḥidushei ha-Rashba*, ed. S. Dickman (Jerusalem, 1995), 552–53, and Nahmanides' *Torat ha-adam* in *Kitvei ha-Ramban*, ed. C. B. Chavel (Jerusalem, 1968), 2:44. Cf. the comment by Ramban's predecessor, Meir ha-Levi (Ramah) Abulafia of Toledo (d. 1236), in *Shitah mekubetset* to BT Bava Kama 116a, s.v. *ve-zu*; Moses Isserles's gloss to *Shulḥan 'arukh, Ḥoshen mishpat* 264:7; and Bernard Septimus, *Hispano-Jewish Culture in Transition* (Cambridge, 1982), 86–87.

19. See above, n. 9. See also Tosafot BT Yevamot 106a, s.v. *ein lo*; and *Tosafot Maharam ve-Rabenu Perets 'al masekhet Yevamot* 106a, s.v. *tol dinar ve-ha'avireni*, ed. H. Porush (Jerusalem, 1991), 236, where R"I's reasoning is extended to include someone who can communicate effectively with the ruling powers on behalf of others. Cf. *Teshuvot ha-Rosh*, 105:1.

20. On R"I of Dampierre's interest in magic, see my *Peering Through the Lattices: Mystical, Magical, and Pietistic Dimensions in the Tosafist Period* (Detroit, 2000), 191–95. This interest was shared by several of the other tosafists who discussed *shadkhanim*, including Barukh of Mainz and his son Samuel Bamberg, Simḥah of Speyer, Isaac Or Zarua', and Meir of Rothenburg; see *Peering Through the Lattices*, 102–6, 208, 221–26, 234–39. For Ashkenazic descriptions of miraculous medical practices (typically on the part of Christian healers), see Joseph Shatzmiller, "Doctors and Medical Practice in Germany Around the Year 1200: The Evidence of Sefer Hasidim," *Journal of Jewish Studies* 33 (1982): 583–93; Ephraim Shoham-Steiner, "'This Should Not Be Shown to a Gentile': Medico-Magical Texts in Medieval Franco-German Jewish Rabbinic Manuscripts," in *Bodies of Knowledge: Cultural Interpretations of Illness and Medicine in Medieval Europe*, ed. S. Crawford and C. Lee (Oxford, 2010), 53–59; S. Emanuel, "Ivaron ke-'eilah le-gerushin," *Masekhet* 6 (2007): 31–42. Cf. Joseph Shatzmiller, *Jews, Medicine, and Medieval Society* (Berkeley, Calif., 1994), 66–67, 122–23; E. E. Urbach, *Ba'alei ha-tosafot* (Jerusalem, 1980), 1:262–63; Aryeh Leibowitz, "Doctors and Medical Knowledge in Tosafist Circles," *Tradition* 42 (2009): 19–34; Tosafot BT Mo'ed Katan 11a, s.v. *kavra'*.

21. See Grossman, *Ḥasidot u-mordot*, 113–15. Additional reasons proposed by Grossman (115–17) are the increasing number of divorces in Ashkenaz from the mid-thirteenth century—which would not explain the proliferation of *shadkhanim* already in the second half of the twelfth century—as well as the development of the professional rabbinate which accounts, as Grossman notes, only for developments in the late fourteenth and fifteenth centuries. Cf. S. Shilo, "Ha-Shadkhan ba-mishpat ha-'ivri," 363–64; Y. Y. Yuval, *Ḥakhamim be-doram* (Jerusalem, 1989), 33–34, 327–28, 398–400. Marriage of grooms below the age of thirteen was uncommon in most areas of medieval Europe. The allowance issued by northern French tosafists (see Tosafot BT Yevamot 62b, s.v. *samukh*; BT Yevamot 96b, s.v. *nasa'*; Tosafot BT Sanhedrin 76b, s.v. *samukh*; *Sefer mitsvot katan le-Yitshak mi-Corbeil* [Constantinople, 1820], sec. 183, fol. 22b; and cf. Grossman, *Ḥasidot u-mordot*, 65, דלא הויא בעילתו בעילת זנות) appears to be a mitigating argument rather than support for a prevalent policy, and German halakhists were even less

permissive. See, e.g., *Ma'aseh ha-geonim*, ed. A. Epstein (Berlin, 1910), 61–62; *Sefer Rabiah*, ed. D. Deblitzky (Bnei Brak, 2008), 3:173–77 (#940). Maimonides' explicit prohibition (*Mishneh Torah, hilkhot isurei bi'ah*, 21:25) impacted the scholars of Sepharad; see, e.g., *Teshuvot ha-Rashba*, 1:803, 1:1181, and 4:207; Grossman, *Ḥasidot u-mordot*, 99–100 (and n. 22, below); and cf. Y. D. Gilat, "Nisu'ei katan: Halakhah u-metsi'ut," *Meḥkerei Talmud* 3, ed. D. Rosenthal and Y. Sussmann (Jerusalem, 2005), 153–68. On balance, Grossman's assessment (*Ḥasidot u-mordot*, 80–81) that the marriage of *ketanim* was a "rare phenomenon" seems quite accurate; although cf. Pinchas Roth, "Ḥakhmei Provens ha-me'uḥarim: Halakhah u-foskei halakhah bi-derom Tsarfat, 1215–1348" (Ph.D. diss., Hebrew University of Jerusalem, 2012), 221–29, 236, for more widespread evidence within southern France during the thirteenth century, despite the disqualification of the *kidushin* of a *katan* in the late twelfth century by Isaac ben Abba Mari of Marseilles in his *Sefer ha-'itur, ot kuf—kidushin* (Warsaw, 1885), pt. 2, fol. 77d.

22. See Grossman, *Ḥasidot u-mordot*, 63–64, 69–75; idem, "Mi-morashatah shel yahadut Sefarad: Ha-yaḥas el ha-ishah ha-'katlanit' bimei ha-benayim," *Tarbiz* 67 (1998): 539–40; A. A. Neuman, *The Jews of Spain*, 2:22–23; Y. T. Assis, *The Golden Age of Aragonese Jewry*, 257–58. Grossman (71n.25) notes the numerous Spanish responsa from the twelfth and thirteenth centuries that refer to the marriage of girls under the age of twelve. Indeed, Rashba rules in a responsum (4:174) that if someone swore that he would marry off his daughter as a *ketanah*, he should do so even if she refuses; see also *Teshuvot ha-Ran*, no. 32, and *Teshuvot ha-Rivash*, no. 198. Only Rashba's student, R. Moses Ḥallawa, suggested that it was preferable for the father gently to convince his daughter to get married and not to force her, even though he would be within his halakhic rights. See *Teshuvot Maharam Ḥallawa*, ed. M. Hershler (Jerusalem, 1987), no. 129, pp. 129–31. (On R. Moses's keen awareness of Ashkenazic materials, see Israel Ta-Shma, *Minhag Ashkenaz ha-kadmon* [Jerusalem, 1992], 301.) For the geonic roots of the Andalusian and Spanish rabbinic view to permit the marriage of *ketanot*, see, e.g., *Teshuvot ha-geonim sha'arei tsedek*, חלק ג', שער ג', סי' יב (p. 40, in a responsum by Sa'adia Gaon): מעשה שהיה במקומנו ראובן היו לו שתי בנות ושידך שמעון לאחת מהם ונתרצה לו. וכן המנהג במקומנו בשעה שהוא רוצה לקדש את הנערה. אם בוגרת היא, מרשת את אביה לקבל קידושיה. ואם קטנה היא מקבל קדושיה מדעתו כמנהג חכמים. ובאין הקהל לבית הכנסת שמתפלל שמה אבי הנערה ומקבל קידושי בתו בבית הכנסת. See also *Otsar ha-Geonim*, ed. B. M. Levin, *Yevamot* (Jerusalem, 1925), 7:190–94. Maimonides held that marrying off a *ketanah*, while technically permitted, was not a good idea (*ein ra'ui la'asot ken*; see *Mishneh Torah, hilkhot ishut*, 3:10, 10:15, and *Beit Yosef* to *Even ha-'ezer* 56, end), but he does not appear to have been influential in Spain in this instance. Cf. *Ḥidushei ha-Ritva* (below, n. 33); and Goitein, *A Mediterranean Society*, 3:76–79.

23. See below, n. 39. Baumgarten's unpublished paper was delivered at the University of Pennsylvania's Center for Advanced Jewish Studies in December 2012. She also cited evidence from *Sefer ḥasidim* and *Sefer ha-ma'asim* that will not be discussed here. I was present at Prof. Baumgarten's talk, and I thank her for providing me with a copy.

24. See Tosafot BT Kidushin 41a, s.v. *asur le-adam* (Grossman, *Ḥasidot u-mordot*, 76).

25. See Grossman, *Ḥasidot u-mordot*, 76n.39, citing *Kol bo*, ed. D. Avraham (Jerusalem, 2001), sec. 75, p. 78: והר"פ כתב וה"מ בימיה' שהיו ישראל רבים במקום אחד. אבל עתה שאנו מתי מעט, רגילין אנו לקדש אפי' קטנה שמא יקדמנו אחה, בשם הר"מ ז"ל. See also *Orḥot ḥayim* (New York, 1959), pt. 2, p. 45 (*hilkhot kidushim*, sec. 6), where this passage appears in the names of ר"ף [רבינו פרץ] and רמנ"ע [ר"מ נוחו עדן].

26. See Urbach, *Ba'alei ha-tosafot*, 2:632 (nn. 47–48).

27. See *Hagahot rabenu Perets le-sefer mitsvot katan*, 183.4, *yom revi'i*, fol. 21a. Dr. Judah Galinsky was kind enough to provide me with photocopies of this passage from the earliest

manuscripts of the *Hagahot rabenu Perets* (Bodl. 877; Nimes 26; Paris 643; Parma 1940), which attribute the ruling to הר"מ (or הר"ם; the ruling is unattributed in Leipzig 9). Based on other references within *Hagahot rabenu Perets*, it is clear that the reference to ר"מ here is to R. Moses of Evreux, in whose *beit midrash* Rabbenu Perets studied (see, e.g., Urbach, *Ba'alei ha-tosafot*, 2:576; and Emanuel, *Shivrei luḥot*, 193–97), rather than to R. Perets's senior colleague, Meir (Maharam) of Rothenburg. Indeed, later in this same section (183.4, fol. 22a), R. Perets refers to Maharam by name, as R. Meir. See also, e.g., *Hagahot rabenu Perets*, 11.3 (fol. 4b); 11.2 (fol. 4a); 93.4 (fol. 84b); 144.5, 146.2 (*yom shlishi*, fols. 7a–b); 185.1 (fol. 42a); 193.6 (fol. 48a); 196.2 (fol. 51b); 221.1 (*yom ḥamishi*, fol. 20b). Cf. my *Peering Through the Lattices*, 236n.46. The sixteenth-century *Shitah mekubetset* (to BT Ketubot 57b, s.v. *ein poskin*) cites a version of this ruling in the name of *rabanei Tsarfat/talmidei ha-R"I*. See Urbach, *Ba'alei ha-tosafot*, 1:480, who suggests that Moses and Samuel of Evreux studied with two of R"I's leading students, R. Samson of Sens and his brother, Ritsba of Dampierre, respectively. In any case, no immediate student of R"I is associated with this ruling. In a responsum composed in Padua in the late fifteenth century (see *Teshuvot Mahari Mints*, ed. A. Siev [Jerusalem, 1995], no. 2, pp. 4–6), Judah Mintz maintains that Rav's position (not to betroth a *ketanah*) should be followed in practice. He cites the gloss of Rabbenu Perets to *Semak* (in the name of Moses of Evreux) that allowed the betrothal of minor girls, but concludes that its application is limited (*she-bistama' ein lomar ken*). Cf. Y. Y. Yuval, *Ḥakhamim be-doram*, 254–55; and Shim'on ben Zemah Duran, *She'elot u-teshuvot tashbets* (Lemberg, 1891), pt. 4, fol. 6b (*ha-tur ha-rishon*, no. 19).

28. See Urbach, *Ba'alei ha-tosafot*, 1:482–84, 2:632; I. Ta-Shma, *Kneset meḥkarim* (Jerusalem, 2004), 2:112–17; and see also *Teshuvot u-piskei Maharik ha-ḥadashim* (Jerusalem, 1970), 14–15 (ותדע שכן הוא שהרי מצינו בתו' שיטה תלמידי רבינו פרץ שכתבו וכו'); ms. Vercelli C235, fol. 308d; ms. Cambridge Or. 71, fol. 24r (=ms. Bodl. 672, fol. 21v, and ms. Hamburg 194, fol. 20v) =Tosafot Evreux le-Bava' Batra', in *'Olat Shelomoh le-zikhro shel S. D. Stuzki* (Petach Tikva, 1989), 1:68–69; ms. Bodl. 672, fol. 54r (=ms. Hamburg 194, fol. 55r) =Tosafot BT Beitsah 22a, s.v. *ein mekhabin* (Urbach, *Ba'alei ha-tosafot*, 2:612, identifies Tosafot Beitsah as Tosafot rabenu Perets, and notes the phrase *ube-shitah me-Evreux tirets*, which appears in Tosafot BT Beitsah 3a, s.v. *R. Yoḥanan*); ms. Bodl. 672 (=Tosafot BT Beitsah 9a, s.v. *galgal*, end); ms. Hamburg 194, fol. 57r: ואומ' הר"ר פרץ נ"ע דיש לדחות את מה שפי' ר"י . . . עכ"ל תוס' שיטה. (=Tosafot BT Beitsah 34a, s.v. *ein nofḥin*); ms. Bodl. 672, fol. 73r and fol. 74r: עוד מצאתי שם משם ר' יצחק מאייברא . . . כל זה לשון שיט' תוס' שיט'. See also my "Between Ashkenaz and Sefarad: Tosafist Teachings in the Talmudic Commentaries of Ritva," in *Between Rashi and Maimonides: Themes in Medieval Jewish Thought, Literature, and Exegesis*, ed. E. Kanarfogel and M. Sokolow (New York, 2010), 262–70.

29. See *Kitsur Semag*, ed. Y. Horowitz (Jerusalem, 2006), sec. 32, pp. 79–80: שמעתי מפי ה"ר טוביה עכשיו כי ידי השרים מושלות עלינו בעוונותינו אין לאסור הדבר הזה, לפי שכל אחד משיא בתו בעוד שהיכולת בידו. On R. Tuvyah, see Urbach, *Ba'alei ha-tosafot*, 1:486–92, and my "R. Tobia de Vienne et R. Yehiel de Paris: La créativité des Tossafistes dans une période d'incertitude," *Les cahiers du judaisme* 31 (2011): 5–9. Another contemporary of the brothers of Evreux, Moses of Coucy, supports the ruling of Rav, but then suggests that there is ample halakhic justification for a father to marry off his minor daughter. This appears, however, to be a theoretical discussion of underlying talmudic sources rather than a practical ruling. See *Sefer mitsvot gadol*, *'aseh* 48, fol. 124d.

30. *Tosafot ha-Rosh* (which is based in large measure on Tosafot Rash mi-Shants, below, n. 49), ed. D. Metzger (Jerusalem, 2006), 325–26; Tosafot R. Samuel ben Isaac, in *Shitat ha-kadmonim 'al Kidushin*, ed. M. Y. Blau (New York, 1970), 109; *Tosafot Tukh Kidushin*, ed. A. Z. Scheinfeld (Jerusalem, 1982), 85. (On the provenance of these collections, see Urbach, *Ba'alei ha-tosafot*, 2:630–33, and Binyamin Richler, "Kitvei ha-yad shel tosafot 'al ha-Talmud," *Ta-Shma:*

Studies in Judaica in Memory of Israel M. Ta-Shma, ed. M. Idel et al. [Alon Shevut, 2011], 811–14.) As a typical example of what appears in earlier Tosafot texts, see ms. Rome Angelica 73 (IMHM no. 11692), fol. 21a. This passage begins with the issue of *tan du* (just as the standard Tosafot to Kidushin does), ending with the phrase אם היתה גדולה לא היתה מתרצית, which is precisely where the reference to the present-day situation begins in the standard Tosafot. Shalem Yahalom, "Mokh: Tikhnun ha-mishpaḥah be-Tsarfat uve-Kataloniyah," *Pe'amim* 128 (2011): 117, links a theoretical formulation by Rabbenu Tam (see *Mordekhai li-Yevamot*, sec. 3) to a passage in *Tosafot Yeshanim ha-shalem 'al masekhet Yevamot* (12b, s.v. *gimel nashim*), ed. A. Shoshana (Jerusalem, 1994), 74–75, which assumes that marriages to *ketanot* actually occurred. However, this collection of Tosafot is also associated with the *beit midrash* at Evreux (see the editor's introduction, 24–26), and there is no evidence that Rabbenu Tam ever presumed this practice.

31. See *Sefer Mordekhai le-masekhet Ketubot*, sec. 179 (to BT Ketubot 57b): ובפ"ק דמכליתא פירש ר' אליהו טעם משום שאנו עתה מעוטי עם חיישינן שמא יקדמנו אחר. לכן אנו נוהגין לקדש כשהיא קטנה. See also *Mordekhai ha-gadol*, ms. Sassoon 534 (=Toronto Feinberg 5–011 [IMHM no. 9334]), fol. 171r, in a marginal gloss: משום שאנו עתה מעט עם. (R. Elijah's comment is not found in a number of the earliest manuscripts of *Sefer Mordekhai* to *Ketubot*. See ms. Vatican Ebr. 141 [IMHM no. 11627], fol. 189v; ms. Budapest [National Library] 1 [IMHM no. 31445], fol. 286v; ms. JTS Rab. 674 [IMHM no. 41419], fol. 143r; ms. Vienna 73 [IMHM no. 1470], *Mordekhai ha-gadol*, fol. 373v.) This *Mordekhai* passage refers to the statement by R. Elijah as a part of his comments to the first chapter of Tractate Ketubot; I have not been able to identify an earlier source for his comment there. (*Sefer Mordekhai* typically cites R. Elijah of Paris simply as R. Elijah; cf. *Sefer Mordkehai le-masekhet Gittin*, ed. M. A. Rabinowitz [New York, 1990], sec. 204, p. 788; *Sefer Mordekhai ha-shalem 'al masekhet Pesaḥim*, ed. Y. Hurwitz [Jerusalem, 2008], sec. 571, p. 55; *Sefer Mordekhai ha-shalem 'al masekhet Megilah*, ed. Rabinowitz [Jerusalem, 1997], sec. 65, p. 102). Nonetheless, R. Elijah is mentioned several times in Tosafot Ketubot. See Urbach, *Ba'alei ha-tosafot*, 1:123, Samuel Cohen, "R. Mordekhai b. Hillel ha-Ashkenazi," *Sinai* 14 (1944): 316; Tosafot BT Ketubot 54b, s.v. *af 'al pi*; *Tosafot ha-Rashba mi-Shants*, ed. A. Liss (Jerusalem, 1973), 131; *Tosafot ha-Rosh*, ed. A. Lichtenstein (Jerusalem, 1999), 367–68, s.v. *im ratsah le-hosif*; *Piskei ha-Rosh*, 5:1; *Sefer Mordekhai le-masekhet Ketubot*, sec. 174. See also Tosafot BT Ketubot 58a, s.v. *hanhu*; Tosafot BT Ketubot 63a, s.v. *be-omer*; *Tosafot Shants*, 167; *Tosafot ha-Rosh*, ed. A. Lichtenstein, 434; *Piskei ha-Rosh*, 5:3. On R. Elijah's position about the kind of occupation a husband must undertake to support his wife (and the competing view of Rabbenu Tam), see my *Jewish Education and Society in the High Middle Ages* (Detroit, 1992), 28–30. This series of comments by R. Elijah on aspects of marital commitments suggests that he may well have composed his own Tosafot to parts of Ketubot. On his involvement in the tosafist enterprise more broadly, see my *The Intellectual History and Rabbinic Culture of Medieval Ashkenaz* (Detroit, 2012), 99–101, 452–53.

32. R"I's ruling is recorded in *Hagahot Maimuniyot*, *hilkhot gerushin*, 11.1.1. See also *Teshuvot Maimuniyot le-sefer Nashim* no. 14 (= *Teshuvot Maharam defus Prague*, no. 569). Cf. A. Grossman, *Ḥasidot u-mordot*, 80, and S. Yahalom, "Kovtsei ha-tosafot le-Kidushin be-sifriyat ha-Ramban," *Sidra* 27–28 (2013): 158.

33. See *Sefer Mordekhai* to Ketubot (above, n. 31, prior to the formulation of Elijah of Paris). See also Rashi to BT Ketubot 57b, s.v. *aval poskin*, as well as Tosafot BT Ketubot 57b, s.v. *bagrah*; *Tosafot ha-Rosh*, ed. Lichtenstein, 392–93; *Tosafot Rash mi-Shants*, ed. Liss, 145, s.v. *poskin*; cf. *Ḥidushei ha-Ritva*, ed. M. Goldstein, 454–55. These tosafist texts all presume that it is either prohibited for a *ketanah* to be married or that it was not commonly done. Regarding their provenance, see Urbach, *Ba'alei ha-tosafot*, 2:625–29; B. Richler, "Kitvei ha-

yad shel tosafot," 801–5. Rashi to Genesis 24:57 comments that "from here we learn that one does not marry a woman without her consent," another instance in which his interpretation supports the position of Rav; see below, n. 63. The *Mordekhai* passage also records a comment by Barukh ben Samuel of Mainz, who offered support for Rabbenu Tam's questioning of Rashi from another talmudic passage toward the end of Tractate Nidah; see also ms. Vatican 141, fol. 189v; ms. Vercelli C235, fol. 308d. For Barukh of Mainz's responses to positions taken by Rabbenu Tam, see S. Emanuel, *Shivrei luḥot*, 108–9, 115, 133n.137, and my "The Development and Diffusion of Unanimous Agreement in Medieval Ashkenaz," *Studies in Medieval Jewish History and Literature*, ed. I. Twersky and J. Harris (Cambridge, Mass., 2000), 3:28. Cf. *She'elot u-teshuvot tashbets*, above, n. 27. Another formulation by Barukh of Mainz in a related matter also reflects a theoretical, interpretive position rather than a practical one; see below, n. 40. On the practice in Germany, which was indeed different than in northern France, see below, n. 37. For Rabbenu Tam's positive view of marital choice, see below, n. 60.

34. See Grossman, *Ḥasidot u-mordot*, 78 and 104n.66, based on *Sefer ha-yashar, ḥelek ha-teshuvot*, ed. Schlesinger, 209–10 (no. 101). A version of this discussion is also found in *Kitsur Semag*, ed. Horowitz, sec. 32, p. 79; Tosafot BT Kidushin 45b, s.v. *be-ferush*; *Sefer Mordekhai 'al masekhet Kidushin*, ed. Roth, sec. 518, pp. 227–28. Cf. S. Yahalom, "Kovtsei ha-tosafot le-Kidushin be-sifriyat ha-Ramban," 155; *Sefer Kol bo*, ed. Avraham, sec. 75, 84–85. E. E. Urbach notes (*Ba'alei ha-tosafot*, 1:147–48) that this was put forward by R. Menaḥem of Joigny as one of three questions against positions of *Halakhot gedolot* that he considered to be "beyond his understanding." Thus, his main interest was to question geonic methodology and not merely to address an unusual situation in his own day; see also *Sefer ha-yashar*, 209n.3.

35. Several versions of this discussion make no reference to a minor; see Tosafot BT Kidushin 52a, s.v. *ve-hilkheta'*; *Sefer mitsvot gadol*, *'aseh* 48, fol. 125d; *Sefer mitsvot katan*, sec. 183, fol. 22a; S. Emanuel, "Bitul shidukhin," 162n.13; *Hagahot Maimuniyot, hilkhot ishut*, 9.1.1 (=ms. Moscow 155, fols. 60a–61a, sec. 42), citing Rabiah and R. Simhah of Speyer; *Teshuvot ha-Geonim sha'arei tsedek*, חלק ג', שער ג', סי' יב (42–43, end). Rabbenu Tam held that any prior indication of which daughter was involved (including the assumption that the oldest daughter was intended) is sufficient to remove the element of doubt, while Menaḥem of Joigny contended that such clarifications are insufficient and a *get* (bill of divorce) must be given to each of the sisters. The Tosafot passage concludes, however, that Rabbenu Tam had second thoughts, and did not act according to his suggested lenient approach in practice. Eli'ezer of Metz, another student of Rabbenu Tam, describes a situation in Troyes (which is apparently a fuller version of the case alluded to by Tosafot Kidushin) that came before the rabbinic court of Rabbenu Tam involving an Isaac ben Oshayah, the grandson of R. Menaḥem. Isaac committed himself to marry the minor daughter of the wealthy R. Morel of Ingletira (אינגליטיר"א), who actually had three such daughters. See *Sefer yere'im ha-shalem*, ed. A. Schiff (Vilna, 1892), sec. 7; and *Hagahot Maimuniyot, hilkhot ishut*, 9:1:1. Ingletira most likely connotes England, although it may refer to a portion of southwestern France (south of the Loire River) that was under English rule (the house of Plantagenet) around this time. See S. Emanuel, *Shivrei luḥot*, 309–10, and Joshua Prawer, *Ha-Tsalbanim: Deyokna shel ḥaverah koloni'alit* (Jerusalem, 1975), 303. Some wished to allow the marriage to proceed on the presumption that the groom had in mind that daughter to whom he had committed originally, but those who did not allow the marriage to take place prevailed, and a *get* was given to each of the three minor daughters. The *Hagahot Maimuniyot* passage concludes with its compiler, Meir ha-Kohen, relating a similar episode that was brought before his brother-in-law, Mordekhai ben Hillel, in which the groom had designated one

daughter to be his bride, but then said at the point of betrothal only that "your daughter is betrothed to me," without specifying her name. In this instance as well, the father had three minor daughters. Meir of Rothenburg ruled in accordance with the view of Eli'ezer of Metz, requiring the groom to give a *get* to all three.

36. See S. Emanuel, *Shivrei luḥot*, 180–81, and my *Peering Through the Lattices*, 107–9, 225–27.

37. See *Perushim u-pesakim le-R. Avigdor Katz*, ed. Harerei Qedem (Jerusalem, 1996), 6 (*pesak* 15): אע"פ שהייתה עדין קטנה, מכאן נהגו בצרפת להשיא בנותיהם כשהן קטנות ולקדשם משום צניעות. See also *Sefer Ḥasidim* (Parma), sec. 1084, p. 275, which instructs against marrying *ketanot*; A. Grossman, *Ḥasidot u-mordot*, 81n.60 and below, nn. 62, 63, 64, 65.

38. See above, n. 35, for the more complex case involving minor daughters brought before Maharam's student, Mordekhai ben Hillel.

39. See *Teshuvot Maharam defus Berlin*, 45 (no. 293): נ"ל דמותר לקדש בתו קטנה. דאע"ג דאמרי' דאסור לאדם לקדש בתו כשהיא קטנה, ה"מ כשהוא בעצמו קבל הקידושין. אבל נתן לה רשות לקבל את קדושיה והיא מקבלתה, מותר. וכן עשיתי בבתי הקטנה אמרתי לה בתי קבלי קדושיך אם את חופצת. ושלום מאיר בן ברוך שיח'. Since Maharam was also a student at Evreux (Urbach, *Ba'alei ha-tosafot*, 2:528), it is tempting to suggest that he was following northern French sensibilities here, but R. Meir's insistence that his daughter had to agree appears to move beyond what the Evreux passages formally required when marrying off a *ketanah*. See also *Teshuvot ha-Rashba*, 1:867; and S. Emanuel, *Teshuvot Maharam mi-Rothenburg ve-ḥaverav*, 281n.7, who notes that this *kidushin* occurred when Maharam's father was still alive. This perhaps suggests that Maharam conducted himself in this way in this instance in order to allow his elderly father to be present at his granddaughter's wedding. Cf. *Teshuvot ba'alei ha-tosafot*, ed. Agus, 176–78 (no. 92). Maharam's approach is noted by Israel Isserlein in *Terumat ha-deshen*, no. 213; and in *Pesakim u-ketavim*, sec. 33. Cf. Grossman, *Ḥasidot u-mordot*, 75–76.

40. Barukh of Mainz, in another theoretical context (in this instance, to correlate tannaitic positions), maintains that a *ketanah* must explicitly agree to her father's choice of a husband for her before the *kidushin* can be accepted. See *Mordekhai 'al masekhet Kidushin*, sec. 517, ed. Roth, 222–25 and above, n. 33.

41. See *Teshuvot geonei mizraḥ u-ma'arav*, ed. J. Mueller (Berlin, 1888), sec. 195, p. 52 (end): שאין בדור הזה לא בושת ולא פגם, שנהוג העולם כמה אנשים מדברים בבנות ישראל לקחתן ואינן נשאות אלא למי שעולות בגורלן. לפי שזיווג אשה לאיש אינו אלא מעשה שמים. וראובן זה שחוזר אחריה לקחתה מה לעשות, לא היתה בגורלו, כבר אמרו חכמים [יומא לח ע"א] אין אדם נוגע במה שמוכן לחבירו. On Ibn Avitur as the author of this responsum, see A. Grossman, "Teshuvot ḥakhmei Sefarad she-nishtamru bi-ketav yad Montefiore 98," *'Atarah le-ḥayim* (*Zalman Dimitrovsky*), ed. D. Boyarin et al. (Jerusalem, 1980), 279–80; idem, *Ḥasidot u-mordot*, 91, 96n.32.

42. See *Teshuvot ha-Geonim sha'arei tsedek*, חלק ג', שער ג', סי' יב; S. Emanuel, "Bitul shidukhin," 164–65.

43. See *Sefer ha-shetarot le-R. Yehudah bar Barzilai ha-Bartseloni*, ed. S. Z. H. Halberstam (Jerusalem, repr. 1967), 72–73, 128; A. Grossman, *Ḥasidot u-mordot*, 91; A. A. Neuman, *The Jews of Spain*, 27–29.

44. See *Mishneh Torah, hilkhot mekhirah*, 11:8, כשהיו חכמי ספרד רוצים להקנות באסמכתא כך היו עושין . . . על דרך זו היינו עושין בכל התנאין שבין אדם לאשתו בשידוכין ובכל דברים הדומים להם. Cf. Emanuel, "Bitul shidukhin," 158.

45. See above, n. 1.

46. See BT Bava Kama 91a; *Mishneh Torah, hilkhot ḥovel u-mazik*, 3:5; *Piskei ha-Rosh* to *Bava Kama*, 8.14; cf. *Ketsot ha-ḥoshen*, 207.7.

47. See *Sefer Or Zarua'*, *Piskei Bava metsi'a* (65b), sec. 188, ed. Machon Yerushalayim, vol. 3, fol. 264a; S. Emanuel, "Bitul Shidukhin," 158n.3; Grossman, *Ḥasidot u-mordot*, 92n.16.

48. See *Sefer Or Zarua'*, *Piskei Sanhedrin*, sec. 28 (vol. 3, fol. 525a, end): כשחוזר בו מבייש את חבירו ומשום דמתבייש חבירו גמרי ומקני אהדדי.

49. See *Tosafot ha-Rosh le-masekhet Sanhedrin* 24b, s.v. *kolki* (=*Sanhedrei gedolah 'al masekhet Sanhedrin*, vol. 3, ed. Y. Lifshitz [Jerusalem, 1970], 97). On the relationship between Tosafot ha-Rosh and Tosafot Rash mi-Shants, see Israel Ta-Shma, *Ha-sifrut ha-parshanit la-Talmud* (Jerusalem, 2000), 2:81–82, 103–7.

50. *Sefer mitsvot gadol*, *'aseh* 82, fol. 159c. See also Tosafot BT Bava Metsi'a 66a, s.v. *manyumei*; Tosafot BT Nedarim 27b, s.v. *ve-hilkheta'*; *Mordekhai ha-shalem 'al masekhet Sanhedrin*, ed. Y. Horowitz (Jerusalem, 2009), sec. 691, pp. 39–42.

51. See *Sefer Mordekhai 'al masekhet Bava Metsi'a*, sec. 322 (כ"כ ראב"י העזרי). See also ms. Vatican 141, fol. 56v; ms. Vercelli C 235, fol. 46c; ms. Sassoon, fol. 37r; ms. Paris BN 407 (IMHM no. 27901), fol. 94r; ms. Parma 929 (IMHM no. 13795), fol. 144r. Cf. ms. JTS Rab. 674, fol. 39c (where Rabiah is not mentioned by name); ms. Budapest 1, fol. 132v.

52. See *Hagahot Maimuniyot, hilkhot mekhirah* 11.13.8. This passage indicates that Rabiah's formulation comes from his (no longer extant) *Sefer Avi'asaf.*

53. See *Teshuvot Rashi*, ed. Elfenbein, 266 (no. 238): וכ"ש על שידוכי אשה שהנהיגו הראשונים כן שלא לבייש בנות ישראל ויש מן הדין לקונסו [ב]ממון ובריודי הגוף. See also S. Emanuel, "Bitul shidukhin," above, n. 52; A. Grossman, *Ve-hu yimshol bakh*, 60–61.

54. See *Teshuvot R. Ḥayyim Or Zarua'*, ed. Abittan, no. 152, fol. 141. In another responsum (no. 242, fol. 230), R. Ḥayyim notes that the payment to be made by those who back out was ordained already by (unidentified) Geonim. Since, however, there is no evidence within geonic literature for this fine as a reflection of *boshet*, and R. Ḥayyim refers only to Ashkenazic rabbinic figures in this responsum (Rashi, R"I, and his teacher, Meir of Rothenburg), it would seem that the term "geonim" here refers to R. Ḥayyim's venerable predecessors in Ashkenaz, who strongly supported this approach; see above, nn. 52, 53, 54, 55, 56, 57, and 58. For the use of the term "geonim" in a broader, more generic way, see Isadore Twersky, *Introduction to the Code of Maimonides* (New Haven, Conn., 1980), 82; Septimus, *Hispano-Jewish Culture in Transition*, 88. On the absence of such a conception during the geonic period, see, e.g., Goitein, *A Mediterranean Society*, 3:69–88; M. A. Friedman, "Shidukhin ve-'erusin le-fi te'udot ha-geniza ha-Kahirit," *Proceedings of the Seventh World Congress of Jewish Studies—Talmud, Halakhah and Midrash* (Jerusalem, 1977), 157–63; Menahem Ben-Sasson, *Tsemiḥat ha-kehilah ha-yehudit be-artsot ha-Islam, 800–1057* (Jerusalem, 1997), 111–14.

55. See *Sefer tashbets*, ed. Machon Yerushalayim, sec. 458, pp. 255–56: לפי שבייש אותו שלא יכול למצוא זיווג כל כך בטוב כמו שהיה עושה קודם לכן. See also *Orḥot Ḥayim*, pt. 2, 59–60 (sec. 18); A. Grossman, *Ḥasidot u-mordot*, 96; idem, *Ve-hu yimshol bakh*, 329–31; S. Emanuel, "Bitul shidukhin," 160–61; A. A. Neuman, *The Jews of Spain*, 28–29.

56. See above, n. 22. Menaḥem ha-Meiri of Perpignan maintained a similar position; see A. Grossman, *Ḥasidot u-mordot*, 100, 105–6.

57. See Grossman, *Ḥasidot u-mordot*, 106–10, and idem, *Ve-hu yimshol bakh*, 268–69.

58. See *Sefer Ḥasidim* (Parma), sec. 1084, p. 275, and sec. 1894, p. 458; A. Grossman, *Ḥasidot u-mordot*, 81, 100.

59. See *SHP*, sec. 1102 and 1104, p. 280, sec. 1131, p. 286, sec. 1897, p. 459; Grossman, *Ḥasidot u-mordot*, 101–3; idem, *Ve-hu yimshol bakh*, 193–96; above, n. 7.

60. See *Tosafot Maharam ve-rabenu Perets 'al masekhet Yevamot*, ed. Porush, 117. Cf. Tosafot BT Yevamot 43b, s.v. *shani*, and Tosafot BT Ketubot 4a, s.v. *aval.*

61. See Michael Satlow, *Jewish Marriage in Antiquity* (Princeton, N.J., 2001), 111–16; Adiel Schremer, *Zakhar u-Nekevah Bera'am: Ha-Nisu'im be-shilhei yemei ha-bayit ha-sheni ubi-tekufat ha-Mishnah veha-Talmud* (Jerusalem, 2003), 42–47; below, nn. 67, 69, 70. Cf. Israel Abrahams, "Marriages Are Made in Heaven," *Jewish Quarterly Review*, o.s., 2 (1890): 172–77, and E. E. Urbach, *Ḥazal: Pirkei emunah ve-de'ot* (Jerusalem, 1983), 247. See also the short treatise בענין זיווג מן השמים, by Meir ben Moses (a teacher of Zedekiah ben Abraham ha-Rofe', author of *Shibolei ha-leket*), published in *Seder erusin ve-kidushin*, ed. S. E. Stern (Bnei Brak, 1990), 11–15, from ms. Vatican 285 (IMHM no. 8632), fols. 127v–129a (=ms. JTS 2499 [IMHM no. 28752], fols. 29r–33r). This text is also found in *Shibolei ha-leket, ḥelek sheni*, ed. M. Z. Hasida (Jerusalem, 1969), sec. 50, pp. 107–9 (=*din 'inyan kidushin*), and was published from the JTS manuscript in *Menorat ha-ma'or le-R. Yisra'el al-Nakawa*, ed. H. G. Enelow (New York, 1932), 4:561–66.

62. See Tosafot BT Yevamot 61b, s.v. *ve-khen*; *Tosafot yeshanim*, ed. Shoshana, ad loc., 569–70: מכאן קשה לפירוש הקונטרוס דבפירושו בחומש כתב דרבקה בת ג' שנים היתה, דהכא משמע דגדולה היתה. לכך הגיה ה"ר שמואל החסיד בסדר עולם שהיתה בת י"ד שנים ומייתי ראיה מספרי וכו' (=*Tosafot Maharam verabenu Perets*, ed. Porush, 178–79); ms. Paris BN 167, fols 55r–v (=ms. Moscow 362, fols. 128r–v; *Tosafot ha-shalem*, ed. Gellis [Jerusalem, 1984], sec. 4, vol. 3, p. 6); *Perushei ha-Torah le-R. Yehudah he-ḥasid*, ed. Lange, 35–36; *Perush ha-Rokeaḥ 'al ha-Torah*, 1:177–78; ms. JTS Lutzki 794, fol. 2v; ms. Florence, Laurenziana, Plut. 2.20 (IMHM no. 20365), fols. 159v–160r; *Perushei R. Ḥayim Palti'el 'al ha-torah*, ed. Y. S. Lange (Jerusalem, 1981), 66–67; *Moshav zekenim*, ed. S. Sassoon (Jerusalem, 1982), 36 (=*Tosafot ha-shalem*, ed. Gellis, sec. 3, vol. 3, p. 5). See my "Midrashic Texts and Methods in Tosafist Torah Commentaries," in *Midrash Unbound: Transformations and Innovations*, ed. M. Fishbane (Oxford, 2013), 300–305, for further discussion of these exegetical works and their approaches in this matter.

63. Although *Bereshit rabbah* (60.12) derives from Genesis 24:57 ("let us call the *na'arah* and ask her") that an orphaned girl may be married only with her consent (*mi-da'atah*), Rashi on this verse asserts more broadly that consent is required of all women, i.e., even if she has a father. This passage again suggests that Rashi supported the position of Rav (BT Kidushin 41a), that a man should not betroth his minor daughter; see above, n. 33. Two northern French tosafist Torah commentaries from the mid-thirteenth century and beyond, ms. JTS Lutzki 794, fol. 2v, and *Moshav zekenim*, ed. Sassoon, 34 (and see also *Tosafot ha-shalem*, ed. Gellis, vol. 2 [Jerusalem, 1983], sec. 1 and 5, pp. 278–79), note the change from the *Bereshit Rabbah* passage made by Rashi in his commentary, but argue that since Rebecca was only three (according to the standard reckoning of the *Seder 'Olam*, which Rashi accepts), she could have been married off by her father even against her will. These tosafist Torah compilations therefore suggest that since Bethuel had died (as recorded also by Rashi to Gen. 24:55), Rebecca was an orphan, and it is (only) for that reason that her consent was needed. In cases where her father is alive, however, a minor girl's consent is not required, in accordance with the opinion of Samuel at the end of Kidushin (81b–82a) which runs counter to the view of Rav, and supports "the extant practice of one betrothing and marrying off his minor daughters." As far as I can tell, these are the only Ashkenazic sources that reject the view of Rav in legal terms (and not because of deteriorating temporal conditions). See also *Perushei R. David Kimḥi 'al ha-torah*, ed. M. Kamelhar (Jerusalem, 1970), 131; *Seder 'olam*, ed. C. J. Milikovsky (Jerusalem, 2013), 1:220–21; 2:14–18.

64. See *Perush ha-torah asher katav Rashbam*, ed. D. Rosin (Berlin, 1882), 24, and similarly, *Perushei R. Yosef Bekhor Shor 'al ha-torah*, ed. Y. Nevo (Jerusalem, 1995), 41.

65. See *Perush ha-Rashbam*, ed. Rosin, 25.

66. See *Perush rabenu Baḥya 'al ha-torah*, ed. C. D. Chavel (Jerusalem, 1994), 1:214–15.

67. See *Shitah ʿal Moʿed Katan le-talmido shel R. Yeḥiʾel mi-Paris* (Jerusalem, 2010), 207, although note the more circumspect formulation in Tosafot ha-Rosh.

68. See Tosafot BT Sanhderin 22a, s.v. *arbaʿim yom*. See also Tosafot ha-Rosh (ed. Lifshitz, 85); Tosafot BT Sotah 2a, s.v. *ha*.

69. See *Ḥidushei ha-Ritva ʿal Moʿed katan*, ed. Z. Hirshman (Jerusalem, 1975), 165. For further contextualization of Ritva's approach, see Shim'on ben Zemah Duran, *She'elot u-teshuvot Tashbets*, 2:1.

70. See *Ḥidushei ha-Ran ʿal masekhet Mo'ed Katan*, ed. S. B. Verner (Jerusalem, 1993), 75; *Nimukei Yosef* (to Alfasi's *Halakhot*, fol. 10b, s.v. *be-raḥamim*): אף שבסוף תתק"ם הגזירה שיגרשנה האיש שהתפלל עליה או ימות במהרה וישאנה איש שהוא בן זוגה אח"כ; JT Taʿanit 1:8 (end); JT Beitsah 5:2 (אפילו כן לא קיימה).

71. See G. D. Cohen, "Messianic Postures of Ashkenazim and Sephardim," *Studies of the Leo Baeck Institute*, ed. M. Kreutzberger (New York, 1967), 117–56. For a more precise analogue to the Ashkenazic position described here, see my "Ashkenazic Messianic Calculations from Rashi and His Generation Through the Tosafist Period," in *Rashi: The Man and His Work*, ed. A. Grossman and S. Japhet (Hebrew; Jerusalem, 2008), 2:381–401. A more intuitive explanation for at least some of these differences might be proposed, based on the smaller size of the communities in Ashkenaz. However, references to this distinction appear only as a factor in justifying the marriage of minor girls in northern France (above, nn. 25, 31). Moreover, as noted, this practice was actually more prevalent in the generally larger communities of Spain (above, n. 22), suggesting that communal size was not a defining consideration in these matters.

CHAPTER 2. NAHMANIDES' FOUR SENSES OF SCRIPTURAL SIGNIFICATION

1. See, e.g., David Berger, *The Jewish-Christian Debate in the High Middle Ages* (Philadelphia, 1979); Sidney Griffith, *The Church in the Shadow of the Mosque* (Princeton, N.J., 2008); Sarah Kamin, *Jews and Christians Interpret the Bible*, 2nd ed., ed. Sara Japhet (Hebrew; Jerusalem, 2008); Daniel Lasker and Sarah Stroumsa, *The Polemic of Nestor the Priest* (Jerusalem, 1996); Hava Lazarus-Yafeh, *Intertwined Worlds: Medieval Islam and Bible Criticism* (Princeton, N.J., 1992).

2. See, e.g., Mordechai Cohen, *Opening the Gates of Interpretation: Maimonides' Biblical Hermeneutics in Light of His Geonic-Andalusian Heritage and Muslim Milieu* (Leiden, 2011); Rina Drory, *The Emergence of Jewish-Arabic Literary Contacts at the Beginning of the Tenth Century* (Hebrew; Tel Aviv, 1988).

3. See, e.g., Gilbert Dahan, *Les intellectuels chrétiens et les juifs au Moyen Age* (Paris, 1990); Kamin, *Jews and Christians Interpret the Bible*; Deanna Klepper, *The Insight of Unbelievers: Nicholas of Lyra and Christian Readings of Jewish Texts in the Later Middle Ages* (Philadelphia, 2007); Frans van Liere, "Andrew of St. Victor, Jerome, and the Jews: Biblical Scholarship in the Twelfth-Century Renaissance," in *Scripture and Pluralism: Reading the Bible in the Religiously Plural Worlds of the Middle Ages and Renaissance*, ed. Thomas Heffernan and Thomas Burman (Leiden, 2005), 59–75; Eva de Visscher, *Reading the Rabbis: Christian Hebraism in the Works of Herbert of Bosham* (Boston, 2014).

4. This Christian delineation was hardly set in stone, as the four senses are classified differently by different interpreters, with even the exact number of senses varying. See Henri de Lubac, *Exégèse médiéval: Les quatre sens de l'écriture* (Paris, 1961), in English as *Medieval Exegesis: The Four Senses of Scripture*, trans. M. Sebanc (Grand Rapids, Mich., 1998).

5. See Albert van der Heide, "*PARDES*: Methodological Reflections on the Theory of the Four Senses," *Journal of Jewish Studies* 34.2 (1983): 147–59; Moshe Idel, *Absorbing Perfections: Kabbalah and Interpretation* (New Haven, 2002), 429–34; Mordechai Cohen, "Bahya ben Asher," in *Encyclopedia of the Bible and Its Reception*, ed. H. Spieckermann et al. (Berlin, 2011), 3:345–48.

6. See Nina Caputo, *Nahmanides in Medieval Catalonia: History, Community and Messianism* (Notre Dame, Ind., 2007); Robert Chazan, *Barcelona and Beyond: The Disputation of 1263 and Its Aftermath* (Berkeley, Calif., 1992); Daniel Lasker, "Jewish Knowledge of Christianity in the Twelfth and Thirteenth Centuries," in *Studies in Medieval Jewish Intellectual and Social History: Festschrift in Honor of Robert Chazan*, ed. D. Engel, L. Schiffman, and E. Wolfson (Leiden; Boston, 2012), 106–7; Eleazar Touitou, "The Controversy with the Christians in Nahmanides' Commentary on the Pentateuch" (Hebrew), *Shnaton: An Annual for Biblical and Ancient Near Eastern Studies* 20 (2010): 137–66.

7. On the close relationship between allegorical and typological interpretation, see, e.g., Sidney Griffith, "Disclosing the Mystery: The Hermeneutics of Typology in Syriac Exegesis," in *Interpreting Scriptures in Judaism, Christianity, and Islam: Overlapping Inquiries*, ed. M. Cohen and A. Berlin (Cambridge, 2016), 46–64.

8. Amos Funkenstein, "Nahmanides' Symbolic Reading of History," in *Studies in Jewish Mysticism*, ed. J. Dan and F. Talmage (Cambridge, Mass., 1982), 129–52.

9. See Bernard Septimus, "'Open Rebuke and Concealed Love': Nahmanides and the Andalusian Tradition," in *Rabbi Moses Nahmanides (Ramban): Explorations in His Religious and Literary Virtuosity*, ed. I. Twersky (Cambridge, Mass., 1983), 11–34.

10. See Moshe Halbertal, *Concealment and Revelation: Esotericism in Jewish Thought and Its Philosophical Implications* (Princeton, N.J., 2007), 83–104; Moshe Idel, "Nahmanides: Kabbalah, Halakhah, and Spiritual Leadership," in *Jewish Mystical Leaders and Leadership in the Thirteenth Century*, ed. M. Idel and M. Ostow (Northvale, N.J., 1998), 15–96; Haviva Pedaya, *Nahmanides: Cyclical Time and Holy Text* (Hebrew; Tel Aviv, 2003); Elliot Wolfson, "By Way of Truth: Aspects of Nahmanides' Kabbalistic Hermeneutic," *AJS Review* 14 (1989): 103–78.

11. See Beryl Smalley, *The Study of the Bible in the Middle Ages* (3rd ed.; Notre Dame, Ind., 1983); see also Alastair Minnis, *Medieval Theory of Authorship: Scholastic Literary Attitudes in the Later Middle Ages* (2nd ed.; Philadelphia, 2010); Christopher Ocker, *Biblical Poetics Before Humanism and Reformation* (Cambridge, 2002); Steven Ozment, *The Age of Reform (1250–1550): An Intellectual and Religious History of Late Medieval and Reformation Europe* (New Haven, Conn., 1980); Jon Whitman, "The Literal Sense of Christian Scripture: Redefinition and Revolution," in Cohen and Berlin, *Interpreting Scriptures in Judaism, Christianity, and Islam*, 133–58.

12. See Alastair Minnis and A. B. Scott with David Wallace, eds., *Medieval Literary Theory and Criticism c. 1100–c. 1375: The Commentary Tradition* (New York, 1988; repr. 2003), 204.

13. See below, n. 38.

14. Smalley, *The Study of the Bible in the Middle Ages*, 2, 41, 85, 88.

15. See de Lubac, *Exégèse médiéval*; see also Alastair Minnis, "Figuring the Letter: Making Sense of *Sensus litteralis* in Late-Medieval Christian Exegesis," in Cohen and Berlin, *Interpreting Scriptures in Judaism, Christianity, and Islam*, 159–82.

16. See Cohen, *Opening the Gates of Interpretation.*

17. Cf. Frank Kermode, "The Plain Sense of Things," in *Midrash and Literature*, ed. G. Hartman and S. Budick (New Haven, Conn., 1986), 190–91.

18. See David Weiss-Halivni, *Peshat and Derash: Plain and Applied Meaning in Rabbinic Exegesis* (New York, 1991), 53–79. A morphological note is in order here. The Hebrew term *pe-*

shuto ("its *peshat*," i.e., the *peshat* of a verse) is attested in this talmudic maxim, often cited by the medieval exegetes. In addition, they regularly employ the fuller expression *peshuto shel mikra* ("the *peshat* of the verse/scripture"), which is not attested in Hebrew in the Talmud; but its Aramaic equivalent *peshateh di-qera* is well attested (see, e.g., BT Ketubot 111b, BT Kidushin 80b, BT Ḥullin 6a).

19. Rashi, commentary on Gen. 3:8, ed. A. Berliner (Frankfurt, 1905), 7–8. On this programmatic statement and its implications, see Sarah Kamin, *Rashi's Exegetical Categorization in Respect to the Distinction Between Peshat and Derash* (Hebrew; Jerusalem, 1986), 62–77.

20. Ivan Marcus has gone so far as to simply define Rashi's commentary as "rewritten midrash." See Marcus, "Rashi's Choice: The Humash Commentary as Rewritten Midrash," in *Studies in Medieval Jewish Intellectual and Social History*, 29–46.

21. See Kamin, *Rashi's Exegetical Categorization*, 209–74.

22. See Sarah Kamin, "Affinities Between Jewish and Christian Exegesis in Twelfth-Century Northern France," in *Jews and Christians Interpret the Bible*, ed. S. Japhet (2nd ed.; Jerusalem, 2008), xxi–xxxv; see also Mordechai Z. Cohen, *The Rule of Peshat: Jewish Constructions of the Plain Sense of Scripture in Their Christian and Muslim Contexts, c. 900–1300* (Philadelphia: forthcoming), chap. 4.

23. James Kugel, *The Bible as It Was* (Cambridge, Mass., 1997), 18. These lists of *middot* aimed to systematize the methods used by the rabbis in the Talmud and midrashic literature to extract meaning from the details of the biblical text.

24. Ibid., 19–20.

25. Ibid., 20–21.

26. For analysis of this important passage, see Kamin, *Rashi's Exegetical Categorization*, 79–86, 123–24; see also Cohen, *Gates of Interpretation*, 205–6, 362–65. Rashi uses the term *peshuto* three more times in his Song of Songs commentary (see on Song 1:4, 2:13, 5:10) to explicitly label the human love story expressed by the literal sense. On the morphology of *peshat/peshuto*, see above, n. 18.

27. Sarah Kamin, "Rashi's Commentary on the Song of Songs and Jewish-Christian Polemic" (Hebrew), in Kamin, *Jews and Christians*, 31–61.

28. See Kamin, *Rashi's Exegetical Categorization*, 158–208.

29. Rashbam, commentary on Gen. 37:2, ed. D. Rosin (Breslau, 1882), 49.

30. See Cohen, *Gates of Interpretation*, 364–65.

31. See Sara Japhet, "The Tension Between Rabbinic Legal Midrash and the 'Plain Meaning' (Peshat) of the Biblical Text—An Unresolved Problem? In the Wake of Rashbam's Commentary on the Pentateuch," in *Sefer Moshe: The Moshe Weinfeld Jubilee Volume*, ed. Ch. Cohen, A. Hurvitz, and Sh. Paul (Winona Lake, Ind., 2004), 403–25.

32. On this programmatic statement and the talmudic maxim Rashbam cites, see Elazar Touitou, *Exegesis in Perpetual Motion: Studies in the Pentateuchal Commentary of Rabbi Samuel ben Meir* (Hebrew; Ramat Gan, 2003), 105.

33. See Mordechai Cohen, "Rashbam Scholarship in Perpetual Motion," *Jewish Quarterly Review* 98 (2008): 394–97.

34. See Hugh White, *Nature, Sex, and Goodness in a Medieval Literary Tradition* (New York, 2000), 77. See also Peter Dronke, "Thierry of Chartres," in *A History of Twelfth-Century Western Philosophy*, ed. P. Dronke (Cambridge, 1988), 358–85.

35. See Cohen, "Rashbam Scholarship," 394–97; Jonathan Jacobs, "Rashbam's Major Principles of Interpretation as Deduced from a Manuscript Fragment Discovered in 1984," *Revue des études juives* 170 (2011): 443–63.

36. *Safah Berurah*, ed. M. Wilensky, *Devir* 2 (1924): 288.

37. See Ibn Ezra, introduction to the Pentateuch, and his short commentary on Exod. 21:8, ed. A. Weiser (Jerusalem, 1975), 1:1, 137; 2:291. Given that Rashbam characterizes midrash using this very term (above, n. 21), it is tempting to regard this as a polemic by Ibn Ezra against his northern French colleague. There is no direct evidence, however, that Ibn Ezra was aware of Rashbam's writings at the time that he wrote his short commentary on Exodus. See Uriel Simon, *The Ear Discerns Words: Studies in Ibn Ezra's Exegetical Methodology* (Hebrew; Ramat Gan, 2013), 65.

38. *Yesod Diqduq*, ed. N. Allony (Jerusalem, 1985), 86. On *asmakhta* in the geonic-Andalusian tradition, see Jay Harris, *How Do We Know This? Midrash and the Fragmentation of Modern Judaism* (Albany, N.Y., 1995), 74–95.

39. See above, n. 29.

40. See Cohen, *Gates of Interpretation*, 74–85.

41. Maimonides, *Sefer ha-miṣwot* (Book of the Commandments), ed. and trans. J. Kafih (Jerusalem, 1971), 14.

42. Ibid., 15. For further details, see Cohen, *Gates of Interpretation*, 247–51, 287–304.

43. See Isadore Twersky, *Introduction to the Code of Maimonides* (New Haven, Conn., 1980), 57–58; Cohen, *Gates of Interpretation*, 431–45.

44. *Hassagot Ramban*, ed. C. Chavel (Jerusalem, 1981), 44.

45. Ibid., 44.

46. Ibid., 37.

47. Ibid., 45.

48. *Kitvei Ramban* (Nahmanides' Writings), ed. C. Chavel (Jerusalem, 1963–64), 1:308. Translation from Septimus, "'Open Rebuke and Concealed Love,'" 21.

49. Compare, e.g., his commentary on Exod. 20:8 with his commentary on Exod. 12:16 and Deut. 25:6. See also *Hassagot Ramban*, 154–56.

50. See Yossi Erel, "Ramban's Approach Toward the Plain Meaning of the Biblical Text vs. His Commitment to Halakhah" (Hebrew), *Jewish Studies Internet Journal* 8 (2009): 117–52. Compare Cohen, *Gates of Interpretation*, 293–300.

51. See Cohen, *Gates of Interpretation*, 375–80.

52. See ibid. 252–76.

53. See Septimus, "'Open Rebuke and Concealed Love,'" 21–22.

54. Nahmanides, commentary on Gen. 12:6, ed. H. D. Chavel (Jerusalem, 1976), 1:77; translation from Moses Nahmanides, *Commentary on the Torah*, trans. C. Chavel (New York, 1971), 1:168–69; the translation used throughout this essay (with slight adjustments).

55. Commentary on Gen. 26:1, ed. Chavel, 1:148.

56. Above, n. 8.

57. Cited in G. W. H. Lampe and K. J. Woollcombe, *Essays on Typology* (Naperville, Ill., 1957), 13. See also B. Darrel Jackson, "The Theory of Signs in Augustine's *De doctrina christiana*," *Revue des études augustiniennes* (1969): 9–49.

58. See Griffith, "Disclosing the Mystery."

59. Nahmanides, "Introduction" to *Commentary on the Torah: Exodus*, ed. and trans. Chavel, 1:279 and 2:3.

60. Compare the observation made about Rashi's innovative usage of the talmudic *peshat* maxim. See Kamin, *Rashi's Exegetical Categorization*, 57–59.

61. Commentary on Gen. 2:3, ed. and trans. Chavel, 1:30–31 and 1:61.

62. See Funkenstein, "Nahmanides' Symbolic Reading of History," 140–41.

63. See Bahya Ibn Paquda, *The Book of Direction to the Duties of the Heart*, trans. M. Mansoor (London, 1973), 106–7; Moses Maimonides, *Guide of the Perplexed*, trans. S. Pines (Chicago, 1963), 3:50, a passage cited by Nahmanides; see *Kitvei Ramban*, 1:144.

64. See Naomi Grunhaus, *The Challenge of Received Tradition: Dilemmas of Interpretation in Radak's Biblical Commentaries* (Oxford, 2013).

65. See, e.g., Radak on Gen. 14:1, 27:1. See also Cohen, "The Qimhi Family," in *Hebrew Bible / Old Testament: The History of Its Interpretation*, vol. 1:2, *The Middle Ages*, ed. M. Sæbø, M. Haran, and C. Brekelmans (Göttingen, 2000), 410–13.

66. See Cohen, "Qimhi Family," 411. The fourteenth-century Provençal exegete and philosopher Levi ben Gershom (Gersonides) brought this endeavor to new heights by systematically deriving a moral lesson (*to'elet*; benefit, use) from each and every biblical narrative.

67. See Cohen, *Gates of Interpretation*, 191–200; idem, *Three Approaches to Biblical Metaphor: From Abraham Ibn Ezra and Maimonides to David Kimhi* (Leiden, 2003), 233–45.

68. Comm. on Gen. 26:20, Chavel ed., 1:152; Chavel trans., 1:334.

69. Chavel ed., 1:3; Chavel trans., 1:9.

70. Chavel ed., 1:7; Chavel trans., 1:15. Naturally, one might ask: If Nahmanides believed it is prohibited to publicize these subjects, how could he disseminate them in his written commentaries? On this question, see Idel, "Nahmanides: Kabbalah, Halakhah, and Spiritual Leadership"; Halbertal, *Concealment and Revelation,* 83–104.

71. See David Berger, "Miracles and the Natural Order," in *Rabbi Moses Nahmanides: Explorations in His Religious and Literary Virtuosity*, ed. I. Twersky (Cambridge, Mass., 1983), 112–13; Septimus, "'Open Rebuke and Concealed Love,'" 21. See also Wolfson, "By Way of Truth," 131–42.

72. See Rashi's commentary on Deut. 25:6 and Ibn Ezra's short comm. on Exod. 21:8 (Weiser ed., 2:291–92). For the comparison between Rashi, Ibn Ezra, and Nahmanides, see Cohen, *Gates of Interpretation*, 348–51, 391–94.

73. Nahmanides reveals a bit more of his intention in his commentary on Gen. 38:8, where he explains the "great mystery" (*sod gadol*) of the law of the levirate marriage.

74. For other examples, see references cited by Berger and Septimus (n. 80, below). See also Mordechai Cohen, "Interpreting 'The Resting of the *Shekhinah*': Exegetical Implications of the Theological Debate Among Maimonides, Nahmanides, and *Sefer ha-Hinnukh*," in *The Temple of Jerusalem: From Moses to the Messiah*, ed. S. Fine (Boston, 2011), 237–74.

75. See Septimus, "'Open Rebuke and Concealed Love,'" 18; see also James A. Diamond, "Nahmanides and Rashi on the One Flesh of Conjugal Union: Lovemaking vs. Duty," *Harvard Theological Review* 102 (2009): 193–94.

76. Commentary on Gen. 1:2, Chavel ed., 1:15; Chavel trans., 1:15.

77. Commentary on Gen. 3:22, Chavel ed., 1:42; Chavel trans., 1:86.

78. *Kitvei Ramban*, 2:295–97. For a discussion of this passage and its implications, see Wolfson, "By Way of Truth," 122–23.

79. See Wolfson, "By Way of Truth," 120.

80. This sort of conceptual transfer is often associated with the technique of allegory, as opposed to typology. See Jon Whitman, "From the Textual to the Temporal: Early Christian 'Allegory' and Early Romantic 'Symbol,'" *New Literary History* 22 (1991): 161–76.

81. See Nahmanides, commentary on Gen. 1:1, ed. Chavel, 9–10.

82. See Hannanel Mack, "*Shiv'im panim la-Torah: Le-mahalakho shel biṭuy*," in *Rabbi Mordechai Breuer Festschrift*, ed. M. Bar-Asher (Jerusalem, 1992), 2:449–62.

83. See Kamin, "Jewish and Christian Exegesis," xxxii–xxxiii.

84. Septimus, "'Open Rebuke and Concealed Love,'" 19.

85. See Funkenstein, "Nahmanides' Symbolic Reading of History," 134–39.

86. Rita Copeland, "Rhetoric and the Politics of the Literal Sense in Medieval Literary Theory: Aquinas, Wyclif, and the Lollards," in *Rhetoric and Hermeneutics in Our Time*, ed. W. Jost and M. J. Hyde (New Haven, Conn., 1997), 340.

87. Minnis, *Theory of Authorship*, ix.

88. Ibid., x.

89. See Alastair Minnis, "Material Swords and Literal Lights: The Status of Allegory in William of Ockham's *Breviloquium* on Papal Power," in *With Reverence for the Word: Scriptural Exegesis in Judaism, Christianity, and Islam*, ed. J. McAuliffe, B. Walfish, and J. Goering (Oxford, 2010), 292–308.

90. See Minnis, *Theory of Authorship*, 73–112.

CHAPTER 3. BIBLE AND POLITICS

This research was supported by the I-CORE Program of the Planning and Budgeting Committee and The Israel Science Foundation (1754/12).

1. Oxford, Bodleian Library, 27/1, fol. 4a (from 1358); Munich, 50, fol. 16b, which was copied in 1552, and is merely an expanded copy of the book *Pa'aneah Raza* (the quotations here follow MS. Oxford).

2. See Ephraim E. Urbach, *The Tosafists* (Hebrew; Jerusalem, 1980), esp. 60–113; Avraham (Rami) Reiner, "Rabbenu Tam: His (French) Teachers and His Pupils from Germany" (Hebrew; M.A. thesis, Hebrew University, 1997); idem, "Rabbenu Tam and His Contemporaries" (Hebrew; Ph.D. diss., Hebrew University, 2002).

3. On Rashbam's ties with non-Jewish scholars, see Meir (Martin) Lokshin, *Commentary to the Torah of Rabbenu Samuel ben Meir* (Hebrew; Jerusalem, 2009), 27–28; Sara Japhet, "Did Rashbam Know the Vulgate Translation of the Song of Songs?," *Textus* 24 (2009): 263–67, and the reference in n. 16. See also Elazar Touitou, *Exegesis in Perpetual Motion: Studies in the Pentateuchal Commentary of Rabbi Samuel Ben Meir* (Hebrew; Ramat Gan, 2003), 11–33; Sarah Kamin, "Rashbam's Conception of the Creation in the Light of the Intellectual Currents of His Time," in *Jews and Christians Interpret the Bible* (2nd ed.; Jerusalem, 2008), xxxvi–lxxiv; Martin Lockshin, "*Peshat* or Polemics: The Case of Genesis 36," in *New Perspectives on Jewish-Christian Relations in Honor of David Berger*, ed. E. Carlebach and J. J. Schacter (Leiden, 2012), 437–53.

4. Ḥayyim Joseph David Azulai, *Shem ha-gedolim* (Jerusalem, 1994), 188.

5. Samuel Poznanski, *Introduction to the French Sages, the Bible Commentators*, appended to *Commentary on Ezekiel and the Twelve Minor Prophets of Eliezer of Beaugency* (Hebrew; Warsaw, 1913), 54.

6. Benjamin Richler, "Rabbeinu Tam's 'Lost' Commentary on Job," in *The F. Talmage Memorial Volume*, ed. B. Walfish (Haifa, 1993), 191–202.

7. Israel M. Ta-Shma, "The Commentary by Rabbenu Tam to the Book of Job" (Hebrew), *Kobez al Yad* 13.23 (1996): 193–233.

8. Avraham Shoshana, *The Book of Job with the Commentaries of Rashi, Rabbenu Jacob b. Meir Tam, and a Disciple of RaSHI* (Hebrew; Jerusalem, 2000). This edition contains the text

of the commentary, following MS. Oxford, Opp. Add. fol. 22 (Neubauer 298), while making use of MS. Moscow, Ginzburg Collection, 1657.

9. Menahem Banitt, *Le Glossaire de Leipzig* (Jerusalem, 2005).

10. Ibid., 1345, s.v. *ve-olalti* (Job 16:15). Cf. Gedalia Lasser, "Rabbeinu Tam's Resolution Treatise on the Confrontation between Menahem ibn Saruq and Dunash ben Labrat: Editing the Composition and Analyzing the Exegetical Method of Rabbeinu Tam Based upon His Composition" (Hebrew; Ph.D. diss., Bar-Ilan University, 2011), 355; Banitt, *Glossaire*, 1405, s.v. *ve-orkiy* (Job 30:17). Cf. Lasser, "Resolution Treatise," 360; Banitt, *Glossaire*, 1463, s.v. *kidodei* (Job 41:11). Cf. Lasser, "Resolution Treatise," 41; Banitt, *Glossaire*, 1465, s.v. *ve-agmon* (Job 41:12). Cf. Lasser, "Resolution Treatise," 218–19.

11. Banitt, *Glossaire*, 1291, s.v. *u-fakadeta* (Job 5:24); cf. Shoshana, *Book of Job*, 36. In this case, each of the two works brings a different biblical example in the interpretation of the word. Banitt, *Glossaire*, 1331, s.v. *lo tishmor al hatati* (Job 14:16). The interpretation mentioned there does not appear in Rabbenu Tam's commentary to Job. Banitt, *Glossaire*, 1333, Job 14:18–19; cf. Shoshana, *Book of Job*, 89–90. In this case, the interpretations differ in their understanding of the entire question.

12. See the interpretations of Rashi and Rabbenu Tam to Job 6:7, 12:4, 13:27, 15:4. At times the author of the commentary attributed to Rabbenu Tam rejects an understanding that appears in the commentary of Rashi, without mentioning "*yesh mefarshim.*" See, e.g., Job 3:4.

13. S.v. *nita'u* (Job 4:10): the commentary attributed to Rabbenu Tam is ascribed to "*yesh mefarshim*," while Rashi's commentary is silent on this; clearly, then, the reference is not to Rashi For additional instances, see 14:19, 15:26, 16:15, 19:29, and more.

14. See Job 6:6 (Lasser, "Resolution Treatise," 271); Job 24:18 (Lasser, "Resolution Treatise," 310); Job 24:20 (Lasser, "Resolution Treatise," 39); Job 39:30 (Lasser, "Resolution Treatise," 362).

15. See Job 9:5 (cf. Lasser, "Resolution Treatise," 65); Job 30:17 (cf. Lasser, "Resolution Treatise," 359); Job 41:12 (cf. Lasser, "Resolution Treatise," 218).

16. Job 16:15 (cf. Lasser, "Resolution Treatise," 403); Job 29:7 (cf. Lasser, p. 36); Job 30:22 (cf. Lasser, "Resolution Treatise," 399); Job 41:11 (cf. Lasser, "Resolution Treatise," 40).

17. Job 15:27 (cf. Lasser, "Resolution Treatise," 155); Job 16:15 (cf. Lasser, "Resolution Treatise," 351).

18. On the use of the expressions "the land of Canaan" and "the language of Canaan," and on the history of the research, see Roman Jakobson and Morris Halle, "The Term 'CANAAN' in Medieval History," in *For Max Weinreich on His Seventieth Birthday: Studies in Jewish Languages, Literature, and Society* (The Hague, 1964), 147–72. See Marcus Nathan Adler, *The Itinerary of Benjamin of Tudela* (London, 1907), 80: "Thence extends the land of Bohemia, called Prague. This is the commencement of the land of Slavonia, and the Jews who dwell there call it Canaan, because the men of that land (the Slavs) sell their sons and their daughters to the other nations." It is noteworthy that Rashi and R. Joseph Kara (Rashi's student and Rabbenu Tam's teacher) refer a number of times to "the language of Canaan"; see Jakobson and Halle, "'CANAAN,'" 151–53.

19. On Rabbenu Tam's students who came to study in his study hall from Bohemia, see Reiner, "Rabbenu Tam: His (French) Teachers," 125–39.

20. On this controversy, see Shelomo Morag, "The Controversy Between Menahem and Dunash and the Revival of the Hebrew Language," *Pe'amim* 56 (1993): 4–19 (Hebrew); Angel Saenz-Badillos, "Early Hebraists in Spain: Menahem ben Saruq and Dunash ben Labrat," *Hebrew Bible/Old Testament* 1.2 (2000): 96–109. See also Ezra Fleischer, "On the Emergence of

Hebrew Secular Poetry in Spain," in *Culture and Society in Medieval Jewry: Studies Dedicated to the Memory of Haim Hillel Ben-Sasson*, ed. Menahem Ben-Sasson, Robert Bonfil, and Joseph H. Hacker (Hebrew; Jerusalem, 1989), 197–225.

21. See Lasser, *Resolution Treatise*, 26–35.

22. *Sepher ha-Galuj von R. Joseph Kimchi*, pub. H. J. Mathews (Berlin, 1887), 2–3.

23. Poznanski, *Introduction*, 54.

24. Urbach, *Tosaphists*, 107.

25. See Yehiel Michel Orlean, *Sefer ha-gan . . . by R. Aaron b. R. Yose ha-Kohen* (Hebrew; Jerusalem, 2009), 26–27, 323, 344.

26. *Sefer Moshav Zekenim al ha-Torah: Collected Interpretations of Our Masters, the Tosafists, of Blessed Memory*, ed. Solomon Sassoon (Hebrew; Letchworth, 1959).

27. BT Kidushin 30a; BT Avodah Zarah 19a.

28. BT Sanhedrin 24a, and Tosafot, s.v. *belulah*.

29. *Sefer ha-yashar, She'eilot u-teshuvot*, ed. Shraga Rosenthal (Berlin, 1898), 46, p. 87.

30. On the influence by Jewish sages and the reception of their teachings among their Christian contemporaries, see Beryl Smalley, *The Study of the Bible in the Middle Ages* (Oxford, 1952), 101–6, 149–72; Aryeh Grabois, "The *Hebraica veritas* and Jewish-Christian Relations in the Twelfth Century," *Speculum* 50 (1975): 613–34. See also David Berger, "Mission to the Jews and Jewish-Christian Contacts in the Polemical Literature of the High Middle Ages," *American Historical Review* 91 (1986): 576–91; Louis H. Feldman, "The Jewish Sources of Peter Comestor's Commentary on Genesis in His *Historia Scholastica*," in *Studies in Hellenistic Judaism* (Leiden; New York; Cologne, 1996), 317–47; Ephraim Kanarfogel, *The Intellectual History and Rabbinic Culture of Medieval Ashkenaz* (Detroit, 2013), 84–110. It seems that Rashbam was a natural choice for such questions; like his brother Rabbenu Tam, he was an inhabitant of Champagne. Rashbam, however, died most likely in the second half of the 1160s, while Rabbenu Tam passed away in the summer of 1171; the exact time of the correspondence has not been determined. On the dating of Rashbam's death, see Reiner, "Rabbenu Tam: His (French) Teachers," 22n.67.

31. Isaac H. Weiss, "*Toledot Rabbenu Yaakov Tam*" (The History of Rabbenu Jacob Tam), *Beit Talmud* 3 (1883): 257.

32. *Sefer ha-yashar, She'eilot u-teshuvot*, 78, p. 176.

33. Ibid. 79, p. 177. "Though ministers meet and consult with me" is based, albeit with altered meaning, on Ps. 119:23.

34. *Sefer ha-yashar, She'eilot u-teshuvot* 15, p. 26.

35. *Sefer zekhirah* (The Book of Memoirs: Penitential Prayers and Lamentations of Rabbi Ephraim bar Jacob of Bonn), ed. Abraham M. Habermann (Jerusalem, 1946), 121. On the literary fashioning of this story, see Ivan Marcus, "Jews and Christians Imagining the Other in Medieval Europe," *Prooftexts* 15 (1995): 209–26.

36. Robert Chazan, *Medieval Jewry in Northern France: A Political and Social History* (Baltimore, 1973), 58–60.

37. This correspondence might have been between Rabbenu Tam and Theobald, Henry's father, who was count of Champagne between the years 1125 and 1152. The character of the inquirer, however, as it emerges from the sources cited below, is more suitable to that of Henry than to his father.

38. See Henri Gross, *Gallia Judaica: Dictionnaire geographique de la France d'apres les sources rabbiniques* (Amsterdam, 1969), 224.

39. See Anne E. Lester, "Gender and Social Networks in Medieval France: The Convents of the County of Champagne" (Ph.D. diss., Princeton University, 2003), 36–40.

40. John F. Benton, "The Court of Champagne as a Literary Center," in *Culture, Power and Personality in Medieval France* (London, 1991), 3–43.

41. Ibid., 15–18.

42. Ibid., 25–27.

43. See, e.g., *The Targum Attributed to Jonathan ben Uzziel*, ed. David Rieder (Hebrew; Jerusalem, 1984), 19.

44. See, e.g., *Enoch I*, 72–81 (trans. E. Isaac, in *The Old Testament Pseudepigrapha*, vol. 1: *Apocalyptic Literature and Testaments*, ed. James H. Charlesworth [Garden City, N.Y., 1985], 50–59); *Jubilees* 4:16–17 (trans. O. S. Wintermate, in *Old Testament Pseudepigrapha*, vol. 2: *Expansions of the "Old Testament" and Legends . . . ,* 62).

45. *Bereshit rabbah* 25, ed. Theodor-Albeck (Jerusalem, 1965), 238–39.

46. *Pesiqta de-Rav Kahana*, ed. Bernard Mandelbaum (New York, 1987), BT Rosh Hashanah 11a, p. 344; *Vayikra rabbah*, ed. Mordecai Margulies (New York, 1993), 29:11, 680.

47. *Bereshit rabbah* 25, ed. Theodor-Albeck, 238.

48. BT Yoma 22b.

49. The centrality of the homage in lord and vassal relations had been noted by scholars of this era. See Marc Bloch, *Feudal Society*, trans. L. A. Manyon (London, 1965), 145–47, 227–30; Francois L. Ganshof, *Feudalism*, trans. Philip Grierson (New York, 1961), 72–82. For a critical appraisal of Ganshof's work, see Fredric L. Cheyette, "'Feudalism': A Memoir and an Assessment," in *Feud, Violence and Practice: Essays in Medieval Studies in Honor of Stephen D. White*, ed. Belle S. Tuten and Tracey L. Billado (Farnham, 2010), 119–33. The concept of homage, as well as the feudal system in general, as applied by these scholars to mediaeval society has been disputed. See Susan Reynolds, *Fiefs and Vassals* (Oxford, 2001), 22–34.

50. For a detailed account of sociopolitical conditions during the lifetime of Rabbenu Tam and Henry the Liberal, see Theodore Evergates, *The Aristocracy in the County of Champagne, 1100–1300* (Philadelphia, 2007), 15–31, 63–81; idem, *Feudal Society in the Bailliage of Troyes Under the Counts of Champagne, 1152–1284* (Baltimore, 1975), 16–30.

51. See Ganshof, *Feudalism*, 73.

52. *Sefer ha-yashar, She'eilot u-teshuvot* 34, p. 59.

53. Ganshof, *Feudalism*, 92–93; Bloch, *Feudal Society*, 220; Evergates, *Feudal Society*, 27.

54. *Sefer ha-yashar, She'eilot u-teshuvot* 78, p. 176.

55. Ibid., 79, p. 177.

56. A number of sources teach of additional, and sporadic, ties between Rabbenu Tam and non-Jewish scholars, but the identity of his correspondents cannot be determined from them, and therefore remains beyond the scope of the current discussion. See *Torah Commentaries by R. Ḥayyim Paltiel*, ed. Isaak S. Lange (Hebrew; Jerusalem, 1981), 82: "A *sar* [minister?] asked Rabbenu Tam"; p. 108 (*Tosafot Rosh* on Berakhot 12b, ed. Yisrael Sklar [Jerusalem, 2007], p. 59): "A *hegemon* [high church official] asked Rabbenu Tam."

57. See, e.g., BT Avodah Zarah 59a, s.v. *be-tzar*: "Rabbenu Tam says that our lands are under lien to the lords . . . and therefore are not ours"; BT Bava Kama 58a, s.v. *iy nami*: "And those Jews who flee from their city, and the lord holds their lands, which are not liable for taxes . . . R. Isaac says . . . that this is not the law of the land, but [simply] theft, for we have seen in the land around us that the Jews have the legal standing to move freely wherever they please. The law of the land understands that the ruler may not seize the holdings of the Jews when they leave his city, and this was the practice in all the land of Bourgogne. If a *sar* [one of high standing] were to come and change the law as he sees fit, this is not the law of the land, for this is not law, it is not at all proper."

58. *Shittah mekubetzet*, Hullin, MS. Moscow 946, fol. 160b. The passage also appears in *Tosafot ha-Rosh*, Hullin, ed. Eliyahu Lichtenstein (Jerusalem, 2002), 264n.527. My thanks to Prof. Simcha Emanuel for drawing my attention to the first source.

59. See Lasser, "Resolution Treatise," 115: "The bird hunters take them and bind them to a peg inserted in the ground. They put nets or glue around it, and they are trapped." See also Leor Jacobi, "Jewish Hawking in Medieval France: Falconry, Rabbenu Tam, and the Tosafists," *Oqimta* 1 (2013): 421–504.

CHAPTER 4. RABBIS, READERS, AND THE PARIS BOOK TRADE

The research for this study was supported by the Israel Science Foundation (grant no. 1474/12). I would like to thank the editors of this volume, and also Adam Davis and Lesley Smith for their very helpful comments and suggestions. I would also like to thank David Ruderman for creating the ideal academic environment that allowed me to explore the ideas presented here during my stay at the Katz Center.

1. See Judah Galinsky, "Between Ashkenaz (Germany) and Tsarfat (France): Two Approaches Towards Popularizing Jewish Law," in *Jews and Christians in Thirteenth-Century France*, ed. Elisheva Baumgarten and Judah Galinsky (London, 2015).

2. One of the issues that I relate to throughout this essay is the question of the various literacy levels within the Jewish community. Clearly, even if a good amount of Jews were able to read the liturgical text, this did not mean that they could comprehend a work of religious law written in Hebrew, even a relatively simple one.

3. For a description of the tosafist dialectical approach to the Talmud, see Haym Soloveitchik, *Collected Essays* (Oxford, 2013), 1:3–10.

4. See Yisrael M. Ta-Shma, *Keneset meḥkarim* (Jerusalem, 2010), 4:259–70.

5. A clear exception to this was El'azar of Worms' *Rokeaḥ;* he, however, belonged to the German Pietists (Ḥasidei Ashkenaz) and cannot be considered part of the mainstream legal writing of the time. See more in my essay "Between Ashkenaz (Germany) and Tsarfat (France)."

6. In the earlier study I suggested that although this Rhineland attitude was prevalent during the high Middle Ages, it was only fully articulated at the beginning of the fifteenth century.

7. See, e.g., Israel M. Ta-Shma, *Creativity and Tradition: Studies in Medieval Rabbinic Scholarship, Literature and Thought* (Cambridge, Mass., 2006), 1, and David Malkiel, *Reconstructing Ashkenaz: The Human Face of Franco-German Jewry, 1000–1250* (Berkeley, 2009), preface, ix. For a more nuanced approach that differentiates between various contexts, see Ephraim Kanarfogel, *The Intellectual History and Rabbinic Culture of Medieval Ashkenaz* (Detroit, 2013), 2–9.

8. See Avraham Grossman, *Ḥakhmei tsarfat ha-rishonim* (Jerusalem, 1995), 545–86; on the relationship with Spanish culture, see 554–71.

9. Ibid., 580–81.

10. On the Seder of R. Amram and its popularity in Europe, see Robert Brody, *The Geonim of Babylonia and the Shaping of Medieval Jewish Culture* (New Haven, Conn., 1998), 191–92.

11. On the *Maḥzor Vitry*, see Y. M. Ta-Shma, *Ha-Tefilla ha-ashkenazit ha-kedumah* (Jerusalem, 2004), 15–25.

12. On Jacob's maḥzor, see Grossman, *Ḥakhmei tsarfat,* 417–18, and for that of Shema'ya, see 395–403.

13. On Joseph, see ibid., 46–81. On the evidence that he authored a maḥzor, see 75.

14. See ibid., 73–75, 77–78.

15. See above, nn. 8 and 13. On the French willingness to absorb cultural influence from other Jewish centers, see Grossman, *Ḥakhmei tsarfat,* 572–86.

16. See A. Grossman, *Ḥakhmei ashkenaz ha-rishonim* (Jerusalem, 1989). More than 400 pages of this work are devoted to reconstructing the talmud-centric culture of Germany from the end of the tenth until the end of the eleventh century. On the scholars as leaders of the community, see 5–6, 18–23.

17. See Grossman, *Ḥakhmei tsarfat,* 34–42.

18. Although it is worth noting that, according to H. Soloveitchik's important studies on pawnbroking and wine, it emerges that in the second half of the twelfth century the Franco-Jewish community was no longer self-conscious about its religiosity. See Soloveitchik, *Collected Essays,* 1:259–77.

19. Within this context one may consider Rashi's great exegetical project of making the Talmud and the Pentateuch more accessible to the reader.

20. Even if one can argue for the relatively quick recovery of these communities in the economic and social spheres, culturally the impact of these massacres seems to have been far-reaching; see Grossman, *Ḥakhmei ashkenaz,* 435–40.

21. For a description of the tosafist dialectical approach see above, n. 3. On the relationship between the early beginning of the tosafist approach in Germany and its development in France, see Grossman, *Ḥakhmei tsarfat,* 439–54; Haym Soloveitchik, *Yenam* (Tel Aviv, 2003), 22–25; and idem, *Collected Essays,* 1:26–29.

22. Mention, however, should be made of Eli'ezer of Metz's work the *Yere'im.* Eli'ezer may have written his work in Germany but he was a product of the French tosafist school. Although his work does include sections that can be considered as halakhic treatments, as a whole the *Yere'im* cannot be considered in my mind a work of religious law. The goal of the work, as the author explains in his introduction, is to inculcate in the student of Talmud the awareness of God as the one who commands men to perform the *mitsvot.* See Judah Galinsky, "The Significance of Form: R. Moses of Coucy's Reading Audience and His *Sefer ha-Mizvot,*" *AJS Review* 35 (2011): 305–8.

23. See Yoel Friedemann, "Sefer ha-terumah le-rabenu Barukh ben R. Yitsḥak: Megamot mivneh ve-nusaḥ" (Ph.D. diss., Hebrew University, 2013), 1.

24. Simcha Emanuel, "'Ve-ish al mekomo mevo'ar shmo': le-toldotav shel R. Barukh b. Yitsḥak," *Tarbiz* 69 (2000): 427–29.

25. See Soloveitchik, *Collected Essays,* 1:9, 17–18, and Simcha Emanuel, *Shivrei luḥot: Sifrei halakhah avudim shel ba'alei ha-tosafot* (Jerusalem, 2006), 6–8.

26. This, of course, does not eliminate the possibility of other external factors that may motivate authors to compose works of law such as exile and decline. See, e.g., Isadore Twersky, *Introduction to the Code of Maimonides (Mishneh Torah)* (New Haven, Conn., 1980), 62–65, and Judah Galinsky, "Of Exile and Halakhah: Fourteenth-Century Spanish Halakhic Literature and the Works of the French Exiles Aaron ha-Kohen and Jeruham b. Meshulam," *Jewish History* 22 (2008): 81–96.

27. Barukh ben Isaac, *Sefer ha-terumah* (Warsaw, 1897), 196.

28. The complete list of topics treated in *Sefer ha-terumah* as it appears in most manuscripts and in the printed version is as follows: 1. *Sheḥita, Terefot* (laws relating to ritual slaugh-

ter), and *Issur ve-hetter* (laws relating to food preparation); 2. *Ḥallah* and *Niddah* (laws relating to challah and family purity); 3. *Gittin* and *Ḥalitsah* (laws relating to divorce and levirate marriage); 4. *'Avodah zarah* and *Yen nesekh* (laws relating to idolatry); 5. *Sefer torah* and *Tefillin* (laws relating to ritual writing of Torah and tefillin); 6. *Erets Yisra'el* (laws relating to the Land of Israel); 7. *Shabbat* (laws relating to the Sabbath). Friedemann, "*Sefer ha-terumah*," 158–60, has recently suggested that he chose these topics because they belonged to the tractates that he wrote Tosafot on. It is difficult to verify such a theory but I would suggest a modified approach, that these were the tractates that he studied personally with his revered teacher Isaac of Dampierre.

29. See Ephraim E. Urbach, *Ba'alei ha-tosafot* (Jerusalem, 1980), 466–71, and J. D. Galinsky, "R. Moshe mi-Kutsi ke-ḥasid, darshan u-fulmusan" (master's thesis, Yeshiva University, 1993), and Galinsky, "The Significance of Form," 298–99.

30. We find him participating in the Talmud trial of 1240 that took place in Paris. On Moses and the Talmud trial see J. R. Woolf, "Some Polemical Emphases in the Sefer Miswot Gadol of Rabbi Moses of Coucy," *Jewish Quarterly Review* 89 (1998): 86–93, and J. D. Galinsky, "Mishpat ha-talmud bi-shenat 1240 be-Paris: 'Vikuaḥ R. Yeḥi'el' ve-'sefer ha-mitsvot' shel R. Moshe mi-Kutsi," *Shenaton ha-mishpat ha-'ivri* 22 (2001–3): 45–69. This would also appear to be the case based on a report of a contemporary who wrote, "So said Karshavya [or more accurately Kreshbeya] Ha-nakdan . . . in the days of R. M. of Coucy and R. Jehiel of Paris; I was in the city of Paris in the presence of R. Jehiel" (Ephraim Kupfer, *Teshuvot u-fesakim* [Jerusalem, 1973], 325).

31. See Y. M. Peles in his introduction to *Sefer mitsvot gadol ha-shalem* (Jerusalem, 1993), 1:23.

32. On the importance of the division into two parts and the influence of Maimonides list of *mitsvot* see Galinsky, "The Significance of Form," 304–10, esp. 308–10. Moses of Coucy did not have access to Maimonides' own *Sefer ha-mitsvot* but did have his list of commandments found in the preface to *Mishneh Torah*, which was copied from that work, and the listing arranged according to the order of *Mishneh Torah* appended to the beginning of each section.

33. On his goal to produce a "French" version of the Maimonidean code, see Jeffery R. Woolf, "Maimonides Revised: The Case of the '*Sefer Miswot Gadol*,'" *Harvard Theological Review* 90 (1997): 175–205, and Galinsky, "The Significance of Form," 300–304.

34. On Maimonides' goal see below, n. 62.

35. On the various types of medieval readers, including this reader, Jacob Molin (Maharil), a German scholar active at the beginning of the fifteenth century, described the various types of readers as part of his critique of accessible works of law. He wrote: "For we are distraught over the previous ones [legal handbooks written in Hebrew]—because every layman who is able to read Rashi's commentary on the Pentateuch or [one who can read the material] from the maḥzor or [those who studied] the interpretation (*shitah*) [the tosafist's glosses to the Talmud] in their youth but had ceased [studying] days and years ago, or those who never apprenticed with an established scholar (*lo shimmesh talmidei ḥakhamim*)": *She'elot u-teshuvot Maharil ha-ḥadashot,* ed. Isaac A. Satz (Jerusalem, 1977), 93, 92–93.

36. See most recently Kanarfogel, *The Intellectual History*, 360–61 and 533–37.

37. On the existence of such a group of readers see Maharil's description of readers, above, n. 35.

38. On some of these theological aspects see Y. Galinsky, "'Ve-lihyot lefanekha 'eved ne'eman kol ha-yamim': Perek be-haguto ha-datit shel R. Moshe mi-Kutsi," *Da'at* 42 (1999): 13–31.

39. *Sefer mitsvot gadol, mitsvot ʻaseh*, 1–96, ed. Elyakim Shlezinger (Jerusalem, 1995), 11.

40. Other such indications were including some of his sermons within the work and description of the heavenly visions he received. For these and other indications see Galinsky, "The Significance of Form," 298–99.

41. See Urbach, *Ba'alei ha-tosafot*, 475, to name the most prominent proponent of this approach.

42. Toward the end of his first introduction he describes his own preparations before heading out on his preaching mission. He writes about "arranging the commandments by-heart . . . the basis of each of the commandments, without all of their ramifications, so that I would not err in my rebuke": *Sefer mitsvot gadol ha-shalem* (Jerusalem, 1993), 1:13.

43. See Urbach, *Ba'alei ha-tosafot*, 571.

44. See Norman Golb, *The Jews in Medieval Normandy: A Social and Intellectual History* (Cambridge, 1998), 526–27, and Emanuel, *Shivrei luḥot*, 193–98. See as well E. Kanarfogel, *Peering Through the Lattices: Mystical, Magical, and Pietistic Dimensions in the Tosafist Period* (Detroit, 2000), 90–91 and n. 176.

45. On Isaac as a rabbinic authority see Pinhas Roth, "Ḥakhmei Provans ha-me'uḥarim: halakhah u-foskei halakhah bi-derom Tsarfat, 1215–1348" (Ph.D. diss., Hebrew University, 2012), 214–19, and Emanuel, *Shivrei luḥot*, 198–207 and 210–11. That Isaac was not a Talmud master for advanced students see Emanuel, *Shivrei luḥot*, 211.

46. On the year the work was completed see Emanuel, *Shivrei luḥot*, 198, and on the year of his death, see 199.

47. The report of Isaac of Strasburg was first printed in the first printing of *ʻAmudei golah* (Constantinople, 1510), and again from Budapest manuscripts in S. Kohn, "Die hebraeischen Handschriften des Ungarischen Nationalmuseums zu Budapest," *MWJ* 4 (1876): 102–4.

48. The report continues: "Later, his disciples stood up and asked him to write for each (and every) commandment explanations and rulings (*perisha u-fesakim*) that are appropriate to be included (and he acquiesced)."

49. Based on a reference by the copyist to Meir of Rothenburg's imprisonment, and praying that God should free him. Meir was jailed in 1286 and died in prison in 1293.

50. Nimes—Bibliotheque Seguier Municipale 26, fol. 2v. The manuscript is accessible online at http://bibliotheque-numerique.nimes.fr/notices/104576/gallery/.

51. It is worth noting that in the continuation of Isaac of Strasburg's report it is mentioned that many people copied the list of commandments directly into their prayer books. A medieval manuscript that preserves this practice was described by Collette Sirat, «Le livre hébreu: Rencontre de la tradition juive et de l'esthétique française," in *Rashi et la culture juive en France du Nord au Moyen Age*, ed. G. Dahan et al. (Paris-Louvain, 1997), 245.

52. The third part of the program that does not interest us here was his plan to enforce via communal sanction the rabbinic obligation to complete the reading of the weekly Torah reading with its Aramaic translation (or with Rashi's commentary).

53. The letter-introduction can be found in all the standard printings of the work. See the opening page of *ʻAmudei golah*, Constantinople, 1510, and Crimona, 1556.

54. It is worth noting that in one of his letters of introduction Isaac also encouraged women to study his work, to gain knowledge of the laws that they were obligated to keep. At the end of the introduction, one of Isaac's students adds: "He also wrote further to tell the women about the commandments that apply to them, [both] positive and negative *mitsvot*. He said that reading (*keri'ah*), study (*talmud*) and meticulous (*dikduk*) [comprehension] of them will benefit them, just as activity of Talmud study benefits men."

55. See E. Kanarfogel, "Prayer, Literacy, and Literary Memory in the Jewish Communities of Medieval Europe," in *Jewish Studies at the Crossroads of Anthropology and History*, ed. Ra'anan S. Boustan et al. (Philadelphia, 2011), 250–70.

56. Paul Saenger, "Book of Hours and the Reading Habits of the Later Middle Ages," in *The Culture of Print: Power and the Uses of Print in Early Modern Europe*, ed. Roger Chartier, trans. Lydia Cochrane (Princeton, 1989), 141–73, esp. 142.

57. See above, n. 33.

58. See the comments by Yitzḥak Shelat in his edition of *Igerot ha-Rambam* (Jerusalem, 1995), 1:196–203, and his introduction to his *Rambam meduyyak, mada'* (Maaleh Adumim, 2004), 2n.10. I thank Professor Bernard Septimus for these references.

59. The earliest known citation of *Mishneh Torah* in France is from 1203 to 1204, during the Resurrection controversy. The three major figures of that event were Meir ha-Levi Abulafia of Toledo, Aharon of Lunel, and Samson of Sens. On this event, see Bernard Septimus, *Hispano-Jewish Culture in Transition: The Career and Controversies of Ramah* (Cambridge, Mass., 1982), 39–60. See as well Ephraim Kanarfogel and Moshe Sokolow, "Rashi ve-Rambam nifgashim ba-geniza ha-kahirit," *Tarbiz* 67 (1998): 411–16. For a nice summary of all the evidence, see Menachem Ben-Sasson, "Mishneh Torah le-Rambam: Le-darkhei yetsirat kanon be-ḥaye meḥaber," in *Ha-Kanon ha-samuy min ha-'ayin: Ḥikrei kanon u-geniza*, ed. M. Ben-Sasson, Y. Brody, A. Lieblich, and D. Shalev (Jerusalem, 2010), 167 and n. 101.

60. Galinsky, "The Significance of Form," 311–20.

61. See Soloveitchik, *Collected Essays,* 1:31–38.

62. Maimonides' desire to popularize the law can be seen from his two primary legal works, his commentary to the Mishnah and his code *Mishneh Torah*. In his introduction to the latter he states that he wrote the book in a way that law should be accessible to the "young and old." See "Introduction to *Mishneh Torah,*" in *A Maimonides Reader*, ed. Isadore Twersky (Springfield, N.J. , 1972), 40. See as well Sarah Stroumsa, *Maimonides in His World: Portrait of a Mediterranean Thinker* (Princeton, N.J., 2009), 53–69.

63. One can make the argument that despite Isaac's lack of overt borrowing from *Mishneh Torah* in his *Semak*, his handbook was actually much closer in spirit to the Maimonidean popularization project than Moses of Coucy's work was.

64. Both Israel Ta-Shma and Ephraim Kanarfogel have written extensively on the influence of the Pietists outside of Germany whereas Haym Soloveitchik has demurred. See H. Soloveitchik, "Piety, Pietism and German Pietism: Sefer Hasidim I and the Influence of Hasidei Ashkenaz," *Jewish Quarterly Review* 92 (2002): 455–84. See as well *Jewish Quarterly Review* 96 (2006) (Forum: *Sefer Hasidim*), which is devoted to clarifying the issue.

65. See Kanarfogel, *Peering,* 59–72.

66. Ibid., 81–92

67. See Y. M. Ta-Shma, "*Mitsvat talmud torah ki-ve'aya ḥevratit–datit be-sefer ḥasidim,*" in his *Halakhah, minhag, u-metsi'ut be-Ashkenaz, 1000–1350* (Jerusalem, 1996), 112–29, and his article in *Keneset meḥkarim*, 1:317–44, esp. 331–36. See as well H. Soloveitchik, "Three Themes in the Sefer Ḥasidim," *AJS Review* 1 (1976): 339–44, where the author independently came to this conclusion about the pietists' religious ideology, without, however, linking it to the broader developments of legal works in France and Germany.

68. See Emanuel, *Shivrei luḥot*, 4–6.

69. See Kanarfogel, *Peering*, 89. As Kanarfogel has already noted (88n.166), there is a striking parallel between Isaac and *Sefer Ḥasidim* (Parma) # 835 with regard to teaching women the laws relevant to them.

70. An additional factor that should be considered is the surprising drop in high scholarly activity in Germany, especially in the Rhineland circa 1230–60, as Simcha Emanuel has recently shown. See S. Emanuel, "The Rabbis of Germany in the Thirteenth Century: Continuity or Crisis" (Hebrew), *Tarbiz* 82 (2014): 549–67.

71. Laura Light, "The Bible and the Individual: The Thirteenth-Century Paris Bible," in *The Practice of the Bible in the Middle Ages: Production, Reception and Performance in Western Christianity*, ed. Susan Boynton and Diane J. Reilly (New York, 2011), 229.

72. The main sources for the following section were Christopher De Hamel's review essay, "The European Medieval Book," in *The Oxford Companion to the Book*, ed. Michael F. Suarez and H. R. Woudhuysen (Oxford, 2010), 38–51, and Lesley Smith, *Masters of the Sacred Page: Manuscripts of Theology in the Latin West to 1274* (Notre Dame, Ind., 2001). And finally mention must be made of all the groundbreaking studies on the Paris book trade by R. H. Rouse and M. A. Rouse. To note just one of their works, *Manuscripts and Their Makers: Commercial Book Producers in Medieval Paris, 1200–1500* (Turnhout, 2000).

73. See De Hamel, "The European Medieval Book," 41b–42a.

74. Ibid, 42a.

75. Ibid.

76. Ibid, 43.

77. See Smith, *Masters of the Sacred Page,* 14–15.

78. See Ian P. Wei, *Intellectual Culture in Medieval Paris: Theologians and the University, c. 1100–1330* (Cambridge, 2012), 109–10.

79. See De Hamel, "The European Medieval Book," 43b–44a, and Smith, *Masters of the Sacred Page,* 24–27 and 113–16. See as well Andrew Taylor, *Textual Situations: Three Medieval Manuscripts and Their Readers* (Philadelphia, 2002), 148–51.

80. See Smith, *Masters of the Sacred Page*, 33, and see the examples at 41–48.

81. See John W. Baldwin, *Masters, Princes, and Merchants: The Social Views of Peter the Chanter and His Circle* (Princeton, N.J., 1970), and Mark Zier, "Sermons of the Twelfth Century Schoolmasters and Canons," in *The Sermon*, ed. Beverly Mayne Kienzle (Turnhout, 2000), 325–52.

82. See David L. d'Avray, *The Preaching of the Friars: Sermons Diffused from Paris Before 1300* (Oxford, 1985), 13–28; Nicole Bériou, "Les sermons latins aprés 1200," in *The Sermon*, 363–443; and Ronald J. Stansbury, "Preaching and Pastoral Care in the Thirteenth Century," in *A Companion to Pastoral Care in the Late Middle Ages (1200–1500)*, ed. R. J. Stansbury (Leiden, 2010), 23–39.

83. R. H. Rouse and M. A. Rouse, "Biblical Distinctions in the Thirteenth Century," *Archives d'histoire doctrinale et littéraire du Moyen Âge* 40 (1974): 27–37.

84. For a general overview of these developments see R. N. Swanson, *Religion and Devotion in Europe c. 1215–1515* (Cambridge, 1995), 21–41 and 52–82.

85. See the various studies by Leonard E. Boyle and Joseph Goering. A good place to begin is Joseph Goering, "Leonard E. Boyle and the Invention of *Pastoralia,*" in *A Companion to Pastoral Care*, 7–20.

86. See, e.g., Bériou, "Les sermons latins," and many of the other essays in *The Sermon.*

87. For a general overview, see Lester K. Little, *Religious Poverty and Profit Economy in Medieval Europe* (London, 1978), 151–58. On the relationship between the Dominicans' own *Studium Generale* to the schools of the "secular" in Paris and the difference in the curriculum, see Michèle Mulchahey, *"First the Bow Is Bent in Study": Dominican Education Before 1350*

(Toronto, 1998), 351–84. With regard to the Franciscans see Neslihan Senocak, "Franciscan *Studium Generale*: A New Interpretation," in *Philosophy and Theology in the Studia of the Religious Orders and at the Papal Court*, ed. K. Emery Jr. et al. (Turnhout, 2012), 221–36, and her *The Poor and the Perfect: The Rise of Learning in the Franciscan Order, 1209–1310* (Ithaca, N.Y., 2012).

88. See d'Avray, *The Preaching*, 64–90.

89. See ibid., 3–4, 160–63.

90. See Light, "The Bible," 228–46, esp. 236–39.

91. See De Hamel, "The European Medieval Book," 44. For examples of preaching aids, see Smith, *Masters of the Sacred Page*, 61–68. For other types of works written for preachers and parish priests, see 137–66.

92. See De Hamel, "The European Medieval Book," 44b–45a.

93. Ibid., and see as well Stella Panayotova, "The Illustrated Psalter," in Boynton and Reilly, *The Practice of the Bible in the Middle Ages*, 247–71, and Eamon Duffy, *Marking the Hours: English People and Their Prayers, 1240–1570* (New Haven, Conn., 2006).

94. On lay literacy see d'Avray, *The Preaching*, 29–43 and 25–26, on lay piety.

95. An initial examination of the thirteenth- and fourteenth-century copies of the work has revealed that their height ranges between 310 and 350 mm.

96. On the medieval meaning of this phrase, see Taylor, *Textual Situations*, 95.

97. Sarit Shalev-Eyni, *Jews Among Christians: Hebrew Book Illumination from Lake Constance* (London, 2010), 14–16, has already begun this exploration regarding Isaac's *Semak*.

98. An initial examination of the thirteenth- and fourteenth-century copies of the work has revealed that although some of the copies are quite substantial, such as 300 mm, 326 mm, and even 334 mm high, most of them are smaller, with their height ranging between161 mm and 240 mm.

99. In the passage I have taken the liberty of paraphrasing Laura Light, "The Bible," 229.

100. For a similar argument, albeit relating to the production of Hebrew medieval manuscripts in northern France, see Collette Sirat, "Le livre hébreu," 243–59. See as well Justine Isserles, "Les parallèles esthétiques des manuscrits hébreux askenazes de type liturgico-légal et des manuscrits latins et vernaculaires médiévaux," in *Manuscrits hébreux et arabes: M*élanges en l'honneur de Colette Sirat, ed. Nicolas de Lange and Judith Olszowy-Schlanger (Turnhout: Brepols, 2014), 77–113.

101. It is worth noting that with professional stationers it was possible to create a personal miscellany tailor-made according to one's interests, at times even "off the shelf" or "off the peg"; see Taylor, *Textual Situations*, 94–99, and Smith, *Masters of the Sacred Page*, 95.

CHAPTER 5. THE MADRASA AND THE NON-MUSLIMS OF THIRTEENTH-CENTURY EGYPT

1. *Al-ittifāq al-gharīb al-ʿajīb*; see subsection "Ibn al-Nabulusi's 'Strange and Wondrous Coincidence.'"

2. Abu ʿAli Hasan al-Tusi Nizam al-Mulk, *Siyar al-muluk (Siyasat nameh)*, ed. H. Darke (Tehran, 1994), 213–42; idem, *Book of Government*, trans. H. Darke (London, 1960), 158–87; Muhammad ibn al-Walid al-Turtushi, *Siraj al-muluk*, ed. J. al-Bayati (London, 1990), 402–3 (in the first printing [n.p., n.d.] the relevant passage is at 136–37). The latter work also contains

a version of the "Pact of 'Umar," once thought to be the earliest extant, and much other material advocating rather stern treatment of non-Muslim subjects.

3. S. D. Goitein, *A Mediterranean Society: The Jewish Communities of the Arab World as Portrayed in the Documents of the Cairo Geniza* (Berkeley, Calif., 1967–93), 2:303.

4. In highlighting this trend I do not intend to occlude study of non-Muslims' concomitant agency and strategies for navigating a shifting social climate, conversion not least among them, or dogmatically to maintain that the "religious community" should function as our primary unit of analysis. Representative studies of the trend: Mark Cohen, *Under Crescent and Cross* (Princeton, N.J., 1994), 67–68; Emmanuel Sivan, "Notes sur la situation des chrétiens à l'époque ayyubide," *Revue de l'histoire des religions* 172 (1967): 117–30; C. E. Bosworth, "The 'Protected Peoples' (Christians and Jews) in Medieval Egypt and Syria," *Bulletin of the John Rylands University Library* 62 (1979–80): 11–36; Claude Cahen, "Dhimma," in *The Encyclopaedia of Islam*, ed. P. Bearman et al. (2nd ed.; Leiden, 1960), 2:227–31; Tamer El-Leithy, "Coptic Culture and Conversion in Medieval Cairo, 1293–1524 A.D." (Ph.D. diss., Princeton University, 2004); Moshe Perlmann, "Notes on Anti-Christian Propaganda in the Mamluk Empire," *Bulletin of the School of Oriental and African Studies* 10.4 (1942): 843–61; Norman Stillman, "The Long Twilight: The Jews of Arab Lands in the Later Middle Ages," chap. 4 in *The Jews of Arab Lands: A History and Source Book* (Philadelphia, 1979); idem, "The Non-Muslim Communities: The Jewish Communities," in *The Cambridge History of Egypt*, vol. 1: *Islamic Egypt, 640–1517*, ed. C. Petry (Cambridge, 1998), 198–210 ("The Mamlūk period marks the nadir of medieval Egypt [*sic*] Jewry" [210]); Terry Wilfong, "The Non-Muslim Communities: The Christian Communities," in *The Cambridge History of Egypt*, 1:175–97 ("During Mamlūk rule of Egypt . . . the Egyptian Christians were most vulnerable to oppression . . . the status and number of Christians continued to decline" [196]); Gaston Wiet, "Ḳibṭ," in *Encyclopaedia of Islam*, 2:990–1003. See also *The Legal Status of Dhimmis in the Islamic West (8th–15th centuries)*, ed. M. Fierro and J. Tolan (Turnhout, 2013).

5. George Makdisi, *The Rise of the Colleges: Institutions of Learning in Islam and the West* (Edinburgh, 1981). A recent, provocative addition to the discussion: Christopher Beckwith, *Warriors of the Cloisters: The Central Asian Origins of Science in the Medieval World* (Princeton, N.J., 2012).

6. Gary Leiser, "The *Madrasa* and the Islamization of the Middle East: The Case of Egypt," *Journal of the American Research Center in Egypt* 22 (1985): 29–47.

7. See, among many other examples, Devin Stewart's corrective words concerning the *ijāzat al-tadrīs wa-l-iftā'* in his "The Doctorate of Islamic Law in Mamluk Egypt and Syria," in *Law and Education in Medieval Islam: Studies in Memory of Professor George Makdisi*, ed. J. Lowry, D. Stewart, and S. Toorawa (Chippenham, UK, 2004).

8. For further studies see, in addition to those cited in this essay, the multipage bibliographical footnote in Devin Stewart, "The Students' Representative in the Law Colleges of 14th-Century Damascus," *Islamic Law and Society* 15 (2008): 187–89n.3. See also more recently Jonathan Berkey, "'There are *'Ulamā'*, and Then There Are *'Ulamā'*," in *Histories of the Middle East: Studies in Middle Eastern Society, Economy, and Law in Honor of A. L. Udovitch*, ed. R. Margariti, A. Sabra, and P. Sijpesteijn (Leiden, 2010), 9–22; Ronnie Ellenblum, *The Collapse of the Eastern Mediterranean: Climate Change and the Decline of the East, 950–1072* (Cambridge, 2012), 120–22.

9. See, e.g., R. Stephen Humphreys, "Women as Patrons of Religious Architecture in Ayyubid Damascus," *Muqarnas* 11 (1994): 35–54.

10. Yehoshu'a Frenkel, "Political and Social Aspects of Islamic Religious Endowments (*awqāf*): Saladin in Cairo (1169–73) and Jerusalem (1187–93)," *Bulletin of the School of Oriental and African Studies* 62.1 (1999): 1–20.

11. The sincere piety that Mamluk military elites could display is highlighted in Jonathan Berkey, "The Mamluks as Muslims: The Military Elite and the Construction of Islam in Medieval Egypt," in *The Mamluks in Egyptian Politics and Society*, ed. T. Philipp and U. Haarmann (Cambridge, 1998), 163–73. See also the fifth chapter of his *The Transmission of Knowledge in Medieval Cairo* (Princeton, N.J., 1992), 128–60. But pious fervor among foreign ruling elites was by and large the exception.

12. Leiser, "The *Madrasa*," passim, esp. 29.

13. Makdisi, *Rise of Colleges*, 22.

14. Makdisi scarcely acknowledged the fact that *waqfs* were often made with public property, not private. Makdisi, *Rise of Colleges*, 35, 199, 225, 227, 281.

15. Kenneth Cuno, "Ideology and Juridical Discourse in Ottoman Egypt: The Uses of the Concept of *Irṣād*," *Islamic Law and Society* 6.2 (1999): 136–63, esp. 146 and references there.

16. The alleged Fatimid preference for non-Muslim officials, a commonplace of modern historiography, has received a long-overdue challenge in Marina Rustow, *Heresy and the Politics of Community: The Jews of the Fatimid Caliphate* (Ithaca, N.Y., 2008), 120–25. The section refers to dozens of Jewish state officials under the Fatimids and demonstrates the extent to which invective against highly placed Jewish and Christian officials was intermixed.

17. Goitein and others would include much of the Ayyubid period in this golden age for non-Muslim officials (*Mediterranean Society*, 2:374).

18. Leiser, "The *Madrasa*," 29.

19. Ibid., 35.

20. Ibid., 36.

21. Ibid.

22. Ibid.

23. Leiser (ibid.) promises "three specific ways" in which this process operated, but the first two resist disentanglement.

24. Ibid., 37.

25. By surveying a variety of Arabic sources, for instance, Leiser is able to highlight the significance of Alexandria and its madrasas for both phenomena, noting in passing Goitein's observation that antisemitism, though relatively infrequent in the geniza documents, crops up in relation to that city in the same period (ibid., 40). Leiser's point regarding the conflation of Ash'arism (of a militant strain, on his reading, 43) with Sunni Islam in toto in the Coptic martyrdom of John of Phanijōit, which follows Casanova, is probably mistaken (see now Jason R. Zaborowski, *The Coptic Martyrdom of John of Phanijōit: Assimilation and Conversion to Islam in Thirteenth-Century Egypt* [Leiden, 2005], 138–39).

26. On Ibn al-Nabulusi and his work see Luke Yarbrough, "'Uthmān b. Ibrāhīm al-Nābulusī" and "*Tajrīd sayf al-himma li-istikhrāj mā fī dhimmat al-dhimma,*" in *Christian-Muslim Relations: A Bibliographical History*, ed. D. Thomas and A. Mallett (Leiden, 2012), 4:310–16. It is now clear, on the basis of the single firsthand prosopographical account of his life, which remains unpublished, that his name should be given as "Ibn al-Nabulusi," not "al-Nabulusi," *pace* Claude Cahen ('Abd al-Mu'min al-Dimyati, *Mu'jam al-shuyukh*, Ms. Bibliothèque Nationale de Tunisie 12909, fol. 75r–v).

27. Claude Cahen, "Histoires coptes d'un cadi médiéval," *Bulletin de l'Institut français d'archéologie orientale* 59 (1960): 137–50. The quotation is from Leiser, "The *Madrasa*," 35.

28. See Joseph Sadan, "Some Literary Problems Concerning Judaism and Jewry in Medieval Arabic Sources," in *Studies in Islamic History and Civilization in Honor of Professor David Ayalon*, ed. M. Sharon (Jerusalem, 1986), 353–98.

29. I am currently preparing a full edition/translation of the work, and here thank the Herbert D. Katz Center for Advanced Judaic Studies for its support of this project in the fall of 2012. The edition/translation is under contract with New York University Press in the Library of Arabic Literature series.

30. Claude Cahen and Carl Becker, "Kitāb luma' al-qawānīn al-muḍiyya fī dawāwīn al-diyār al-miṣriyya," *Bulletin d'études orientales* 15 (1955–57), appendix (68–74). My translations are based on the in-preparation critical edition referred to above, which here does not differ significantly from the text established by Cahen.

31. Cahen and Becker, "Kitāb luma' al-qawānīn," 68.

32. This is the *Izhar ṣan'at al-Hayy al-Qayyum fi tartib bilad al-Fayyum* (=*Ta'rikh al-Fayyum wa-biladihi*, ed. B. Moritz [Cairo, 1898]). This work is the subject of an ongoing collaborative project, "Rural Society in Medieval Islam: 'History of the Fayyum,'" led by Yossef Rapoport; see http://www2.history.qmul.ac.uk/ruralsocietyislam/index.html.

33. Leiser, "The *Madrasa*," 45.

34. Konrad Hirschler, *Medieval Arabic Historiography: Authors as Actors* (London, 2006), 23. See the preceding section of this study for an incisive discussion of the mechanism of patronage and advancement, *ṣuḥba/mulāzama*.

35. Patricia Crone, *Pre-Industrial Societies* (Oxford, 1989), 58–61. For Islamicate contexts, see the classic study of Roy Mottahedeh, *Loyalty and Leadership in an Early Islamic Society* (rev. ed.; New York, 2001); for a more recent contribution, see Marina Rustow, "Formal and Informal Patronage Among Jews in the Islamic East: Evidence from the Cairo Geniza," *al-Qanṭara* 29.2 (2008): 341–82; idem, "Patronage in the Context of Solidarity and Reciprocity: Two Paradigms of Social Cohesion in the Premodern Mediterranean," in *Patronage, Production, and Transmission of Texts in Medieval and Early Modern Jewish Cultures*, ed. M. E. Alfonso and J. Decter (Turnhout, 2014), 13–44.

36. Cf. Goitein, *Mediterranean Society*, 2:375: Before the thirteenth century, "business and industry offered more lucrative and less dangerous opportunities than the often humiliating and mostly precarious service of the sultans. . . . From the thirteenth century on, however, when the economy became increasingly monopolized by the state, the clamoring Muslim candidates for government posts became ever stronger, and the minority groups had to give way."

37. R. I. Moore, "The Eleventh Century in Eurasian History: A Comparative Approach to the Convergence and Divergence of Medieval Civilizations," *Journal of Medieval and Early Modern Studies* 33.1 (2003): 11.

38. Rustow, *Heresy*, 122; M. G. Carter, "The *Kātib* in Fact and Fiction," *Abr-Nahrain* 9 (1971): 47–48; Maaike Van Berkel, "Accountants and Men of Letters: Status and Position of Civil Servants in Early Tenth Century Baghdad" (Ph.D. diss., University of Amsterdam, 2003), chap. 3.

39. Perlmann, "Notes"; El-Leithy, "Coptic Culture."

40. Nothing on the scale of the rigorist *furū' al-fiqh* work *Ahkam ahl al-dhimma* by Ibn Qayyim al-Jawziyya (d. 751/1350) seems previously to have existed in the literature. The relevant section of al-Khallal's *Kitab al-Jami'* is limited to presenting the response of Ahmad ibn Hanbal, while earlier works by Abu Ya'la ibn al-Farra' and Abu l-Shaykh al-Isbahani, though lost, seem to have been shorter and more narrowly retrospective. On the last works see Yarbrough, "'Uthman" and "*Tajrīd*."

41. For a sense of the diversity that characterized the sumptuary strictures that non-Muslims were supposed to observe in the early Islamic period (specifically the *ghiyār*), see Luke

Yarbrough, "Origins of the *ghiyār*," *Journal of the American Oriental Society* 134.1 (2014): 113–21. The requirements of the *ghiyār* edicts issued, for example, by the later caliphs al-Mutawakkil and al-Ḥākim, are far from uniform. For the famous eleventh-century Iraqi scholar al-Mawardi the *ghiyār* was not "demanded" (*mustaḥaqq*) but only "preferred" (*mustaḥabb*) (al-Mawardi, 'Ali ibn Muhammad, *al-Ahkam al-sultaniya* [Cairo, 1966], 145). Scholars of the documentary geniza have concluded that the *ghiyār* rules were imposed only rarely (e.g., Rustow, *Heresy*, 120). I would argue that the *ghiyār* and other "discriminatory measures" are most accurately conceptualized not as fixed doctrines of a reified Islamic law that periodically lapsed in practice, but rather as persistent strands within the developing aspirational Islamic legal discourse that were reactivated and asserted at particular historical moments, for reasons peculiar to those moments.

42. Al-Mawardi, *Ahkam*, 27, 116.

43. Abu Salim Muḥammad ibn Talha al-Nasibi, *al-'Iqd al-farid li-l-malik al-sa'id*, ed. M. R. Muhannā (Mansoura, 2000), 173.

44. Abu Yusuf Ya'qub ibn Ibrahim, *Kitab al-kharaj* (Cairo, 1933/34).

45. Aḥmad ibn 'Ali al-Khatib al-Baghdadi, *Ta'rikh madinat al-salam*, ed. B. 'A. Ma'ruf (Beirut, 2001), 7:280; Ibn Muflih, Muhammad al-Maqdisi, *al-Adab al-shar'iya*, ed. 'I. al-Ḥaristani (Beirut, 1997), 1:275.

46. For brief treatments, see, e.g., Antoine Fattal, *Le statut légal des non-musulmans en pays d'islam* (2nd ed.; Beirut, 1995), 236–40; Mun'im Sirry. "The Public Role of Dhimmīs During 'Abbasid Times," *Bulletin of the School of Oriental and African Studies* 74.2 (2011): 187–204.

47. Cahen and Becker, "Kitāb luma' al-qawānīn," 73–74.

48. Daphna Ephrat, *A Learned Society in a Period of Transition: The Sunni 'Ulama' of Eleventh-Century Baghdad* (Albany, N.Y., 2000), 113.

49. Michael Milton Chamberlain, *Knowledge and Social Practice in Medieval Damascus, 1190–1350* (Cambridge, 1994). Chamberlain's study should be read alongside cautionary words from Devin Stewart and Jonathan Berkey (reviews in, respectively, *Comparative Education Review* 50.3 [2006]: 531–33, and *American Historical Review* 101.4 [1996]: 1254–56). See also Stewart, "Doctorate of Islamic Law"; idem, "Students' Representative."

50. Leiser, "The *Madrasa*," 46.

51. Chamberlain, *Knowledge*, 52.

52. Ibid., 66.

53. Ibid., 90.

54. Ibid., 177.

55. Cf. Jonathan Berkey, "Culture and Society During the Late Middle Ages," in *The Cambridge History of Islamic Egypt*, 1:379: "The boom in the construction of *madrasas* . . . represented an effort to give formal structure to and exert control over social channels by which Islamic religious and legal knowledge were transmitted."

56. Chamberlain, *Knowledge and Social Practice*, 100, reading *manṣib* for *manṣab*. Cf. on the scholarly side Berkey, "Culture and Society," 402: "Altercations among the scholars were frequent, and generally resulted from a complex mixture of genuine doctrinal or ideological disputes and intense, sometimes vituperative personal or professional animosity."

57. Chamberlain, *Knowledge and Social Practice*, 175.

58. Ibid., 93.

59. Ibid., 97.

60. For an independent account of this patronage culture (many more might be cited): Tarif Khalidi, *Arabic Historical Thought in the Classical Period* (Cambridge, 1994), 191–93.

61. For other titles, see Yarbrough, "'Uthmān" and "*Tajrīd*."

62. R. I. Moore, *The Formation of a Persecuting Society* (1987; 2nd ed., Oxford; Malden, Mass., 2007). I am not the first to draw parallels in general terms between Moore's work and "persecution" in Islamic societies; Moore himself touched on the matter (*Formation*, 149ff.) and Mark Cohen also engaged with it, both in ways more general than the parallelism I highlight here. See Cohen, *Under Crescent and Cross*, 169–70.

63. For critiques of Moore's view, see David Berger, *Persecution, Polemic, and Dialogue: Essays in Jewish-Christian Relations* (Boston, 2010), 20–23; David Nirenberg, *Communities of Violence: Persecution of Minorities in the Middle Ages* (Princeton, N.J., 1996), 242n.40.

64. Moore, *Formation*, 141.

65. Brigitte Bedos-Rezak, "The Confrontation of Orality and Textuality: Jewish and Christian Literacy in Eleventh and Twelfth-Century Northern France," in *Rashi 1040–1990: Hommage à Ephraïm E. Urbach*, ed. G. Sed-Rajna (Paris, 1993), 554.

66. Walter Pakter, *Medieval Canon Law and the Jews* (Ebelsbach, 1988), esp. 221–47 (quotation on 247).

67. Moore, *Formation*, 167–68.

68. Ibid., 168–69.

69. Ibid., 171.

CHAPTER 6. JEWS IN AND OUT OF LATIN NOTARIAL CULTURE

I thank Kenneth Stow, Pinchas Roth, Sol Cohen, Paola Tartakoff, Josh Halpern, and the editors of this volume for their contributions to my developing thought in this chapter. I also wish to thank Arthur R. Lepage for supporting History Department research projects, the Theology Institute of Villanova University for a 2013 inaugural summer grant, and the Dean's office of the College of Liberal Arts and Sciences at Villanova for a faculty development grant to conduct research in French and Spanish archives during the summer of 2014. Finally, I thank Dr. Christine Langé and members of her team—Benjamin Marty, Denis Fontaine, and Magali Rieu at the Archives Départementales des Pyrénées Orientales and Dr. Josep Baucells i Reig at the Arxiu Capitular de la Catedral de Barcelona—for supporting my research.

1. N.B. Paleographical conventions: Abbreviations that I have extended are indicated by <angle brackets>, while lacunae in the text or words only partially legible with a quartz lamp or suggested by the editor are indicated by [square brackets]. Insertions into the text in the line above are indicated by (above:). The beginnings of new lines are indicated by Arabic numerals. All folio numbers not otherwise marked are rectos. Perpignan, *Archives Départementales des Pyrénées Orientales* (ADPO) 3E1 Register 1, fol. 23 (12 August 1261): 1. ij Idus Aug<us>ti. Jacob us de Mo<n>t<e>p<essu>la<n>o iud<e>us (above: et Jucef filius eius h<ab>ita<tor>es P<er>pin<iani>) profiteor et recog<nosco> t<ibi> B<er>n<ardo> Boshom filio condam P<etri> B ono h<om>i<n>o (sic: Bonhominis) de Toyrio quod tu satisfe[cisti nobis ad] 2. vol<un>tate<m> de om<n>ibus debitis q<ue> nobis fecisti et fid<e>iussio<n>i<bu>s usque in hu<n>c d ie< m> (above: cu<m> carta et sin<e> carta etc.) et si carta vel carte de[bitis] 3. et fideiussio<n>ibus inveniretur de cetero n<u>lli<u>s si<n>t volor<em> (sic: valorem) s<cilicet> p<ro> cancelat<a> etc. de q<ua> sat<i>sfac<t>io<n>e [---] 4. יעקב דמונפשליר מודה יוסף מודה בנו 5. t<estes> G. Vin<e>a de Toyrio et Ruben fili<us> Abrae d<e> Mo<nte>p<essu>la<n>o et Mosse Sa<m>iel 6. Hoc vi d<enarios> P<etrus> Cal<vet> vi d<enarios>.
1. B<er>n<ardus> Bonushomo filius condam P<etri> Bonihomini[s] de Toyrio solvo et diffinio

vo<bi>s Jacob de Mont<e>p<essu>la<n>o et Jucef [---] 2. Ab omnibus usuris q<uibus> a me recipistis et habuistis (above: cum carta et sine carta aliquo modo usque in hu<n>c di<em>) recognosc<en>s vo<bi>s q<uod> satisfecisiti[s] mihi pl<e>narie [---] 3. Pactu<m> de no<n> pet<iv>ero aliquid p<ro>p<ter> d<i>c<t>is etc. t<estes> qui supra G<uillelmus> Vinea de Toyr et G<uillelmus> Vallespir. 4. Pro lau<datio> vi d<enarios>. H<oc> vi d<enarios>.

2. RelMin on line database: Concilium Lateranense IV[c. 67]: "graves et immoderatas usuras" http://www.cn-telma.fr/relmin/extrait30315/; accessed 2 August 2014. I agree with John C. Moore's translation of this phrase in his "Pope Innocent III and Usury," in *The Pope, the Church and the City: Essays in Honour of Brenda M. Bolton,* ed. Francis Andrews, Christoph Eggers, and Constance M. Rousseau (Leiden, 2004), 70.

3. Jean Régné, *History of the Jews in Aragon: Regesta and Documents 1213–1327,* ed. Yom Tov Assis (Jerusalem, 1978), no. 625, pp. 62–63; Richard W. Emery, *The Jews of Perpignan the Thirteenth Century: An Economic Study Based on Notarial Records* (New York, 1959), 88–89, 130 (for the dowry figures); Barcelona, *Arxiu de la Corona d'Aragó* (ACA) Canc., register 20, fol. 266v (23 June 1275).

4. Ecclesiastical judgments against Jewish creditors were ongoing; see Emery, *Jews of Perpignan,* 89–95. Emery estimates that for 1261–87 there were "some 500 cases of papal intervention, and about 1500 cases of compromise between Jews and their Christian debtors." See also Philip Daileader, *True Citizens: Violence, Memory and Identity in Medieval Perpignan* (Leiden, 2000), 28.

5. Asunción Blasco Martínez, "Notarios-Escribanos Judíos de Aragón (Siglos XIV–XV)," in *Rashi: 1040–1990 Homage à Ephraïm E. Urbach: Congrès européen des Études* juives, ed. Gabrielle Sed-Rajna (Paris, 1993), 655: "Es evidente que en Aragón el notariado judío se hallaba menos evolucionado que el cristiano, aunque no cabe la menor duda de que en los siglos xiv y xv los judíos aragoneses tenían sus proprios escribanos para los contratos matrimoniales y dotales, libelos de repudio y testamentos."

6. ADPO 3E1 Register 1 (1260–61), Pere Calvet notary: fols. 4v, 7v, 9, 11, 14v (two register entries), 20v, 21v, 23, 25v, 26v, 29, 31v, 32, 38; ADPO 3E1 Register 2 (1266), Arnau Miró notary: fols. 14 and 25v (two register entries).

7. Emery, *The Jews of Perpignan,* 7.

8. Uriel I. Simonsohn, *A Common Justice: The Legal Allegiances of Christians and Jews Under Early Islam* (Philadelphia, 2011), 10. Simonsohn argues convincingly that the reason the Jews of eleventh-century Palestine did not abide by the mandate of the Geonim forbidding them from bringing cases between Jews before Islamic courts was because it was to their advantage to use these courts.

9. See, e.g., Kenneth Stow, "Writing in Hebrew, Thinking in Italian," in his *Jewish Life in Early Modern Rome: Challenge, Conversion and Private Life* (Aldershot, 2007), 1–14, as well as Kirsten A. Fudeman, *Vernacular Voices: Language and Identity in Medieval French Jewish Communities* (Philadelphia, 2010).

10. Both regions were closely related to the Crown of Aragon: Marseilles was in Provence, the place of origin of some of the Jews settled in mid-thirteenth-century Perpignan, and Sicily was under the rule of the kings of Aragon from 1282. Juliette Sibon, "Notables juifs et noblesse urbaine chrétienne à Marseille au XIVe siècle: Frontières labiles et limites de la marginalité," in *L'histoire des minorités est-elle une histoire marginale?* ed. Stéphanie Laithier and Vicent Vilmain (Paris, 2008), 60: ". . . la trace de formules laconiques écrites en caractères hébraïques dont la raison d'être est purement symbolique, selon l'interprétation proposée par Annliese Nef à partir d'exemples comparables dans les archives siciliennes du xve siècle." On 60n.7, Sibon

gives the archival references for the two Hebrew notations: ADBDR 3 B 69 fol. 23v, 19 August 1328, and ADBDR 381 E 67 fol. 58v, 27 February 1364. Sibon does not reveal what they say. Annliese Nef, "La langue écrite des Juifs de Sicile au xve siècle," in *Mutations d'identités en Mediterranée: Moyen Age et époque contemporaine,* ed. Henri Bresc et Christiane Veauvy (Paris, 2000), 85–95.

11. For a discussion of the *ius commune* in the Crown territories see Marie A. Kelleher, *The Measure of Woman: Law and Female Identity in the Crown of Aragon* (Philadelphia, 2010), 20–24.

12. Robert I. Burns, *Jews in the Notarial Culture: Latinate Wills in Mediterranean Spain, 1250–1350* (Berkeley, Calif., 1996), 39.

13. For the notariate in a larger village see Gregory B. Milton, "The Transition from Ecclesiastical *scribania* to Professional Notariate in Santa Coloma de Queralt," *Journal of Medieval History* 39.1 (2013): 1–19.

14. For more on Christian notaries in the Crown of Aragon see José Bono, *Historia del derecho notarial español,* 2 vols. (Madrid, 1979–82); Robert I. Burns, "The Notariate," in *Diplomatarium of the Crusader Kingdom of Valencia: The Registered Charters of Its Conqueror Jaume I, 1257–1276,* vol. 1: *Society and Documentation* (Princeton, N.J., 1985), 33–37; Burns, *Jews in the Notarial Culture,* 38–43; Francesch Carreras y Candi, "Desenrotllament de la institució notarial a Catalunya en el segle XIII," *Ier Congrés d'Historia de la Corona de Aragó dedicat al rey en Jaume I y a la seva época* (Barcelona, 1913), 2:751–89; Rafael Conde y Delgado de Molina, "El pas de l'escrivà al notari," *Actes del I Congrés d'Història del Notariat Català* (Barcelona, 1994), 439–46; Kathryn L. Reyerson and Debra A. Salata, eds. and trans., *Medieval Notaries and Their Acts: The 1327–1328 Register of Jean Holanie* (Kalamazoo, Mich., 2004); Rodrigue Tréton, "Preludi a la història del notariat públic a Perpinyà i el comtat de Rosselló (1184–1340)," *Afers. fulls de recerca i pensament* 22.58 (2007): 551–609.

15. Kenneth Stow, *The Jews in Rome,* vols. 1 (1536–1551) and 2 (1551–1557) (2nd ed.; Leiden, 1997); idem, *Theater of Acculturation: The Roman Ghetto in the Sixteenth Century* (Seattle, 2001); idem, *Jewish Life in Early Modern Rome: Challenge, Conversion, and Private Life* (Ashgate, 2007).

16. E.g., see Blasco Martínez, "Notarios-Escribanos Judíos de Aragón," 645–56, and Jaume Riera i Sans, "Notaris jueus i sarraïns," in M. T. Ferrer i Mallol and J. Riera i Sans, "Miscel-lània de documents per a la història del notariat als estats de la corona catalano-aragonesa," *Estudios históricos y documentos de los archivos de protocolos* (Miscelànea en Honor de Raimundo Noguera de Guzmán) 4 (1974): 434–38, 444–45.

17. For the Jewish *sofer hakahal* during the thirteenth century, see Yom Tov Assis, *Golden Age of Aragonese Jewry: Community and Society in the Crown of Aragon, 1213–1327* (Leiden, 1997), 132–35; Robert I. Burns, *Jews in the Notarial Culture,* 43–49; Isidore Epstein, *The "Responsa" of Rabbi Solomon Ben Adreth of Barcelona (1235–1310): As a Source of the History of Spain* (New York, 1925; repr. 1968), 40–42; and Elka Klein, *Hebrew Deeds of Catalan Jews/Documents hebraics de la Catalunya medieval: 1117–1316* (Barcelona, 2004), esp. 13–20.

18. Fragments of *pinkasim* from fourteenth-century Girona have recently been found in the bindings of Christian notaries' protocols. See Mauro Perani, "The 'Girona Geniza': An Overview and a Rediscovered Ketubah of 1377," *Hispania Judaica Bulletin* 7 (2010): 137–73. The record book of Isaac Solomon Bendit, the Jewish notary in charge of surveying the community for the payment of a tax in 1413, is also extant as MS 21 of the Médiathèque centrale / Bibliothèque Municipale of Perpignan. Discussed by Isidore Loeb, "Histoire d'une taille levée sur les juifs de Perpignan en 1413–1414," *Revue des études juives* 27 (1887): 55–79.

19. Elka Klein has identified six individuals as specializing in the drafting of *shetarot,* either summaries of proceedings of *batei din* or witnesses' statements on behalf of individuals in civil cases, in thirteenth-century Barcelona; Klein, *Hebrew Deeds,* 14.

20. S. D. Goitein, *A Mediterranean Society: The Jewish Communities of the Arab World as Portrayed in the Documents of the Cairo Geniza* (Berkeley, Calif., 1978), 2:228–30.

21. Malachi Beit Arié, "English Summary," *Hebrew Codicology: Historical and Comparative Typology of Hebrew Medieval Codices Based on the Documentation of the Extant Dated Manuscripts from a Quantitative Approach,* pre-publication, Internet version 0.1 (2012): 5–6.

22. *She'elot u-teshuvot ha-Rashba* (Jerusalem, 1996), 1:729.

23. Burns, *Jews in the Notarial Culture,* 44.

24. E.g., see ACA, Register 43, fol. 114 (26 January 1285), cited in Yom Tov Assis, *Jewish Economy in the Medieval Crown of Aragon 1213–1327* (Leiden, 1997), 96.

25. Judah ben Barzillay Bartzeloni, *Sefer ha-Shetarot,* ed. S. Z. Halberstam (Berlin, 1898). For more on Bartzeloni, see Klein, *Hebrew Deeds,* 17; and idem, *Jews, Christian Society, and Royal Power in Medieval Barcelona* (Ann Arbor, 2006), 28–29.

26. Emery, *Jews of Perpignan,* doc. 137. Rebecca Winer, *Women, Wealth, and Community in Perpignan c. 1250–1300* (Aldershot, 2006), 78, 189: "de schientia ebraica."

27. Technically, these Jews often wrote in semi-cursive. Malachi Beit Arié, "Hebrew Script in Spain," in *Moreshet Sepharad* (Jerusalem, 1992), 1:282–317.

28. ADPO 3E1 Register 1, fols. 11, 29 and Register 2, fol. 25v.

29. The degree of Latin knowledge Jewish businesspeople possessed has not been the subject of serious study. Jewish physicians and intellectuals' familiarity with Latin, on the other hand, has attracted scholarly attention. The emerging consensus concerning the Crown of Aragon and its neighbors suggests that in southern France there were some medical translations from Latin to Hebrew before the fifteenth century and that in northern Spain there may have been even broader scholarly exchange. See Alexander Fidora, Resianne Fontaine, Gad Freudenthal, Harvey J. Hames, and Yossef Schwartz, "Latin-into-Hebrew: Introducing a Neglected Chapter in European Cultural History," in *Latin-into-Hebrew: Texts and Studies,* vol. 2: *Texts in Context,* 1–10.

30. ADPO 1B 334 (1406–1410): the four parchments in this container from 1408 are s.n.

31. For more on Astruc Roven of Barcelona and his siblings, see below.

32. Joseph Shatzmiller, *Cultural Exchange: Jews, Christians, and Art in the Medieval* Marketplace (Princeton, N.J., 2013), 14.

33. Klein, *Hebrew Deeds,* 19, notes that most *shetarot* survive because they were preserved by Christian owners of property that had previously been in Jewish hands. That said, she gives a list of the types of documents extant for Catalonia on 189–90, and of eighty-two *shetarot* at least sixty concern real property in a direct way, and even more do so indirectly.

34. David Abulafia, *A Mediterranean Emporium: The Catalan Kingdom of Majorca* (Cambridge, 1994), 94: "The value of these [extant Latin notarial] documents as a record of all Jewish economic activity must be seriously doubted."

35. For examples, see Richard J. H. Gottheil, "Some Spanish Documents," *Jewish Quarterly Review* 16.4 (1904): 702–14.

36. Assis cites an instance in 1311 where the Jews of Valencia protested to the Crown the high rates two subcontractors to the *sofer hakahal* were charging. Assis, *Golden Age of Aragonese Jewry,* 133.

37. See Elizabeth Kolsky's introduction in "Forum: Maneuvering the Personal Law System in Colonial India," *Law and History Review* 28.4 (2010): 973–78.

38. This case is analyzed in Abigail Agresta, "The Doctor and the Notary: A Latinate Jewish Will from Fourteenth-Century Catalonia," *Viator* 46.1 (2015): 229–48. I thank Ms. Agresta, a Ph.D. student at Yale University, for allowing me to read this article in draft.

39. Winer, *Women Wealth and Community*, 95.

40. Abulafia, *Kingdom of Majorca*, 94.

41. Winer, "Marriage, Family and the Family Business: Links Between the Jews of Medieval Perpignan and Girona," in *Temps i espais de la Girona Jueva: Actes del Simposi Internacional celebrat a Girona 23, 24 i 25 de març de 2009* (Girona, 2011), 250.

42. For the general history of the region see Thomas Bisson, *The Medieval Crown of Aragon: A Short History* (Oxford, 1991).

43. Régné, *History of the Jews*, no. 28, pp. 5–6, lists multiple manuscripts from Catalonia that register this legislation of 26 February 1241; one is the Archives Municipales de Perpignan, *Livre vert mineur* (1183–1413), fols. 27–29.

44. For more on the Jewry oath, see Amnon Linder, "The Jewry-Oath in Christian Europe," in *Jews in Early Christian Law, Byzantium and the Latin West, 6th–11th centuries*, ed. J. V. Tolan, N. de Lange, L. Foschia, and C. Nemo-Pekelman (Leiden, 2014), 311–58.

45. Régné, *History of the Jews*, no. 4, pp. 1–2.

46. Some moneylending was still done solely by pawn without contract. See Emery, *Jews of Perpignan*, 31–33; and Shatzmiller, *Cultural Exchange*, 14.

47. Daileader, *True Citizens*, 115; *Les Coutumes de Perpignan*, ed. J. Massot-Reynier (Marseilles, 1848; repr. 1976), article 54, p. 29.

48. F. Bofarull y Sans, ed., *Los judios en el territorio de Barcelona (segles x-xiii): Reinado de Jaime I (1213–1276)* (Barcelona, 1910), document 143, p. 113.

49. Daileader, *True Citizens*, 127, citing ADPO 1B 94, fol. 89v (9 May 1326).

50. *Arxiu Històric de Girona*, Castelló d'Empúries (AHG Ca) 44: "Primo liber Jassie Ravalia et filii eius Vitalis" (30 March 1324–5 March 1328). In her honors thesis "A Medieval Moneylender: One Jewish Family's Microlending Business in Castelló d'Empúries (1323–1331)" (Swarthmore College, 2011), 6, Hannah Purkey corrects the dates to 1323–31.

51. ADPO 3E1, Register 8 (October 1276–March 1287).

52. Emery, *Jews of Perpignan*, 11.

53. Sibon, "Notables juifs," 60: "Les notables juifs marseillais s'affichent discrètement dans les documents comme une minorité religieuse consciente d'ellemême, notamment par l'usage parcimonieux du terme *hebreus* en lieu et place de celui de *judeus* que le notaire, lui, n'omettait jamais, et par la présence d'annotations en caractères hébraïques, rencontrées exceptionnellement dans la marge des écrits latins."

54. ADPO 3E1, Register1, fols. 11, 14v (twice), 29; Register 2, fol. 14.

55. ADPO 3E1, Register1, fol. 4v and Register 2, fol. 25v.

56. ADPO 3E1, Register1, fol. 26v.

57. ADPO 3E1, Register1, fols. 20v, 23, 25v, 31v and Register 2, fol. 25v. In four others the entry is damaged and the creditor's name is incomplete or missing: ADPO 3E1, Register1, fols. 7v, 9, 32, 38.

58. Emery, *Jews of Perpignan*, 67.

59. ADPO 3E1 Register 1, fol. 1v.

60. Between 19 and 22 August 1261 Ruben, son of Abrae Mosse de Montpellier, rented a house in Perpignan for one year for twenty-five sous; see ADPO 3E1 Register 1, fol. 25.

61. ADPO 3E1 Register 1, fol. 11 (24 June 1261) (one inch missing on right margin of register.) 1. viii K<alendas> Julii. 2. Mosse de Soal et pro eo Mosse Samiel. [et] Vital<is> Sal-

amo <nis> tibi B<ernardo> Be<ne>dicto xvi libr<as> minus [ii ---] 2. [ad festum] omni s<anc>torum [words crossed out: da<m>p<num> t<estes> G. Vallespir] . . . juro osta. (above: supra lege) et cogere et micionis curie ad d[ampnum] 3. t<estes> P<etrus> Vall<es>pir, G<uillelmus> Vall<e>spir clericus et B<ernardus> Carl<e>s, B<ernardus> Dura<n>, R<aimundus> Carl<e>s מושה דשואל 4. Vitalis Salamonis viiii K<alendas> Julii.

62. Mossé de Soal signs when he is the primary debtor, but not as guarantor, for all three transactions; see ADPO 3E1, Register 1, fols. 1v, 11, and 29.

63. Emery, *Jews of Perpignan*, 23.

64. ADPO 3E1 Register 1, fol. 21v [Nonas Augustii] (5 August 1261): 1. Bonjuses filius Mosse Catala<n>i (above: condam) profiteor et recog<nosco> v<o>b<is> L<e>oni de Elna. Davino Bon<e>to de Biterris (above: secretariis universitatis judeorum P<er>p<inia>ni) me v<o>b<is> dixisse<m> veritate<m> i<n> 2. [sup]er f<a>c<t>a q<ues>t<ion>e jud<e>orum de bo<n>is m<e>is de q<ui>b<us> bo<n>is m<e>is tradidi v<o>b<is> memorial<em> in quada<m> sedula (above: signata manu mea p<ro>p<ri>a) et si a<li>a 3. [omni]a debita p<os>t illa qu<e> sunt scripta i<n> d<ic>ta sedula q<ue> m<e> d<e>b<e>nt<ur> usque i<n> hu<n>c die<m> in t<er>ra Ross<illione> v<el> i<n> t<er>ra C<er>itanie 4. [---] lucris illa si<n>t d<om>ini Reg<is> et illa possit ip<s>e vel sui pot<estat>e et h<ae>c et recup<er>ar<e> ta<m>quam sua p<ro>p<ri>a ced<e>ndo actio-5. [nis ---] solvis mi<h>i d<i>c<ti>s debit<is> q<u>o<rum> v<o>b<is> [----] memorial<em> tradidi et solvo mi<h>i honore<m> m<e>u<m> et solvis debitis et 6. feci diffinicione<m> (above: sin<e> fraud<e>) fr<atr>i m<e>o Vitali et nepoti m<e>o Mosse et Mosse d<e> Narb<on>a n<omin>e d<ic>ti nepotis m<e>i et 7. [2 words missing?] debitis q<ue> s<un>t f<ac>ta i<n> n<omi>ne m<e>o q<uorum> h<ab>et i<n>str<umen>ta Vives Davinus sororius m<e>us et Vital<is> Salamon<is> sororius m<e>us 8. [2-3 words] juro etc t<estes> P<etrus> de Podio. B<ernardus> Carles (R crossed out) B<ernardus> Bruge<t>is (below: Leoni jud<e>o redd<ere>) 9. יהודה קטאלן מודה.

65. The list is termed a "sedula" in the Latin; in modern Spanish "cédula" means a tax or residence certificate, but in this context it probably indicates that Catalan's list was on a loose sheet of paper or parchment.

66. Régné, *History of the Jews in Aragon,* no. 25, p. 5, ACA, Canc., register 13, fol. 163 (27 April 1264).

67. ADPO Series 1B 334: "אני החתום מודה".

68. Klein, *Hebrew Deeds*, no. 7, p. 44 and no. 9, p. 48.

69. *Arxiu Capitular de la Catedral de Barcelona* (ACB) Pergamins 1-6-419 (4[?] June 1251); ACB Pergamins 1-6-546 (6 March 1238); Pergamins 1-6-573 (10 September 1240); ACB Pergamins 1–6-835 (16 July 1256); ACB Pergamins 1-6-1928 (21 February 1240); ACB Pergamins 1-6-2843 (30 September 1239); ACB Pergamins 1-6-3048 (20 March 1240); ACB Pergamins 1-6-3170 (15 November 1238); ACB Pergamins 1-6-3192 (4 June 1248) and ACB Pergamins 1-6-3209 (8 May 1233). For Elka Klein's analysis of these parchments see Klein, *Jews, Christian Society and Royal Power,* 175 and 274n.29, and her "Power and Patrimony: The Jewish Community of Barcelona, 1050–1250" (Ph.D. diss., Harvard University, 1996), 292.

70. As Stephan Escasset did in a hand much larger and less regular than that of the notary, on 15 November 1238, 21 February 1240, and 20 March 1240 (ACB Pergamins 1-6-3170 "n<omen> Stephani Escasseti," ACB Pergamins 1-6-1928 and ACB Pergamins 1-6-3048); and Guillem Eimeric on 6 March 1238 ACB (Pergamins 1-6-546).

71. ACB Pergamins 1-6-2843.

72. Yale doctoral student Sarah Ifft Decker is currently working with other bilingual parchments in the Arxiu de la Cathedral in Barcelona and says that Jewish witnesses signed in

Hebrew in at least two other thirteenth-century Barcelona parchments. I thank her for her corroboration.

CHAPTER 7. FROM CHRISTIAN DEVOTION TO JEWISH SORCERY

This project grew out of discussions during our time together at the Herbert D. Katz Center for Advanced Judaic Studies at the University of Pennsylvania. We would like to thank Galit Noga-Banai, Joshua Byron Smith, Katherine Aron-Beller, and all those who commented on early presentations of this material. We are also grateful to Sarah Blick, Sarah Brown, Alexandra Lesk, and Roger Rosewell for graciously providing us with photographs for this project.

1. Cf. David Nirenberg, *Anti-Judaism: The Western Tradition* (New York, 2013).

2. The figurines are identified in the sources by several Latin terms, including *simulacrum*, *effigies*, *idolum*, *similitudo*, *instar*, *figura*, *analogia figurata*, *imago* (also spelled *ymago*), *sculptile*, and *statua*, which in this context all convey the semantic range of image/likeness/representation and are mostly interchangeable. We have not systematically distinguished between these various terms in our translations. Note that some of these terms can also describe two-dimensional representations, and the meaning must be determined from the context.

3. The notion of "sympathy," associated with James George Frazer, has fallen out of favor among some scholars. We still find the term to be the easiest shorthand for an efficacious connection established through resemblance or analogy. Note that Frazer used magical figurines as one of his key examples for this notion in *The Golden Bough*, vol. 1: *The Magic Art and the Evolution of Kings* (London, 1911), 55–78.

4. See esp. Fabiana Fabbri, "Votivi anatomici dell'Italia di età medio e tardo-repubblicana e della Grecia di età classica: Due manifestazioni cultuali a confronto" *Bollettino di archeologia on line* 1 (2008), Poster Session 3, available at http://www.bollettinodiarcheologiaonline.beniculturali.it/documenti/generale/4_FABBRI.pdf (accessed 8 September 2014); F. T. van Straten, "Gifts for the Gods," in *Faith, Hope and Worship: Aspects of Religious Mentality in the Ancient World*, ed. H. S. Versnel (Leiden, 1981), 65–151, esp. 105–46; Alexandra L. Lesk, "The Anatomical Votive Terracotta Phenomenon in Central Italy: Complexities of the Corinthian Connection," in *SOMA 2001: Symposium on Mediterranean Archaeology*, ed. G. Muskett, A. Koltsida, and M. Georgiadis (Oxford, 2002), 193–202; and the sources cited in David Freedberg, *The Power of Images: Studies in the History and Theory of Response* (Chicago, 1989), 466n.1.

5. See, e.g., Christopher A. Faraone, "Binding and Burying the Forces of Evil: The Defensive Use of 'Voodoo Dolls' in Ancient Greece," *Classical Antiquity* 10.2 (1991): 165–205; Fritz Graf, *Magic in the Ancient World*, trans. F. Philip (Cambridge, Mass., 1997), 118–74; Daniel Ogden, "Binding Spells: Curse Tablets and Voodoo Dolls in the Greek and Roman Worlds," in *Witchcraft and Magic in Europe*, vol. 2: *Ancient Greece and Rome*, ed. B. Ankarloo and S. Clark (Philadelphia, 1999), 1–90, esp. 71–79. Relevant primary sources are collected in John G. Gager, *Curse Tablets and Binding Spells from the Ancient World* (New York, 1992), nos. 19, 27–28, 30, 41, 64, 107–8, 141–44, 165; Daniel Ogden, *Magic, Witchcraft, and Ghosts in the Greek and Roman Worlds* (2nd ed.; Oxford, 2009), nos. 16, 55, 67, 89–91, 98–99, 207, 209, 236–40, 242–46.

6. Theodoret of Cyrrhus, *Theodoreti Graecarum affectionum curatio*, ed. J. Raeder (Leipzig, 1904), 8.64, p. 217; Marvin Meyer and Richard Smith, *Ancient Christian Magic: Coptic Texts of Ritual Power* (San Francisco, 1994), nos. 110, 128; Sophronius, *Los* Thaumata *de Sofronio*, ed. N. Fernández Marcos (Madrid, 1975), 35.9–10, p. 321.

7. Virgil, *Eclogues*, 8.75, 80–81; Horace, *Epodes*, 17.76; *Satires*, 1.8.30–44; Ovid, *Amores*, 3.7.29–30, 79–80; *Heroides*, 6.91–92; cf. *Fasti*, 2.575–79; Angelo Mai, *Iulii Valerii V.CI.* Res gestae Alexandri Macedonis *translatae ex Aesopo graeco*, in *Classicorum auctorum e Vaticanis codicibus editorum* (Rome, 1835), 1.1, pp. 7:61–62.

8. Apuleius of Madauros, *Pro se de magia (Apologia)*, ed. V. Hunink (rev. ed.; Amsterdam, 1997), 63.6, p. 1:79. The Latin is quoted above in the epigraph.

9. Charles de Clercq, *Concilia Galliae, a. 511 – a. 695*, CCSL 148A (Turnhout, 1963), c. 3, p. 265: "Nec sculptilia aut pede aut hominem [*var.* homine] ligneo [*var.* lineo] fieri penitus praesumat." We are inclined to accept the variant *homine* and to read *pede* and *homine* as ablatives of quality. This excerpt, as well as many of those that follow, has been cited frequently throughout secondary literature. In general, see Freedberg, *Power of Images*, 136–37; Valerie I. J. Flint, *The Rise of Magic in Early Medieval Europe* (Princeton, N.J., 1991), 210–12, 254–55; Bernadette Filotas, *Pagan Survivals, Superstitions and Popular Cultures in Early Medieval Pastoral Literature* (Toronto, 2005), 34, 87–88, 143, 169, 201, 208–9, 242, 264.

10. Gregory of Tours, *Liber vitae patrum opere Georgi Florenti Gregori Toronici*, ed. B. Krusch, MGH SRM 1.2 (new ed.; Hannover, 1969), 6.2, p. 231.

11. Dado of Rouen, *Vita Eligii episcopi Noviomagensis*, ed. B. Krusch, MGH SRM 4 (Hannover, 1902), 2.16, p. 708.

12. Pirmin, *Scarapsus*, ed. E. Hauswald (Hannover, 2010), §22, pp. 78–79.

13. Georg Pertz, *Indiculus superstitionum et paganiarum*, MGH Leges 1 (Hannover, 1835), 20; Alfred Boretius, *Capitularia regum Francorum*, MGH Leges 2.1 (Hannover, 1883), 223.

14. Anne-Marie Bautier, "Typologie des ex-voto mentionnés dans des textes antérieurs à 1200," in *La piété populaire au Moyen Age*, Actes du 99e Congrès national des Sociétés savantes, Section de philologie et d'histoire jusqu'à 1610 (Paris, 1977), 237–82.

15. Ronald C. Finucane, *Miracles and Pilgrims: Popular Beliefs in Medieval England* (London, 1977), 96.

16. Bautier, "Typologie," 246; Finucane, *Miracles and Pilgrims*, 95.

17. Bautier, "Typologie," 244–46, 252–53.

18. Ibid., 248.

19. O. Holder-Egger, *Ex translatione SS. Chrysanti et Dariae*, MGH SS 15.1 (Hannover, 1887), §17, p. 375.

20. Uffingus of Werden, *Ex vita S. Idae auctore Uffingo monacho Werthinensi*, ed. G. Pertz, MGH SS 2 (Hannover, 1829), 1.12, p. 573.

21. Gerhard of Augsburg, *Vita sancti Oudalrici episcopi*, ed. G. Waitz, MGH SS IV (Hannover, 1841), 2.7, p. 420.

22. Gerhard of Augsburg, *Vita*, 2.22, p. 423. See Andrzej Pleszczyński, *The Birth of a Stereotype: Polish Rulers and Their Country in German Writings c. 1000 A.D.*, trans. R. Bubczyk (Leiden, 2011), 72–83, who identifies the figure in question as Mieszko I of Poland.

23. O. Holder-Egger, *Ex translatione et miraculis S. Firmini Flaviniacensibus*, MGH SS 15.2 (Hannover, 1888), Miracles 2.4, p. 807.

24. Bautier, "Typologie," 244–45.

25. Adriano Duque, "Wax Candles," in *Encyclopedia of Medieval Pilgrimage*, ed. L. J. Taylor et al. (Leiden, 2010), 818.

26. Pierre André Sigal, "L'ex-voto au Moyen Age dans les régions du nord-ouest de la Méditerranée (XIIe–XVe siècles)," *Provence historique* 33 (1983): 19–20.

27. Late antique figurines used for sorcery range from about 3 to 18 centimeters, according to the catalogue in Faraone, "Binding and Burying," 200–205.

28. Bautier, "Typologie," 253.

29. Ibid., 259.

30. Ibid., 247, 260, 261.

31. Ibid., 19–22.

32. Finucane, *Miracles and Pilgrims*, 98. See also the December 1307 letter to Clement V, which gives the combined number of wax bodies and limbs as 1,424. Printed in *Acta Sanctorum*, 2 October, 1:595A, §297.

33. See, e.g., U. M. Radford, "The Wax Images Found in Exeter Cathedral," *Antiquaries Journal* 29.3/4 (1949): 164–68; D. R. Dendy, *The Use of Lights in Christian Worship* (London, 1959), 115–16; Finucane, *Miracles and Pilgrims*, 97–99; Vauchez, *Sainthood in the Later Middle Ages*, trans. Jean Birrell (Cambridge, 1997), 456–59; Fabio Bisogni, "Ex voto e la scultura in cera nel tardo medioevo," in *Visions of Holiness: Art and Devotion in Renaissance Italy*, ed. A. Ladis and S. E. Zuraw (Athens, Ga., 2001), 67–91; Roberta Panzanelli, "Compelling Presence: Wax Effigies in Renaissance Florence," in *Ephemeral Bodies: Wax Sculpture and the Human Figure*, ed. R. Panzanelli (Los Angeles, 2008), 13–39 (and see the references cited at 32n.9); Sarah Blick, "Votives, Images, Interaction and Pilgrimage to the Tomb and Shrine of St. Thomas Becket, Canterbury Cathedral," in *Push Me, Pull You: Physical and Spatial Interaction in Late Medieval and Renaissance Art*, ed. S. Blick and L. D. Gelfand (Leiden, 2011), 2:21–58.

34. Megan Holmes, "Ex-votos: Materiality, Memory, and Cult," in *The Idol in the Age of Art: Objects, Devotions and the Early Modern World*, ed. M. W. Cole and R. Zorach (Farnham, 2009), esp. 159–61, 167–68, 179.

35. Franco Sacchetti, *Il Trecentonovelle*, ed. V. Marucci (Rome, 1996), Novella 109.8, pp. 330–31. Translation expanded from Holmes, "Ex-votos," 159.

36. Cf. Freedberg, *Power of Images*, who has emphasized the efficacy attributed to resemblance (e.g., 157–59, 201–5), and the ways in which representational images can substitute for the presence of person (e.g., 204–6, 215–16, 227, 232, 260, 262). See also Vauchez, *Sainthood*, 458, who discusses votives as a commutation for the self. Cf. Holmes, "Ex-votos," 160, 162–63; Panzanelli, "Compelling Presence," 30.

37. Holmes, "Ex-votos," 161–62. See also Panzanelli, "Compelling Presence," 30–31. On medieval ideas of wax and impressions, see Katharine Park, "Impressed Images: Reproducing Wonders," in *Picturing Science, Producing Art*, ed. C.A. Jones and P. Galison (New York, 1998), 254–71. Aristotle employed the example of wax in *De anima*, 2.1, 2.12. On the significance of wax's similarity to skin, see David Freedberg, *The Power of Images*, 157, 212–31; Fabio Bisogni, "Ex voto," 85.

38. A less developed version of this argument is suggested by Nilson, "Medieval Experience," 107.

39. See esp. Elliott Horowitz, *Reckless Rites: Purim and the Legacy of Jewish Violence* (Princeton, N.J., 2006); Cecil Roth, "The Feast of Purim and the Origins of the Blood Accusation," *Speculum* 8.4 (1933); T. C. G. Thornton, "The Crucifixion of Haman and the Scandal of the Cross," *Journal of Theological Studies* 37.2 (1986); David W. Chapman, *Ancient Jewish and Christian Perceptions of Crucifixion* (Tübingen, 2008), 238–39; John Tolan, "The Rites of Purim as Seen by the Christian Legislator: Codex Theodosianus 16.8.18," in *Ritus infidelium: Miradas interconfesionales sobre las prácticas religiosas en la edad media*, ed. J. Martínez Gázquez and J. Tolan (Madrid, 2013), 165–73.

40. See Kathleen Corrigan, *Visual Polemics in the Ninth-Century Byzantine Psalters* (Cambridge, 1992); Mary Cunningham, "Polemic and Exegesis: Anti-Judaic Invective in Byzantine Homiletics," *Sobornost* (1999): 46–68; Stephen Gero, *Byzantine Iconoclasm During the Reign of*

Leo III (Louvain, 1973), 60–64; Alexander Alexakis, *Codex Parisinus Graecus 1115 and Its Archetype* (Washington, D.C., 1996), nos. 26, 31–33, pp. 183–84, 188–92.

41. Gregory of Tours, *Glory of the Martyrs*, trans. R. Van Dam (Liverpool, 1988), 40. The Pseudo-Athanasian tale, together with this citation, is found in the ninth-century Theodore the Studite's *Antirrheticus*, PG 99, 2.9, p. 365, translated by C. P. Roth in *On the Holy Icons* (New York, 1981), 55. On the history of the legend, see Michele Bacci, "'Quel bello miracolo onde si fa la festa del santo Salvatore': studio sulle metamorfosi di una leggenda," in *Santa Croce e Santo Volto. Contributi allo studio dell'origine e della fortuna del culto del Salvatore (secoli IX–XV)*, ed. G. Rossetti (Pisa, 2002), 7–86.

42. Celebrated on 9 November as *Passio Imaginis* or *Sancti Salvatoris*. Bacci, "'Quel bello miracolo,'" 23–31.

43. Its use on the feast day (14 September) is described by Bacci, "'Quel bello miracolo,'" 25–26. For iconoclasm and desecration of the cross, see Richard Landes, "La vie apostolique en Aquitaine en l'an mil. Paix de Dieu, culte de reliques et communautés hérétiques," *Annales ESC* 46.3 (1991): 573–93.

44. Rachel Fulton, *From Judgment to Passion: Devotion to Christ and the Virgin Mary, 800–1200* (New York, 2002), 60–106; Richard Landes, *Relics, Apocalypse, and the Deceits of History: Ademar of Chabannes, 989–1034* (Cambridge, Mass., 1995), esp. 285–327; Daniel F. Callahan, "Ademar of Chabannes, Millenial Fears and the Development of Western Anti-Judaism," *Journal of Ecclesiastical History* 46.1 (1995): 19–35.

45. Ademar of Chabannes, *Chronicon*, ed. P. Bourgain, R. Landes, and G. Pon, CCCM 129 (Turnhout, 1999), 3.59, pp. 165–66; Rodulfus Glaber, *Historiarum libri quinque*, ed. and trans. J. France (Oxford, 1989), 2.5, pp. 64–67. On these events, see Fulton, *From Judgment to Passion*, 64–66.

46. See Glaber, *Historiarum libri quinque*, 2.11, p. 91, discussed by Michael Frassetto, "Heretics and Jews in the Early Eleventh Century: The Writings of Radulphus Glaber and Ademar of Chabannes," in *Christian Attitudes Toward the Jews in the Middle Ages: A Casebook*, ed. M. Frassetto (New York, 2007), 50.

47. See Daniel F. Callahan, "The Cross, the Jews, and the Destruction of the Church of the Holy Sepulchre," in *Christian Attitudes Toward the Jews*, 15–23; Phyllis G. Jestice, "A Great Jewish Conspiracy? Worsening Jewish-Christian Relations and the Destruction of the Holy Sepulchre," in *Christian Attitudes Toward the Jews*, 25–42; Regula Meyer Evitt, "Eschatology, Millenarian Apocalypticism, and the Liturgical Anti-Judaism of the Medieval Prophet Plays," in *The Apocalyptic Year 1000: Religious Expectation and Social Change, 950–1050*, ed. A. Gow, D. C. Van Meter, and R. landes (Oxford, 2003), 205–12.

48. Ademar of Chabannes, *Chronicon*, 3.52, p. 171, on which see also Bacci, "'Quel bello miracolo,'" 31–38. The sermon is found in Paris, Bibliothèque nationale de France, lat. 3784 following the markedly anti-Jewish *Gospel of Nicodemus*, on which see Callahan, "Ademar of Chabannes," 24.

49. See Horowitz, *Reckless Rites*, 163–67. For later cases, see Joseph Shatzmiller, "Desecrating the Cross: A Rare Medieval Accusation" (Hebrew), *Studies in the History of the Jewish People and the Land of Israel* 5 (1980): 159–73; idem, "Profaner la Saint-Croix: Une rare accusation anti-juive au Moyen Age," in *Identités juives et chrétiennes: France méridionale, XIVe–XIXe siècle*, ed. G. Audisio, R. Bertrand, M. Ferrières, and Y. Grava (Aix-en-Provence, 2003), 39–45; Christoph Cluse, "Stories of Breaking and Taking the Cross: A Possible Context for the Oxford Incident of 1268," *Revue d'histoire ecclésiastique* 90 (1995): 396–442.

50. On the origins of the miracle collections, see Richard W. Southern, "The English

Origins of the 'Miracles of the Virgin,'" *Medieval and Renaissance Studies* 4 (1958): 176–216; Benedicta Ward, *Miracles and the Medieval Mind* (London, 1982), 142–55.

51. The prominence of the stories featuring Jews from the beginnings of the genre has been noted by Robert Worth Frank, "Miracles of the Virgin, Medieval Anti-Semitism and the Prioress' Tale," in *The Wisdom of Poetry: Essays in Early English Literature in Honor of Morton W. Bloomfield*, ed. L. D. Benson and S. Wenzel (Kalamazoo, Mich., 1982), 59–65; Anthony Bale, *The Jew in the Medieval Book: English Antisemitisms, 1350–1500* (Cambridge, 2007), 55–104; Adrienne Williams Boyarin, *Miracles of the Virgin in Medieval England: Law and Jewishness in Marian Legends* (Cambridge, 2010).

52. Albert Poncelet, "Index miraculorum B. V. Mariae quae saec. VI-XV latine conscripta sunt," *Analecta Bollandiana* 21 (1902): 283. For edited versions of the Latin story, see *Miracula Sanctae Virginis Mariae*, ed. Elise Dexter (Madison, Wisc., 1927); *Miracula Beate Marie Virginis (Ms. Thott 128 de Copenhague): Una fuente paralela a Los Milagros de Nuestra Señora de Gonzalo de Berceo*, ed. A. Carrera de la Red and F. Carrera de la Red (Logroño, 2000); Vincent of Beauvais, *Speculum historiale; Speculum maius* (Douai, 1624), 4.81, p. 250.

53. Dexter, *Miracula*, 39.

54. Ibid.

55. William of Malmesbury, *De laudibus et miraculis Sanctae Mariae*, ed. J. M. Canal (Rome, 1968), 74. Our sincere thanks go to Michael Winterbottom and Rodney Thomson for allowing Kati Ihnat to see a preliminary draft of their new edition and translation, William of Malmesbury, *The Miracles of the Blessed Virgin Mary* (Woodbridge, 2015).

56. For example, in London, British Library, Arundel 346, Add. 35112; Oxford, Balliol Library, MS 240; Oxford, Bodleian Library, Laud. Misc. 410; Paris, BnF, lat. 2873, 3177, 3809A, 14463, 18168; Gil de Zamora, *Liber de Jhesu et Mariae*; Vincent of Beauvais, *Speculum historiale* (1624).

57. There is also some evidence for a potential historical source for this particular story, namely the persecution of Jews in Toledo following the death of Alfonso VI, on 29 June 1109. Cf. Yitzhak Baer, *A History of the Jews in Christian Spain* (Philadelphia, 1992), 1:51. See Peter Carter, "The Historical Content of William of Malmesbury's Miracles of the Virgin Mary," in *The Writing of History in the Middle Ages: Essays Presented to Richard William Southern*, ed. J. M. Wallace-Hadrill and R. H. C. Davis (Oxford, 1981), 145–46.

58. Some of the best-known later versions include Gil de Zamora, *Liber Jhesu et Mariae* (Madrid BN 9503, fol. 109), John of Garland, *Stella Maris*, ed. E. Wilson (Cambridge, 1946), 107; Adgar, *Marienlegenden nach der Londoner Handschrift Egerton 612*, ed. C. Neuhaus (Heilbronn, 1886), 58–62; Adgar, *Le Gracial*, ed. P. Kunstmann (Ottawa, 1982), 143–47; Gonzalo de Berceo, *Los milagros de nuestra señora*, ed. B. Dutton (London, 1971), 3.18, pp. 139–41, with translation in *The Collected Works of Gonzalo de Berceo in English Translation,* trans. J. K. Bartha, A. G. Cash, and R. T. Mount (Tempe, Ariz., 2008), 77–79.

59. *Recueil des historiens des gaules et de la France,* ed. L. Delisle (Paris, 1877), 12:407.

60. Ferdinando Ughelli, *Italia sacra sive De episcopis Italiae et insularum adiacentium* (Rome, 1644–62), 6:852. Cecil Roth reads more into the account, placing the events at Good Friday and in the synagogue. Cecil Roth, *The History of the Jews of Italy* (Philadelphia, 1946), 72.

61. Arnold of Lübeck, *Chronica Slavorum*, MGH SS 21 (Hannover, 1869), 190–91.

62. Ibid., 190.

63. Thomas of Monmouth, *The Life and Miracles of St William of Norwich*, ed. and trans. A. Jessop and M. R. James (Cambridge, 1896), 15, and 93–94 for the ritual element. See esp. Gavin Langmuir, "Thomas of Monmouth: Detector of Ritual Murder," in *Towards a Definition*

of Antisemitism (Berkeley, Calif., 1990), 209–36; John M. McCulloch, "Jewish Ritual Murder: William of Norwich, Thomas of Monmouth, and the Early Dissemination of the Myth," *Speculum* 72.3 (1997): 698–740; Simon Yarrow, *Saints and Their Communities: Miracle Stories in Twelfth-Century England* (Oxford, 2006), 122–68; Yuval, *Two Nations*, 167–89; Jeffrey J. Cohen, "The Flow of Blood in Medieval Norwich," *Speculum* 78.1 (2004): 26–65. See now Thomas of Monmouth, *The Life and Passion of William of Norwich*, trans. Miri Rubin (London, 2014).

64. Miri Rubin, *Gentile Tales: The Narrative Assault on Late Medieval Jews* (Philadelphia, 2004).

65. Dwayne E. Carpenter, *Alfonso X and the Jews: An Edition of and Commentary on Siete Partidas 7.24 de los Judios* (Berkeley, Calif., 1986), 7.24.2, pp. 63–66. See also Joseph F. O'Callaghan, *The Learned King: The Reign of Alfonso X of Castile* (Philadelphia, 1993), 110–11.

66. Alfonso X, *As Cantigas de Loor de Santa María (edición e comentario)*, ed. E. Fidalgo Francisco et al. (Santiago de Compostela, 2004), 88–89, translated in Kathleen Kulp-Hill, *The Songs of Holy Mary by Alfonso X, the Wise: A Translation of the Cantigas de Santa Maria* (Tempe, Ariz., 2000), 19. On Jews in the stories, see, among others, Albert Bagby, "Jews in the Cantigas of Alfonso X," *Speculum* 46.4 (1971): 670–88; Vikki Hatton and Angus Mackay, "Anti-Semitism in the *CSM*," *Bulletin of Hispanic Studies* 60 (1983): 189–99; Dwayne E. Carpenter, "Social Perception and Literary Portrayal: Jews and Muslims in Medieval Spanish Literature," in *Convivencia: Jews, Muslims, and Christians in Medieval Spain*, ed. V. B. Mann, T. F. Glick, and J. D. Dodds (New York, 1992), 61–82; Maria Dolores Bollo-Panadero, "Heretics and Infidels: The Cantigas de Santa Maria as Ideological Instrument of Cultural Codification," *Romance Quarterly* 55.3 (2008): 163–74.

67. Around the early fifth century, Servius described the practice in his commentary on *Eclogue* 8.80. In 875, Anastasius Bibliothecarius produced a Latin translation of Sophronius's *Miracles of Cyrus and John*, which includes an account of sorcery with a figurine. This passage, however, was not influential. Additionally, the nineteenth-century scholar Benjamin Thorpe misinterpreted three legal documents from Anglo-Saxon England, wrongly claiming that these were references to piercing wax figurines. Finally, there are legendary accounts of sorcery with figurines that concern the tenth and eleventh centuries, but they were all composed in the twelfth century or later.

68. L. J. Downer, *Leges Henrici primi* (Oxford, 1972), c. 71.1, pp. 226–27.

69. John of Salisbury, *Policraticus I–IV*, ed. K.S.B. Keats-Rohan, CCCM 118 (Turnhout, 1993), 1.12, pp. 58–59. Translation from Joseph B. Pike, *Frivolities of Courtiers and Footprints of Philosophers* (Minneapolis, 1938), 41–42.

70. Peter of Blois, *Epistolae*, ep. 65 ("Ad soicum et amicum"), PL 207:192A; Hélinand of Froidmont, *Chronicon*, bk. 48, s.a. 1150, PL 212:1057B-C; William of Auvergne, *De universo*, in *Guilielmi Alverni episcopi Parisiensis . . . opera omnia* (Paris, 1674), 1.1.46, p. 1:661b (C-D).

71. G. Waitz, *Gesta Treverorum*, MGH SS 8, pp. 111–200 (Hannover, 1848), §32, p. 174.

72. See esp. Eva Haverkamp, "'Persecutio' und 'Gezerah' in Trier während des Ersten Kreuzzugs," in *Juden und Christen zur Zeit der Kreuzzüge*, ed. A. Haverkamp (Sigmaringen, 1999), 49–50.

73. Waitz, *Gesta Treverorum*, Additamentum et continuatio prima, §8, p. 182; on the dating, see 116, 118, 125–28 (the redaction appears in Recensions B and C); Thomas Heinz, *Studien zur Trierer Geschichtsschreibung des 11. Jahrhunderts* (Bonn, 1968), 23–25; Haverkamp, "Persecutio," 35. The story is expanded in Johannes Trithemius, *Annales Hirsaugienses* (St. Gall, 1690), s.a. 1059, pp. 1:203–4. Note that the term *lychnus* ("lamp, torch, candle") can also refer specifically to wicks that were measured in order to be made into votive candles. See R. E. Latham,

D. R. Howlett, and R. K. Ashdowne, *Dictionary of Medieval Latin from British Sources* (Oxford, 1975–2013), s.v. *lychnus* 2b.

74. Cf. Freedberg, *Power of Images*, 82–98 on the consecration of images, and 263–70 on magical images.

75. On magical use of the eucharist, see esp. Peter Browe, "Die Eucharistie als Zaubermittel im Mittelalter," *Archiv für Kulturgeschichte* 20.2 (1930): 134–54; Richard Kieckhefer, *European Witch Trials: Their Foundations in Popular and Learned Culture, 1300–1500* (Berkeley, Calif., 1976), 26, 50, 64, 111, 129, 140–41; Miri Rubin, *Corpus Christi: The Eucharist in Late Medieval Culture* (Cambridge, 1991), 338–41. The contemporary understanding of superstition and idolatry relied on Augustine, *De doctrina christiana*, esp. 2.20(30) and 2.23(36).

76. E.g., Robert of Flamborough, *Liber poenitentialis*, ed. J. J. F. Firth (Toronto, 1971), 3.3.159, p. 158; Joseph Hansen, *Quellen und Untersuchungen zur Geschichte des Hexenwahns und der Hexenverfolgung im Mittelalter* (Bonn, 1901), 44; Claude Devic and Joseph Vaissète, *Histoire générale de Languedoc avec des notes et les pièces justificatives* (Toulouse, 1872–92), 8:987–88 (fifteen-volume edition) or 6:405–6 (ten-volume edition); Bernard Gui, *Practica inquisitionis heretice pravitatis*, ed. C. Douais (Paris, 1886), 5.6, pp. 292–93; 5.7.12, p. 301; Philipp Jaffé, *Annales Colmarienses maiores*, MGH SS 17 (Hannover, 1861), s.a. 1279, p. 206. Cf. the (likely spurious) passage that has been attributed to Marbode of Rennes in Harmening, *Superstitio*, 222.

77. On the trial, see esp. Alain Provost, *Domus diaboli: Un évêque en procès au temps de Philippe le Bel* (Paris, 2010).

78. Paris, Archives nationales, Trésor des Chartes, J 438 B, n°6, p. 64 (deposition of Lorin de la Chambre).

79. Abel Rigault, *Le procès de Guichard, évêque de Troyes (1308–1313)* (Paris, 1896), 61–62, 67–68, 77–80. Cf. G. Mollat, "Guichard de Troyes et les révélations de la sorcière de Bourdenay," *Le Moyen Age* 21 (2nd ser., 12) (1908): 310–16.

80. Nearly all studies rely on the faulty description of the events given in Edmond Albe, *Autour de Jean XXII: Hugues Géraud, évêque de Cahors: L'affaire des poisons et des envoûtements en 1317* (Cahors, 1904). Our analysis is based on the unpublished trial records in Rome, Archivio Segreto Vaticano, Camera Apostolica, Collectoriae 493, fols. 1r–45r.

81. Rome, ASV, Collect. 493, fol. 30v (deposition of Pierre Moret, 9 September 1317).

82. Rome, ASV, Collect. 493, fol. 21r (deposition of Pierre Fouquier, 6 July 1317).

83. This latter point was highlighted again in Robert of Mauvoisin's trial in Avignon, which began before Hugues's trial had finished. See Joseph Shatzmiller, *Justice et injustice au début du XIVe siècle: L'enquête sur l'archevêque d'Aix et sa renonciation en 1318* (Rome: École française de Rome, 1999).

84. Parma, Biblioteca Palatina, Parm. 2342 (Richler 1542), fols. 286v–287r.

85. Parma, Parm. 2342, fol. 287r: וימצא הצלם דונג בתוכה וזה משפטו ידיו על חלציו ומסמרות בין ברכיו וכפות רגליו כרותות.

86. The chapter on Jews (7.24.2) is discussed above. The condemnation of wax images in sorcery appears in 7.23.2. See Alfonso X, *Las Siete Partidas del Rey Don Alfonso el Sabio*, ed. La Real Academia de la Historia (Madrid, 1807), 3:668.

CHAPTER 8. NICOLAS DONIN, THE TALMUD TRIAL OF 1240, AND THE STRUGGLES BETWEEN CHURCH AND STATE IN MEDIEVAL EUROPE

I wish to thank Marina Rustow for commenting on a previous draft of this essay, the editors for their insightful advice and suggestions, and Katelyn Mesler for her invaluable help in the final redaction. All errors or omissions are mine alone. All transcriptions from manuscripts and translations of sources are mine unless otherwise indicated.

1. Bull *Lacrimabilem iudeorum in regno Francie commorantium* by Gregory IX (5 September 1236); Shlomo Simonsohn, *The Apostolic See and the Jews. Documents: 492–1404* (Toronto, 1988), 163–65, nos. 154–55. On this issue, and on the purported burning of Maimonides' works in Montpellier in 1232 or 1233, see Jeremy Cohen, *The Friars and the Jews: The Evolution of Medieval Anti-Judaism* (Ithaca, N.Y., 1982), 52–61.

2. Translation of the main sources in Robert Chazan, Jean Connell Hoff, and John Friedman, *The Trial of the Talmud: Paris, 1240* (Toronto, 2012).

3. On Jews in Aragon see Yom Tov Assis, *The Golden Age of Aragonese Jewry: Community and Society in the Crown of Aragon, 1213–1327* (London, 1997); Robin Vose, *Dominicans, Muslims and Jews in the Medieval Crown of Aragon* (Cambridge, 2009); Paola Tartakoff, *Between Christian and Jew: Conversion and Inquisition in the Crown of Aragon, 1250–1391* (Philadelphia, 2012).

4. On the categorization of Jews as infidels and heretics in canon law in the years around the Paris Talmud trial, see Benjamin Z. Kedar, "Canon Law and the Burning of the Talmud," *Bulletin of Medieval Canon Law* n.s. 9 (1979): 79–82.

5. On these events, see Mark G. Pegg, *A Most Holy War: The Albigensian Crusade and the Battle for Christendom* (Oxford; New York, 2008); idem, *The Corruption of Angels: The Great Inquisition of 1245–1246* (Princeton, N.J., 2001); Jean-Louis Biget, *Hérésie et inquisition dans le midi de la France* (Paris, 2007); Cohen, *The Friars and the Jews*, 59 and 236n.35; Robert Moore, *The Formation of a Persecuting Society: Authority and Deviance in Western Europe 950–1250* (2nd ed.; Oxford, 2007), 26–42.

6. *Monumenta Germaniae Historica. Leges, Legum section IV*, Tomus II, ed. L. Weiland (Hannover, 1896), 274–76n.204.

7. Thomas of Cantimpré (d. 1272) stated in his *Bonum universale de proprietatibus apum*, I, 3 (Cologne, c. 1478–80 [GW M46647], 7b–8a; cf. idem, *Bonum universale de apibus*, ed. G. Colvenerius [Douai, 1627], 17–18), that the execution of the sentence of 1240 was delayed because the Jews succeeded in bribing one archbishop who was one of the king's counselors. For a full reappraisal of the question, see P. L. Rose, "When Was the Talmud Burnt at Paris? A Critical Examination of the Christian and Jewish Sources and a New Dating: June 1241," *Journal of Jewish Studies* 62.2 (2011): 324–39.

8. I think André Tuilier is right in ascribing this renewal of the church's anti-talmudic policy to the conflict between Innocent IV (and his conception of the unity of Christendom and the church's supreme authority within it) and secular rulers (especially Frederick II, who in the spring of 1244 was threatening central Italy). Such a threat would have prompted the pope to refuse even Louis IX's mediation. See André Tuilier, "La condamnation du Talmud par les maîtres universitaires parisiens, ses causes et ses conséquences politiques et idéologiques," in *Le brûlement du Talmud 1242–1244*, ed. G. Dahan and E. Nicolas (Paris, 1999), 59–78. See also Daniela Müller, "Die Pariser Verfahren gegen den Talmud von 1240 und 1248 im Kontext von Papsttum und Französischem Königtum," in *Interaction Between Judaism and Christianity in*

History, Religion, Art and Literature, ed. M. Poorthuis, J. Schwartz, and J. Turner (Leiden, 2009), 181–99.

9. Thus in Paris, Bibliothèque nationale de France, MS Lat. 16558, fol. 234a (*Sententia Odonis*).

10. Henri Gross, *Gallia Judaica. Dictionnaire géographique de la France d'après les sources rabbiniques* (Paris, 1897), 560–61. The name Donin appears in some manuscripts of Yitsḥak of Corbeil's *Sefer Mitsvot Katan* (*Small Book of Commandments*, 1277), in a sample bill of divorce (*get*) written "according to the order of our teacher Perets" (i.e., the tosafist Perets of Corbeil). Both the place (in northern France) and the date of issue of the *get* vary in the manuscripts (Bray-sur-Seine, Corbeil, Ramerupt; 1247, 1290, 1295, 1342), but the name of the husband repudiating his wife appears consistently as "Matatyah known as Donin, son of Rabbi Ya'akov." I am grateful to Judah Galinsky for calling my attention to the manuscripts of the *Sefer Mitsvot Katan* and granting me precious information about them. At the end of the Moscow manuscript (Rossiiskaya Gosudarstvennaya Biblioteka, MS Günzburg 1390, fol. 101b) Donin is given the apparently Italian diminutive nickname "Nicoletto" (הנקרא ניקולטו).

11. *Sefer Vikuaḥ rabenu Yeḥi'el mi-Paris*, ed. S. Grünbaum (Grynboym) (Thorn, 1873), reprinted with further mistakes in *Vikuaḥ rabenu Yeḥi'el mi-Pariz*, ed. R. Margaliot (Lwów, 1922). For a presentation and discussion of the manuscript tradition of the *Vikuaḥ* see Piero Capelli, "Il *Wikkuaḥ Rabbenu Yeḥi'el*: Problemi di storia del testo," *Sacra Doctrina* 51 (2006): 148–66; idem, "Editing Thirteenth-century Polemical Texts: Questions of Method and the Status Quaestionis in Three Polemical Works," *Henoch* 37.1 (2015): 43–52; Judah Galinsky, "The Different Hebrew Versions of the 'Talmud Trial' of 1240 in Paris," in *New Perspectives on Jewish-Christian Relations: In Honor of David Berger*, ed. E. Carlebach and J. J. Schacter (Leiden, 2012), 109–40.

12. Paris, Bibliothèque nationale de France, MS Hébr. 712, fol. 44a–b: ומה מצאתם בנו להביאנו עד פה לעמוד על נפשינו להלחם על תורתינו, לחוטא הלז אשר כפר בדברי חכמים, זה ט"ו שנה ולא היה מאמין רק בכתוב בתורת משה בלא פתרון. ואתם ידעתם כי לכל דבר צריך פשר, ועל כן הבדלנוהו ונדינוהו, ומאז ועד עתה חשב רעה עלינו לעקור הכל ולשוא (emphases mine).

13. MS Paris Hébr. 712, fol. 46a: מיום שנפרדת ממנו זה ט"ו שנה בקשת תאנה עלינו להתגולל בעלילות רשע, והיא לא תצלח (emphasis mine).

14. MS Moscow Günzburg 1390, fols. 87a (וזה הטמא כבר עבר ט"ו שנה שלא האמין רק בתורה שב כתב תורה בלא פתרון ויתרון ובעת הבינו בו רבותי' נדנוהו והבדלנוהו מעל עדת ישראל) and 88a (ט"ו שנה שנתת לבך על כל הדברי' האלה מיום שנפרדת ממנו).

15. Robert Chazan, "The Letter of R. Jacob Ben Elijah to Friar Paul," *Jewish History* 6.1–2 (1992): 51–63.

16. Trans. Solomon Grayzel, *The Church and the Jews in the XIIIth Century: A Study of Their Relations During the Years 1198–1254* (Philadelphia, 1933), 339–40 (emphasis mine), from the edition by Joseph Kobak, "Igeret (vikuaḥ) R. Ya'akov mi-Venetsi'ah," *Jeschurun* 8.2 (1868): 1–34 (here 29–30).

17. Thus Adolf Lewin, "Die Religionsdisputation des R. Jechiel von Paris 1240 am Hofe Ludwigs des Heiligen, ihre Veranlassung und ihre Folge," *Monatsschrift für Geschichte und Wissenschaft des Judentums* 18.3–5 (1869): 97–110, 145–56, 193–210. For a less convincing identification with Pope Gregory IX (based on terminological correspondence with sources from other periods and places), see Joseph Shatzmiller, "Ha-im he'elil ha-mumar Nicolas Donin et 'alilat ha-dam?" *Studies in the History of the Jewish People and the Land of Israel* 4 (1978): 176–82 (here 181–82).

18. Thus Jacob Mann, "Une source de l'histoire juive au XIIIe siècle: la lettre polémique de Jacob b. Elie à Pablo Christiani," *Revue des études juives* 82 (1926): 63–77.

19. Grayzel, *The Church*, 340, followed by, e.g., Ben-Zion Dinur, *Yisra'el ba-golah*, vol. 2.2 (Tel Aviv; Jerusalem, 1966), 54n.7.

20. Christian Hünemörder, "Thomas v. Cantimpré," in *Lexikon des Mittelalters*, vol. 8 (Stuttgart, 1997), cols. 711–14.

21. *Bonum universale de proprietatibus apum*, II, 28 (ed. Cologne, c. 1478–1480 [GW M46647], 65a; cf. idem, *Bonum universale de apibus*, ed. G. Colvenerius [Douai, 1627], 305).

22. I am grateful to Katelyn Mesler for her suggestions on Cantimpré's passage and its context.

23. *Sefer Yosef ha-Mekane' le-R. Yosef ben R. Natan Ofitsi'al*, ed. J. Rosenthal (Jerusalem, 1970), 53–54 (§36).

24. I thank Luca Benotti for helping me to understand this passage.

25. Gilbert Dahan, "Un dossier latin de textes de Rashi autour de la controverse de 1240," *Revue des études juives* 151.3–4 (1992): 321–36 (here 324n.19); idem, "Les traductions latines de Thibaut de Sézanne," in *Le brûlement du Talmud à Paris: 1242–1244*, ed. G. Dahan (Paris, 1999), 95–120 (here 99–106).

26. On Donin and the blood libel see the discussion in Chen Merchavia, *The Church Versus Talmudic and Midrashic Literature (500–1248)* (Hebrew; Jerusalem, 1970), 226–38; Shatzmiller, "Ha-im he'elil"; Chen Merchavia, "Kelum he'elil Donin et 'alilat ha-dam?," *Tarbiz* 49.1–2 (1979–80): 111–21.

27. For the date of the burning, see Rose, "When Was the Talmud Burnt."

28. Merchavia, *The Church*, 307–9.

29. The Latin text of the accusations was published by Isidore Loeb, "La controverse de 1240 sur le Talmud," *Revue des études juives* 1 (1880): 247–61; 2 (1880): 248–70; 3 (1881): 39–57; English translation by Jean Connell Hoff in Chazan, Hoff, and Friedman, *The Trial*, 102–21. The prooftexts from the Talmud and Rashi are listed in Judah M. Rosenthal, "The Talmud on Trial: The Disputation at Paris in the Year 1240," *Jewish Quarterly Review* n.s. 47 (1956): 58–76, 145–69 (here 145–66).

30. The text of both "confessions" was published by Loeb, "La controverse," 3 (1881): 55–57, and again by Merchavia, *The Church*, 453–55; English translation by Hoff in Chazan, Hoff, and Friedman, *The Trial*, 122–25.

31. Partially edited by Gilbert Dahan, "Rashi, sujet de la controverse de 1240. Edition partielle du ms. Paris, BN Lat. 16558," *Archives juives* 14.3 (1978): 43–54 (glosses to Genesis), and idem, "Un dossier latin" (glosses to Proverbs and excerpts from the glosses to Exodus, Joshua, and 1 Samuel). Some of the glosses to Genesis and some other scattered ones (from Exodus, Deuteronomy, 1 Samuel, Ecclesiastes, and Obadiah) were edited by Herman Hailperin, *Rashi and the Christian Scholars* (Pittsburgh, 1963), 118–28. See Piero Capelli, "Rashi nella controversia parigina sul Talmud del 1240," in *"Ricercare la sapienza di tutti gli antichi" (Sir 39,1). Miscellanea in onore di Gian Luigi Prato*, ed. M. Milani and M. Zappella (Bologna, 2013), 441–48; Görge K. Hasselhoff, "The Parisian Talmud Trials and the Translation of Rashi's Bible Commentaries," *Henoch* 37.1 (2015): 29–42.

32. Thus Chazan in Chazan, Hoff, and Friedman, *The Trial*, 46.

33. Merchavia, *The Church*, 307; Dahan, "Les traductions latines," 118.

34. Thus Dahan, "Un dossier latin," 328–39.

35. See Robert Chazan, "Trial, Condemnation, and Censorship: The Talmud in Medieval Europe," in Chazan, Hoff, and Friedman, *The Trial*, 17, 20.

36. Joseph Shatzmiller, *La deuxième controverse de Paris. Un chapitre dans la polémique entre chrétiens et juifs au Moyen Age* (Paris; Louvain, 1994), 21. See also Ursula Ragacs, *Die zweite Talmuddisputation von Paris 1269* (Frankfurt am Main, 2001).

37. Fols. 56b–57b and 66b–68a. The first edition of this text is being prepared by Philippe Bobichon, to whom I am grateful for sharing with me in advance the results of his research.

38. Edition in Shatzmiller, *La deuxième controverse*, 44.

39. The *kaf* (= 20) of the MS (fol. 102b) bears a mark of deletion (Shatzmiller, *La deuxième controverse*, 17, 45n.14, 58n.5).

40. The similitude is taken from a saying of Ben 'Aza'i in BT Bekhorot 58a.

41. Shatzmiller, *La deuxième controverse*, 45. The last clause echoes 1 Kings 12:10.

42. Emile Littré, "Notices succinctes sur divers écrivains, de l'an 1286 à l'an 1300," *Histoire littéraire de la France*, Tome XXI (Paris, 1847, repr. 1895), 293. For Donin as a purported Franciscan, see already Lewin, "Die Religionsdisputation," 106n.4. Thus also Alexander Kisch, "Die Anklageartikel gegen den Talmud und ihre Verteidigung durch Rabbi Jechiel ben Joseph vor Ludwig dem Heiligen in Paris," *Monatsschrift für Geschichte und Wissenschaft des Judentums* 23.1–5 (1874): 10–18, 62–75, 123–30, 155–63, 204–12 (here 126n.5); Charles Singer, "Hebrew Scholarship in the Middle Ages Among Latin Christians," in *The Legacy of Israel*, ed. E. R. Singer and C. J. Bevan (Oxford, 1928), 295; Merchavia, *The Church*, 237; Judah M. Rosenthal, "Donin, Nicholas," in *Encyclopaedia Judaica*, vol. 6 (Jerusalem, 1971), cols. 167–68 (here 167); Philippe Bobichon, "Juifs et convertis engagés dans les controverses médiévales," in *Les juifs méditerranéens au Moyen Age, culture et prosopographie*, ed. D. Iancu-Agou (Paris, 2010), 83–125 (here 111).

43. The Franciscan sources are the *Chronicon XIV vel XV Generalium Ministrorum Ordinis fratrum Minorum seu Catalogus «Gonsalvinus» dictus Genelalium* [*sic*] *Ministrorum Ordinis fratrum Minorum* and the *Chronica XXIV Generalium Ordinis Minorum*, both edited by Quinctianus Müller in *Analecta Franciscana sive Chronica Aliaque Varia Documenta ad Historiam Fratrum Minorum Spectantia edita a Patribus Collegii S. Bonaventurae*, vol. 3 (Quaracchi, 1897), 693–707 (Appendix IV, here 703, ll. 20–22) and I–XXVII, 1–575 (here 408 lines 14–16). On Nicholas of Ghistelle, see André Callebaut, "Les provinciaux de la province de France au XIIIe siècle. Notes, documents et études," *Archivum Franciscanum Historicum* 10 (1917): 289–356 (here 346–47). On the whole question, see Stefano Brufani, "Matteo d'Acquasparta generale dell'ordine francescano," in *Matteo d'Acquasparta francescano, filosofo, politico. Atti del XXIX Convegno storico internazionale. Todi, 11–14 ottobre 1992* (Spoleto, 1993), 51–77 (here 68–69).

44. Görge K. Hasselhoff, *Dicit Rabbi Moyses. Studien zum Bild von Moses Maimonides im Lateinischen Westen vom 13. bis zum 15. Jahrhundert* (Würzburg, 2004), 123–24, states that after conversion Donin became a Dominican or was at least close to the Dominican order, but this only on the basis of Donin's possible closeness to the activity of the Dominican Thibaut de Sézanne as the translator of the *Extractiones*.

45. Grayzel, *The Church*, 340; Yitsḥak Baer, "Le-bikoret ha-vikuḥim shel R. Yeḥi'el mi-Paris ve-shel R. Mosheh ben Naḥman," *Tarbiz* 2.2 (1931): 172–87 (here 173); Bernard Blumenkranz, "Jüdische und Christliche Konvertiten im Jüdisch-Christlichen Religionsgespräche des Mittelalters," in *Judentum im Mittelalter. Beiträge Zum Christlich-Jüdischen Gespräch*, ed. P. Wilpert and W. P. Eckert (Berlin, 1966), 264–82 (here 279–80); Simon Schwarzfuchs, *Les juifs de France* (Paris, 1975), 80; Anna Sapir Abulafia, *Christians and Jews in Dispute: Disputational Literature and the Rise of Anti-Judaism in the West (c. 1000–1150)* (Aldershot; Brookfield; Singapore; Sidney, 1998), 80; Hasselhoff, *Dicit Rabbi Moyses*, 124; Fausto M. Parente, *Les juifs et l'église romaine à l'époque moderne (xve–xviiie siècle)*, ed. M. Anquetil-Auletta and D. Tollet (Paris, 2007), 251 and 262.

46. Salo W. Baron, *A Social and Religious History of the Jews* (2nd ed.; New York; London; Philadelphia, 1965), 9:64 and 270n.12; Cohen, *The Friars*, 61; Robert Chazan, "The Condem-

nation of the Talmud Reconsidered," *Proceedings of the American Academy for Jewish Research* 55 (1988): 11–30 (here 16); cf. Marina Rustow, "Karaites Real and Imagined: Three Cases of Jewish Heresy," *Past and Present* 197 (2007): 52.

47. Thus Hasselhoff, *Dicit Rabbi Moyses*, 122–29. For Donin as a Maimonist, cf. Kisch, "Die Anklageartikel," 125–26.

48. Merchavia, *The Church*, 233–34; Rosenthal, "Donin, Nicholas," 167; Kurt Schubert, "Apostasie aus Identitätskrise—Nikolaus Donin," *Kairos. Zeitschrift für Judaistik und Religionswissenschaft* 30/31 (1988/89): 1–10 (here 4).

49. Milan Žonca, "Apostasy and Authority: The Transformation of Christian Anti-Jewish Polemic in the Twelfth and Thirteenth Centuries," *Focus Pragensis* 9 (2009): 61–88 (here 79).

50. Personal communication, November 2011.

51. Here, the reading "you cannot deny" from the now lost Strassburg manuscript transcribed by Johann Christoph Wagenseil in his editio princeps of the *Vikuaḥ* (included in his *Tela ignea Satanae* [Altdorf, 1681]) is probably preferable.

52. MS Paris, fol. 44a (emphases mine): וילבש צור אמונים גבורה, ויאמר אל המין: על מה תריבני, ומה זה תשאלני? ויאמר המין: על דבר ישן אשאלך, כי בזה לא אכפור כי התלמוד מד' מאות שנה. ויאמר הרב: יותר מט"ו מאות שנה. ויאמר אל המלכה: אנא אדונתי, אל נא תכריחני לענות לדבריו, אחרי כי הודה אשר הוא ישן נושן. ועד הלום אין דובר עליו דבר והנה קד' יריומא הגלח ידע כל תורתינו התלמוד והכל כאשר נודע לכל הגלחות, ואם היה בו דופי לא היה מניחו עד כה, ועוד הכי עד הלום לא היו גלחים ומשומדים חשובים כאלה? ואין אומר ואין דברים בלי נשמע קולם זה ט"ו מאות שנה.

53. Israel Moses Ta-Shma, "Rabbi Yéhiel de Paris: l'homme et l'œuvre, religion et société (XIIIe siècle)," *Annuaire—Ecole pratique des hautes études, Section-sciences religieuses* 99 (1991): 215–19 (here 217).

54. Lewin, "Die Religionsdisputation," 101n.1; Merchavia, *The Church*, 232.

55. See Naḥman Danzig, "Mi-Talmud 'al-peh le-Talmud bi-khtav," *Bar-Ilan: Sefer ha-shanah le-mada'ei ha-yahadut ve-ha-ruaḥ shel Universitat Bar-Ilan* 30–31 (2006): 49–112; Robert Brody, *The Geonim of Babylonia and the Shaping of Medieval Jewish Culture* (New Haven, Conn.; London, 1998), 230–32.

56. Talya Fishman, *Becoming the People of the Talmud: Oral Torah as Written Tradition in Medieval Jewish Cultures* (Philadelphia, 2011), esp. chaps. 4–5.

57. Galinsky, "The Different Hebrew Versions," 113 and n. 21 (fifteenth century); Shatzmiller, *La deuxième controverse*, 9 (second half of the fourteenth century).

58. Ms. Moscow Günzburg 1390, fol. 87a (תורתינו הנכונה אשר עבר ט"ו מאות שנה שהעתיקוה רבינא ורב אשי למען כי בימיהם נטמעטו הלבבות ולא היו יכולין לקיימה על פה כבראשונה).

59. Ms. Moscow Günzburg 1390, fol. 98b (כל דבריהם דברי רוח וראויים לישרף, כי פעם אחת עשו כן בימי אספסיינוס קיסר ושרף התורה).

60. Ms. Moscow Günzburg 1390, fol. 101a (ועל אשר אמרת ששרפו התורה בימי אספסיינוס קיסר לא התלמוד לבדו שרפו אלא כל התורה שרפו שהרי עדיין לא נכתב התלמוד עד לאחר כמה שנים בימי רבינא ורב אשי).

61. Ms. Moscow Günzburg 1390, fol. 101b (התלמוד ישן נושן מיותר מאלף שנים ועד עתה לא דבר עליו שום אדם דבר רע).

62. In the Barcelona disputation of 1263 Nahmanides would resort to the same talmudic dating, placing Rav Ashi's compilation of the Talmud "around four hundred years after Jesus" (*Sefer Vikuaḥ ha-Ramban*, ed. M. Steinschneider [Berlin, 1860], 6).

63. On the issue of the dating of the Talmud see my "Dating the Talmud in Medieval Europe" (forthcoming).

64. Hailperin, *Rashi and the Christian Scholars*, 103–4 (emphasis mine).

65. Or that, in Jacob Katz's wording, "was expressed almost entirely in religious terms"

(*Exclusiveness and Tolerance: Studies in Jewish-Gentile Relations in Medieval and Modern Times* [New York, 1962], 76).

66. Shlomo Simonsohn, *The Apostolic See and the Jews: History, Studies and Texts* (Toronto, 1991), 279.

67. Hermannus quondam Iudaeus, *Opusculum de conversione sua*, ed. G. Niemeyer (Weimar, 1963), 100, 105, and chap. 13.

68. Caroline W. Bynum, *Jesus as Mother: Studies in the Spirituality of the Middle Ages* (Berkeley, Calif.; London, 1982), 85.

69. Schubert, "Apostasie aus Identitätskrise," 8 (emphasis mine).

70. Rosenthal, "Donin, Nicholas," 167.

71. MS Moscow Günzburg 1390, fol. 84b (לסוף היה נהרג בבית ע"ז שלו). Cf. Grayzel, *The Church and the Jews*, 340.

72. וגם דת רומה לא היה מאמין... הכה ומת אין לו דמים. Cf. Kisch, "Die Anklageartikel," 126n.5.

73. Yossef Schwartz, "Images of Revelation and Spaces of Discourse: The Cross-Cultural Journey of Iberian Jewry," in *Christlicher Norden—Muslimischer Süden. Ansprüche und Wirklichkeiten von Christen, Juden und Muslimen auf der Iberischen Halbinsel im Hoch- und Spätmittelalter*, ed. A. Fidora and M. M. Tischler (Munich, 2011), 267–87 (here 285), based on Bill Hillier and Alan Penn, "Visible Colleges: Structure and Randomness in the Place of Discovery," *Science in Context* 4.1 (1991): 23–49.

74. The first instance I know is Johannes Pfefferkorn (1469–1523) and his polemics against Johannes Reuchlin about the prosecution and destruction of Jewish books; see David H. Price, *Johannes Reuchlin and the Campaign to Destroy Jewish Books* (Oxford, 2011).

75. John V. Tolan, "*Lachrymabilem Judeorum questionem*: La brève histoire de la communauté juive de Bretagne au XIIIe siècle," in *Hommes, cultures et paysage de l'antiquité à la période moderne : Mélanges offerts à Jean Peyras*, ed. I. Pimouguet-Pédarros, M. Clavel-Levêque, and F. Ouachour (Rennes, 2013), 417–32 (here 428–29). In the end, Pierre de Dreux moved to the Crusade only in 1239. See in general William C. Jordan, *The French Monarchy and the Jews: From Philip Augustus to the Last Capetians* (Philadelphia, 1989); Müller, "Die Pariser Verfahren," 181–99.

76. MS Paris Hébr. 712, fol. 51b: ויען הנבל: הלא כמה רבבות נפלו מכם בחרב ברטיינא ואניוב ופוייטוב ואיה הם הנפלאות והאות אשר עשה לכם אלהיכם אם אתם עם סגולה כאשר אמרתם? Cf. the mention of the massacres of 1236 in the *Chronicon Britannicum* (or *Britanniae*) quoted by Tolan, "*Lachrymabilem Judeorum questionem*," 432n.35.

77. Simonsohn, *The Apostolic See*, 162–63 (nos. 154–55).

78. Cohen, *The Friars and the Jews*, 52–61. The source is translated in Grayzel, *The Church and the Jews*, 227.

79. See Piero Capelli, "Conversion to Christianity and Anti-Talmudic Criticism from Petrus Alfonsi to Nicolas Donin and Pablo Christiani," in *Transcending Words: The Language of Religious Contact Between Buddhists, Christians, Jews, and Muslims in Premodern Times*, ed. G. K. Hasselhoff and K. M. Stünkel (Bochum, 2015), 89–102.

CHAPTER 9. CULTURAL IDENTITY IN TRANSMISSION

1. There are five manuscripts of the letters. While we are in need of a new critical edition, the best available version is the one printed in Itzhak Blumenfeld, ed., *Otsar Neḥmad* (Vienna, 1863), 2:124–42.

2. Moritz Guedemann, *Geschichte des Erziehungswesens und der Cultur der abendländischen Juden wärend des Mittelalters und der neueren Zeit* (Vienna, 1884), 2:152–75; Hermann Vogelstein and Paul Rieger, *Geschichte der Juden in Rom* (Berlin, 1896), 1:415–20. Joseph Sermoneta and Aviezer Ravitzky wrote doctoral dissertations on Hillel and Zeraḥyah, respectively. Each dedicated substantial parts to the debate, analyzing it from the different perspectives of our two protagonists. See Joseph B. Sermoneta, "Rabbi Hillel ben Shemu'el of Verona and His Philosophical Doctrine" (Hebrew; Ph.D. diss., Hebrew University of Jerusalem, 1962), 33–39, 167–75; Aviezer Ravitzky, "R. Zerahiah b. Isaac b. Shealtiel Hen and the Maimonidean-Tibbonian Philosophy in the Thirteenth Century" (Hebrew; Ph.D. diss., Hebrew University of Jerusalem, 1977), 269–92.

3. Kirsten A. Fudeman, *Vernacular Voices: Language and Identity in Medieval French Jewish Communities* (Philadelphia, 2010), 26–59.

4. Cyril Aslanov, "From Latin into Hebrew Through the Romance Vernaculars: The Creation of an Interlanguage Written in Hebrew Characters," in *Latin-into-Hebrew: Texts and Studies,* vol. 1: *Studies,* ed. Resianne Fontaine and Gad Freudenthal (Leiden, 2013), 69–84, here 74.

5. For an overview of the translations and preliminary general analysis, cf. Mauro Zonta, "Medieval Hebrew Translations of Philosophical and Scientific Texts: A Chronological Table," and Gad Freudenthal, "Arabic and Latin Cultures as Resources for the Hebrew Translation Movement: Comparative Considerations, Both Quantitative and Qualitative," both in *Science in Medieval Jewish Cultures,* ed. Gad Freudenthal (Cambridge, 2011), 17–73 and 74–105, respectively.

6. Sarah Stroumsa, "The Muslim Context of Medieval Jewish Philosophy," in *The Cambridge History of Jewish Philosophy: From Antiquity Through the Seventeenth Century,* ed. Steven Nadler and Tamar Rudavsky (Cambridge, 2009), 39–59.

7. Joseph Shatzmiller, *Jews, Medicine, and Medieval Society* (Berkeley, Calif., 1994).

8. On the basic esoteric mechanism common to different late medieval Jewish spiritual trends, see Moshe Halbertal, *Concealment and Revelation: Esotericism in Jewish Thought and Its Philosophical Implications,* trans. Jackie Feldman (Princeton, N.J., 2007), 60–134.

9. Mauro Zonta, *The Jewish Mediation in the Transmission of Arabo-Islamic Science and Philosophy to the Latin Middle Ages: Historical Overview and Perspectives of Research,* in *Wissen über Grenzen, Arabisches Wissen und lateinisches Mittelalter,* Miscellanea Mediaevalia 33, ed. A. Speer and L. Wegener (Berlin and New York, 2006), 90–105; idem, *Medieval Hebrew Translations: Methods and Textual Problems,* in *Les traducteurs au travail: Leurs manuscrits et leurs méthodes,* ed. J. Hamesse (Turnhout, 2001), 129–142.

10. Aslanov, "From Latin into Hebrew Through the Romance Vernaculars," 79.

11. Freudenthal, "Arabic and Latin Cultures as Resources for the Hebrew Translation Movement."

12. For concrete test case, see Yossef Schwartz, "Thirteenth Century Hebrew Psychological Discussion: The Role of Latin Sources in the Formation of Hebrew Aristotelianism," in *The Letter Before the Spirit: The Importance of Text Editions for the Study of the Reception of Aristotle,* ed. Aafke M. I. van Oppenraay and Resianne Fontaine (Leiden, 2012), 173–94, here 186.

13. Out of the approximately 570 philosophic texts gathered by Zonta and analyzed by Freudenthal, fifty-seven belong to Averroes and forty to Alfarabi, almost 20 percent of the total number of translated works and 29 percent of the Arabic-to-Hebrew translations. If we count only Arabic non-Jewish works, then the translations of Alfarabi and Averroes represent more than a third (36 percent) of the total number.

14. Averroes' *Tahāfut al-tahāfut*, a polemic against Algazali's work that entails large portions of Algazali's own text, was first translated from Arabic into Latin in 1328 by Kalonymos ben Kalonymos ben Meir and from Arabic into Hebrew at about the same time by Kalonymos ben David ben Todros.

15. Mauro Zonta, "Avicenna in Medieval Jewish Philosophy," in *Avicenna and His Heritage*, Ancient and Medieval Philosophy, vol. 28, ed. Jules Janssens and Daniël De Smet (Leuven, 2002), 267–79; Warren Zev Harvey, "Maimonides' Avicennianism," *Maimonidean Studies* 5 (2008): 107–19; Steven Harvey, "Avicenna's Influence on Jewish Thought: Some Reflections," in *Avicenna and His Legacy: A Golden Age of Science and Philosophy,* Cultural Encounters in Late Antiquity and the Middle Ages, vol. 8, ed. Tzvi Langerman (Turnhout, 2009), 327–40, esp. 335–38. On the later fourteenth-century Hebrew translation of Avicenna, see Gabriella Elgrably-Berzin, *Avicenna in Medieval Hebrew Translation: Todros Todrosi's Translation of Kitāb al-najāt, on Psychology and Metaphysics* (Leiden, 2015).

16. Serafín Vegas González, *La Escuela de traductores de Toledo en la historia del pensamiento* (Toledo, 1998); Charles Burnett, "The Coherence of the Arabic-Latin Translation Program in Toledo in the Twelfth Century," *Science in Context* 14 (2001): 249–88; Alexander Fidora, *Die Wissenschaftstheorie des Dominicus Gundissalinus: Voraussetzungen und Konsequenzen des zweiten Anfangs der aristotelischen Philosophie im 12. Jahrhundert* (Berlin, 2003).

17. Dag Nikolas Hasse, *Avicenna's 'De anima' in the Latin West: The Formation of a Peripatetic Philosophy of the Soul, 1160–1300* (London; Turin, 2000).

18. Monica Green is about to publish a detailed research of the reception of Gerard's medical translations. Preliminary results were introduced during a conference held at the Israel Institute for Advanced Studies at the Hebrew University of Jerusalem on 9–11 December 2013 (Medical Texts in Hebrew Contexts: Jewish Physicians and the Dynamics of Cultural Transfer in Pre-Modern Europe), and I am grateful to her for sharing those preliminary results with me.

19. It is typical that the early Jewish Hebrew reception of the psychology of Avicenna, so influential in early scholastic thought, was mediated through the Hebrew translation of its Christian Latin paraphrase composed by Gundissalinus; see Schwartz, "Thirteenth Century Hebrew Psychological Discussion."

20. David Wirmer's detailed study of the Hebrew reception of Avicenna's Canon is now in the process of publication.

21. On the parallel cross-disciplinary relations between medicine and theology in Christian culture, see Joseph Ziegler, "Religion and Medicine in the Middle Ages," in *Religion and Medicine in the Middle Ages*, ed. Peter Biller and Joseph Ziegler (York, 2001), 3–14, esp. 10–11. Describing Arnau de Vilanova's "double career as a scholastic physician and a visionary mystic," Ziegler points to the turn of the fourteenth century as the earliest period in which physicians crossed disciplinary boundaries.

22. On Hillel's biography, see Moritz Steinschneider in Hillel's *Tagmulei ha-nefesh*, ed. Solomon J. Halberstamm, 7–27; Sermoneta, "Rabbi Hillel"; Mauro Zonta, "Hillel di Samuel da Verona," *Dizionario Biografico degli Italiani* 61 (2004); Cartina Rigo, *Routledge Encyclopedia of Philosophy*, 431.

23. Sermoneta, "Rabbi Hillel," 6–17. Sermoneta follows and further develops the basic assessment offered by Yitzhak Baer in *A History of the Jews in Christian Spain* (Philadelphia, 1961), 1:401. Warren Harvey was one of the first to raise doubts regarding Sermoneta's negative attitude toward the reliability of Hillel's testimonies; see Harvey's review article on Sermoneta's edition of *Tagmulei ha-nefesh*, *Tarbiz* 52.3 (1983): 529–37, here 535.

24. The later date is clearly the result of a wrong (over)interpretation of Hillel's statement

that he had studied with Jonah Girondi in Barcelona until Jonah's departure to Toledo. Since the general context of the narrative relates to Jonah's role during the Maimonidean controversy of the 1230s, Hillel immediately proceeds to describe Jonah's indecent death at Toledo, caused by the fact that he did not fulfill his oath to travel further to Maimonides' grave in order to repent for the terrible sin he had committed against him in his youth. Steinschneider, Vogelstein/Rieger, Sermoneta, and others have assumed that Jonah moved to Toledo immediately before his death, about 1264, and therefore have dated Hillel's stay in Barcelona to the early 1260s. But this is not at all asserted in the text. Hillel, who wrote his testimony many decades after the narrated events took place, simply asserts that he was with his teacher until the very last moment of his master's presence in Barcelona. He does not mention how long Jonah stayed in Toledo before he died there, but the logic of his argument certainly implies that Jonah spent some years in Toledo since his "sin" lay precisely in the fact that he did not proceed immediately with his promised pilgrimage to Maimonides' grave. If we turn to scholars of Iberian legal tradition to seek some biographic details on Rabbi Jonah, then it becomes clear that we do not know when exactly Jonah arrived at Toledo (Septimus), and his arrival clearly took place between the early 1240s (Ta-Shma) and the early 1250s (Galinsky). For the dates of Jonah's residence in Barcelona, see Israel M. Ta-Shma, *Ha-Nigle she-banistar: Le-heker shkiei ha-halakha be-sefer ha-zohar* (Tel Aviv 2001), 52; Judah D. Galinsky, *The Four Turim and the Halakhik Literature of 14th Century Spain: Historical, Literary and Halakhic Aspects* (Ph.D. thesis, Bar Ilan University 1999), 18n.18.

25. See Vogelstein/Rieger, *Geschichte der Juden in Rom*, 1:401.

26. If we combine Hillel's self-testimony concerning his studies under Jonah Girondi—one of the central figures among the anti-Maimonideans of the 1230s, the son-in-law of Nahmanides, and a the author of widely known moral treatises—with the one provided by Abraham Abulafia in his book *Otsar 'eden ganuz*, composed during the early 1280s, it seems that during the 1260s Hillel was at least partially close to kabbalist circles.

27. These works were edited by Halberstamm and Steinschneider in 1874, and *Sefer tagmulei ha-nefesh* was reedited by Joseph Sermoneta in 1981: see *Sefer tagmulei ha-nefesh*, ed. Solomon J. Halberstamm (Lyck, 1874); *Sefer tagmulei ha-nefesh* (Book of the Rewards of the Soul), Critical Edition with Introduction and Commentary by Joseph Sermoneta (Jerusalem 1981).

28. Ravitzky, "R. Zerahiah b. Isaac b. Shealtiel Hen," 66; Steinschneider, *Otsar Neḥmad,* 2:229–45.

29. Ravitzky, "R. Zerahiah b. Isaac b. Shealtiel Hen," 71.

30. Moritz Steinschneider, *Die Hebräische Übersetzungen des Mittelalters und die Juden als Dolmetscher* (Gratz, 1893), 113. Steinschneider suggested possible identification of Judah ben Solomon with Judah Salmon, with whom Abraham Abulafia corresponded.

31. MS Cambridge, Cambridge University Library, Add. 1235, fol. 91a–b.

32. Steinschneider gloomily suggested that there is nothing new under the sun; see *Otsar Neḥmad*, 2:238.

33. Vogelstein/Rieger, *Geschichte der Juden in Rom*, 1:415.

34. James T. Robinson, "The Ibn Tibbon Family: A Dynasty of Translators in Medieval Provence," in *Be'erot Yitzhak: Studies in Memory of Isadore Twersky,* ed. Jay M. Harris (Cambridge, Mass., 2005), 193–224; Carlos Fraenkel, „From Maimonides to Samuel ibn Tibbon: Interpreting Judaism as a Philosophical Religion," in *Traditions of Maimonideanism*, ed. Carlos Fraenkel (Leiden, 2009), 177–212.

35. Gilles Deleuze and Félix Guattari, *What Is Philosophy?*, trans. Graham Burchell and Hugh Tomlinson (New York, 1994), 61–84.

36. Perhaps the most paradigmatic case would be Johann Franz Buddeus's "Philosophic Dissertation on Spinozism Before Spinoza" (*Dissertatio philosophica de Spinozismo ante Spinozam,* 1701); see Haim Mahlev, "Der Spinozismus vor Spinoza: Johann Franz Buddes Erwiderung auf Johann Georg Wachters *Der Spinozismus im Jüdenthumb,*" *Scientia Poetica* 15 (2011): 67–91.

37. On Zeraḥyah's commentary, see Steinschneider, *Die Hebräische Übersetzungen*, 113.

38. Hillel, *First Letter to Maestro Gaio (Itzhak ben Mordechai ha-Rofe)*, *Ḥemda Genuza*, ed. Shmuel Edelmann (Königsberg, 1856), 20a.

39. *Tagmulei ha-nefesh*, ed. Sermoneta, 116f., ll. 160–66.

40. Ibid., 167f., ll. 167–76.

41. Dag Nikolas Hasse, *Avicenna's De Anima in the Latin West: The Formation of a Peripatetic Philosophy of the Soul, 1160–1300* (London; Turin, 2000), 154–65.

42. Herbert A. Davidson, *Alfarabi, Avicenna and Averroes on Intellect* (New York, 1992), 118–22.

43. Hasse, *Avicenna's De Anima in the Latin West*, 156; Thomas Aquinas, *De veritate* 12.3: "Praeterea ad prophetiam non requiruntur nisi tria, scilicet claritas intelligentiae et perfectio virtutis imaginativae et potestas animae ut ei materia exterior oboediat ut Avicenna ponit in .iv. de naturalibus"; Davidson, *Alfarabi, Avicenna and Averroes on Intellect*, 122ff.: "In addition to intellectual prophecy and imaginative prophecy, both of which are cognitive phenomena, Avicenna recognizes the possibility of man's effecting changes in the physical world through an act of sheer will, and he calls that phenomenon prophecy as well."

44. *Otsar Neḥmad*, 2:135.

45. Ibid.: "Since what you have said, that the holy tongue was given to Adam naturally, this is a fictive lie, according with both experience and logic, which reject this kind of reality found by you and other week minds." Irene Zwiep, *Mother of Reason and Revelation: A Short History of Medieval Jewish Linguistic Thought* (Amsterdam, 1997), 165–77.

46. Arno Borst, *Der Turmbau von Babel: Geschichte der Meinungen über Ursprung und Vielfalt der Sprachen und Völker* (Stuttgart, 1957–63), II/2, 756; Adam de Salimbene, *Chronica*, ed. Oswald Older-Egger (Monumenta Germaniae Historica 32) (Hannover, 1913), 350; Ernst Kantorowitz, *Kaiser Friedrich der Zweite* (Berlin, 1927), 325ff.

47. Zwiep, *Mother of Reason and Revelation*, 171–72.

48. Robinson, "The Ibn Tibbon Family," 193–95.

49. I intend to dedicate a full study to these translations elsewhere. On the general phenomenon of multiple translations to one and the same text see Jean-Pierre Rothschild, "Traductions refaites et traductions révisées," *Latin-into-Hebrew: Studies and Texts*, vol.1: *Studies*, ed. Resianne Fontaine and Gad Freudenthal (Leiden, 2013), 391–420. Rothschild mentions Hillel and Zeraḥyah's parallel translations of the *Book of Causes* but does not stress the fact that they were done simultaneously nor provides any account of the fact that the two authors translated parallel medical texts as well.

50. Alfredo Focà, *Maestro Bruno da Longobucco* (Calabria, 2004); Antonio Maria Adorisio, *I codici di Bruno da Longobucco* (Casamari, 2006).

51. Steinschneider, *Die Hebräische Übersetzungen*, 788. For the adaptation of this dating in modern scholarship, see Gerrit Bos, "Novel Medical and General Hebrew Terminology from the 13th Century," *Journal of Semitic Studies*, Supplement 27 (Oxford, 2011), 12n.53.

52. Steinschneider, *Die Hebräische Übersetzungen*, 660; Suessmann Muntner, *Moshe ben Maimon (Maimonides) Medical Works* (Jerusalem, 1987), 2:XXVII; Bos, "Novel Medical and General Hebrew Terminology," 10.

53. Benjamin Richler, "Another Letter from Hillel Ben Samuel to Isaac the Physician?," *Kiryat Sefer* 62.1–2 (1988–89): 450–52; Shatzmiller, *Jews, Medicine, and Medieval Society*, 46.

54. The occupation that eventually made him such a fortunate man is well represented in his popular short poem on medical praxis; see Bos, *Novel Medical and General Hebrew Terminology*, 14ff.

55. Steinschneider, *Die Hebräische Übersetzungen*, 734.

56. Moritz Steinschneider et al., eds., *Hebraeische Bibliographie* (Berlin, 1863), 6:110–14.

57. Jean-Pierre Rothschild, "Le *Livre des causes* du latin à l'hébreu: textes, problèmes, réception," in *Latin-into-Hebrew: Texts and Studies*, vol. 2: *Texts in Contexts,* ed. Alexander Fidora, Harvey Hames, and Yossef Schwartz (Leiden, 2013), 47–84, here 50, 84.

58. Richard C. Dales, *The Problem of the Rational Soul in the Thirteenth Century* (Leiden, 1995), 113–91; Yossef Schwartz, "Divine Space and the Space of the Divine: On the Scholastic Rejection of Arab Cosmology," *Représentations et conceptions de l'espace dans la culture medieval,* ed. Tiziana Suarez Nani and Martin Rohde (Scrinium Friburgense, 30) (Berlin, Boston, 2011), 89–119, esp. 100–102, 117–19.

59. Gerrit Bos, ed., *Aristotle's 'De anima' Translated into Hebrew by Zeraḥyah ben Isaac Shealtiel Ḥen: A Critical Edition with an Introduction and Index* (Leiden, 1994).

60. On the institutional aspects of medical education in Islamic lands, see S. D. Goitein, *A Mediterranean Society: An Abridgment in One Volume*, rev. and ed. Jacob Lassner (Tel Aviv, 1999), 248–89; Goitein, *A Mediterranean Society* (Berkeley, 1967), 2:240–72. Regarding the problematization of medicine as reflected in its location within Alfarabi's classification of sciences and different receptions among post-Maimonidean Jewish authors, see Sara Stroumsa, "Al-Farabi and Maimonides on Medicine as Science," *Arabic Sciences and Philosophy* 3 (1993): 235–49.

61. Cf. Bos, "Novel Medical and General Terminology," 49. The work was translated into Hebrew in the year 1259.

62. *Ozar Nehmad*, 2:142; Bos, "Novel Medical and General Terminology," 122.

63. See Michael McVaugh, *The Rational Surgery of the Middle Ages* (Florence, 2006), 25.

64. James T. Robinson, *Samuel Ibn Tibbon's Commentary on Ecclesiastes* (Tübingen, 2007).

65. Ottfried Fraisse, *Moses ibn Tibbons Kommentar zum Hohelied und sein poetologisch-philosophisches Programm. Synoptische Edition, Übersetzung und Analyse* (Berlin, 2004). As I have demonstrated elsewhere, it is no coincidence that the most prolific Christian university theologian to choose the biblical commentary form for his philosophic speculation—the German Dominican and Parisian theology professor Meister Eckhart—did so under the heavy influence of Maimonides' *Guide*; see Yossef Schwartz, "Meister Eckhart and Moses Maimonides: From Judaeo-Arabic Rationalism to Christian Mysticism," in *A Companion to Meister Eckhart*, Brill's Companions to the Christian Tradition 36, ed. Jeremiah M. Hackett (Leiden, 2012), 389–414.

66. Apparently the existing manuscript tradition was rooted in Zeraḥyah's circle, which might explain the fact that Hillel's text was totally omitted.

67. *Otsar Nehmad*, 2:142.

68. Ibid.

69. Immanuel von Rom, *The Cantos of Immanuel of Rome* (*Maḥberot Immanuel Haromi*), ed. Dov Yarden (Jerusalem, 1957), 2:558.

70. *Otsar Nehmad*, 2:124.

71. Bernard Septimus, "Piety and Power in Thirteenth-Century Catalonia," in *Studies in Medieval Jewish History and Literature*, ed. Isadore Twersky (Cambridge, Mass., 1979), 197–230.

CHAPTER 10. MATTER, MEANING, AND MAIMONIDES

The manuscript that lies at the core of this study has been a tough nut to crack, particularly paleographically. I am grateful to several members of my cohort at the Katz Center for Advanced Judaic Studies at the University of Pennsylvania—Esperanza Alfonso, Piero Capelli, Elisabeth Hollender, Rami Reiner, and Uri Shachar—who very graciously spent time looking at some of the owners' marks with me, as well as to Haggai Ben-Shammai and Malachi Beit-Arié, who also consulted with me on these matters during their sojourns at the Katz Center. I am likewise grateful to David Shyovitz and David Wachtel for helping me to identify and contextualize some of the Ashkenazic paleographic issues and onomastic elements; and to Shamma Boyarin, Ross Brann, Dorothy Kim, Eilis Monahan, Karl Steel, and David Wacks, as well as to the anonymous reviewers of this chapter and the anonymous reviewers of the related one that will appear in my forthcoming monograph, for their thoughtful comments and discussion on the bigger thematic and theoretical issues raised here. It is usually pro-forma for an author to accept responsibility for all errors and absolve anyone whose help she has received, but I think it is especially important to highlight this in a chapter that comes to some quite admittedly speculative conclusions about the nature of the ownership of this book: any errors, oversights, questionable judgment calls, or general insufficiencies are entirely my own responsibility and not theirs. I am grateful to the editors of this volume for their unusual forbearance with my ongoing and extensive delays in completing this chapter. And finally, it is a pleasure to be able to acknowledge the generosity of Ione Apfelbaum Strauss, who endowed the Louis Apfelbaum and Hortense Braustein Apfelbaum Fellowship that I held at the Center that allowed me to complete the research reflected here.

1. My original conception of this type of writing was as fiction; however, as I have begun to reconsider whether that is the best framework, I have tried to refrain from referring to the colophon and the other texts that I discuss in this chapter as fiction. The present study is more concerned with the ownership history of the manuscript; for a more considered discussion of genre and the place of fiction in understanding this kind of paratextual element, please see the discussion in the aforementioned monograph in progress, *No Achievement But Through Arabic: Judah ibn Tibbon and the Culture of Andalusi Reading in Exile* (Bloomington, Ind., 2017). Here, I have taken the notion of fantasy from the framework of *Rabbinic Fantasies* (New Haven, Conn., 1990), a volume edited by David Stern and Mark Jay Mirsky that anthologizes "imaginative" Hebrew literary texts, some from an Arabizing, Sephardic literary tradition and others not.

2. The notion that any life of Alexander is more surely a reflection of the author's interests than a biography of its subject is a well-attested one. For example, we hear echoes of Johann Gustav Droysen's nineteenth-century advocacy for German unification under Prussian rule in his coining of the term "Hellenizing" to describe Alexander's cultural influence over vast swaths of Asia. Parallels abound in the writing of the historians, travelers, and bureaucrats of Victorian England who cast Alexander as the consummate colonial administrator. And in a more contemporary turn Rory Stewart, denizen of the recent Western military efforts in Afghanistan that were defined, at least in part, by a dramatic lack of knowledge of the local cultures, sums up the issue and creates one more example of it when he writes, "The more we produce about Alexander the less we seem to understand him."

3. The main question identified with the Maimonidean controversies is the esotericism of Maimonides' summa, the *Guide of the Perplexed*, and the appropriate interpretive ciphers for it.

Ancillary issues include questions about the nature of the soul, of bodily resurrection of the dead, and divine anthropomorphism in Scripture. A good overview of the issues and the thinkers who drew them out may be found in David Jeremy Silver, *Maimonidean Criticism and the Maimonidean Controversy* (Leiden, 1965). For more recent work, see, inter alia, Idit Dobbs-Weinstein, "The Maimonidean Controversy," in *History of Jewish Philosophy*, ed. Daniel Frank and Oliver Lehmann (New York, 1997), 275–90; Sarah Stroumsa, "The Maimonidean Controversy in Baghdad," in *Self, Soul, and Body in Religious Experience*, ed. A. Baumgarten and G. Stroumsa (Leiden, 1998), 313–34; and the first chapter of Harvey J. Hames, *The Art of Conversion: Christianity and Kabbalah in the Thirteenth Century* (Leiden, 2000).

4. Geertz's work has been particularly important in the Judaeo-Arabic, Arabizing Hebrew, and Sephardic worlds since S. D. Goitein described it in the epilogue to his *A Mediterranean Society* as crucial in driving him from a more philological interest in the texts of the Cairo Geniza to the concern for the social-historical picture they paint; although this study is a literary and codicological history, it is indebted both to Goitein's centering of Geertz within discourse on the Judaeo-Islamic Mediterranean world as well as to literary criticism's accepting engagement with anthropological methodologies.

5. A different brand of entanglement theory, borrowed from yet another field of study, has also become popular of late in comparative literature and medieval studies. I mention it here for the sake of completeness and because of some interesting correspondences with other moments within the history of the field of Judaic studies, but ultimately I do not find it to be particularly useful for explicating this material text. This second version of entanglement theory, known as "quantum entanglement" theory, attempts to read text for and in light of its scientific accuracy and to subject text and culture to the methodologies of the cutting edge of physics, calling its toolkit for studying the "intra-actional" relationship between texts and their material supports "agential realism." The foundational work of quantum entanglement theory is Karen Barad, *Meeting the Universe Halfway: Quantum Physics and the Entanglement of Matter and Meaning* (Durham, N.C., 2007). A forthcoming issue of the journal *Rhizomes* will offer a variety of studies on Barad and her work, some that will make enthusiastic use of it and others that are more cautious in their approach. The notion of using the critical tools from a scientific discipline in the service of literary and historical questions is particularly interesting within the field of Jewish studies, juxtaposed against the legacy of the *Wissenschaft des Judentums*, an intellectual movement that cast itself as a mode of scientific and scientifically precise inquiry into text and history, bringing to light many details that allowed later scholars to continue to piece together the panorama and to reshape and refine a narrative. Quantum entanglement theory might have been particularly of interest with respect to this present study of that Alexander manuscript because, beside its debts to the field of anthropology, I also locate this work, if anachronistically, within a *Wissenschaft*-type framework, addressing questions of manuscript, textual transmission, and text in a descriptive manner as a way of setting the stage for further research, shedding light on the parts in the interest of facilitating a discussion of the whole even in the absence of a definitive resolution to the question at hand. This mode is founded upon a recognition that any kind of identification like that of the rank-and-file readers and owners of this peculiar Hebrew Alexander romance is made piecemeal and that there is value in putting the pieces out in the light and beginning a discussion. Some of what is new in this study is, indeed, speculative. It is a step forward within the science of Judaic studies but cannot benefit from a framework that assumes that "quantum physics . . . asks all the right questions" (Barad, *Meeting the Universe Halfway*, 6), as quantum entanglement theory does, an idea that runs roughshod over the academic study of text and upholds the increasingly popular and problematic notion of the superi-

ority of scientific fields of inquiry and their automatic ability to inhere in and supplant literary study. This work, then, is a cultural-historical, anthropological study of a manuscript but is also, ultimately, quietly, a defense of literature and literary criticism.

6. Ian Hodder, *Entangled: An Archaeology of the Relationships Between Humans and Things* (Oxford, 2012), 208. See also Bruno Latour, *Reassembling the Social: An Introduction to Actor-Network Theory* (Oxford, 2007); and Alfred Gell, *Art and Agency* (Oxford, 1998).

7. This Hebrew text draws, more specifically, on the Latin recensions of *Historia de proeliis* usually called I2 and I3 in the standard scholarly stemma. For more on the relationship between versions and sub-versions, the textual stemmata, and Alexander bibliography, see Wout van Bekkum, *A Hebrew Alexander Romance According to MS London, Jews College 145* (Leuven, 1992), 16–21; later, esp. Eli Yassif, "The Hebrew Tradition of Alexander of Macedon," *Tarbiz* 75 (2005): 76–123; and Saskia Doenitz, "Alexander the Great in Medieval Hebrew Traditions," in *A Companion to Alexander Literature in the Middle Ages*, ed. Z. David Zuwiyya (Leiden, 2011), 21–39, where the relationship between one of the source texts, *Sefer Yosifon*, and the Alexander romance under discussion, is reassessed.

8. Van Bekkum, *A Hebrew Alexander Romance According to JCL 145*, 25–26.

9. Ibid.

10. Moses Maimonides, "Letter to Samuel ibn Tibbon on the Matter of Translating the Guide," in *Letters of the Rambam*, vol. 2, ed. Isaac Shailat (rpt.; Maale Adumim, 1995), 512–46. A partial English translation of the letter by Hermann Adler is available in *Miscellany of Hebrew Literature,* ed. David Solomon (London, 1872).

11. Joel Kraemer and Josef Stern, "Shlomo Pines on the Translation of Maimonides' Guide of the Perplexed," *Journal of Jewish Thought and Philosophy* 8 (1999): 13–24, at 21.

12. For the origins of this discussion in the late antique and early Islamic periods see Dimitri Gutas, *Greek Thought, Arabic Culture* (New York, 1998).

13. A variety of other texts in translation are falsely attributed to Samuel. Notable among these include Maimonides' introduction to the tenth chapter of Mishnah Sanhedrin and 'Alī ibn Ridwan's commentary on Galen's *Ars parva*.

14. Transcription from Van Bekkum's edition of the text, pp. 204–5.

15. Literally "from the Hagarite language." A considerable amount of scholarship on the relevant terminology derived from biblical onomastica has been carried out. For the development of these terms, *Ishmaelite* and *Hagarite*, in biblical and ancient texts, and particularly for a consideration of whether the two terms refer to the same group of people in those texts, see Israel Eph'al, "Ishmael and the Arab(s): A Transformation of Ethnological Terms," *Journal of Near Eastern Studies* 35.4 (1976): 225–35. For an overview of this terminology in rabbinic literature, consult Carol Bakhos, *Ishmael on the Border: Rabbinic Portrayals of the First Arab* (Albany, N.Y., 2006). Nehemia Allony considers the linguistic-terminological function of the biblical figure of Hagar, Ishmael's mother, in "Sarah and Hagar in the Poetry of Spain," in *Studies in the Bible and the History of Israel* (Jerusalem, 1979), 168–85. In "The Muslim in the Ideologies of Spain," in *Saracens: Islam in the Medieval European Imagination* (New York, 2002), 174–93, John Tolan assesses the representation of Muslims in the Iberian Latin and early Romance literature of the twelfth and thirteenth centuries, though his terminological interests run more toward the uses of the epithet *moro*.

16. Beinecke Heb. Suppl. MS 103. 35v. The phrase in italics represents a significant departure in reading and translation from the work of previous scholars. This is discussed thoroughly in the following pages.

17. In the interest of space I refrain from listing the well-documented intertextual depen-

dencies that make up this version of the Alexander romance and complement the major source, namely the *Historia de proeliis*. These connections and dependencies are discussed in detail in the works of Van Bekkum, Bowman, and Doenitz cited here. Moritz Steinschneider's contention in his discussion of the text in the *Hebraische Übersetzungen* that Samuel ibn Tibbon could not have been the translator because such a text was beneath his dignity is a less compelling argument against his involvement.

18. For a discussion of this word, see Steven Bowman, review of Van Bekkum, "A Hebrew Alexander Romance According to MS Héb. 671.5 Paris, Bibliothèque Nationale," *Journal of Jewish Studies* 48.1 (1997): 166–68.

19. Moritz Steinschneider, *Hebraische Übersetzungen*, 899.

20. Adolf Neubauer, *Catalogue of the Hebrew Manuscripts in Jews' College, London* (Oxford, 1886).

21. Adolf Neubauer, "An Inedited Version of the Legend of Alexander the Great," *Jewish Quarterly Review* 4.4 (1892): 687.

22. Israel Levi, "Sefer Toledot Alexander," *Sammelband kleinter Beitraege aus Handschriften*, vol. 2 (Berlin, 1886), xi. See also Levi's "Les traductions hébraiques de l'histoire légendaire d'Alexandre," *Revue des études juives* 7 (1883): 238–65.

23. Van Bekkum, *A Hebrew Alexander Romance*, 23.

24. See the discussion of this term in Steven Bowman's review of Van Bekkum's editions of the Paris and London manuscripts of the Hebrew Alexander romance.

25. Shamma Boyarin, "Diasporic Culture and the Makings of Alexander Romances" (Ph.D. diss., University of California, Berkeley, 2008), 96–102.

26. For a discussion of the extent to which later medieval readers, both Jewish and Christian, associated Maimonides with Aristotle, see Angel Sáenz-Badillos, "Late Medieval Jewish Writers on Maimonides," in *Traditions of Maimonideanism*, ed. Carlos Fraenkel (Leiden, 2009), 223–43.

27. Malachi Beit-Arié, *The Makings of the Medieval Hebrew Book* (Jerusalem, 1993), 12ff.

28. Henri Gross, *Gallia Judaica* (Amsterdam, 1897; rpt., 1969), 430.

29. Beinecke Heb. Suppl. MS 103, 3r.

30. Steven M. Lowenstein, *The Berlin Jewish Community: Enlightenment, Family, and Crisis* (Oxford, 1994).

31. The following manuscripts in the Jews' College London catalogue are not indicated as having been owned by Itzig but in fact bear his stamp and/or his signature: JCL MSS 27, 44, 63, 64, 69, 75, 84, 88, 89, 91, 97, 106, 116, 117, 122. These are the manuscripts that Neubauer correctly identifies as having belonged to Itzig: JCL MSS 2, 10, 18, 29, 47, 65, 77, 93, 96, 100, 103, 145.

32. Late nineteenth-century cataloguing issues aside, the LSJS library is badly in disarray and its present state illustrates both the need and wisdom in selling off the manuscript collection that it could no longer maintain. In attempting to establish a more secure history of the provenance of the manuscript under present discussion, I visited the LSJS library in the summer of 2013. I found it in very poor condition, not climate-controlled, infested with bugs, badly catalogued, and with little institutional memory at the human or archival level to guide any library users through the materials that remained and to indicate what had been removed. Two years prior to the sale at Christie's, there had been an attempt to transfer much of its archive to the Metropolitan Archives of London, but the loss and chaos were already so severe that there was little to send from the library's sleepy Hendon site to central London; and there is, to this day, little to be found in the six folders and boxes that survived to make it to the Met. Appar-

ently the only indication of the transfer is a letter of agreement I found shoved at the bottom of a librarian's desk drawer, under volumes of Maimonides, spare office supplies, informational requests from high school students and researchers in countries with even poorer library facilities, invoices, and twenty-year-old applications for an assistant librarianship long since filled and vacated. Scant evidence remains to indicate that this once-illustrious institution had held a significant collection of late medieval and early modern Hebrew manuscripts: this includes a handwritten missive from Jerusalem inquiring whether the college would be interested in acquiring a manuscript that had been discovered in that capital of an alternate world during the hostilities of the Great War and a few letters from a bygone era of library practice, inquiring whether the manuscripts might be lent out for a few days, accompanied by promises that they would be kept in locked—and in one instance, fireproof—rooms.

33. Sale 9192 results, lot 6. http://www.christies.com/lotfinder/lot/alexander-the-great-the-book-of-the-1525472-details.aspx?from=salesummary&intObjectID=1525472&sid=626203b8-15d6-4ee3-ab40-6458c369dabf.

34. Christie's New York, *Important Hebrew Manuscripts and Printed Books: Wednesday 23 June 1999*, 22–23.

35. Pers. comm., Gaia Gazzi, May 2014.

36. http://www.textmanuscripts.com/descriptions_manuscripts/description_220.pdf.

37. http://dla.library.upenn.edu/dla/schoenberg.

38. The Library of the Earls of Macclesfield Removed from Shiburn Castle, Part 12. http://www.sothebys.com/en/auctions/2008/the-library-of-the-earls-of-macclesfield-removed-from-shirburn-castle-part-twelve-continental-books-and-manuscripts-l08406.html.

39. Yale catalogue record.

40. Perhaps a more serious cataloguing discrepancy is found in the catalogue entry written by Les Enlumineurs, which claims that the paper on which the manuscript is written contains a watermark that is consistent with the one identified in Briquet's classic album, *Filigranes*, as exemplar 5923. Neither that watermark nor any other may presently be found in the codex.

41. Hodder, *Entangled*, 3.

42. For considerations of space and avoiding repeating myself in print, the present study has focused most centrally upon the manuscript history; the literary history and questions of genre, in other words, the subject of this very brief final section, is the more central focus of a related but distinct chapter in my forthcoming monograph.

43. Diana Lobel, *A Sufi-Jewish Dialogue: Philosophy and Mysticism in Baḥya ibn Paqūda's Duties of the Heart* (Philadelphia, 2007), ix–x.

44. Index of Manuscripts, Colette Sirat, "Une liste de manuscripts: Préliminare à une nouvelle edition du dalālat al-Ḥāyryn," in *Maimonidean Studies*, ed. Arthur Hyman (New York, 2000), 4:109–33; Jacob Diestag, "Maimonides' *Guide for the Perplexed*: A Bibliography of Editions and Translations," in *Occident and Orient*, ed. Robert Dan (Leiden, 1988), 95–128.

45. The *Treatise on Resurrection*, itself born out of charges that Maimonides had denied the possibility of bodily resurrection, has been the subject of speculation that it, too, was a pseudepigraphical text falsely attributed to Maimonides. Sarah Stroumsa has roundly quelled this speculation, though; see her *Maimonides in His World* (Princeton, N.J., 2009), 165–66.

46. The text, based on Bodeian MS Opp. Add. 4to 164.3 (Neubauer 2496.3), fol. 124, is published in Joshua Finkel, "Moses Maimonides' Treatise on Resurrection," *Proceedings of the American Academy for Jewish Research* 9 (1938): 80–83. A more detailed discussion of the fictional character of this preface to the *Treatise* is forthcoming.

47. Marc Bloch, *The Historian's Craft* (Manchester, 1954; rpt., 2004), 77.

48. Daniel Jeremy Silver, *Maimonidean Criticism and the Maimonidean Controversies* (Leiden, 1965).

49. Joseph Dan, "Ashkenazi Hasidism and the Maimonidean Controversy," *Jewish Mysticism* 2 (1998): 180–81.

50. Steven Harvey, "Did Maimonides' Letter to Samuel ibn Tibbon Determine Which Philosophers Would Be Studied by Later Jewish Thinkers?," *Jewish Quarterly Review* 58.2 (1992): 51–70.

51. Dan, "Ashkenazi Hasidism," 187.

52. An edition of the text appears in Joseph Dan, *Studies in the Litertature of the Ashkenazi Pietists* (Ramat Gan, 1975), 159–60. For a discussion, see Dan, "Ashkenazi Hasidism," 190–93. For more on the relationship between the Ashkenazic pietists and other types of Spanish texts, see Ephraim Kanarfogel, *The Intellectual History and Rabbinic Culture of Medieval Ashkenaz* (Detroit, 2012), esp. chap. 3.

53. In a 1931 study, "Reste neuplatonischer Spekulation in der Mystik der deutschen Chassidim und ihre Vermittlung durch Abraham bar Chija," *Monatsschrift für Geschichte und Wissenschaft des Judentums* 75 (1931): 172–91, Gershom Scholem offers a related example with a crucial difference that raises some interesting questions about the nature of fiction itself. Scholem notes that in one of the print editions of a commentary on *Sefer Yetsirah* by the author identified as a pseudo-Sa'adia's, the work claims to cite from a certain esoteric work known as *Sefer Tsaḥ ve-Ashur* where more correctly transcribed editions cite the work of Abraham bar Ḥiyya, a scientist and philosopher who was active in mid-twelfth-century Barcelona. This unusual coinage is in fact still referring to Abraham bar Ḥiyya's book and that the invented Hebrew title of the book represents a corruption of Bar Ḥiyya's honorific title, *ṣāḥib al-shurṭā'* (chief of police). And so we see that the movement of Spanish works of philosophy into Ashkenazic realms in ways that could be acceptable to Ashkenazic readers happens along a continuum that runs from error to fiction and raises interesting questions about the relationship between those two termini. The juxtaposition of error against fiction and the way in which an erroneous transcription makes its way into an edition of the text, thereby accidentally creating what becomes a fictional transmission history, here is quite striking.

54. Elchanan Reiner, "The Attitude of Ashkenazi Society to the New Science in the Sixteenth Century," *Science in Context* 10.4 (1997): 589–91.

55. Ibid., 589.

CHAPTER 11. POLLUTION AND PURITY IN NEAR EASTERN JEWISH, CHRISTIAN, AND MUSLIM CRUSADING RHETORIC

1. Mary Douglas, *Purity and Danger: An Analysis of the Concepts of Pollution and Taboo* (London, 1966), 115–21; idem, *Risk and Blame: Essays in Cultural Theory* (London, 1992), esp. 38–55; Jonathan Z. Smith, "What a Difference a Difference Makes," in *"To See Ourselves as Others See Us": Christians, Jews, "Others" in Late Antiquity*, ed. J. Neusner and E. S. Frerichs (Chico, Calif., 1985), 46–48.

2. Jonathan Z. Smith, *To Take Place: Toward Theory in Ritual* (Chicago, 1987), 62ff.

3. Jonathan Z. Smith, *Relating Religion: Essays in the Study of Religion* (Chicago, 2004), 231; Jonathan Klawans, "Pure Violence: Sacrifice and Defilement in Ancient Israel," *Harvard Theological Review* 9.2 (2001): 133–35; Saul M. Olyan, "Purity Ideology in Ezra-Nehemiah as a

Tool to Reconstitute the Community," *Journal for the Study of Judaism in the Persian, Hellenistic, and Roman Period* 35.1 (2004): 1–2.

4. Tikva Frymer-Kensky, "Pollution, Purification, and Purgation in Biblical Israel," in *The Word of the Lord Shall Go Forth: Essays in Honor of David Noel Freedman*, ed. C. Meyers and M. O'Connor (Winona Lake, Ind., 1983), 400–401; Jacob Milgrom, *Leviticus 1–16: A New Translation with Introduction and Commentary* (New York, 1991), 745, 768; Joan R. Branham, "Blood in Flux, Sanctity at Issue," *RES: Anthropology and Aesthetics* 31 (1997): 59–60; David Biale, *Blood and Belief: The Circulation of a Symbol Between Jews and Christians* (Berkeley, Calif., 2007), 39–40. *Henoch* has devoted a special volume to explore the work that blood did in separating and connecting communities, where the editors set up the problem proclaiming that the use of blood as a marker of Jewish and Christian difference in late antiquity relied heavily on a shared and deeply polemical symbolic vocabulary; see Ra'anan Boustan and Annette Yoshiko Reed, introduction to "Blood and the Boundaries of Jewish and Christian Identities in Late Antiquity," *Henoch* 30.2 (2008): 229–34.

5. John Tolan, *Saracens: Islam in the Medieval European Imagination* (New York, 2002), 16–20, 120; Richard Southern, *Western Views of Islam in the Middle Ages* (Cambridge, 1962), 3; Norman Daniel, *Islam and the West: The Making of an Image* (Edinburgh, 1960), 338–41; Tomaž Mastnak, *Crusading Peace: Christendom, the Muslim World, and Western Political Order* (Berkeley, Calif., 2002), 128–29; and Penny Cole, "'O God, the Heathen Have Come into Your Inheritance' (Ps. 78.1): The Theme of Religious Pollution in Crusade Documents, 1095–1188," in *Crusaders and Muslims in Twelfth-Century Syria*, ed. M. Shatzmiller (Leiden, 1993), 84–111.

6. Southern, *Western Views of Islam*, 15, 26.

7. Raymond d'Aguilers, *Historia Francorum qui Ceperunt Iherusalem*, ed. J. Hill and L. Hill (Paris, 1969), 144–45. Emphasis added.

8. Composed around 1106–8, Robert the Monk's chronicle is arguably the most popular medieval account of the First Crusade; see Carol Sweetenham, *Robert the Monk's History of the First Crusade* (Burlington, 2005), 4–6; and *The Historia Iherosolimitana of Robert the Monk*, ed. D. Kempf and M. Bull (Woodridge, 2013), 34–39.

9. Robert the Monk, *Historia Iherosolimitana*, ed. Kempf and Bull, 4–6. Emphasis added.

10. Ibid., 5–6.

11. In Fulcher of Chartres, who settled in the east after the First Crusade, we find a precursor to this sentiment. Writing in the 1120s, Fulcher accommodates the notion of pollution that is a result of unbelief. Having conquered Jerusalem, the Franks are said to have desired that it be "cleansed from the contagion of the heathen inhabiting it at one time or another, so long contaminated by their superstition [tamdiu superstitione eorum contaminatus]." He shared, however, with his predecessors the conviction that the conquest put an immediate end to this contaminating presence, as the city "was restored to its former rank by those believing and trusting in Him." Fulcher of Chartres, *Historia Hierosolymitana*, ed. H. Hagenmeyer (Heidelberg, 1913), 306; idem, *A History of the Expedition to Jerusalem*, trans. F. Ryan (Knoxville, Tenn., 1969), 123.

12. On this trope, see Misgav Har-Peled, "Animalité, pureté et croisade: Etude sur la transformation des églises en étables par les musulmans durant les croisades (XIIe–XIIIe siècles)," *Cahiers de civilisation médiévale* 52 (2009): 113–36; Pascal Buresi, "Les conversions d'églises et de mosquées en Espagne aux XIe–XIIIe siècles," in *Religion et société urbaine au Moyen âge*, ed. P. Boucheron and J. Chiffoleau (Paris, 2000), 333–50; Julie Harris, "Mosque to Church Conversions in the Reconquest," *Medieval Encounters* 3 (1997): 158–72; Amy Remensnyder,

"The Colonization of Sacred Architecture: The Virgin Mary, Mosques, and Temples in Medieval Spain and Early Sixteenth-Century Mexico," in *Monks and Nuns, Saints and Outcasts: Religion in Medieval Society: Essays in Honor of Lester K. Little*, ed. S. Farmer and B. Rosenwein (Ithaca, N.Y., 2000), 189–219.

13. William appears to have reconstructed the pope's speech on the basis of the account found in the *Gesta Francorum* as well as the chronicles written by Raimond of Aguiler, Baldric of Dol, Fulcher of Chartres, and Albert of Aachen (or the main source that Albert had used); see Edbury and Rowe, *William of Tyre*, 47–50. Emily Babcock and A. C. Krey mention Walter the Chancellor for the events surrounding Antioch; see their introduction to William of Tyre, *A History of Deeds Done Beyond the Sea*, ed. Emily Babcock and A. C. Krey (New York, 1943), 29. Comparing the various extant accounts of the speech, Dana Munro posited that William's account shares many of the brute facts with the other versions, but is unlike any other in style, tone, and interpretation; see Dana Carleton Munro, "The Speech of Pope Urban II at Clermont 1095," *American Historical Review* 11.2 (1906): 234.

14. Guillaume de Tyre, *Chronique*, ed. R. B. C. Huygens (Turnhout, 1986), 131–32 [1:15]; William of Tyre, *A History of Deeds*, ed. Babcock and Krey, 1:90.

15. Guillaume de Tyre, *Chronique*, 1.15, p. 132. William of Tyre, *A History of Deeds*, ed. Babcock and Krey, 1:90.

16. Guillaume de Tyre, *Chronique*, 1.15, p. 132. William of Tyre, *A History of Deeds*, ed. Babcock and Krey, 1:90.

17. Guillaume de Tyre, *Chronique*, 1.15, p. 132. William of Tyre, *A History of Deeds*, ed. Babcock and Krey, 1:90.

18. Carole Hillenbrand, "Jihad Poetry in the Age of Crusades," in *Crusades: Medieval Worlds in Conflict*, ed. T. F. Madden et al. (Burlington, 2010), 17–20.

19. One notable exception to this chronology is Abu Ḥasan al-Sulami (d. 1106), who shortly after the First Crusade started preaching on jihad near Damascus and compiled his teachings on the subject in a treatise, *Kitāb al-Jihad*. Recent studies view al-Sulami's choice to circulate these ideas in the cultural and intellectual outskirts of Damascus, as a sign of his recognition that his authority as a legal scholar was contested and that his ideas on the subject were marginal. See Niall Christie, *The Book of Jihad: Text, Translation, and Commentary* (Farnham, 2013); idem, "Parallel Preachings: Urban II and al-Sulami," *Al-Masaq* 15.2 (2003): 139–48.

20. See Suleiman Mourad and James Lindsay, *The Intensification and Reorientation of Sunni Jihad Ideology in the Crusader Period: Ibn 'Asakir of Damascus (1105–1176) and His Age* (Leiden, 2013), 33–34. Among the few jihad poems composed before mid-century, most notable are al-Adhimi's verse addressed to the rulers of Mardin and Aleppo, and Ibn al-Nahawi's "al-Qasida al-Munfarija," both from the 1120s. See Muhammad Sayyid Kilani, *Al-Ḥurūb al-ṣalībīyya wa-Atharuhā fī-l-Adab al-'Arabī fī Miṣr wa-l-Shām* (Cairo, 1989), 301–12, and Nizar Hermes, *The [European] Other in Medieval Arabic Literature and Culture* (New York, 2012), 160–61.

21. Josef Meri, *The Cult of Saints Among Muslims and Jews in Medieval Syria* (Oxford, 2002), 15.

22. See, e.g., Ibn 'Asakir's eighty-volume encyclopedia about Damascus and its environs, *Tā'rīkh Madinat Dimashq* (Beirut, 1995), and Ibn al-'Adim's encyclopedic enterprise on Aleppo, *Bughyat al-ṭalab fi tā'rīkh Ḥalab* (Damascus, 1988).

23. The relative sanctity of Jerusalem in Muslim theology and worship is contested both in medieval commentary and in modern scholarship; see Amikam Elad, *Medieval Jerusalem and Islamic Worship: Holy Places, Ceremonies, Pilgrimage* (Leiden, 1995), 29–33; Ofer Livne Kafri, "The Muslim Traditions 'in Praise of Jerusalem' (Faḍā'il al-Quds): Diversity and Complexity,"

Annali 58 (1998): 165–92; Niall Christie, "Jerusalem in the Kitab al-Jihad of 'Ali ibn Tahir al-Sulami (d. 1106)," *Medieval Encounters*, 13.2 (2007): 209–21. Carole Hillenbrand criticizes Emmanuel Sivan for dismissing the efforts of the Fatimid and Seljuk regarding Jerusalem, and therefore undervaluing the sanctity of Jerusalem in the Muslim consciousness in the pre-crusade period, in her "Ayyubid Jerusalem: A Historical Introduction," in *Ayyubid Jerusalem: The Holy City in Context, 1187–1250*, ed. R. Hillenbrand and S. Auld (London, 2009), 6–7; Emmanuel Sivan, *L'Islam et la Croisade: Idéologie et propagande dans les réactions musulmanes aux Croisades* (Paris, 1968), 9–22. For examples of some key representatives of this genre, see Muḥammad b. Aḥmad al-Wāsiṭī, *Faḍa'il al-Bayt al-Muqaddas*, ed. I. Hasson (Jerusalem, 1979); Muḥammad b. 'Abd al-Wahid al-Maqdisii, *Faḍā'il Bayt al-Maqdis* (Damascus, 1988); Abu al-Ma'ali al-Maqdisi, *Faḍā'il Bayt al-Maqdis wa-l-Khalil wa-faḍā'il al-Shām*, ed. O. Livne-Kafri (Shefar'am, 1995).

24. Sivan, *L'Islam et le Croisade*, 62, 85, 104, 115; Carole Hillenbrand, *The Crusades: Islamic Perspectives* (Edinburgh, 1999), 285–301; idem, *Jihad Poetry in the Age of Crusades*, 17; Alexandra Cuffel, *Gendering Disgust in Medieval Religious Polemic* (Notre Dame, 2007), 145–49.

25. For a comprehensive treatment of impurity in early Islam, see Marion Katz, *Body of Text: The Emergence of the Sunnī Law of Ritual Purity* (Albany, N.Y., 2002), 162–63n.50. On the question of contagion in ritual purity laws, see Ze'ev Maghen, "Close Encounters: Some Preliminary Observations on the Transmission of Impurity in Early Sunni Jurisprudence," *Islamic Law and Society* 6.3 (1999): 348–92; and idem, *Virtues of the Flesh: Passion and Purity in Early Islamic Jurisprudence* (Leiden, 2005), 68.

26. For a word play that draws on the near homonymity between '*kufūr* [villages]' and '*kafūr* [infidel/ungrateful],' which denotes a certain ingratitude and lack of appreciation toward the divine, see Qur'an 22:66 or 43:15.

27. Abu Shamah, *Kitāb al-Rawḍatayn fī akhbār al-dawlatayn al-Nūriyyah wa-l-Ṣalāḥiyyah*, ed. I. al-Zaybaq (Beirut, 1997), 1:279–81.

28. Kevin Reinhart, "Impurity / No Danger," *History of Religion* 30 (1990): 15–16; on the distinction between the various purification procedures, see John Burton, "The Quran and the Islamic Practice of Wuḍu," *Bulletin of the School of Oriental and African Studies* 51.1 (1988): 21–58.

29. On the place of anti-Byzantine verses that celebrate the early conquest of al-Sham in twelfth-century Syrian literature, or more generally on the problem of using poetry in historical studies, see Suleiman Mourad, "Poetry, History, and the Early Arab-Islamic Conquests of al-Sham (Greater Syria)," in *Poetry and History: The Value of Poetry in Reconstructing Arab History*, ed. R. Baalbaki et al. (Beirut, 2011), 175–83.

30. Bonner, *Aristocratic Violence*, 53.

31. Nadia El Cheikh-Saliba, *Byzantium Viewed by the Arabs* (Cambridge, 2004), 83–84.

32. The term "Holy Land [*al-arḍ al-muqaddasah*]" appears in Qur'an 5:21. Reuven Firestone's study on the Abraham "legend" traces the history of the way the notion of "holy land" came to be appreciated by generations of Muslim exegetes. His study unfolds the intertextual environment within which Muslim interpreters appropriated foundational concepts from the Bible, and ultimately he shows that in Muslim exegesis it was taken to refer to Mecca and its sacred precinct. See Reuven Firestone, *Journeys in Holy Lands: The Evolution of the Abraham-Ishmael Legends in Islamic Exegesis* (Albany, N.Y., 1990), 61n.1.

33. 'Ali b. Muḥammad b. Nabih, *Diwan Ibn al-Nabih*, ed. U. al-As'ad (Beirut, 1969), 456–58; see Hillenbrand's brief discussion and partial translation of this verse, *The Crusades: Islamic Perspectives*, 308.

34. Younys Mizra, "Abraham as an Iconoclast: Understanding the Destruction of 'Images'

Through Qur'anic Exegesis," *Islam and Christian-Muslim Relations* 16.4 (2005): 413–28; for a more comprehensive treatment of exegetical traditions surrounding the role of Abraham in the formation of the Muslim monotheistic legacy, see Firestone, *Journeys in Holy Lands*; and John Van Seters, *Abraham in History and Tradition* (New Haven, Conn., 1975). As with many of the Quranic stories pertaining to Abraham, the one involving his smashing the idols also has rabbinical roots; see *Bereshit Rabbah* 38, ed. J. Theodor and C. Albeck (Jerusalem, 1996), 361–64, as well as Shari Lowin's treatment of this episode in its wider narrative setting and the way it was deployed in post-biblical and early-Muslim literature, *The Making of a Forefather: Abraham in Islamic and Jewish Exegetical Narratives* (Leiden, 2006), 176–207.

35. Abu Ja'far Muhammad al-Tabari, *Tafsir al-Tabari*, ed. A. al-Turki (Riyad, 2003), 16:212–37.

36. Emmanuel Sivan discusses part of this poem in *L'Islam et le croisade*, 115.

37. Literally: "and shed upon it / blood, which when you intersperse, [*al-Quds*] becomes clean."

38. Abu Shamah, *Kitāb al-Rawḍatayn*, 2:450–51.

39. Anne-Marie Eddé, *Saladin*, trans. J. Todd (Cambridge, 2011), 218.

40. Mustansir Mir, "Irony in the Qur'ān: A Study of the Story of Joseph," in *Literary Structures of Religious Meaning in the Qur'an*, ed. I. J. Boullata (London, 2000), 173–87; see also Ayaz Afsar, "Plot Motifs in Joseph/Yūsuf Story: A Comparative Study of Biblical and Qur'ānic Narrative," *Islamic Studies* 46.2 (2006): 167–89.

41. For the most recent treatment of al-Qaysarānī's war poetry, see Hermes, *The [European] Other*, 161–68.

42. Quran 1:125, translation Sahih International, with slight changes.

43. On this episode, and more generally on al-Nasir Da'ud's reign, see Joseph Drory, "Al-Nasir Dawud: A Much Frustrated Ayyubid Prince," *Al-Masaq* 15.2 (2003): 161–87, esp. 169–70; for another account of al-Nasir's ill-fated conquest of Jerusalem, see Peter Jackson, "The Crusades of 1239–1241 and Their Aftermath," *Bulletin of School of Oriental Asian Studies* 50 (1987): 39.

44. Ibn Waṣil, *Mufarrij al-kurūb fi akhbār Bani Ayyub*, 5:249. For other contemporary and Mamluk chroniclers who documented this episode, see Ahmad b. 'Ali al-Maqrizi, *Kitāb al-sulūk li-ma'rifat duwal al-mulūk*, ed. M. Ziyadah (Cairo, 1934), 1:284, 292; al-Yunini, *Dhayl Mir'at al-Zamān*, ed. A. 'Abbas (Abu Dhabi, 2007), 1:142; Muhammad b. Ahmad al-Dhahabi, *Tārīkh al-Islām*, ed. U. Tadmuri (Beirut, 1999), 243.

45. *Gesta Francorum et aliorum Hierosolymitanorum*, ed. R. Hill (London, 1962), 10.38, p. 92.

46. Raimond d'Aguilers, *Historia Francorum qui Ceperunt Iherusalem*, 127–28.

47. *The Historia Iherosolimitana of Robert the Monk*, ed. Kempf and Bull, 8.7, p. 87.

48. Raimond d'Aguilers, *Historia Francorum qui Ceperunt Iherusalem*, 150–51.

49. Guillaume de Tyre, *Chronique*, 8.20, p. 412.

50. For scholarly debates on dating the translation of William's chronicle into Old French, see Issa, *La version latine de Guillaume de Tyr*, 13–15; Bernard Hamilton, "The Old French Translation of William of Tyre as an Historical Source," in *The Experience of Crusading: Defining the Crusader Kingdom*, ed. P. Edbury and J. Phillips (Cambridge, 2003), 93–112; Edbury and Rowe, *William of Tyre*, 4; Margaret Ruth Morgan, *The Chronicle of Ernoul and the Continuations of William of Tyre* (Oxford, 1973), 119, 172.

51. *Recueil des historiens des croisades* [*RHC*] (Paris, 1844), 1:355.

52. "La Continuation de Guillaume de Tyr, 1184–1197," in *Documents relatifs à l'histoire des croisades*, ed. M. Morgan (Paris, 1982). Emphasis added.

53. Sibt ibn al-Jawzi, *Mir'at al-Zamān fī Tā'rīkh al-A'yan*, ed. J. Jewett (Chicago, 1907), 7:2, p. 656 and 8:1, p. 397; Ibn al-Athir, *Al-Kāmil fī al-Tā'rīkh*, ed. C. Tornberg (Leiden, 1851), 11:365; 'Imād al-Dīn Muḥammad al-Isfahānī, *Al-Fatḥ al-Qussi fī al-Fatḥ al-Qudsi* (Cairo, 1965), 47.

54. "*Sapientibus*" is the author's rendering of the term *'ulama'*, the class of scholars of Islamic law. This phrase may indicate an appreciation for the complex relations between *'ulama'* and rulers, whose history goes back to the earliest Islamic polities. See Patricia Crone and Martin Hinds, *God's Caliph: Religious Authority in the First Centuries of Islam* (Cambridge, 1986), 43–57; for the Ayyubid context, see Michael Chamberlain, *Knowledge and Social Practice in Medieval Damascus: 1190–1350* (Cambridge, 1994), 69–90.

55. *De Expugnatione Terrae Sanctae per Saladinum Libellus*, ed. J. Stevenson (London, 1875), 246.

56. Ibid., 246.

57. Ibid., 248.

58. Ibid., 248; cf. Acts 1:18.

59. *De Expugnatione terrae sanctae*, 248. Emphasis added.

60. Ibid., 249.

61. Ibid., 247.

62. "*Beithalla*" derives from Bayt Allah, the house of God.

63. *De Expugnatione terrae sanctae*, 249.

64. Ibid., 249.

65. Ibid., 250.

66. For scholarship on the immigration to Palestine in the beginning of the thirteenth century, see Ephraim Kanarfogel, "The 'Aliyah of 'Three Hundred Rabbis' in 1211: Tosafist Attitudes Toward Settling in the Land of Israel," *Jewish Quarterly Review* 76.3 (1986): 191–215; Samuel Krause, "L'*Emigration de 300* Rabbins en Palestine en l'an 1211," *Revue des études juives 82* (1926): 343–46.

67. Uri Shachar, "Dialogical Warfare: Figurations of Pious Belligerence Among Christian, Muslim, and Jewish Authors in the Crusading Near East" (Ph.D. diss., University of Chicago, 2014), 171–234.

68. MS Darmstadt, Hessisches Landes- und Hochschulbibliothek, Cod. Or. 25, fol. 14r.

69. MS Darmstadt 25, fol. 14v. Emphasis added.

70. Cuffel, *Gendering Disgust*, 21–35, with a special emphasis on questions of female purity and menstruation; Jacob Neusner, "History and Purity in First-century Judaism," *History of Religions* 18.1 (1978): 1–17; Eva Levavi Feinstein, "Sexual Pollution in the Hebrew Bible: A New Perspective," in *Bodies, Embodiment, and Theology of the Hebrew Bible*, ed. T. Kamionkowski and W. Kim (New York, 2010), 114–45.

71. There is a large body of literature that discusses Nahmanides' attitude toward the Land of Israel and the obligation to live in it. See Haviva Pedaia, "Erets shel Ruaḥ ve-Erets shel Mamash: R. Ezra, R. Azriel ve-haRamban," in *The Land of Israel in Medieval Jewish Thought*, ed. M. Halamish and A. Ravitzky (Jerusalem, 1991), 233–89, and, in the same volume, Michael Zvi Nehorai, "Erets Yisra'el be-Toratam shel haRambam ve-haRamban," 123–37.

72. Nahmanides, *Commentary on the Torah*, ed. and trans. C. Chavel (Brooklyn, 1973), 3:473.

73. Nahmanides, "Homily for the New Year," in *Kitvei rabenu Mosheh ben Naḥman*, ed. C. Chavel (Jerusalem, 1963–64), 1:250; Nahmanides, *Commentary on the Torah*, 3:269.

74. Parma, Biblioteca Palatina, MS 2342 (Richler 1542; IMHM 13218), fol. 205r. Another contemporaneous example comes from the thirteenth-century manifestation of the RaSHBI cycle, *Secrets of RaSHBI*: "Immediately he [Messiah] signals for them [the army of immigrants] and gathers all of Israel, and brings them up to Jerusalem, and fire will come down from the heaven and consume Jerusalem three cubits [underground] and will displace the uncircumcised, and the impure and the foreigners from its midst," Parma MS. 3122 (Richler 701; IMHM 12284), fol. 230v.

75. Oxford, Bodleian Library, Opp. Add. Qu. 140, fol. 75r.

CHAPTER 12. ADOPTION AND ADAPTATION

1. For an analysis of how this assumption has shaped historiography, see David J. Malkiel, *Reconstructing Ashkenaz: The Human Face of Franco-German Jewry, 1000–1250* (Stanford, Calif., 2009), 3–33.

2. Ismar Schorsch, *From Text to Context: The Turn to History in Modern Judaism* (London, 1994), 71–92.

3. Ephraim Kanarfogel, *The Intellectual History and Rabbinic Culture of Medieval Ashkenaz: Expanding Horizons and Innovating Traditions* (Detroit, 2012).

4. Cf., e.g., Saskia Dönitz, *Überlieferung und Rezeption des Sefer Yosippon* (Tübingen, 2013).

5. For a discussion of the complexity of cultural transfer and the inadequacy of its terminology, see Peter Burke, "Translating Knowledge, Translating Cultures," in *Kultureller Austausch in der Frühen Neuzeit*, ed. M. North (Vienna, 2009), 69–77.

6. Note the difference in cases where functions rather than texts were imported, as per the introduction of quantitative meter into Hebrew poetry by Dunash ben Labrat, and where external value systems would influence long-standing cultural functions. For an inspiring analysis of such cases, see Rina Drory, *Models and Contacts: Arabic Literature and Its Impact on Medieval Jewish Culture* (Boston, 2000).

7. Dov Yarden, *The Liturgical Poetry of Rabbi Yehuda ha-Levi* (Hebrew; Jerusalem, 1978–85), 913–18.

8. Cf. Moshe Gil and Ezra Fleischer, *Yehuda ha-Levi and His Circle: 55 Geniza Documents* (Hebrew; Jerusalem, 2001), 235n.230. This author would like to thank Prof. Tova Beeri (Tel Aviv University) for pointing out the importance of the relative dating of Judah ha-Levi's poem and the likelihood of its late date.

9. The ease with which Ashkenazic and Tsarfatic liturgies placed Sephardic liturgical poetry (*piyyutim*) into slots that differed from the composition's original purpose raises the likelihood that the personal lament by Judah ha-Levi was recast as a liturgical text in Tsarfat or Ashkenaz. For a different opinion, see Avraham Fraenkel, "Masoret ashkenazit ʿal hagiʿato shel R. Yehuda ha-Levi li-Yerushalayim," *Ha-Ma'ayan* 53.3 (2013): 5–14. Without a doubt, most of the Sephardic *piyyutim* that were adopted into Ashkenazic rites were transferred from Sepharad through Tsarfat, including *piyyutim* by Judah ha-Levi. Yet the fact that "Zion, Will You Not Inquire" is not included in *minhag* Roma or in the Balkan rites that were influenced by Sephardic traditions lowers the probability that its adoption as a liturgical poem was propagated via the Iberian Peninsula.

10. While it seems likely that complete liturgical manuscripts came from Sepharad to Provence, there is no indication that more than selected texts were brought into Tsarfat and Ashkenaz.

11. Only one medieval Ashkenazic manuscript that transmits *kinnot* is written in a calligraphic semi-cursive hand (Jerusalem, private collection C); it was obviously produced at a lower cost than those copied with ample margins and in square script. That outstanding manuscript includes a standard collection of *piyyutim*. Cf. also Ms Parma Palatina 2962 (de Rossi 589), a manuscript that contains the entire Book of Job and three rarely transmitted Zionides, two of which are also in the printed rites; they obviously represent an addendum to a rite that did not originally include these texts. None of the informal manuscripts that would have served as interim sources for precentors have been preserved; however, in rare cases, the existence of such manuscripts can be reconstructed from the orthography of formal manuscripts; cf. Elisabeth Hollender, "Die anonyme ashkenazische Seliḥa אלהים אל דמי אל נקשר בשמי: Fragen zu Text und Subtext," *Frankfurter Judaistische Beiträge* 35 (2009): 85–113.

12. The number of Jewish communities in Ashkenaz increased throughout the thirteenth century, especially during its latter half; see, e.g., Christoph Cluse, Rosemarie Kosche, and Matthias Schmandt, "Zur Siedlungsgeschichte der Juden im Nordwesten des Reiches während des Mittelalters," in *Geschichte der Juden im Mittelalter von der Nordsee bis zu den Südalpen: Kommentiertes Kartenwerk*, ed. A. Haverkamp (Hannover, 2002), 40–43; Rainer Barzen, "Zur Siedlungsgeschichte der Juden im mittleren Rheingebiet bis zum Beginn des 16. Jahrhunderts," in *Geschichte der Juden im Mittelalter von der Nordsee bis zu den Südalpen. Kommentiertes Kartenwerk*, ed. A. Haverkamp (Hannover, 2002), 62–63 (especially in the Middle Rhine area, growth continued through the early fourteenth century; see 63–64).

In some cases, liturgical manuscripts were commissioned by individuals; see, e.g., the first section of the Worms Maḥzor (1272) and the Nuremberg Maḥzor (1331). While the Worms Maḥzor seems to reflect an established synagogue rite, the Nuremberg Maḥzor was apparently commissioned to gather more *piyyutim* than would usually be performed.

13. In his seminal study of the tosafists who composed *piyyutim*, Kanarfogel, *Intellectual History*, 393–443, mentions seventeen twelfth- and thirteenth-century liturgical poets who used quantitative meter, beginning with Rabbenu Tam and Eli'ezer ben Samson of Cologne. This survey omits tosafists who composed fewer than four *piyyutim* and specialized poets who did not author works in other genres that were part of the greater tosafist enterprise. Those authors in the scope of Kanarfogel's study include a comparative high number of Tsarfatic authors, mirroring the likely travel route of Sephardic *piyyutim* and poetic techniques from the Iberian peninsula via Provence and northern France to the Rhineland.

14. Four of these adaptations are transmitted in both the eastern and western Ashkenazic rites; see Daniel Goldschmidt, *Seder ha-kinnot le-Tisha be-Av ke-minhag Polin* (Jerusalem, 1968), 14. Adaptations of "Zion, Will You Not Inquire" were also composed in other Jewish communities that adopted Judah ha-Levi's lament into their liturgies, e.g., Benjamin Bar Tikwa, *Genres and Topics in Provençal and Catalonian Piyyut* (Hebrew; Beer Sheva, 2009), 400–403.

15. They are ציון יי לכס בחר מעוניך (צ 277) by Yaqar ben Samuel ha-Levi; ציון אלהים אביר יעקב בעוז יגביר (צ 279), identical to ציון אשר יאמרו אף כל מדניך (צ 282) by Abraham ben Jacob; ציון אשר הללוך תמיד אבותי (צ 281) by Simḥa (unpublished); ציון במר תבכי עלי בתוליך (unpublished); ציון במשפט לכי לך עם מעונניך (צ 283) by Josef ha-Kohen ben Ḥayyim (might be slightly later); ציון בעת זכרי חבלך ויצירך (צ 284) by Judah (unpublished); ציון גברת לממלכות מציריך (צ 286); ציון הלא תדרשי לשלום ידידיך בשבי הלא הלכו עמך יחידיך (צ 290) by Judah ben Shen'ur; ציון הלא תשאלי לשלום אמוניך (צ 291) by Abraham ben Joseph, who was killed in southern Germany in 1298 (unpublished); ציון הלא תשאלי

לשלום עלוביך שלם בכי (צ 294) by El'azar ben Judah of Worms; ציון ידידות ידיד צעיר לשריך (צ 299) by Jacob; ציון יפה נוף כליל יופי הדריך by Joseph ben Qalonymos ha-Naqdan (unpublished); צוון מכון שבתך נהרס ונחרב לאי (צ 308) by Abraham ha-Levi on the 1298 persecutions; ציון מעון קדשי ארכו זמנייך by Meir ben Judah ben Joseph ben David (unpublished); ציון עטרת צבי שמחת המוניך (צ 314) by El'azar ben Moses ha-Darshan from Würzburg; ציון צפירת פאר חדות אגודיך (צ 316) by Meir ben El'azar ha-Darshan; ציון קחי כל צרי גלעד לציריך (צ 318), sometimes ascribed to Abraham ha-Ḥoze; ציון שארית בני יעקב (צ 319) by Samuel ben Isaak; and שאלי שרופה באש (ש 132) by Meir ben Barukh from Rothenburg (Maharam) on the burning of the Talmud in Paris 1244. Reference numbers follow Israel Davidson, *Thesaurus of Medieval Hebrew Poetry* (New York, 1924–33). For a scholarly edition of the Zionides in the Eastern Ashkenazic rite, see Goldschmidt, *Seder ha-Kinnot*.

16. In a survey of thirty-seven manuscripts from the thirteenth through the fifteenth centuries, these were the following: Prague, Narodni Knihovna v Praze VI Ea 2 (thirteenth-fourteenth centuries); Arras, Bibliothèque d'Arras, Ms 560 (thirteenth century); Karlsruhe, Badische Landesbibliothek, Cod. 309 (1292); Oxford, Bodleian Library MS Can. Or. 70 (fourteenth century); Berlin, Staatsbibliothek, Or. fol. 1224 (Erfurt 18) (thirteenth-fourteenth centuries); Oxford, Bodleian Library MS Opp. 649 (fourteenth century); Oxford, Bodleian Library MS Opp. 173 (fourteenth century); Hamburg, Staats- und Universitätsbibliothek Cod. hebr. 233; (fourteenth century) Berlin, Staatsbibliothek Or. Qu. 798 (fourteenth-fifteenth centuries); Munich, Bayerische Staatsbibliothek Cod. hebr. 21 (thirteenth-fourteenth centuries).

17. Three manuscripts transmit "Zion, Were You to Take All the Balms of Gilead" with Judah ha-Levi's lament alone, namely Copenhagen, Royal Library Cod Hebr. Add. III/49; Parma, Biblioteca Palatina Cod. Parm. 2886 (de Rossi 585); and Leiden, Universiteitsbibliotheek Leiden Acad. 214, II. The *kinna* by El'azar of Worms is the sole Ashkenazic Zionide in two manuscripts: Oxford, Bodleian Laud Or 321 (Neubauer 2373), and Warszaw, Uniwersytet, Inst. Orientalistyczny 258.

18. Oxford, Bodleian Library MS Mich 571 (Neubauer 1097); Cremona, Archivo Municipale, fragment 34 (only fragments of this manuscript have been preserved; it may have included other Zionides as well); Erlangen, University Library, Ms 2601; Dresden, Sächsische Landesbibliothek Eb A 46a; Vatican, Biblioteca Apostolica ebr. 312.

19. A comparison of early modern choices and the resulting contrasts between the liturgies of eastern and western Ashkenaz extends beyond the scope of this article, but this author is currently preparing a monograph on Sephardic traces in the Ashkenazic rites. With the exception of the few Zionides that were clearly established within fourteenth-century Ashkenazic rites, namely Judah ha-Levi's lament, El'azar ben Judah's Zionide, the anonymous "Zion, Were You to Take All the Balms of Gilead," and Maharam's שאלי שרופה באש, which were all transmitted in at least ten medieval manuscripts and included in the printed rites, the number of extant manuscripts that include a given Ashkenazic Zionide is not a reliable predictor of its inclusion in the printed rites. Twelve of the nineteen Ashkenazic Zionides composed during the thirteenth century appear in the printed rites; they are transmitted in one (5), two (1), three (1), four (1), five (1), ten (1), twelve (1), or twenty-one (1) manuscripts. The other Zionides are known from one (4), two (2), or three (1) manuscripts. The number of occurrences is generally not correlated to their time of composition, i.e., older Zionides are not necessarily attested to more often than later ones. E.g., ציון יי לכס בחר מעונך (צ 277) by Yaqar ben Samuel ha-Levi from Cologne, who served as "Judenbischof" in the closing years of the thirteenth century, is transmitted in five extant manuscripts, whereas ציון צפירת פאר (צ 316) by Meir ben El'azar, purportedly composed during the first third of the thirteenth century, appears in only one manuscript. If we agree that roughly 5 percent of medieval Hebrew manuscripts are available to modern scholar-

ship, these transmission numbers may not accurately reflect the medieval library. Yet it is unlikely that the modern custom of burning the *kinnot* booklets after the Ninth of Av, symbolizing the hope for redemption (that would render these texts irrelevant), was practiced during the Middle Ages when parchment or paper were expensive commodities.

20. Rabbenu Tam's compositions in his exchange of poems with Abraham ibn Ezra (see, e.g., Isaac Meiseles, *Shirat Rabbenu Tam: The Poems of Rabbi Jacob ben Rabbi Meir. Critical Edition with Commentary* [Hebrew; Jerusalem, 2012], 140–44) have been interpreted as showing deference to the qualitative superiority of Sephardic poetry, but they can just as plausibly be read as standard panegyrics, possibly spiced with sarcasm. While Rabbenu Tam undoubtedly regarded Ibn Ezra as a fine poet, that would not have induced this versatile Ashkenazic scholar to regard himself or his literary tradition as inferior. Rabbenu Tam's poems in response to Ibn Ezra demonstrate his grasp of the Sephardic tradition of poetic responses and his ability to engage in it. In the case of אבי עזרי ישיבוהו סעפיו (א 191), he picked up the meter from Ibn Ezra's poem, skillfully reversed the opening letters of the hemistichs from א-ו-ו-ו to ו-א-א-א, and added to the rhyme scheme of the hemistichs, converting it from a-b-c-b to a-a-b-a, compelling Ibn Ezra to employ that rhyme scheme in response, הנכון אל אביר. The astonishing number of biblical and talmudic allusions that Rabbenu Tam incorporated in these two distichs displays his mastery of Ashkenazic poetics and his desire to weave some of its features into his answer to Ibn Ezra. I would like to thank Dr. Avraham (Rami) Reiner (Ben Gurion University of the Negev) for discussing Rabbenu Tam and his character with me.

21. *Ha-Mitpashet* is a meter that combines long (-) and short (˘) syllables into a fourteen-syllable stich: - - ˘ - / - ˘ - / - - ˘ - / - ˘ - . Early Ashkenazic metered poetry typically followed *mishkal ha-tenu'ot*, i.e., using only long syllables (with full vowels). Ashkenazic Zionides sometimes contain metrical errors, although that may in some cases be due to their interpretation of Hebrew grammar and pronunciation. A few examples in manuscripts that employ pre-Ashkenazic vocalization systems, which do not differentiate long and short vowels such as *kamats* and *pataḥ* (cf. Ilan Eldar, *Masoret ha-keri'ah ha-kedam-ashkenazit: Mahutah vi-yesodot ha-meshutafim lah u-le-masoret Sepharad* [Jerusalem, 1989], vol. 1) show how those texts found ways to follow the metrical rules in cases where a Tiberian vocalization, based on biblical Hebrew, would break the meter.

22. E.g., the *kinna* מעוני שחקים (מ 1987) by Menaḥem ben Jacob of Worms (d. 1204) is described as being sung to the Sephardic *niggun* in Arras, Bibliothèque municipale Ms 560, and Oxford, Bodleian Library Can Or 139 (Neubauer 1027).

23. For a discussion of this rhyme syllable and its possible connotations in Ashkenaz, see Elisabeth Hollender, "ציון שארית בני יעקב: An Ashkenazic Qina in Sephardic Garb," *Masoret ha-Piyyut* 6 (forthcoming).

24. An important "Sephardic feature" of several Ashkenazic Zionides is the presence of biblical language without a link to its original literary context. Sephardic poets did not always separate biblical expressions from their literary settings; however, in contrast to classical liturgical poets and their Ashkenazic followers, the Sephardic poets were more likely to quote biblical phrases that could readily be identified with specific verses without providing an indication of their textual references or narrative sources. Whereas this approach may have been appealing as a path toward new poetic options, the Ashkenazic authors who applied it in their Zionides or other derivations of Sephardic models never used it in their "classical" or unmetered *piyyutim*.

25. Cf. Elisabeth Hollender, "Late Ashkenazic Qinot in the Nuremberg Maḥzor," in *Giving a Diamond: A Festive Volume for Joseph Yahalom on the Occasion of His Seventieth Birthday*, ed. W. van Bekkum and N. Katsumata (Boston, 2011), 265–78.

26. In addition to twenty verbs in the first-person singular, the personal pronoun "I" appears twice, plus over ten nominal and verbal forms with a first-person singular suffix. The closing section, which expresses hope for redemption, is written in the third-person singular form, parallel to Psalm 1.

27. The communities took measures to reduce the tension between the first person voice in the kinna and the communal character of the service, thus late fourteenth-century rubrics in manuscripts indicate that "Zion, Will You Not Inquire" was recited by "the most honored man" in the community. For a discussion of the use of the first-person singular in Ashkenazic Zionides, cf. Elisabeth Hollender, "Angepasste Nachdichtungen: Vom Umgang mit innerjüdischer Differenz in der mittelalterlichen liturgischen Poesie," in *Diversität - Differenz - Dialogizität: Religion in pluralen Kontexten*, ed. S. Alkier and C. Wiese (Boston, forthcoming).

28. The famed "*'aliya* by 300 rabbis" originated in France; cf. Ephraim Kanarfogel, "The 'Aliyah of 'Three Hundred Rabbis' in 1211: Tosafist Attitudes Toward Settling in the Land of Israel," *Jewish Quarterly Review* 76.3 (1986): 191–215. While Rebekka Voß, "Rom am Rhein: die SchUM-Gemeinden im jüdischen messianischen Denken," in *Die SchUM-Gemeinden Speyer - Worms - Mainz; auf dem Weg zum Welterbe*, ed. P. Heberer and U. Reuter (Regensburg, 2013), 327–44, argues that Maharam's attempted emigration to Israel may have been motivated by messianic expectations, it was an unusual act in Ashkenaz.

29. Yudah L. Fleischer, "Kama ḥakhamim hayu lanu be-shem R. Abraham ha-Ḥoze?," *Horeb* 11 (1951): 256–68; Shraga Abramson, "Navi, ro'eh, ve-Ḥoze—R. Abraham ha-Ḥoze," in *Rabbi Mordecai Kirshblum Jubilee Book*, ed. D. Telsner (Hebrew; Jerusalem, 1983), 117–39.

30. Abraham Rosenfeld, trans. and ed., *The Authorized Kinot for the Ninth of Av Including the Prayers for the Evening, Morning and Afternoon Services, Reading of the Law and the Blessing of the New Moon: According to the Ashkenazic Rite* (London, 1965), 154–55.

31. On this discussion, cf. Sasha Stern, *Calendar and Community: A History of the Jewish Calendar, Second Century BCE–Tenth Century CE* (Oxford, 2001), 161n.19.

32. Cf. ibid., 161.

33. Cf. ibid., 207.

34. It seems that they may have been available, as recent studies show; see Reimund Leicht, "The Reception of Astrology in Medieval Ashkenazi Culture," *Aleph: Historical Studies in Science and Judaism* 13.2 (2013): 201–34.

35. Rosenfeld, *The Authorized Kinot*, 154.

36. H. Freedman, trans., *Midrash Rabbah. Genesis* (London, 1951), 1:126.

37. Rosenfeld, *The Authorized Kinot*, 154.

38. Cf. Ariel Zinder, *"Is This Thy Voice?" Rhetoric and Dialogue in Solomon Ibn-Gabirol's Liturgical Poems of Redemption (piyyutei ge'ulah)* (Hebrew; Jerusalem, 2012).

39. This would explain why topics that this Zionide introduces (e.g., R. Pinḥas ben Ya'ir's pious ass and the intercalation of the calendar being conducted in Jerusalem) are taken up by later poets.

40. Cf. Isaac Meiseles, *Shirat ha-Rokeaḥ: The Poems of Rabbi El'azar ben Yehudah of Worms. Critical Edition with Commentary* (Hebrew; Jerusalem, 1993).

41. For the image cf. Midrash Tehillim, Ps 9, § 13; a discussion of this topic in Ashkenazic memorial literature of the 1096 persecutions and martyrdom is presented by Israel J. Yuval, "Vengeance and Damnation, Blood and Defamation: From Jewish Martyrdom to Blood Libel Accusations" (Hebrew), *Zion* 58 (1993): 33–90.

42. The eastern Ashkenazic rite, discussed by Joseph Soloveitchik, does not include this Zionide, which may have led him to characterize Zionides as *kinnot* that recall "the beautiful life

of Jerusalem before the destruction. The *Tsiyon Kinot* all describe in glorious terms the beauty and holiness of Jerusalem and the wisdom of her people." Samuel Posner, ed., *The Koren Mesorat haRav Kinot with Commentary on the Kinot Based upon the Teachings of Rabbi Joseph B. Soloveitchik* (Jerusalem, 2010), 559.

43. On the use of this "return" here and in another Zionide, cf. Hollender, "An Ashkenazic Qina in Sephardic Garb."

44. Rosenfeld, *The Authorized Kinot*, 152.

45. Ibid., 153.

46. Based on the development of this genre as described in Elisabeth Hollender, *Piyyut Commentary in Medieval Ashkenaz* (Berlin, 2008), the absence of extant commentaries on Ashkenazic Zionides and the limited number of commentaries on "Zion, Will You Not Inquire" (marginal commentary in Berlin, Staatsbibliothek [Preussischer Kulturbesitz] Or. Qu. 799 [Steinschneider 177], fols. 208v–209v; marginal commentary in Oxford, Bodleian Library MS Can. Or. 86, fol. 154r–v; glosses in Hamburg, Staats- und Universitätsbibliothek Cod. hebr. 239a [Steinschneider 130], fols. 161v–162v) should be read as an indication neither that these texts were easily understood nor that comprehending them was not a priority. Studying *piyyutim* and their commentaries was a key element of thirteenth- and fourteenth-century Ashkenazic education, as the volume of manuscripts that include this material demonstrates; however, the *piyyutim* that were relatively late inclusions in the Ashkenazic rite, including the Zionides, did not receive significant attention from commentators.

47. The selections from Judah ha-Levi's liturgical poetry that have been in Ashkenazic liturgies range in their usage; some appear in the liturgical positions for which they were composed (e.g., *ge'ulot, ofanim,* and *reshuyot* for *Kaddish* or *Barkhu*), whereas others are linked to different positions (e.g., יום ליבשה נהפכו מצולים [י 1814], which appears as a *ge'ula* for the seventh day of Passover in the Sephardic rites, is associated in Ashkenaz with that same placement and for a Sabbath when a circumcision takes place).

48. Moses Mendelssohn, "Elegie an die Burg Zion gerichtet. Aus dem Hebräischen," in *Beschäftigungen des Geistes und des Herzens, Zweyter Band*, ed. J. G. P. Müchler (Berlin, 1756), 111–14. The fact that the young Jewish philosopher, when invited to contribute to a German periodical, responded with a German rendering of "Zion, Will You Not Inquire" and another Hebrew Andalusian poem, is evidence of the "myth of Sephardic supremacy" that dominated eighteenth- and nineteenth-century German Jewish views of medieval Judaism; see Schorsch, *From Text to Context*, 71–92.

49. For an in-depth analysis of Mendelssohn's translation, cf. Maren R. Niehoff, "Moses Mendelssohn's Translation of Judah ha-Levi's Elegy on Zion" (Hebrew), in *The Land of Israel in Modern Jewish Thought*, ed. A. Ravitsky (Hebrew; Jerusalem, 1998), 313–25.

50. Moses Mendelssohn, *Schriften zum Judentum IV*, Gesammelte Schriften Jubiläumsausgabe 10,1, ed. W. Weinberg (Stuttgart; Bad Cannstatt, 1985), lxxiv.

Contributors

Elisheva Baumgarten is Professor Yitzhak Becker Chair of Jewish Studies at the Hebrew University of Jerusalem. Her most recent book is *Practicing Piety in Medieval Ashkenaz: Men, Women, and Everyday Religious Observance* (University of Pennsylvania Press, 2014).

Piero Capelli is Associate Professor of Hebrew at Ca' Foscari University, Venice, Italy. His most recent book is *Il male: Storia di un'idea nell'ebraismo dalla Bibbia alla Qabbalah* (Evil: History of an Idea in Judaism Between the Bible and Kabbalah) (Società Editrice Fiorentina, 2012).

Mordechai Z. Cohen is Associate Dean and Professor of Bible at the Bernard Revel Graduate School of Jewish Studies at Yeshiva University. His most recent book is *Opening the Gates of Interpretation: Maimonides' Biblical Hermeneutics in Light of His Geonic-Andalusian Heritage and Muslim Milieu* (Brill, 2011), and his next book, *The Rule of Peshat,* is forthcoming from the University of Pennsylvania Press.

Judah Galinsky is Senior Lecturer in the Talmud Department at Bar-Ilan University. Most recently he has edited, with Elisheva Baumgarten, *Jews and Christians in Thirteenth-Century France* (Palgrave Macmillan, 2015).

Elisabeth Hollender is Professor of Jewish Studies at the Goethe University, Frankfurt, Germany. She works mainly on Ashkenazic *piyyut* and *piyyut* commentary with a focus on inner-Jewish cultural transfer.

Kati Ihnat is a postdoctoral research assistant at the University of Bristol, having received her Ph.D. at Queen Mary, University of London, in 2011. She is completing a monograph entitled *Mother of Mercy, Bane of the Jews:*

The Virgin Mary in Anglo-Norman England (Princeton University Press, forthcoming).

Ephraim Kanarfogel is E. Billi Ivry University Professor of Jewish History, Literature and Law at the Bernard Revel Graduate School of Jewish Studies at Yeshiva University. His most recent book is *The Intellectual History and Rabbinic Culture of Medieval Ashkenaz* (Wayne State University Press, 2013).

Ruth Mazo Karras is Professor of History at the University of Minnesota. Her most recent book is *Unmarriages: Women, Men, and Sexual Unions in the Middle Ages* (University of Pennsylvania Press, 2012).

Katelyn Mesler is a postdoctoral fellow at the Westfälische Wilhelms-Universität in Münster. Her current research concerns the intersections of Hebrew and Latin traditions of magic, science, and medicine.

S. J. Pearce is Assistant Professor in the Department of Spanish and Portuguese Languages and Literatures at New York University. Her first book, *No Achievement But Through Arabic: Judah ibn Tibbon and the Culture of Andalusi Reading in Exile*, is forthcoming from the Indiana University Press.

Avraham (Rami) Reiner is Professor in the Department of Jewish Thought at Ben-Gurion University of the Negev. His research focuses on the history of *halakhah* in Europe during the Middle Ages. His most recent book, with K. Müller and S. Schwarzfuchs, is *Die Grabsteine vom judischen Friedhof in Würzburg aus der Zeit vor dem Schwarzen Tod* (Society of Frankish History, 2011).

Yossef Schwartz is Professor at the Cohn Institute for the History and Philosophy of Science and Ideas at Tel Aviv University. He is the coeditor of *Latin-into-Hebrew: Studies and Texts*, vol. 2: *Texts in Contexts* (Brill, 2013).

Uri Shachar is Assistant Professor in the Department of History and a member of the Center for the Study of Conversion and Inter-Religious Encounters at Ben-Gurion University.

Rebecca Winer is Associate Professor of History at Villanova University. Her research focuses on Jewish, Christian, and Muslim entanglement and gender in the medieval Crown of Aragon.

Luke Yarbrough is Assistant Professor of History at Saint Louis University. His most recent work is the translation of the thirteenth-century polemic by ʻUthman ibn Ibrahim al-Nabulusi, *The Sword of Ambition: Bureaucratic Rivalry in Medieval Egypt* (New York University Press, 2016).

Index

Page numbers in italics refer to illustrations.

Acknowledgments

This volume represents a harvest of joint thinking and individual work on the thirteenth century by the community of scholars fostered by the Katz Center for Advanced Judaic Studies at the University of Pennsylvania. The seminars and events at the Center led to many of the essays within this collection. We are grateful for the opportunity to thank David Ruderman, then the Director of the Katz Center, for creating a place that encourages scholarship and collaborative effort, and activating the magic that made the time we spent together wonderfully productive and thought provoking. The staff at the Katz Center provided the assistance and peace of mind needed for our joint endeavor. We are grateful to Natalie Dohrmann, Carrie Love, Etty Lassman, and all the devoted librarians who took care of all of our needs. We thank Yossi Schwartz, Chaim (Harvey) Hames, and Alexander Fidora for the original proposal that led to the convening of this group.

Our work on this book allowed us to continue to explore themes and ideas we first began discussing at the Center. We thank Jesse Izzo and Noam Sienna for their help copyediting and checking transliterations. Jerry Singerman advised and guided us through the process of creating and producing this book. We also thank Eric Schramm and Erica Ginsburg for their help with production. For comments on a draft of the introduction we thank David Berger, Jeremy Cohen, Mordechai Cohen, Rita Copeland, Elisabeth Hollender, William Chester Jordan, Yossi Schwartz, and Luke Yarbrough. We are grateful to the anonymous readers of the book for the press for their helpful comments and suggestions.

During the preparation of this book, Katelyn Mesler benefited from the support of the Mandel Scholion Interdisciplinary Research Center in the Humanities and Jewish Studies (Hebrew University of Jerusalem). A Grant in Aid of Research from the University of Minnesota allowed the three of us to reconvene in person to continue our work and funded research assistance from Jesse Izzo.

Olivia Remie Constable, admired and beloved colleague, spent a month with our group. It was with great sorrow that we all learned of her untimely death. This book is dedicated to her memory.